EVANGELICAL THEOLOGIES OF LIBERATION AND JUSTICE

EDITED BY
MAE ELISE CANNON
AND **ANDREA SMITH**

Academic

An imprint of InterVarsity Press
Downers Grove, Illinois

InterVarsity Press
P.O. Box 1400, Downers Grove, IL 60515-1426
ivpress.com
email@ivpress.com

InterVarsity Press® is the book-publishing division of InterVarsity Christian Fellowship/USA®, a
movement of students and faculty active on campus at hundreds of universities, colleges, and schools
of nursing in the United States of America, and a member movement of the International Fellowship
of Evangelical Students. For information about local and regional activities, visit intervarsity.org.

All Scripture quotations, unless otherwise indicated, are taken from The Holy Bible, New International
Version®, NIV®. Copyright © 1973, 1978, 1984, 2011 by Biblica, Inc.™ Used by permission of Zondervan.
All rights reserved worldwide. www.zondervan.com. The "NIV" and "New International Version"
are trademarks registered in the United States Patent and Trademark Office by Biblica, Inc.™

Cover design and image composite: David Fassett
Interior design: Daniel van Loon
Images: Grunge paper: © billnoll / E+ / Getty Images
          Phoenix illustration: © CSA Images / Getty Images

ISBN 978-0-8308-5246-8 (print)
ISBN 978-0-8308-7096-7 (digital)

Library of Congress Cataloging-in-Publication Data

A catalog record for this book is available from the Library of Congress.
Library of Congress Control Number: 2019942934

P   25   24   23   22   21   20   19   18   17   16   15   14   13   12   11   10   9   8   7   6   5   4   3   2

Y   37   36   35   34   33   32   31   30   29   28   27   26   25   24   23   22   21   20   19

CONTENTS

Introduction . . . . *vii*
    Mae Elise Cannon and Andrea Smith

PART ONE: LIBERATION METHODOLOGIES

1. Centered Versus Bounded: Moving Beyond Divide and Conquer
    Strategies for Liberation *3*
    Paul Louis Metzger

2. Evangelical Theologies of Liberation *30*
    Soong-Chan Rah

3. Is It Time for a Womanist Theology of Reconciliation? *53*
    Chanequa Walker-Barnes

PART TWO: ENGAGEMENT WITH LIBERATION
THEOLOGY MOVEMENTS

4. Toward a Perspective of "Brown Theology" *75*
    Robert Chao Romero

5. *Justicia Familiar: Misión Integral* in the United States. *96*
    Alexia Salvatierra

PART THREE: RETHINKING SIN

6. A Born-Again Theology of Liberation *111*
    Andrea Smith

7. The Groaning Creation: Animal Liberation and
    Evangelical Theology *130*
    Sarah Withrow King

8. Holy and Acceptable: Liberation from Evangelical Fat Shame. *153*
    J. Nicole Morgan

9. Liberation: Self and Community in Relationship. *170*
    Terry LeBlanc and Jeanine LeBlanc

PART FOUR: THEOLOGICAL RESOURCES FROM THE MARGINS

10. Lean In to Liberating Love: The Birth of Evangelical Theology of
Liberation at Gordon-Conwell's Center for Urban Ministerial
Education   195
Peter Goodwin Heltzel, Pablo A. Jiménez, and Emmett G. Price III

11. Toward an Indian Liberation Theology for the *Shudra* and Dalit . . .   235
Rajkumar Boaz Johnson

12. Strange Freedom: Liberation for the Sake of Others   262
Mae Elise Cannon

PART FIVE: RETHINKING OUR EVANGELICAL HERITAGE

13. Liberating Barabbas: And the Things That Make for Peace   285
Drew G. I. Hart

14. Jubilee, Pentecost, and Liberation: The Preferential
Option of the Poor on the Apostolic Way   306
Amos Yong

15. Sacramental Theology   325
Dominique DuBois Gilliard

Contributor Biographies   345

Scripture Index   354

INTRODUCTION

MAE ELISE CANNON AND ANDREA SMITH

LIBERATION THEOLOGY may be a distant notion for many evangelicals. Some might think that liberation theology, particularly in light of its roots in Latin American Catholicism and African American Protestantism, is antithetical to evangelical theology. Other evangelicals may simply not be familiar with the profound impact of liberation theological traditions on Latin American, African American, and other global subaltern Christian communities.

Liberation theology is a twentieth-century movement that almost simultaneously emerged in the writings and ministry life of Latin American Roman Catholics and African American Protestants. The emphasis of these theological traditions focuses on freedom (or liberation) from political, social, and economic injustices and oppression. Many traditional liberation theologies call on material deliverance from oppression and injustice as a precursor that anticipates the coming of the kingdom of God and ultimately salvation.

While the history of liberation theology is articulated more fully in the essays by Robert Chao Romero and Alexia Salvatierra, in this introduction, to briefly summarize, liberation theology emerges from two independent sources: Latin American movements against neo-colonialism and the black power movement. In the 1960s, while many Latin American countries were living under military rule, generally backed by the US government, many theologians despaired over what seemed to be the silence of churches in light of this oppression and suffering. Gustavo Gutierrez published his germinal *A Theology of Liberation*, which provides the framework for articulating the relationship between God and justice. Many works from other liberation theologians soon followed, which argued that God was on the side of the poor and the oppressed. And thus, to follow God required that one be actively engaged in movements for social justice. Latin American liberation theologians were very engaged in Marxist thought, albeit critically, in keeping with the Marxist underpinnings of the movements against colonialism happening at the time.

Because of its engagement with Marxist thought, white evangelicals tended to reject liberation theology altogether as communist and hence nonbiblical, without sufficiently addressing US complicity, particularly US-evangelical complicity, in supporting repressive governments that were using death squads to brutally repress their citizens. In the twenty-first century, evangelicals have been more critical of their role in this repression. *Christianity Today* published Jeanette Hardage's review of the video *Precarious Peace: God and Guatemala*, which documents the CIA'S overthrow of a democratically elected government and the suppression and massacres of Indigenous peoples. She notes how evangelicals either supported these massacres or refused to take a stand against them.[1] *Christianity Today* critiqued its own support for Efraín Ríos Montt's 1982 military coup that enabled him to gain the presidency, noting that Luis Palau, Jerry Falwell, and Pat Robertson also supported him. The magazine now reflects that his rule was "probably the most violent period of the 36-year internal conflict, resulting in about 200,000 deaths of mostly unarmed

---

[1] Jeanette Hardage, "Witnesses amid War," *Christianity Today*, July 2004, 67-68.

Indigenous civilians."[2] *Christianity Today* also ran an article criticizing the evangelical support of dictator Alberto Fujimori in Peru.[3] However, as the article notes there was little of this evangelical critique during the birth of liberation theology. For instance, former evangelical president of Guatemala Rios Mott received much financial support from Pat Robertson, which went to support Mott's Gospel Outreach campaign to annihilate Indigenous people. Stated one Gospel Outreach pastor, "The Army doesn't massacre the Indians. It massacres demons, and the Indians are demon possessed; they are communists."[4] *Charisma* asserts that the oppression of Indigenous peoples in Guatemala can be traced, not to US policy, but to "demonic power . . . [that has] held Guatemala in bondage."[5] But Christian revival liberates them from oppression. "Before the revival . . . farmers worked just enough to support their drinking habits; today they are investing in topsoil and fertilizers, and some are paying cash for Mercedes trucks and emblazoning them with names such as *Regalito de Dios* ('Little Gift from God')."[6] Pat Robertson justified this genocide with the following:

> These tribes are . . . in an arrested state of social development. They are not less valuable as human beings because of that, but they offer scant wisdom or learning or philosophical vision that can be instructive to a society that can feed the entire population of the earth in a single harvest and send spacecraft to the moon. . . . Except for our crimes, our wars and our frantic pace of life, what we have is superior to the ways of primitive peoples. . . . Which life do you think people would prefer: freedom in an enlightened Christian civilization or the suffering of subsistence living and superstition in a jungle? You choose.[7]

---

[2]Deann Alford, "The Truth Is Somewhere," *Christianity Today*, September 2006, 20-21.
[3]David Miller, "Divorcing a Dictator," *Christianity Today*, February 5, 2001, 22-23. Another article mentioned that evangelicals were also persecuted under this regime (Deann Alford, "Imprisoned Evangelicals Dispute Accusations of Terrorism," *Christianity Today*, February 9, 1998, 94-95); see also David Miller, "Christians to Help Investigate Crimes," *Christianity Today*, January 7, 2002, 27.
[4]Sara Diamond, *Roads to Dominion* (New York: Guilford Press, 1995), 238.
[5]Mell Winger, "The Miracle of Almolonga," *Charisma*, September 1998, 71.
[6]Winger, "The Miracle of Almolonga," 72.
[7]Pat Robertson, *The Turning Tide* (Dallas: Word Books, 1993), 153.

In addition, white evangelicals often portrayed liberation theology as antithetical to evangelicalism and organized against it. In fact, as described by Robert Chao Romero's essay in this volume, many liberation theologians in Latin America were and are evangelical.

Contemporaneously, but independently, black liberation theology also emerged in the wake of the black power movement in the United States. This movement was sparked by the key texts of James Cone, *Black Theology and Black Power* (1969) and *A Black Theology of Liberation* (1970), which argued that, within the context of racial justice struggle, God was on the side of black peoples. Black liberation theology focused more on race than economic justice and hence did not significantly engage Marxist thought, at least at the beginning. And this work did in fact have a significant impact among black evangelicals, particularly with the founding of the National Black Evangelical Association. However, as Soong-Chan Rah notes in this volume, white evangelicals failed to substantively engage the contributions of black theology. And indeed, white evangelicals for the most part (with some exceptions) did not support the black civil rights movement. For instance, when Jerry Falwell described the events that led to the development of the Christian right, his stated reasons were the *Brown v. Board* decision (1954), the decision banning school prayer (1962), and *Roe v. Wade* (1973).[8] Much of the rise of the Christian right was a reaction *against* the civil rights movement.[9] It was in response to this complicity that James Cone argued that "theology's great sin is silence in the face of white supremacy."[10]

While black liberation and Latin American liberation theology initially developed independently, these thinkers began to collaborate

---

[8]Ellen Rosenberg, *Southern Baptists: A Subculture in Transition* (Knoxville: University of Tennessee Press, 1984), 84.

[9]Randall Balmer, "The Real Origins of the Religious Right," *Politico*, May 27, 2014, www.politico.com/magazine/story/2014/05/religious-right-real-origins-107133; Andrea Smith, *Native Americans and the Christian Right: The Gendered Politics of Unlikely Alliances* (Durham, NC: Duke University Press, 2008).

[10]James Cone, "Theology's Great Sin: Silence in the Face of White Supremacy," *Black Theology* 2 (2004): 139-52.

through the development of the Ecumenical Association of Third World Theologians (EATWOT) in 1976. In turn, liberation theologies began to emerge out of Asia and Africa, as well as out of feminist and other racialized peoples in the United States. These theologies, while in dialogue with each other, were also very diverse and often in tension with each other. Some theologies focused more on racism, others on capitalism, and others on religious imperialism. There was considerable debate as to whether gender oppressions should be addressed by many liberation theologians, and in fact EATWOT did not allow women's membership until 1981. There was also debate about whether theology was an academic enterprise: some highlighted what was termed Christian base communities as the source for theological praxis (or reflection and action). Thus, in developing this volume, we concluded that, given the diversity of thought within liberation movements, it did not make sense to proffer a singular evangelical liberation theology. But rather, we offer a space for discussion and debate on what evangelical theologies of liberation and justice might be.

Evangelical Theologies of Liberation and Justice contests the assumption that the pursuit of emancipation from injustice and oppression is antithetical to the core tenets of evangelicalism. Rather, this book wrestles with the question of how evangelical traditions and perspectives intersect and have the potential to be deeply informed by liberation theological traditions. First, as we have noted, evangelicals, while often erased in the genealogies of liberation theologies, have always been part of their development. But second, rather than understanding evangelical faith as necessarily at odds with liberation theology, we hold that evangelical tenets of faith are actually helpful in the development of justice-rooted liberation praxis.

This book brings together Christian authors and speakers from diverse perspectives who present their understanding of evangelical perspectives of liberation. All of the contributors either self-identify as evangelical or have close ties with the evangelical community. With biblical mandates to end oppression (such as Is 58:6-9), one would assume biblically centered evangelicals would have well-developed theologies of liberation. And yet, evangelicals have generally dismissed liberation theology completely, despite the diversities of liberation theologies that currently exist.

At the same time, we are seeing a rise in evangelicalism of those centering on justice work as part of their faith. Such examples include the popularity of the annual Justice Conference and the inclusion of Black Lives Matter at the Urbana15 conference, hosted by InterVarsity Christian Fellowship. And yet evangelical theologians have not developed the theological foundation for this kind of activism.

Evangelical Theologies of Liberation and Justice hopes to fill these gaps by providing multiple voices of those articulating evangelical liberation theologies. We do not offer an uncritical engagement or wholesale acceptance, nor rejection, of liberation theology. Rather, we critically engage liberation theology for what it may be able to offer justice-centered evangelicals. We provide a conversation that can serve as a base for developing a specifically evangelical view of liberation that speaks to the critical social justice struggles of our time.

This book is for individual Christians, specifically evangelicals, who are wrestling with what it means to live out the Christian life and to be advocates of biblical justice. Communities, small groups, seminary or theology classes, and churches who want to engage in personal reflection and action around issues of biblical justice in a group or corporate setting will find this book instructive, insightful, and inspiring as they seek to better love God, their neighbors, and their enemies in a globalized world. The authors present in this book are a mix of academics, activists, and pastors who are uniquely equipped to speak to this relevant issue.

This volume is organized into several sections that seek to parse and better understand points of intersection between evangelicalism and theologies of liberation. The essays in part one point to the importance of seeing liberation as a process and a methodology and not a destination. In particular, given the systemic nature of oppression it is important for evangelicals to be open to new ideas and frameworks that can help provide further insight into helpful ways to address injustice. This requires a stance of humility and the ability to hear from those with which one might have substantial disagreement on a number of issues. Paul Louis Metzger provides a helpful framework that allows for engagement across differences. So often, the fallen powers that be divide and conquer communities that seek liberation. Divisions easily happen in liberation communities because communities emphasize what differentiates them to the detriment of what unites them, sometimes as the result of an overbearing hermeneutic of suspicion. Metzger argues that one of the ways we can break free from such deconstructing strategies is to move from bounded to centered sets of discourse as they pertain to liberation.

Soong-Chan Rah speaks to the limitations of evangelical theologies that focus on boundaries when those theologies are not informed by the work of people of color. Rah asserts that part of the reason why there is no evangelical liberation theology is the inability of white evangelicals to engage with the prophetic strands of African American Christianity. Rah emphasizes that white evangelical's investment in whiteness rather than the gospel limits the ability for the gospel to be manifested in all its fullness.

Chanequa Walker-Barnes builds on Rah's premise to argue that it is not just enough to have a racially inclusive theology, but the methodological approach must be intersectional as well. In particular, Walker-Barnes argues that an intersectional race and gender analysis transforms evangelical theology. Walker-Barnes reviews the historical antecedents of the racial reconciliation paradigm within the Promise Keepers movement. She describes how this legacy not only marginalizes the voices of women of color, but also results in anemic understandings of race, racism, and reconciliation. Using womanist theology as an example, Walker-Barnes argues that the unique perspectives of women of color must be moved from margin to center if we truly hope to work toward reconciliation.

The essays in part two provide a historical context for the relationship between liberation theological movements and evangelicalism. Both Robert Chao Romero and Alexia Salvatierra trace the impact of Latin American liberation theology and note that while there has been evangelical suspicion of this movement, there has also in fact been exchange between evangelicalism and Latin American liberation theologians that has enabled the development of what Romero calls the "brown church." Romero offers a historical overview of four key theologians/theological movements of the brown church: Bartolomé de Las Casas, Latin American liberation theology, *misión integral*, and Latina/o theology. This list of thinkers and movements is by no means exhaustive and in fact just scratches the surface of the theological wealth of the brown church. Nonetheless, it may be enough to encourage the reader to dig deeper and engage on a lifetime of learning from the ecclesial capital of Latina/o Christians across the centuries. Even more, it is hoped that this introduction to Latina/o historical theology may encourage some to *volver*—to return to Jesús. Not the Jesus of the white colonial church, which drapes itself exclusively in *ropa anglo-sajon* (Anglo-Saxon clothing), but the Cristo who has led the brown church in *misión integral* and radical personal and social transformation for more than five hundred years. Alexia Salvatierra similarly reviews how *misión integral*—the evangelical version of liberation theology in Latin America—has manifested itself in the United States. She then moves into the insights that Latinos in the United States are contributing and can contribute to the field of theology as well as the implications for the broader evangelical community.

Centering social justice in evangelical theology then requires us to rethink some of our theological assumptions. In particular, the essays in part three rethink theological concepts of sin and righteousness and how these concepts construct what we consider to be the human. Andrea Smith reconceptualizes sin through the lens of racialization. She argues that sin is not so much the result of bad ideas about race that result in sin, but in fact the whole world is constituted through white supremacy such that an end to racism requires an end to the world as we know it—requiring us to really be born again. Racialization is then more of a verb than a noun; it is the process by which some get marked as human (whiteness) and some fall outside of humanity.

Animal rights activist Sarah King further suggests the importance of theologically questioning the complete divide between animal and human through a focus on animal liberation. King talks about the "groaning of creation" as she seeks to integrate animal liberation and evangelical theology. The verdant planet created by God is now home to close to eight billion human beings. And though we humans share the planet with eighteen billion chickens, three million great whales, half a million elephants, and many billions more nonhuman animals, Euro-American evangelical theologies are rarely attentive to God's other creatures. The consequences—to animals, to the environment, and to our fellow human beings—are disastrous. Human activity has caused and accelerated the extinction of whole species, silencing the worship of the woodland bison of West Virginia, the Culebra parrot of Puerto Rico, and the Rocky Mountain grasshopper, to name just a few. Animals from around the globe are regularly captured from the wild and taken from their families and homes; some are killed so their fur can be used on coat collars, some are used in painful experiments, and others are simply put on display in zoos or aquariums. And in the United States, we have pioneered and exported a system of industrial farming that raises and kills approximately nine billion land animals each year in nightmarish cruelty, exploiting vulnerable workers and poisoning air, land, and water along the way. But what if our theology, and our practice, reflected the reality of the liberation from bondage and the reconciliation of *all* God's creatures back to the Creator? This chapter explores the place of animal and human creatures in God's creation, examines the long-reaching consequences of exercising tyrannical dominion, and suggests some ways that Christians might contribute to the flourishing of every living being.

J. Nicole Morgan looks at how sin becomes embodied in evangelical thought such that some bodies become deemed as inherently sinful—in particular fat bodies. Morgan argues for theology that liberates us from "fat shame" by analyzing the way we name a sinful body and the bondage that creates for both individuals and the church community a whole. She argues that Christian teaching—especially contemporary evangelical teaching—has prioritized a thin body, going so far as to call fat bodies *sinful.* That naming of fat bodies as sinful hinders the ability of individual fat Christians to live into the calling of God on their lives. In addition, body shame breaks the bonds of community within the church and hinders their ability to live their call to be a picture of the kingdom of God on earth. Morgan advocates for a theology and church that is liberated from antifat bias. It should be further noted that the creation of the bad versus good body ideal, as many disability scholars have argued, provides the foundation for racism as the embodiment of those peoples who should be subjected to oppression. It also provides a feminist lens in terms of women seemingly more of the flesh than men.

Similarly to Sarah King, Terry LeBlanc and Jeanine LeBlanc critique the human/creation divide within mainstream evangelical theology, but through centering it on an Indigenous Christian framework. They argue that liberation must be seen in its totality and includes all of creation, not just humans. They also discuss the reality and role of community in the process of liberation, and assert that at times the needs of the overall community must supersede individual needs for the sake of the survival of the community. They challenge white evangelicalism's overemphasis on individualism and autonomy by considering liberation through an Indigenous philosophical and theological lens.

Part of the debate that has arisen among liberation theologians is, Who is the proper source of liberation theology? Must the liberation theologians be academically trained? Or does this presupposition reinforce social hierarchies that devalue the theological contributions of those who do not have the privilege of accessing an academic education? The essays in part four build on this discussion by looking to theological resources from the margins. In their chapter, "Lean In to Liberating Love," Peter Goodwin Heltzel, Pablo A. Jiménez, and Emmett G. Price III celebrate the contributions to contextual urban theological education from the Center for Urban Theological Education at Gordon-Conwell Theological Seminary in Boston, Massachusetts. They contend that the evangelical theology of liberation was born as a theological movement at the center. In particular, the essay highlights the prophetic ministries of courageous leaders such as Rev. Dr. Eldin Villafañe, Rev. Dr. Michael E. Haynes, and Rev. Dr. Dean Borgman, who were instrumental in the development of the emerging evangelical theology of liberation in the United States. Following Jesus, who loved the poor, evangelical theologians of liberation proclaim and embody Christ's righteous reign through joining the liberating Spirit in seeking justice, embodying love, and walking humbly with our Lord (Mic 6:8).

Rajkumar Boaz Johnson writes about his personal narrative of growing up in the slums of New Delhi in chapter eleven. Johnson came to encounter the writings of Pandita Ramabai, a high caste Hindu woman, who died in 1922. Before she died she had done amazing things in India. She had rescued young girls who were forced into prostitution in the harems of Bombay, widows who were treated as untouchables in society, little female infants who were about to be killed, and so many others. The source for Ramabai's faith was her dramatic conversion, in which she had a personal encounter with Jesus. This same Jesus had transformed the lives of many other outcaste men, women, and children. Johnson recounts through moving personal testimony and narrative the liberating effects of the gospel of Christ on the humanity and suffering of numerous communities in India, from the elite Hindu woman Ramabai to the Sikh guru by the name of Bhakt Singh. He tells of the radical transformations after radical encounters with the liberating message of Jesus.

In her chapter, titled after one of Howard Thurman's most profound articles, "A Strange Freedom," Mae Elise Cannon challenges the typical approach in evangelicalism to look beyond a white-centric evangelical theology to more broadly understand the good news of the gospel. Cannon moves from the roots of black liberation theological considerations to the question of how this framework can better help us understand a perspective of liberation related to Israel and the occupied Palestinian territories. Cannon considers how the gospel of Christ must be viewed as a liberating gospel. What does it mean to be liberated through Christ's death on the cross and subsequent resurrection? Does liberation extend beyond just the need of personal redemption and the forgiveness of sins? Cannon argues that at the heart of the good news of the gospel, liberation is expressed by providing opportunities for both existential and material freedom. One must be liberated from oneself through the forgiveness of individual sins and depravity, but also by the shedding of false paradigms, like the need for white liberation from a colonized perspective of privilege and superiority. Looking at lessons from the black liberation struggle in the United States and consulting with liberationists Martin Luther King Jr., Howard Thurman, and Cornel West, Cannon identifies key themes of Christ's proclamation of freedom (Lk 4) and applies them to the contemporary struggles against oppression. Cannon moves beyond a typical approach to evangelicalism to look at theology from the perspective of the poor and the oppressed. Her chapter considers the current geopolitical conflict between Israelis and Palestinians as one example of where liberation must be sought— not only for Palestinians living under the reality of military occupation, but also for those holding positions of power and authority that are used to oppress.

Finally, the essays in part five rethink and reimagine our evangelical heritage(s) through the lens of liberation. Drew Hart does a deep reading of the story of Barrabas to suggest he was a fellow revolutionary. While Jesus may have not supported violent insurrection, Hart argues that Jesus empathized with and understood those who did support it rather than pathologizing it, even as he held on to a nonviolent approach for social change. Hart calls on evangelicals to read the Bible again to discern Jesus' clear commitment to justice.

Amos Yong traces liberation sources within the Pentecostal tradition. According to Yong, recent trends in liberation theology show remarkable diversification compared with the predominant Marxist underpinnings of the first generation's efforts. In the meanwhile, although liberation theologians opted for the poor, the poor opted for Pentecostalism. Yong considers how Pentecostal spirituality, which has served the poor across the majority world, can yet gain further theological traction and specification from sustained engagement with the "many tongues" of liberation theology in the present global context, as refracted through apostolic witness, particularly of the third gospel and its sequel volume.

Dominque Gilliard rethinks sacramental theology to articulate the sacraments as a source for liberation politics. God troubles the waters of belonging through the scandalous nature of the sacraments. The sacraments are divinely ordained to deracinate the imperial ethos of belonging; they are ordained by God to castrate the oppressive hierarchies that empires constitute. The sacraments provide a blueprint for Christian ethics, and this chapter articulates how they should catalyze Christians to participate as colaborers with Christ, pursuing biblical justice and inducing liberation. This chapter explores how the sacraments subpoena Christians to confront evil, combat injustice, and form covenantal bonds of solidarity with the other. This chapter concludes by examining the justice ends that are usually forsaken by our sacramental means.

All of us are in need of liberation. May the pages ahead challenge us and compel us to learn from brothers and sisters in Christ coming from different backgrounds, socioeconomic situations, and cultures.

Christ reminded his followers "whatever you did for one of the least of these . . . you did for me" (Mt 25:40). With that in mind, may we not ignore the profound lessons to be learned from the "least of these" and their subaltern theologies of liberation, which call us not only to personal relationship with Christ, but also to divine liberation from injustice. We hope these essays, while not promising to provide the answer or a singular prescription, can provide further discussion and exchange about the possibilities for developing evangelical theologies of liberation and justice.

PART ONE

LIBERATION METHODOLOGIES

CENTERED VERSUS BOUNDED

Moving Beyond Divide and Conquer Strategies for Liberation

PAUL LOUIS METZGER

SO OFTEN, THE FALLEN POWERS DIVIDE and conquer communities that seek liberation. Divisions easily result in liberation communities because they emphasize what differentiates them to the detriment of what unites them, sometimes as the result of an overbearing hermeneutic of suspicion. One of the ways that we can break free from such deconstructive strategies is to move from bounded to centered sets of discourse for the sake of liberation. In the ensuing discussion, we will argue for a centered-set approach as it pertains to evangelical liberation strategies bearing on caring for the orphan, widow, and alien in their distress. The aim of the essay is to foster ways evangelicals from different theological traditions can come together and not allow various boundaries to sabotage solidarity as they cultivate a more liberating theology. The key is to center the discussion on the gospel of the kingdom in service to those on the margins. The outline for this essay is as follows. First, we will provide definitions of centered and bounded sets of discourse, along with a biblical exposition of these categories, as well as a historical backdrop to extreme versions of bounded sets. Second, we will unpack a centered- over against a bounded-set approach to evangelical liberation theology. This approach will include consideration of the theological underpinnings as well as a brief case study that brings together various atonement theories in service to this centered-set model favoring those on the margins. It will be followed by principles required for consideration in future conversations on liberation theology among evangelicals.

CENTERED- AND BOUNDED-SET
APPROACHES TO THEOLOGY

What is the difference between centered and bounded sets?

A centered-set approach focuses on goals and what brings individuals and groups together. A bounded-set approach focuses on the boundaries and who is in and who is out of the movement. Roger Olson says of the bounded-set model, "The bounded set model ends up allowing little or no distinction between the center (the gospel) and the boundaries (orthodoxy). It also leads inevitably to obsessive boundary maintenance and inquisitorial judgments about whether persons and groups are Christian."[1] The centered-set approach has a great deal to offer the evangelical Christian community in pursuing justice across the evangelical theological spectrum.

Why does a centered-set approach prove more strategic for evangelical theologies of liberation? As a movement, evangelicals need to build momentum that accounts for and draws from our diversity within the broad evangelical tradition. Diversity can and often should be a strength, not a weakness! Focusing on boundaries often holds the evangelical movement back, instead of evangelicals moving forward together in shared justice aims. Many evangelical groups frame partnerships in bounded theological categories or sets. While this has its place in certain quarters at various times, it is likely not

---

[1] Roger E. Olson, *The Mosaic of Christian Belief: Twenty Centuries of Unity & Diversity*, 2nd ed. (Downers Grove, IL: InterVarsity Press, 2016), 49. Paul Hiebert has written about the subject of centered and bounded sets in *Anthropological Reflections on Missiological Issues* (Grand Rapids: Baker Books, 1994).

advantageous in this context that focuses on ethics, not doctrine. Centering on the biblical categories of caring for the alien, widow, and orphan in their distress provides order and direction without having to invest major energies on what distinguishes and perhaps even divides the movement theologically. David Bebbington's centering categories for evangelicalism has merit:

Conversionism: the belief that lives need to be transformed through a "born-again" experience and a life-long process of following Jesus;

Activism: the expression and demonstration of the gospel in missionary and social reform efforts;

Biblicism: a high regard for and obedience to the Bible as the ultimate authority;

Crucicentrism: a stress on the sacrifice of Jesus Christ on the cross as making possible the redemption of humanity.[2]

Still, for the purposes of this volume, it proves more strategic to frame the discussion in terms of a question: What are the biblical and theological resources that help us prophetically address Jesus' gospel of the kingdom care for the orphan, widow, and alien in their distress? While theology is critically important, it makes more sense given the present volume's concrete justice aims to discuss how the Bible and theology inform evangelicalism's respective views of applied justice for the orphan, widow, alien, and the like. With this point in mind, we are reminded of Jesus' challenge to the religious scholar in the story of the Samaritan of exceeding mercy (Lk 10:25-37). Jesus did not tell

---

[2]The National Association of Evangelicals includes Bebbington's important statement(s) depicting evangelicalism on their site: www.nae.net/church-and-faith-partners/what-is-an-evangelical. See David W. Bebbington, *Evangelicalism in Modern Britain: A History from the 1730s to the 1930s* (London: Unwin Hyman, 1989). I prefer this exposition of evangelical theological core sensibilities over against distinctively Reformed or Arminian articulations. For other discussions of evangelical identity, see the following: Donald W. Dayton and Douglas M. Strong, *Rediscovering an Evangelical Heritage: A Tradition and Trajectory of Integrating Piety and Justice*, 2nd ed. (Grand Rapids: Baker Academic, 2014); Mark A. Noll, *American Evangelical Christianity: An Introduction* (Oxford: Wiley-Blackwell, 2000); and George M. Marsden, *Understanding Fundamentalism and Evangelicalism* (Grand Rapids: Eerdmans, 1990).

the religious leader who had come to test him about eternal life to go and think a certain way so that he might live, but to go and act a certain way so that he would live (Lk 10:37).

What are some biblical examples of bounded and centered sets, and how do we discern when and where to apply them?

A great contrast between the bounded-set and centered-set approaches is found in Mark 9:38-41. There we find Jesus' disciples taking exception to someone casting out demons in Jesus' name. Instead of rejoicing, they sought to stop the person. Why? Because he was not part of their circle. They were operating from a bounded-set approach to ministry, whereas Jesus' response to his disciples was a striking example of a centered-set approach:[3]

> John said to him, "Teacher, we saw someone casting out demons in your name, and we tried to stop him, because he was not following us." But Jesus said, "Do not stop him, for no one who does a mighty work in my name will be able soon afterward to speak evil of me. For the one who is not against us is for us. For truly, I say to you, whoever gives you a cup of water to drink because you belong to Christ will by no means lose his reward." (Mk 9:38-41 ESV)

The New Testament includes examples of both bounded-set and centered-set approaches to faith and ministry. Mark 9:38-41 is an example of a centered-set approach (in the case of Jesus, though not his disciples), whereas the Jerusalem Council recorded in Acts 15 is an example of a bounded-set approach. There James, Peter, Paul, Barnabas, and others debated the significance of circumcision in the Christian life, especially for Gentiles. Given the Spirit's movement in Gentile believers' lives through faith apart from circumcision, they

---

[3]Joel Green writes on a parallel passage, Lk 9:49-50, "Jesus had effectively negated conventional issues of status, yet John and his companions had operated within those conventions in order to deny this 'outsider' permission to work in Jesus' name. That is, they had engaged in boundary-making on the basis of conventional notions of perceived honor. He did not belong to the community around Jesus, so his behavior was disallowed." Joel B. Green, *The Gospel of Luke*, The New International Commentary on the New Testament (Grand Rapids: Eerdmans, 1997), 392.

determined that this rite should not be required of Gentile believers, and those who sought to persuade Gentiles to be circumcised should be prohibited. The issue had become a cause of great turmoil and division, and needed to be resolved for the sake of unity in the church at large. Even so, the boundaries that were put in place were ultimately for the sake of unity in mission: instead of excluding the Gentiles unless they were circumcised, they were included as equals through faith alone in Jesus and shared experience of the manifestation of the Holy Spirit.

Another example of a bounded-set approach is 1 John 2:18-27 in conjunction with 1 John 4:1-6. The author of this epistle expressed grave concern over those who had left the fellowship because of their claim that Jesus has not come in the flesh. Their teaching reflected the spirit of the antichrist, not the Holy Spirit. As with the Jerusalem Council, where saving faith in Jesus was accompanied by the manifestation of the Spirit, here doctrinal truth centering on the incarnation was viewed as central to confession in the Spirit. The spirit that denies Jesus' incarnation is not of the Spirit, and not of God (1 Jn 4:2-3). Even here, though, the aim is not doctrine as the end, but as the means to the end of love. It follows that those who deny the incarnation could easily deny embodied love, whereas those who affirm the incarnation must embody love. It supernaturally follows (1 Jn 4:7-21).

The preceding discussion suggests that there is a biblical basis for bounded sets, specifically when trying to navigate teachings that are promoting disunity in the church. However, even in these situations, the aim is not ultimately to exclude, but to foster unity among the faithful for greater impact in life and ministry.

Jesus was not engaged in boundary maintenance at every turn in his ministry. While he engaged in teaching about the kingdom of God, what God is like, and about his own person and work, the aim was never teaching as such. Rather, it was about mission to the world. One of the most striking examples of Jesus' emphasis came in response to John the Baptist and his disciples recorded in Luke 7:18-23. John was in prison and was pondering if Jesus was the long-awaited Messiah. Jesus did not engage in a long doctrinal exercise in answering John. Rather, he placed emphasis on acts of mercy toward those in great need and the proclamation of the gospel to the poor. Only after John's disciples departed did Jesus make the staggering claim that while no one born of woman is greater than John, everyone who belongs to the kingdom of God inaugurated in Jesus' person is greater than John (Lk 7:28). This claim is doctrinally important—Jesus is the center. However, the teaching is not an end in itself. Jesus' aim is proclaiming the gospel of the kingdom to the marginalized and demonstrating it in acts of mercy.

The focus on the proclamation of the gospel of the kingdom also appears in Matthew 9:9-13. This passage records an incident where the Pharisees sought to ensure boundary maintenance and found Jesus failing miserably. Jesus had just called Matthew the tax collector to follow him. He was eating in Matthew's house with fellow tax collectors and sinners.[4] How could Jesus be a legitimate rabbi if he was not maintaining clear boundaries by excluding association with the morally impure? Jesus rebuked the Pharisees: "But when he heard it, he said, 'Those who are well have no need of a physician, but those who are sick. Go and learn what this means: "I desire mercy, and not sacrifice." For I came not to call the righteous, but sinners'" (Mt 9:12-13 ESV).

The irony in this passage is that the Pharisees' emphasis on boundaries related to purity made it impossible for them to reach out to those whom God sought to reach. Moral and doctrinal purity have their place, never as ends in themselves, but always as ends to mercy.

---

[4]Jesus' eating with sinners has been defended as one of the most historically reliable and distinctive aspects of authentic Jesus tradition. See Craig Blomberg, "Jesus, Sinners, and Table Fellowship," *Bulletin for Biblical Research* 19 (2009): 35–62. N. T. Wright argues that "he ate with 'sinners,' and kept company with people normally on or beyond the borders of respectable society—which of course in his day and culture, meant not merely social respectability but religious uprightness, proper covenant behaviour, loyalty to the traditions, and hence to the aspirations of Israel." N. T. Wright, *Jesus and the Victory of God*, Christian Origins and the Question of God, vol. 2 (Minneapolis: Fortress, 1996), 149.

How else do we make sense of God's holiness? In view of Jesus' life, teaching, and example, we see that God's holiness does not entail setting himself apart from sinners. Rather, God's holiness sets him apart from sin for sinners.

Could a case be made for claiming that the false teachers in the New Testament were not simply those whose teaching was off to a degree? Could it be that biblically speaking, false teachers were and are those who use orthodoxy and heterodoxy to oppress and exclude outsiders and the downtrodden, rather than reach out to them compassionately to invite them to share in Jesus' life? In contrast, orthodoxy always aims to include others through faith alone in Jesus apart from status, especially the outsiders and downtrodden. That is why James tells us that biblical religion includes caring for widows and orphans in their distress, and not simply for keeping oneself un-polluted by the world (Jas 1:27). James discounts mere concern for doctrinal truth and personal faith that does not entail robust care for the poor and excluded from society. Faith that matters always works, specifically on behalf of the orphan, widow, and alien in their distress. Thus, personal liberation through faith in response to God's grace always entails works of righteousness.

In answering the question in the subheading above, centered sets reflect a missional heart that reaches out and includes the poor and lower class (Jas 1–2), the moral outcast (Mt 9:9-13), and the Gentile outsider (Gal 2:11-14). Through faith in Jesus, they become one people with the supposed well-to-do, righteous, and insiders. The bounded set of doctrinal and moral purity serves this missional thrust. When the church fails to include the marginalized, such as Gentiles, women, and slaves, excluding them for the sake of the Jews, men, and the free (Gal 3:28), among others, the likes of Paul will stand up and demand inclusion in the faith community, just as he did with Cephas (Gal 2:11-14), and even more so, the Judaizers (see Paul's letter to the Galatians as well as Phil 3). Thus, the bounded rebuke to the legalists, the proto-Gnostics, and those favoring the rich serve to liberate the gospel center from false boundaries. In each of these cases, the boundary is God's will involving new birth through Jesus, whom we receive and in whom we believe, not natural descent or a husband's will (Jn 1:12-13),[5] not circumcision, maleness, Roman citizenship or nonslave status (Gal 3:28), private and esoteric knowledge (Col 2:8, 18-19), ceremonial purity (Mt 9:9-13), or wealth or class (Jas 1; 2).[6]

One could make a case that the legalism addressed in Matthew and Galatians, the proto-Gnosticism challenged in Colossians and 1 John, and the classism confronted in James were all grounded in faulty power dynamics of elitism and exclusion. They run contrary to the gospel, which is a different kind of power—the power of God available to all through faith. As Paul writes in Romans 1,

> I am under obligation both to Greeks and to barbarians, both to the wise and to the foolish. So I am eager to preach the gospel to you also who are in Rome. For I am not ashamed of the gospel, for it is the power of God for salvation to everyone who believes, to the Jew first and also to the Greek. For in it the righteousness of God is revealed from faith for faith, as it is written, "The righteous shall live by faith." (Rom 1:14-17 ESV)

---

[5]See D. A. Carson's discussion on these verses in *The Gospel According to John*, The Pillar New Testament Commentary (Grand Rapids: Eerdmans, 1990), 126.

[6]It would be a grave mistake to assume that Jesus removed all boundaries and proclaimed a gospel of mere tolerance. He required repentance and faith in his person. Jesus reframed sinfulness and renamed sinners through grace and forgiveness. Miroslav Volf puts the matter in this way: "It would be a mistake . . . to conclude from Jesus's compassion toward those who transgressed social boundaries that his mission was merely to demask the mechanisms that created 'sinners' by falsely ascribing sinfulness to those who were considered socially unacceptable. He was no prophet of 'inclusion' . . . for whom the chief virtue was acceptance and the cardinal vice intolerance. Instead, he was a bringer of 'grace,' who not only scandalously included 'anyone' in the fellowship of 'open commensality,' but made the 'intolerant' demand of repentance and the 'condescending' offer of forgiveness (Mark 1:15; 2:15-17). The mission of Jesus consisted not simply of renaming the behavior that was falsely labeled 'sinful' but also in remaking the people who have actually sinned and suffered distortion. The double strategy of renaming and remaking, rooted in the commitment to both the outcast and the sinner, to the victim and the perpetrator, is the proper background against which an adequate notion of sin as exclusion can emerge." Miroslav Volf, *Exclusion and Embrace: A Theological Exploration of Identity, Otherness, and Reconciliation* (Nashville: Abingdon, 1996), 72-73.

What import might this biblical claim have for the cultivation and flourishing of an evangelical liberation theology today? Among other things, it entails reframing the word *evangelical* so that it does not entail power politics that excludes many for the sake of the chosen few, the righteous, and the well-to-do. Rather, it involves returning it to its biblical roots of good news—the evangel—especially for the orphan, widow, and alien in their distress. It involves taking back *evangelical* to the eighteenth and nineteenth centuries in England and the United States—prior to the Scopes Trial and its aftermath in the 1920s and beyond—back to a time when the movement was defined by a biblically based conversionism that involved a form of crucicentrism toward an activism of abolition, not slavery. It also entails going back further in time to the patristic through early Reformation eras, prior to the wars of religion in the 1600s, when religion was not defined primarily in terms of objective propositions to which to assent, but a transformed heart by faith in God's word leading toward virtuous living for the sake of human flourishing.

Where did we go wrong? Historical considerations.

The preceding biblical exposition suggests that orthodoxy is a liberating theology at its core. It is always missional. It always seeks to promote virtue and human flourishing, not in the Aristotelian sense of a noble class of virtuous friends, but one that involves enemy love as well as love for those whom the society deems unattractive.[7] This subject will be treated in the next major section. There consideration will be given to a centered-set theological framework in service to a more liberating evangelical theology.

For now, it is important to highlight the need to safeguard against rigidity and "obsessive boundary maintenance," as Olson notes in his assessment of centered and bounded models, and to account for

---

[7]Refer to the discussion of Aristotle in Leslie Stevenson, David L. Haberman, and Peter Matthews Wright, *Twelve Theories of Human Nature*, 6th ed. (New York: Oxford University Press, 2013), 105-6. See also the excellent comparison of Aristotle and the New Testament on friendship and love on 113-14.

historical contexts where the latter occurred. By understanding the historical backdrop to this problem, it is hoped that we will not have to repeat that historical dynamic again and again.

It is vital that Christian communities throughout the ages place their emphasis on the essentials of the faith, as difficult as the task of discerning essentials and nonessentials can be. For Olson, the center is the gospel, which should be the focus, not orthodoxy, which concerns boundaries. When the distinction is lost, an inquisitive posture can easily move toward an inquisitional stance involving what Olson calls "inquisitorial judgments" toward those who fall outside the parameters of legitimacy. Orthodox boundaries certainly have an important role to play, but always in support of the center.

Against this backdrop, it is wise to keep in mind the oft-quoted statement (wrongly) attributed to St. Augustine: "in essentials unity, in non-essentials liberty, in all things charity." The phrase originates with Rupertus Meldenius, who included it in a tract published during the Thirty Years War in the seventeenth century (1618–1648). Religious strife involving various branches of Christendom played a significant role in that war, or series of wars.[8] The strife was bound up with the dissolution of the Holy Roman Empire and the rise of nation states, along with religious diversification. The peace that was eventually brokered involved various political powers territorializing and privatizing religion by making the different ecclesial bodies serve national territorial interests. When such territorializing and privatizing of faith occurs, it is quite difficult for Christian movements to come together as liberating forces for the sake of human flourishing, including the orphan, widow, and alien in their distress.

While creedal statements date back to the early church, here Christian confessions were reduced to objectified propositions. One of the effects of this move was that such objectification of religious confessions led eventually to a war with science, as scientific terms were also objectified

---

[8]Philip Schaff, *History of the Christian Church*, vol. 7 (repr. Grand Rapids: Eerdmans, 1965), 650-53.

and placed in juxtaposition and opposition to theological claims. Previously, science, or natural philosophy, as it was called during the ancient and medieval periods, was a stepping stone along with mathematics to engaging theology in service to human flourishing. Still another effect was that with the emergence of colonial powers in Europe, the Christian faith was exported to other lands in service to Europe's God and the countries of the West. In addition to the colonization of non-Western peoples, the gospel was also colonized, as it was no longer understood as the theopolitical and cosmic basis and telos for human flourishing and virtue, which concerned all people regardless of their stations in life. The gospel devolved into a privatized system of beliefs as a world religion in competition with other world religions that was useful for the purposes of national territorial expansion.[9]

It is important to note one accompanying historical factor bearing directly on oppression. The development of a global Christian mission involving colonial powers during the late medieval period, followed by the privatizing and replacing of Christian mission with the mission of reason during the modern Enlightenment period made it possible for slavery to accompany colonization. Religion and reason were used one after the other in the subjugation of non-Christian and seemingly nonenlightened peoples of the East and South.[10]

Closer to home and closer in time, the Civil War here in the States as well as the ensuing war between faith and science had an equally damning impact on evangelicalism and the Christian religion more broadly. Mark Noll argued that evangelicalism's decline on the public stage started in the mid-nineteenth century.[11] The Civil War eroded

---

[9]For consideration of this historical trajectory, see Peter Harrison, *The Territories of Science and Religion* (Chicago: The University of Chicago Press, 2015). Refer also to Jason Ānanda Josephson, *The Invention of Religion in Japan* (Chicago: The University of Chicago Press, 2012); Tomoko Masuzawa, *The Invention of World Religions* (Chicago: The University of Chicago Press, 2005).

[10]See Manuela Boatcă, "Colonial Beginnings: The Christian Mission" and "Enlightenment: The Civilising Mission," in *Global Inequalities Beyond Occidentalism*, Global Connections (London: Routledge, 2015). James H. Cone addresses the Enlightenment's oppressive significance for non-Western peoples in *God of the Oppressed* (New York: Orbis Books, 1997), 42-43.

[11]Mark A. Noll, *American Evangelical Christianity: An Introduction* (Oxford: Blackwell, 2001), 202.

public theology as the North and South waged war with the same Bible in hand. It was a conflict over theology as well as a conflict over state and federal rights on the question of slavery.[12]

Just as the North and South were divided over theology and slavery, so many fundamentalist Christians waged war with their more progressive and liberal-minded Christian counterparts on science. The struggle came to a head with the Scopes Trial in 1925. George Marsden wrote, "It would be difficult to overestimate the impact" of this trial "in transforming fundamentalism."[13] While evangelicalism had played a key role in the abolitionist movement in the nineteenth century, increasingly evangelicalism was subsumed under an otherworldly and privatized fundamentalist worldview that was alienated from the public square and failed to address racism and poverty.

This reactionary and escapist impulse eventually led to Carl F. H. Henry's 1947 clarion call challenging the fundamentalist-evangelical movement in *The Uneasy Conscience of Modern Fundamentalism.* Henry called on the movement to engage in rigorous theological reflection and social action: "Fundamentalism is wondering just how it is that a world-changing message narrowed its scope to the changing of isolated individuals."[14] Henry added, "Whereas once the redemptive gospel was a world-changing message, now it was narrowed to a world-resistant message. Out of twentieth-century Fundamentalism of this sort there could come no contemporary version of Augustine's *The City of God.*"[15]

Decades later in 1998, James Montgomery Boice built on Henry's landmark book: "Evangelicals had been avoiding the great social

[12]On the theological crisis bound up with the Civil War, see Mark Noll, *The Civil War as a Theological Crisis*, The Steven and Janice Brose Lectures in the Civil War Era (Chapel Hill: The University of North Carolina Press, 2006).

[13]George Marsden, *Fundamentalism and American Culture: The Shaping of Twentieth-Century Evangelicalism—1870–1925* (Oxford: Oxford University Press, 1980), 184.

[14]Carl F. H. Henry, *The Uneasy Conscience of Modern Fundamentalism* (Grand Rapids: Eerdmans, 1947; reprint, with a foreword by Richard J. Mouw, 2003), 14.

[15]Henry, *Uneasy Conscience*, 19.

issues of the day, above all racism and the plight of the poor, and we were uneasy about it somewhere deep in our inmost thoughts and hearts."[16] Boice went further and claimed that the time had now come for a sequel to be written titled "The Easy Conscience of Modern Evangelicalism." Boice was referring to Martin Marty's claim that the most worldly people in America at the end of the twentieth century would be the evangelicals.[17] Boice concurred: "We have fulfilled his prophecy, and it is not yet the year 2000." Boice asserted that evangelicals have become fixated with gaining this world's kingdom and "have made politics and money our weapons of choice for grasping it."[18] Often, one finds evangelicals calling for being biblically correct, not politically correct. If only we were more politically aware, as our particular approach to biblicism often clouds or covers political agendas, including white middle-class values.

The lack of attention to race and poverty, as well as the politicizing of evangelicals' own racially framed concerns, manifested themselves in the Scopes Trial. Certainly, for many white fundamentalist Christians, their view of theology and morality was hinged to their rejection of evolutionary theory. It was a part of a long-standing struggle to address a crisis of authority.[19] However, their fight with white modernists led them down a path that differed radically culturally from their African American evangelical counterparts. While African American evangelicals shared many of the same theological convictions, they took serious issue with their white counterparts' tolerance for injustice. Entrance into the kingdom of God

---

[16]James Montgomery Boice, "Our All-Too-Easy Conscience," *Modern Reformation* 7, no. 5 (September/October 1998): 44

[17]Boice, "Our All-Too-Easy Conscience," 44.

[18]Boice, "Our All-Too-Easy Conscience," 44.

[19]On evangelicalism and the question of authority, see Molly Worthen, *Apostles of Reason: The Crisis of Authority in American Evangelicalism* (Oxford: Oxford University Press, 2013). Worthen complexifies the culture war phenomenon to make it not simply a political struggle over doctrine, or a war between religious conservatives and secular liberals, but also a conflict within the evangelical movement to bring together faith and reason, and how to lead the nation back to God's righteous ways.

entailed faithfulness on matters of racial justice and equity for many African American evangelicals.[20]

For evangelicals of whatever ethnic background, it is important that we do not stop at doctrine and allow it to divide us. A centered-set approach can assist us in moving through doctrinal similarities and differences toward justice and equity. Doctrinal truth and moral purity both matter to God (1 Tim 4:16; Jas 1:27). What is required is a more liberating evangelical theology.

A CENTERED-SET APPROACH TO AN
EVANGELICAL LIBERATION THEOLOGY

What might a centered-set evangelical liberation theology look like?

The envisioned centered-set approach to an evangelical liberation theology involves a well-reasoned affection toward a certain social

---

[20]See Mary Beth Swetnam Mathews, *Doctrine and Race: African American Evangelicals and Fundamentalism Between the Wars* (Tuscaloosa: The University of Alabama Press, 2017), 87, 96-97. Black evangelicals shared many of the fundamental theological and personal moral convictions that their white counterparts did, but they went further. As Mathews writes elsewhere, "But the A.M.E. and National Baptist Convention writers did not stop there. They also charged that white Christians were not truly Christian because they allowed segregation, discrimination, and violence against African Americans. . . . White fundamentalists had made fundamentalism a racialized term by excluding African Americans from the conversation and doubting their ability to understand Christianity; African Americans evangelicals returned the favor and made salvation contingent on racial equality." Mary Beth Mathews, "The History of Black Evangelicals and American Politics," *Black Perspectives*, March 30, 2017, www.aaihs.org/the-history-of-black-evangelicals-and-american-politics/. Elsewhere Mathews states, "White fundamentalists framed the conflict they had with modernists in an all-or-nothing way. If you, for example, denied the virgin birth or read the Bible as a literary remnant of a long past group of believers, then you had departed the Christian fold. White fundamentalists tended to believe that only people who embraced fundamentalist doctrines were Christians. African-American evangelicals rejected this all-or-nothing approach, even as they issued their own ultimatum—that to be a Christian, one had to treat all people as equals. They had no quarrel with, say, conservative white evangelicals' rejection of modernism's embrace of historical criticism, nor did they wish to see black Christians drinking, dancing, or gambling. But they insisted that a strict reading of the Bible, especially the New Testament, would produce an ecclesiology that taught that only those individuals who preached love and equality could truly claim the mantle of Jesus." Mary Beth Swetnam Mathews, "African-American Christians and Fundamentalism," interview with Thomas S. Kidd, The Gospel Coalition, April 4, 2017; https://blogs.thegospelcoalition.org/evangelical-history/2017/04/04/african-american-christians-and-fundamentalism/. Consider also Jeffrey P. Moran, "Reading Race into the Scopes Trial: African American Elites, Science, and Fundamentalism," *The Journal of American History* 90, no. 3 (Dec. 2003): 898-99; Jeffrey P. Moran, *American Genesis: The Evolution Controversies from Scopes to Creation Science* (Oxford: Oxford University Press, 2012).

end. This well-reasoned affection is the holy love of the triune God embodied in Jesus through the Spirit. It is a love that turns outward because there is no need or lack in the divine communion. This love creates the attraction and so creates the world and ever turns outward toward the world. There are no elitist boundaries to God's covenantal love, which is centered on the lowly. God gives preferential treatment to the poor[21]—not because God plays favorites, but because we all too often discount the poor and lowly in favor of the rich and lofty.

God gives preferential treatment to the poor and lowly? How else does one make sense of the Magnificat (Lk 1:46-55), where Mary proclaims that God brings down the mighty and exalts the lowly, or the cross where God gloriously lowers himself in his incarnate state to the level of a slave through whom he provides salvation or liberation in his resurrection and ascension (Phil 2:5-11)? Jesus came from peasant stock and blessed the poor (Lk 6:20) as well as the poor in spirit (Mt 5:3). The New Testament understanding of poverty is broader than what many conservative evangelicals and liberal Christians envision. One might even say it is unbounded as we center the discussion on Jesus. Gordon Fee and Douglas Stuart have argued that we must account for physical poverty and spiritual poverty if we are to aspire to Jesus' vision:

> In Matthew the poor are "the poor in spirit"; in Luke they are simply "you poor" in contrast to "you that are rich" (6:24). On such points most people tend to have only half a canon. Traditional evangelicals tend to read only "the poor in spirit"; social activists tend to read only "you poor." We insist that *both* are canonical. In a truly profound sense the real poor are those who recognize themselves as impoverished before God. But the God of the Bible, who became incarnate in Jesus

---

[21]On God's preferential option for the poor, see Gustavo Gutiérrez's *A Theology of Liberation: History, Politics, and Salvation,* 15th anniversary edition with new introduction (Maryknoll, NY: Orbis Books, 1988). See also Daniel G. Groody and Gustavo Gutiérrez, ed., *The Preferential Option for the Poor Beyond Theology* (Notre Dame, IN: Notre Dame Press, 2013).

of Nazareth, is a God who pleads the cause of the oppressed and the disenfranchised. One can scarcely read Luke's gospel without recognizing his interest in this aspect of the divine revelation (see 14:12–14; cf. 12:33–34 with the Matthean parallel, 6:19–21).[22]

God is free to liberate the poor and captive, since God is holy and unadulterated love. There is no need in God. God does not need our love, since God is secure in the mutual indwelling love of Father, Son, and Spirit. And yet, that mutual indwelling is not exclusionary, but open and inviting, including those on the margins. The Spirit of God never closes the circle of communion, but reaches out to include us through faith in Jesus. The Spirit completes the Trinity from all eternity, though not in a manner that closes God off from the world God creates. In the words of Colin Gunton, the Spirit who, as Basil states, "completes the divine and blessed Trinity," operates

> not as the one who completes an inward turning circle, but as one who is the agent of the Father's outward turning to the creation in his Son. As the one who "completes," the Spirit does indeed establish God's aseity, his utter self-sufficiency. Yet this aseity is the basis of a movement outwards. . . . The love of the Father, Son and Spirit is a form of love which does not remain content with its eternal self-sufficiency because that self-sufficiency is the basis of a movement outwards to create and perfect a world whose otherness from God— of being distinctly itself—is based in the otherness-in-relation of Father, Son and Spirit in eternity.[23]

God's love is unconditional—agape. As a result, God is free to love the one whom we often deem unworthy of our affection. At the center of God's agape love is the orphan, widow, and alien in their distress. God's inclusive and active liberating love always includes the other,

---

[22]Gordon Fee and Douglas Stuart, *How to Read the Bible for All Its Worth*, 2nd ed. (Grand Rapids: Zondervan), 125.

[23]Colin E. Gunton, *Act and Being: Towards a Theology of the Divine Attributes* (London: SCM Press, 2002), 146.

notably the one deemed ugly, lowly, dispossessed. God's love creates the attraction. As Martin Luther writes, "The love of God does not find, but creates, that which is pleasing to it. The love of man comes into being through that which is pleasing to it."[24]

God's love is always active, flowing from the divine center—not fixated on boundaries, but moving out toward the margins. Orthodox beliefs (orthodoxy) express a heart trajectory (orthopathy) that orients us toward a gospel-centric way of life (orthopraxy) embodied in the church. The church is the triune God's community that operates as a distinct polis in society at large. Rather than bounding the church as exclusionary, these beliefs expressing this heart orientation open us up to include those on the margins, such as the widow, orphan, and alien in their distress.

The church's way of life is never private but public and political. The church is the triune God's kingdom community. The church participates in the missions of God, namely, the Son and Spirit. Jesus extends his incarnate, cruciform, resurrected, and ascended life through the Spirit in the life of the church. While the church can never atone for personal and social sins, it experiences the transformative power of redemption interpersonally and systemically through Jesus' atoning work. The church knows Jesus as its substitute for sin and lives in solidarity with Jesus as he transforms human hearts and structures as well as all creaturely life in the Spirit.

In view of the preceding, how might a centered-set approach bear on the doctrine of atonement in fostering a truly liberating theology? It will prove helpful to consider briefly atonement theories as a case study. It will be argued that apart from a centered-set approach to theology, there is no way to address the human problem of sin and evil in a comprehensive manner bearing on liberation themes.

---

[24]Martin Luther, "Heidelberg Disputation," in *Martin Luther's Basic Theological Writings*, ed. Timothy F. Lull (Minneapolis: Augsburg Fortress, 1989), 48.

How might this centered-set framework be applied to the center or crux of the Christian faith—atonement theory?

In his *Christian Theology*, Millard Erickson writes that penal substitution serves as the central model of the atonement. In his estimation, it includes the merits of all other positions.[25] Regardless of the merits of penal substitution as an atonement model, this orientation does not reflect a centered-set approach. God's being revealed in Jesus' Spirit-filled life action of incarnation, crucifixion, resurrection, and ascension centers us, rather than individual atonement models, all of which operate as facets of Jesus' life work in the community.[26] Moreover, given the thrust of Jesus' life, such centering includes those beyond the boundaries at the margins of society, namely the orphan, widow, and alien in their distress.

While the penal substitution model has a place in the development of an evangelical theology of liberation, it is not the central model. No model is. Though it addresses a core biblical emphasis on sin and guilt and the needed payment through Jesus' substitutionary work, if left in isolation or offered as the dominant model, penal substitution easily leads toward a punitive and individualistic engagement of evil. If left to itself or viewed as an overarching paradigm, it cannot address adequately and even ignores or tolerates various facets of systemic evil. In addition to penal substitution, which addresses individual liberation from the sin and guilt that can easily weigh people down in the fight against oppression, Jesus' cross also serves as an example of God's love for his suffering world (moral influence), and our love for God while identifying with the plight of the world (Socinian). Moreover, victorious suffering in the form of transformative solidarity must also play a part, especially pertaining to persecuted

---

[25]See Millard Erickson's exposition of penal substitution, titled "The Central Theme of the Atonement," in *Christian Theology*, 3rd ed. (Grand Rapids: Baker Academic, 2013), ch. 37.

[26]For an example of this multifaceted and inexhaustible orientation centered in Jesus' storied work of salvation, see Fleming Rutledge's *The Crucifixion: Understanding the Death of Jesus Christ* (Grand Rapids: Eerdmans, 2015).

minority groups in the face of political and religious oppression, as was the case for the early church (Christus victor).[27]

The doctrine of atonement is multifaceted. The problems it addresses and solutions it offers are complex. Jesus addresses personal guilt and existential alienation as well as systemic oppression. He pays the penalty for personal sin and is victorious over existential suffering, as well as over large-scale social injustice. Given this diverse array of themes and dynamics, we must enter into dialogue with theological voices from various religious traditions and cultural backgrounds. Only as we listen and learn from one another can we be in a position to reflect more capably and expansively on the atonement's import for the fullness of life. In this light, consider what James Cone, the father of black theology, conveys about the import of Jesus' cross for the African American community. During an interview titled "Theologians and White Supremacy," Cone says,

> The cross stands at the center of the Christian faith of African-Americans because Jesus' suffering was similar to their American experience. Just as Jesus Christ was crucified, so were blacks lynched. In the American experience, the cross is the lynching tree. The crucifixion of Jesus was a first-century lynching. If American Christians want to understand the meaning of the cross, they have to view it through the image of the lynching tree on which approximately 5,000 mostly (but not exclusively) black people were killed.[28]

---

[27]The argument has been made that the Christus victor model waned in influence during the medieval period as the church went from being a persecuted minority to receiving official status and legitimacy in the empire. As a result, the need to portray Jesus' atoning work as the pivotal point in the cosmic conflict between God and Satan became less significant. See Walter Wink, *The Powers That Be: Theology for a New Millennium* (New York: Galilee Doubleday, 2009), 89-90. For consideration of Christus victor framed more broadly in terms of its significance during the patristic period, see Alan F. Johnson and Robert E. Webber, *What Christians Believe: A Biblical and Historical Summary* (Grand Rapids: Zondervan, 1993), 258-63.

[28]James H. Cone, "Theologians and White Supremacy: An Interview with James H. Cone," *America: The Jesuit Review*, November 20, 2006, www.americamagazine.org/issue/592/article /theologians-and-white-supremacy. See also James H. Cone, *The Cross and the Lynching Tree* (Maryknoll, NY: Orbis Books, 2011).

An evangelical theology of liberation must account for personal conversion from a sinful heart orientation (an evangelical hallmark) as well as conversion of societal structures of evil, a theme often lacking in evangelicalism. Evangelicals often prize individual and personal relational concerns, but fail to account for systemic issues, including matters pertaining to racialization.[29] If we are to move beyond the divide for the sake of greater unity and a more liberating theology, this division must be overcome. The cross must not be viewed as apolitical or indifferent to systemic injustices, nor the weapon or instrument of injustice,[30] but as the transformative instrument of just and equitable solidarity.

How might we continue to cultivate the liberation theological conversation among evangelicals in an open way?

Understand that all theology is contextual and perspectival. This is a point brought home by Robert Jenson. Unfortunately, not everyone recognizes what Jenson calls "historical self-consciousness."[31] At least on race, white theology often fails to account for its racial self-consciousness, or subconsciousness. Evangelical theology is racialized. It is not always what we write, but also what we do not write about or emphasize theologically that reflects racial ideological patterns.

Two of the dynamics or factors that work against a healthy consideration of race are hubris and homogeneity. First, hubris. We must realize that we all struggle with pride and struggle to affirm particularity. Hermeneutical hubris is a problem from which we all require liberation. It must be replaced by hermeneutical humility. It is all too easy to consider our approach to theology and worship the best. In his book, *One Church, Many Tribes: Following Jesus the Way God Made You,* Richard Twiss writes,

---

[29]Michael O. Emerson and Christian Smith, *Divided by Faith: Evangelical Religion and the Problem of Race in America* (New York: Oxford University Press, 2000), 76, 78.

[30]"Where the cross goes, there is never life more abundantly—only death, destruction, and ultimately betrayal." Vine Deloria Jr., *God Is Red: A Native View of Religion* (Golden, CO: Fulcrum Publishing, 1994), 261.

[31]Robert W. Jenson, *Systematic Theology,* vol. 1, *The Triune God* (New York: Oxford University Press, 1997), ix.

Because we are all so prone to be culturally egocentric, the temptation is to consider our worldview the biblical and correct one, shunning all others as unbiblical and wrong. Worse yet is our habit of judging cultural ways—songs, dances, rituals, etc.—to be sinful when there is no clear violation of Scripture.[32]

Vincent Wimbush addresses this point as well, as he chronicles the departure of many African Americans to fundamentalist Christianity and the supposed move from biblical illiteracy:

The sharp criticism of the biblical illiteracy of African Americans is actually quite incredible. Rather than seeing in such criticism a mere reference to the lack of a certain type of education, or knowledge of the pertinent "facts," it should be interpreted as a radical religious re-socialization. It amounts to a deracialization of the African American religious world view, masked, of course, as a legitimate, authoritative, and broad-based, if not universal, race-neutral view and stance. . . . Protestant-defined fundamentalism, with its obvious racial, ethnic, and class origins, was masked as a movement that had transcended all such categories through its fetishization of the Bible as text. As this fundamentalism was embraced by African Americans, African American historical cultural experiences were (depending on the particular strain of fundamentalism or the nature of outside pressures) necessarily backgrounded, rendered invisible, or held in contempt.[33]

In addition to hermeneutical hubris, it is vital that we guard against a premature universalizing or homogenizing tendency. Uniformity is not the same thing as unity, which involves particularity and diversity. It is impossible to acquire a generic and pure gospel free of various cultural dynamics. Lesslie Newbigin maintains, "The idea that one can or could at any time separate out by some process of distillation a pure gospel unadulterated by any cultural

---

[32]Richard Twiss, *One Church, Many Tribes: Following Jesus the Way God Made You* (Ventura, CA: Regal Books, 2000), 113.

[33]Vincent L. Wimbush, *The Bible and African Americans: A Brief History* (Minneapolis: Fortress Press, 2003), 72-73.

accretions is an illusion."[34] The Japanese Christian intellectual Uchimura Kanzo weighs in as well on the matter from his uniquely Eastern context:

> A Japanese by becoming a Christian does not cease to be a Japanese. On the contrary, he becomes more Japanese by becoming a Christian. A Japanese who becomes an American or an Englishman, or an amorphous universal man, is neither a true Japanese nor a true Christian.[35]

Jesus did not become a generic human, but was embodied as a Jewish person in first-century Palestine. The Spirit of God does not wipe out such particularity, but unifies all people in their cultural diversity, through faith in Jesus. Because he was and is particular, we are free to be the particular humans we are. The same goes for theological reflection. The particular narrative involving Israel and the church must not be whitewashed in favor of some Western or Occidental ideal, but shape our theological conversations, including race.[36]

Understand that all theology has the potential to foster or hinder liberation. Theology does not simply disclose or offer information about God and the world. Nor does it simply express religious experience in relation to God and the world. It also provides rules for how we are to speak about God and the world, and how to act accordingly. Now, not all uses of doctrine serve to foster human flourishing. Thus, it is important to discern between appropriate and inappropriate uses in service to the hallmark of evangelical activism noted at the outset of this chapter.

---

[34]Lesslie Newbigin, *Foolishness to the Greeks: The Gospel and Western Culture* (Grand Rapids: Eerdmans, 1986), 4.

[35]Kanzo Uchimura, "Japanese Christianity," in *Sources of Japanese Tradition*, vol. 2, ed. Ryusaku Tsunoda, Wm. Theodore de Bary, and Donald Keene (New York: Columbia University Press, 1958); reprinted in *Religion in the Japanese Experience: Sources and Interpretations*, ed. H. Byron Earhart, The Religious Life of Man Series (Belmont, CA: Wadsworth Publishing Company, 1974), 113.

[36]For more on this subject, see J. Kameron Carter, *Race: A Theological Account* (Oxford: Oxford University Press, 2008).

On the appropriate and inappropriate uses of theology, it is worth drawing attention to George Lindbeck's model for understanding the nature of doctrine. Lindbeck presents three ways of approaching Christian doctrine: cognitive-propositional, experiential-expressive, and cultural-linguistic. He sees certain benefits in each of the former two models, incorporating them into the third type in support of ecumenical discourse. As a postliberal theologian, Lindbeck rejects the conservative theological notion that doctrine ultimately discloses or reveals truths. Lindbeck also maintains that significant doctrinal differences can be reconciled ecumenically. However, he affirms the conservative conviction that doctrinal traditions are important and should be upheld. Lindbeck maintains that doctrines function as linguistic and grammatical devices that orient a community to speak and act appropriately. Without effective communication and accompanying action, we cannot flourish as a community.[37]

This chapter represents a conservative evangelical theological bent by affirming that doctrine does make truth claims (contrary to postliberal and liberal theology respectively). However, it also shares the view that doctrines express religious experiences (in keeping with liberal theology, though not contrary to core evangelical convictions on biblical authority). Finally, this essay takes seriously Lindbeck's emphasis on theology's performative task—doctrine must be applied and used in service to God and the world.

In his short though excellent treatment of Lindbeck's book, fellow evangelical theologian John Frame writes that Lindbeck does not offer us sufficient guidelines for which doctrinal grammatical rules to use. However, if one accepts an orthodox view of Scripture (which

---

[37]See George A. Lindbeck, *The Nature of Doctrine: Religion and Theology in a Postliberal Age* (Philadelphia: Westminster Press, 1984). Another helpful source in accounting for various perspectives in an open manner, especially as it pertains to moral activity, is Jonathan Haidt, *The Righteous Mind: Why Good People Are Divided by Politics and Religion* (New York: Pantheon Books, 2012). Unlike Lindbeck's ecumenical model for approaching doctrine, Haidt accounts for various moral intuitions that conservatives and liberals manifest in search of understanding and more comprehensive moral reasoning in public discourse.

provides the basis for making such determinations on use), one can benefit from Lindbeck's analysis. Frame writes that Lindbeck's model "complements, rather than replaces, the other two" models: "Doctrine is all three things: propositional truth-claims, expressions of the inner experience of regeneration, and rules for the speech and conduct of God's creatures. No one of these is prior to the others." It is often neglected that "the purpose of doctrine is not to be simply repeated, but also to be 'applied-' to be *used* for all of God's purposes in the world. And if we cannot *use* it, we cannot in any serious sense claim to 'understand' it."[38]

If we were to make use of this framework and apply it to the four core evangelical convictions (Bebbington) and case study offered earlier, it could be argued that all the major atonement theories (crucicentrism) have biblical support (biblicism). Furthermore, not only do they disclose facets of God's dealings with the world, but also they express certain cultural and experiential contexts and responses that lay claim to us (conversionism). Moreover, these atonement theories can orient us toward right speech and conduct for the purposes of human flourishing (activism), if applied correctly. A key centrist question posed in this essay would be, How does a particular doctrine (such as an atonement model) serve to advance human flourishing, namely, for the orphan, widow, and alien in their distress?

It is important to ask this question, seeking to find how a given doctrine or theory fosters human flourishing for the marginalized. While not reducing doctrine to usefulness, doctrinal articulations that do not serve the biblical mandate to love God and our neighbor, including the orphan, widow, and alien, must be jettisoned in favor of those who do (Mk 12:30-31; Lk 10:37; Deut 10:18; Zech 7:10; Jas 1:27). The centering is on the performance or action, and the bounding is not on doctrines as such, but uses of doctrine that fail to support

---

[38]John M. Frame, "Review of Lindbeck's *The Nature of Doctrine*," *The Presbyterian Journal* 43 (February 27, 1985): 11-12.

biblical justice. This framework ensures that human liberation flows freely from keen theological reflection.

Understand that all voices are important to the theological conversation, especially those often marginalized. It is important to cultivate an open table conversation. Without intending to delegitimize orthodoxy, it is often the case sociologically that the dominant cultural grouping dictates what is and what is not orthodox. In other words, those who control the terms of debate control the debate. In this light, it is important that dominant theological subcultures ask themselves if they are listening to minority voices to discern what they themselves might be missing and make sure that the minority representatives are not guests, but regular, active participants at the table of discourse. Here I am reminded of what one African American pastor said: he and his fellow African American pastor were invited as guests to predominantly white pastor gatherings in his city, not as full participants with regular table settings.

While dominant cultural and theological traditions may and often do provide invaluable insights into the biblical revelation, each theological tradition must understand that it is limited by human frailty and sin. Thus, dominant cultural voices must encourage and foster dynamics for open table conversations involving a dialogical posture and hermeneutic of humility that seeks to draw from the riches of Scripture and develop an ethic that cultivates human flourishing, especially for those often marginalized.[39]

It is also important that theologians in dominant cultural contexts guard against seeing themselves as experts. Like all others, they are

---

[39]We must guard against hubris and skepticism in hermeneutics. On this subject of hermeneutical humility in seeking to ascertain biblical truth, see the final chapter, "A Hermeneutics of Humility and Conviction," in Kevin Vanhoozer, *Is There A Meaning In This Text? The Bible, the Reader, and the Morality of Literary Knowledge* (Leicester, UK: Apollos, 1998), 455-68. Grant R. Osborne also provides invaluable service to the interpretive task in his work, *The Hermeneutical Spiral: A Comprehensive Introduction to Biblical Interpretation*, rev. and expanded ed. (Downers Grove, IL: IVP Academic, 2007). See, for example, his distinction between polyvalent meaning and polyvalent attitude, and his call for "interpretive realism" that involves "constant dialogue with the various communities of faith in order to reform and reformulate theories on the basis of further evidence or more coherent models" (517-18).

dialogue partners, fellow students, and comrades. While it is important to learn the dominant syntax of a given theological tradition, it is also important to deconstruct it if and when it does not promote a dialogical posture that is open to other voices in pursuit of the biblical mandate to care for the orphan, widow, and alien in their distress.[40]

CONCLUSION: THE LORD'S SUPPER
AND NATIVE TALKING CIRCLES

The best way to account for a dialogical posture is to move from a platform-based model of theological education to one set at a table. The Lord's Table, which takes us into Jesus' atoning work, calls us to envision theological education that is open in posture. Unlike the church in Corinth that misapplied the import of the Lord's Table and displaced those of a lower social class to the periphery, the agape feast exhorts us to keep the circle open, especially to the underside.[41] It involves doing theology from below, just as the Lord washed his disciples' feet. The difference here, though, is that we are all in a position of need in which the Lord alone washes feet in a truly efficacious manner. We are not even worthy to wash one another's feet apart from the Lord's initiative.

What is required is that in the Lord we all take off our outer garments and offer up our dirty feet and souls for cleansing. We must wash one another's feet. This participatory and cathartic act will also involve washing one another's theological perspectives. None of us see the biblical text from a God's-eye point of view. Each of us has limitations of various kinds. At best, we see through a glass dimly.

---

[40]Here I build on the dialogical framework developed in Paulo Freire, *Pedagogy of the Oppressed*, 30th anniversary ed. (New York: Bloomsbury Academic, 2000).

[41]According to Gordon Fee, the Lord's Supper was probably part of a common meal. The "haves" and "have-nots" were likely divided during this celebration, as it was "sociologically natural for the host to invite those of his/her own class to eat" in the dining room. Those not of their class (the less fortunate there in Corinth) ate in the courtyard. Gordon D. Fee, *The First Epistle to the Corinthians*, The New International Commentary on the New Testament, vol. 7 (Grand Rapids: Eerdmans, 1987), 533-34.

Only then shall we see face to face, as Paul writes in his treatment of the Spirit's most excellent gift of love in 1 Corinthians 13.

One of the best ways we can demonstrate love in the Spirit is to listen to one another share our perspectives and deepest values. Native Hawaiians call it "Talk Story." It involves vulnerability, as we share from the heart. I have found occasions to talk story risky, but also life giving. I have experienced a similar communal dynamic in a talking circle that was led by a Native American friend. In a talking circle, each person has opportunity to share without being interrupted, as the talking stick is handed from one person to the next. This practice can serve as an effective means to engage and transform conflict situations involving parties who might not otherwise listen to one another.

The same approach is required in theological reflection today if we are to safeguard against dominant cultural constructs marginalizing minority voices. Everyone is welcome at the table, which is never a platform. All of us should bring a theological dish to share at the agape feast and wash one another's feet with our various perspectives as we seek to account for the biblical mandate to care for the orphan, widow, and alien in their distress. We must also listen deeply, not simply to the words, but also to the breath and soul of each saint as the stick is passed from one person to another. In this way, we gain new insights and are energized and renewed to go out and remain at the margins, led by the same divine Spirit who centers us at the Lord's Table in the open circle.

CHAPTER TWO

EVANGELICAL THEOLOGIES OF LIBERATION

SOONG-CHAN RAH

THE CURRENT ERA OF AMERICAN CHRISTIANITY marks the transition from a Western, white-dominated evangelicalism to an ethnically diverse evangelicalism. Despite this increasing diversity, US evangelicalism has demonstrated a stubborn inability to address the entrenched assumption of white supremacy. When whiteness is viewed as superior, the need to confront captivity to Western white culture is not recognized. This inability to engage cultural captivity allows the status quo of the white dominance of US evangelicalism.

Students of American religion often limit the term *evangelical* to refer to North American Christians of European descent. The dominance of the white evangelical story has often resulted in the exclusion of the story of African American Christianity, despite theological compatibility. This lacuna results in an insufficient understanding of attempts at racial integration and increasing racial diversity among evangelicals in the United States in the latter half of the twentieth century. Despite the projection of a multiethnic future, the assumption of a white-dominated evangelicalism remains entrenched and resistant to liberation.[1]

---

[1]See Soong-Chan Rah, *The Next Evangelicalism* (Downers Grove, IL: InterVarsity Press, 2008).

African American Christianity offers a theological corrective to the problem of the Western white captivity of the church. In the last third of the twentieth century, particularly in the decades of the 1960s and 1970s, African American evangelicals emerged as a burgeoning movement. These self-identified evangelicals held to a conservative theological framework but were often excluded from key areas of evangelical leadership and influence. This chapter focuses on the inability of white evangelicalism to engage the narrative of African American Christianity and the absence of an evangelical theology of liberation because of this inability. The historical problem of engaging African American Christianity reveals the theological problem of white supremacy. How does a cultural captivity to white supremacy result in the inability to engage other narratives within American Christianity, thereby stifling the possibility of an evangelical theology of liberation?

EVANGELICAL IDENTITY

Defining evangelicalism presents an elusive task. The label is used in different contexts as a political, social, ecclesial, or theological term. Is *evangelical* a political designation entangled with the Republican party? Is it defined by sociological categories such as white, Anglo-Saxon, and Protestant? Is it contained in particular denominations or ecclesial traditions? Does it reflect particular theological boundaries? Or is it a cross-section of all of the above? Evangelicalism does not follow the typical rules of an institution with clear boundaries of membership, leadership, and structure. Mark Noll notes that "evangelicalism has always been made up of shifting movements, temporary alliances, and the lengthened shadows of individuals."[2]

Following World War II and in the latter half of the twentieth century, a neo-evangelicalism emerged that diverged from the more strident fundamentalism defining conservative Protestantism in the

---

[2]Mark Noll, *The Scandal of the Evangelical Mind* (Grand Rapids: Eerdmans, 1994), 8.

early half of the twentieth century. In 1942, the National Association of Evangelicals (NAE) was formed with an evangelical identity, rather than a fundamentalist one. In addition to the NAE, evangelicals (sometimes self-identified as neo-evangelicals) formed a number of institutions and organizations. These institutions developed social networks that supported each other's ministries and often transcended denominations. These networks united conservative Protestants and formed "a tighter national network among previously isolated centers of evangelical activity scattered around the country."[3]

Evangelicalism that had been theologically defined with a received heritage from historical Christianity now exhibited an external sociological expression in the twentieth century. Evangelicalism could be viewed from the perspective of its theological tenets, but also from the perspective of being a sociological movement. Evangelicals developed a sociological community bound together by the desire to preserve theological boundaries that sought to reflect historical orthodoxy. By seeing themselves as heirs of a distinct, received, and even unchallengeable tenets, US evangelicals could embrace their exceptional status and stave off challenges to their orthodox assumptions.

Evangelicals perceive themselves in the line of orthodoxy tracing back to biblical times. Evangelicals are the inheritors of orthodox Christianity from the chosen line evident in Genesis, to the chosen nation of Israel, to the New Testament church birthed in Acts 2, to the missionary efforts of Paul, to the early church and their martyrs, to the empowered missionary church, to the faithful remnant in Roman Christendom, to the great Protestant Reformers, to those who seek a pure faith on the canvas of tabula rasa, to the chosen people seeking to establish a city set on a hill, to the experiencers of great revivals, to the great missionaries of the great mission century, to the great

---

[3]Robert Wuthnow, *The Restructuring of American Religion* (Princeton, NJ: Princeton University Press, 1988), 174.

evangelists calling for personal conversion, and to the faithful remnant who serve as cultural warriors in the midst of the collapse of Christendom. Evangelicalism transcends denominations, integrating the Lutheran, Presbyterian, and Reformed churches, which trace their heritage to the Protestant Reformation; the passion of the Pietists, Puritans, and the Pentecostals; the mission emphasis of the Moravians and the Methodists; and those who claim to seek guidance from the Bible only, such as the Baptists and the Brethren. Evangelicals will consistently read the framework of their faith back into the history of Christianity as the inheritors and protectors of orthodoxy.

By viewing itself in the line of orthodoxy, US evangelicals face the temptation to assume that they inherited a completed theology. The goal of evangelical theology, therefore, is the preservation and conservation of received doctrine, rather than a healthy engagement with sociocultural reality. This assumption could lead to a form of cultural captivity as evangelical theology becomes more beholden to a culturally framed theology drawn from a particular context rather than actual engagement with Scripture and with the person and work of Jesus.

The desire to preserve orthodoxy is informed by an evangelical theology that operates from certain key intellectual assumptions. Historian George Marsden points out that Scottish Common Sense philosophy plays a prominent role in the formation of evangelical theology.[4] Scottish Common Sense asserts the human capacity to attain common knowledge through rational thought. Evangelical theology rooted in Scottish Common Sense assumes a level of reasonableness and perspicuity. Even as the culture around them changes, evangelicals assert a positive self-perception of the thought processes that formed their theology. Any adaptation to a changing culture would be rejected, since rationally derived presuppositions should not be challenged.

---

[4]George Marsden, *Fundamentalism and American Culture* (New York: Oxford University Press, 2006), 14-16.

Scottish Common Sense led evangelicals to assert that their fundamentalists roots emerged from rational thinking. Marsden finds that
fundamentalist-evangelical self-perception differed from the public
caricature of the backwater, uneducated, anti-intellectual, rural,
Southern fundamentalist. Fundamentalists viewed their own epistemology as a rational system in contrast to modern liberalism's reliance
on unproven hypotheses. Fundamentalists were not concerned about
all intellectual and scientific thought, but in the specific thought
process employed by modernists. The fundamentalist perspective
emerged from rational thought; therefore, the fundamentals of
evangelical faith served as nonnegotiable tenets of orthodoxy.

In the twentieth century, American evangelicalism was shaped by
concern over the preservation of orthodox faith against the onslaught
of secularism. Evangelicals expressed anxiety when American culture
and society, once believed to be a New Jerusalem, now exhibited
characteristics of fallen Babylon. US cities provided the negative
example of cultural decline. The cities (and the nation) that had been
bastions of white Anglo-Saxon Protestant faith were now home to
Italian Catholics, Orthodox Greeks, and Eastern European Jews. The
Great Migration that resulted in the massive influx of African
Americans into urban centers also challenged the assumption of
American cities as expressions of the superiority of white Protestantism. American cities and consequently American society was
believed to be under attack.

As the self-perceived inheritors of historical orthodoxy, US
evangelicals sought to preserve the integrity of the gospel in a
changing world. The social networks that emerged to strengthen
US evangelicalism in the latter part of the twentieth century served
the high calling of preserving Christian orthodoxy. In turn, they
expressed particular sociological characteristics and a distinct
evangelical identity emerged. This identity is often caricatured as
white middle-class suburbanite Republicans. This particular subset
of evangelicalism engaged the culture in a specific way, primarily

through the self-perception of exceptionalism and expectation of triumphalism.

Toward the end of the twentieth century, US evangelicals awakened as a public political presence. The neo-evangelical movement that emerged after World War II attempted to distance itself from the separatist tendencies of the fundamentalists and began to exhibit greater social engagement. However, despite that effort, the themes of an exceptional expression of Christianity remained entrenched. The social and political engagement of US evangelicals reflected the social characteristics and identity as outlined above. The religious right, therefore, came to represent the dominant expression of evangelical involvement in American society by the close of the twentieth century.

The evangelical self-perception of standing in the stream of historical orthodoxy led to a sense of exceptionalism. As the inheritors of the orthodox heritage, evangelicals felt a particular pressure to maintain the purity of the church. As the culture around them shifted, conservative Protestants rejected the social gospel of their liberal counterparts. Instead, conservative Protestants opted to pit Christ against the surrounding culture. The activist, conversionist impulse of fundamentalist evangelicals remained intact. This impulse, however, now expressed itself as suspicion of the broader culture and sought to rescue as many as possible from the wrecked, sinking vessel.

In the latter part of the twentieth century, when evangelicals began to engage more directly in the political process, the narrative of a fallen world remained entrenched. Twentieth-century evangelicals had embraced the narrative of a world destined for God's ruthless judgment—a perspective that contrasted sharply with the previous centuries' eschatological hope of America as an exceptional nation favored by God. A desire to return to that idealized version of a Christian America would drive many on the religious right. The fundamentalist-modernist controversy of the early twentieth century exasperated that perception, and the religious right would address the belief that something had been lost.

The rapidly changing culture of the latter half of the twentieth century served as an impetus for the formation of the religious right. In *American Grace*, Robert Putnam and David Campbell assert that changing sexual norms, which were particularly evident in American society in the 1960s, contributed to the galvanizing of evangelicals around conservative politics. Putnam and Campbell claim that the 1960s lit the fuse for the culture wars of the following decades. The decade witnessed a seismic generational shift on social issues such as birth control, premarital sex, homosexuality, and abortion. The 1960s also marked the decline of religious participation, amplifying the evangelical perception that American society was deteriorating. Putnam and Campbell argue that concerns about sexual immorality can be closely associated with the rise of evangelicalism. They further argue that the religious right responded to these concerns effectively, which helped to swell its ranks.[5]

Seth Dowland takes a similar approach by identifying anxiety over changing gender roles as a factor in the rise of the religious right. Dowland asserts that the religious right galvanized around the evangelical emphasis on order and authority, which reflects a more patriarchal and traditional model of the family. The religious right's emphasis on family values reveals its insecurity concerning the drastic changes in the culture in the latter half of the twentieth century.[6] Anxiety over these changes spurred the religious right to directly utilize overtly political tools to influence the culture, providing another example of the evangelical ability to use whatever tools are available to further its own agenda. In the same manner that fundamentalists did not hesitate to use the cultural tool of media to

---

[5]Robert Putnam and David Campbell, *American Grace: How Religion Divides and Unites Us* (New York: Simon & Schuster, 2010), 91-133.

[6]Seth Dowland, *Family Values and the Rise of the Religious Right* (Philadelphia: University of Pennsylvania Press, 2015), 1-20.

communicate the gospel, the religious right did not hesitate to use political tools to influence and shape the culture.[7]

The rise of the religious right was predicated on the increasing anxiety over the changing norms evident in American society. An identifiable enemy was needed in order to galvanize American evangelicals, and the prevailing secular worldview would serve that function. Evangelical Christians would combat that dominant narrative of secularism in American society with their own counter-narrative of a Christian worldview.[8]

The work and influence of Francis Schaeffer served as an important centralizing perspective in the face of a changing world. From his perch at L'Abri Fellowship in Switzerland, Schaeffer began to postulate a narrative of the decline of American society. Schaeffer's work tells of a Christian worldview that was under attack in secular American culture. He asserted that in the past Christianity could depend on society to affirm a Christian worldview, but the presuppositions endemic in secular humanism enabled it to operate as a surrogate religion. This reality necessitated the assertion of a Christian worldview.

In *How Should We Then Live?*, Francis Schaeffer offered an "overarching argument about how western culture moved from a Christian worldview at the time of Aquinas to the relativistic secularism, or what he calls simply secular humanism, of the late twentieth century."[9] Barry Hankins summarizes Schaeffer's argument: "Early Christianity was pure and biblical; medieval Roman Catholic Christianity became increasingly corrupt; the Renaissance introduced humanism; then the Reformation recaptured true Christianity and held humanism at bay until the twentieth century."[10] Schaeffer

---

[7]Joel Carpenter, *Revive Us Again: The Reawakening of American Fundamentalism* (New York: Oxford University Press, 1997), xii, 3-12, 245.

[8]Molly Worthen, *Apostles of Reason* (New York: Oxford University Press, 2014), 27-30, 216-19, 259-65.

[9]Barry Hankins, *Francis Schaeffer and the Shaping of Evangelical America* (Grand Rapids: Eerdmans, 2008), 167. See also Francis Schaeffer, *How Should We Then Live?* (Grand Rapids: Fleming H. Revell, 1976).

[10]Hankins, *Francis Schaeffer*, 169.

therefore, operated under the conviction that evangelicalism of the late twentieth century needed to oppose the secular worldview. Hankins recognizes Schaeffer's weakness as an "over-reliance on Enlightenment categories and a tendency to conflate issues of faith with issues of politics and American patriotism."[11]

While lacking formal education and depth in his analysis, Schaeffer exerted considerable influence as one of evangelicalism's key thought leaders. Molly Worthen states that "he was a brilliant demagogue who offered up all of Western history in an hour's lecture, stripped of confusing nuance."[12] His lectures at Christian colleges made sweeping generalizations about American society that led to apocalyptic conclusions, while stirring the hearts of evangelicals who were troubled by the crumbling of a Christendom they believed had existed at one point in American history. Francis Schaeffer's son, Franky Schaeffer, claims that his own desire to launch a movie career led to the production of movies that would popularize his father's teaching.[13] Francis Schaeffer's lectures and movies provided the intellectual fodder (as shallow as it was) for the evangelical masses.

The Christian worldview purported by Francis Schaeffer viewed the reality of abortions in the United States as particularly problematic. Initially seen as an issue for the Roman Catholic Church, political conservatives surmised that the issue of abortion could serve as a rallying issue for evangelicals. The image of dolls floating in a lake, used by Franky Schaeffer in a documentary on abortion, sought to portray how far American society had fallen and to what extent a secular worldview had shaped that decline. For evangelicals, abortion exhibited the depths of America's fall and became their central political issue.

---

[11]Hankins, *Francis Schaeffer*, 238.

[12]Worthen, *Apostles of Reason*, 212.

[13]Frank Schaeffer, *Crazy for God: How I Grew Up as One of the Elect, Helped Found the Religious Right, and Lived to Take All (or Almost All) of It Back* (Cambridge, MA: DeCapo, 2007), 242-64.

Because the world had fallen captive to secular humanism, evangelicals needed to hang on to a God-honoring worldview, which they believed was rapidly slipping away. Toward that end, the Republican Party sought out issues that tapped into the evangelical sense of cultural decline. Conservative positions on abortion, prayer in schools, and the separation of church and state provided the necessary ammunition to bring theological conservatives into the politically conservative camp.

Randall Balmer argues that the 1973 *Roe v. Wade* decision was less critical to the formation of the religious right than the *Green v. Connally* case, in which the IRS sought to deny tax-exempt status to a racially segregated school in Mississippi. Balmer claims that the federal government's power to enforce the Civil Rights Act sparked the early formation of the religious right, and a subsequent case against Bob Jones University's policy of segregation served to further raise the ire of fundamentalist evangelicals. He maintains that the fear of government encroachment on church rights (including the right to resist racial integration) moved evangelicals toward the larger agenda of the Republican Party.[14] The formation of the religious right pivoted on a narrative that a Christian worldview must hold fast against the machinations of secular culture.

In response to this potential encroachment, evangelicals began to utilize the infrastructures of media and education that had grown after the Scopes Trial and over the course of the twentieth century. While the culture may have declined during the twentieth century, the tools of that culture could be co-opted. Evangelical activists found an outlet not only in the task of personal evangelism but also in cultural transformation through political activism. Because evangelicals from Whitefield, Finney, and McPherson to Graham had used the tools of culture to advance Christianity, the transition to political activism—one of the most significant tools of culture—to express active, conversionist faith proved to be relatively smooth.

---

[14]Randall Balmer, *Thy Kingdom Come* (New York: Basic Books, 2006), 11-17.

Old-time fundamentalist gospel preacher Jerry Falwell formed the Moral Majority and attempted to use the tools of American politics to impact issues like church rights, abortion, and prayer in schools. Pentecostal televangelist Pat Robertson ran for president of the United States as a Republican and successfully dabbled in media and higher education to assert that elusive Christian worldview. Throughout the last quarter of the twentieth century, the religious right successfully incorporated secular cultural tools into the toolbox of evangelicalism to combat what they perceived to be a crumbling culture. Christ would stand against the culture, and the church would defeat the culture on its own terms.

The self-perception of exceptionalism and the need for victory and triumph isolated US evangelicalism. It not only isolated evangelicals from those who held a secular worldview and proposed a secular agenda, but it also prevented a deeper connection with like-minded spiritual siblings. Evangelicals could easily dismiss the theological liberals as possessing a secular worldview. But what would happen in an encounter with a theologically like-minded community that emerged from a different historical narrative, but most importantly, possessed a different racial identification? How would theology and race intersect in the evangelical world?

AFRICAN AMERICAN CHRISTIANITY

African American Christianity as a transformative presence in American church history began with the onset of the transatlantic slave trade and the establishment of a contextualized religion within the reality of the institution of slavery. Christian faith on the plantation reveals an authentic expression of faith by slaves in the midst of tremendous suffering, and the lament of slave religion provides a counternarrative to the triumphalistic narrative of Anglo Christianity in North America. Continuing through the Civil War and the Emancipation Proclamation, African American Christianity demonstrated the power of spiritual freedom and liberation. Post–Civil War African

American Christianity, extending through the Great Migration and through the two World Wars, points toward the emergence of a faith that greatly valued and asserted human agency in the face of an oppressive system of slavery, Jim Crow laws, and urban segregation. The Great Migration to the eastern and northern cities resulted in the growth of an autonomous black church in the urban setting. The ability to contextualize the Christian message without falling into cultural captivity reveals the ability to engage a narrative of biblical justice without the limits imposed by evangelical individualism.

Many of these African American churches were steeped in a biblicism that mirrored evangelical theology. However, in terms of social-historical affiliation, they did not find integration with the emerging American evangelical ethos in the twentieth century. African American churches, while holding a conservative theology, differed from their white counterparts in the positive assertion of God's justice in the public square and were not obsessed with an exclusively personal evangelism approach to ministry. Theological affinity existed between the African American church with the larger Protestant church, but numerous distinctions emerged differentiating the two threads of American religion.

The strong, distinct, and separate African American church community in the United States points to the historic failure of the dominant culture's ability to embrace the work of the Spirit in that community. Instead of offering the acceptance Peter exemplified toward Cornelius, the white church in America rejected the presence of African Americans in their churches (and most certainly in their homes and in their lives). The black church, therefore, arose out of racism that sought to keep African Americans as second-class citizens or completely excluded by the majority culture church. Instead, the African American church arose in a hostile context but provided an enduring institution despite significant obstacles.

Deep levels of racism, cultural insensitivity, and cultural incompetence resulted in a rift between different communities in the United

States. Not only did explicit examples of racism generate animosity and mistrust, but implicit approval of racism and passive inactivity toward injustice perpetuated the racial divide. The social, political, and cultural gulf between the historic black churches and the white churches continued to widen as the experiences of the white church diverged significantly from the experiences of the black church. Segregation in the church was exacerbated by segregation in society and vice versa. This lack of integration allowed racism to become a rampant problem not only in society but within the church. With primary relationships and connections built along racial lines, affinity toward one's own racial group took precedence over a Christian community that could bridge the racial divide.

Segregation in the church fostered the growth of unique and specific traditions. As Sweeney notes, "Black Christians developed their own ecclesiastical traditions. . . . The Africans' full-bodied, improvisational, communal worship and praise; their dynamic preaching methods; their commitment to biblical justice; even dozens of their spirituals have leavened the evangelical movement here and abroad."[15] Over the years, these unique cultural expressions of Christianity arising out of the African American church became another point of disconnect between black and white Christians.

The divergence between the black church and the white church became even more pronounced during the civil rights movement. As African Americans were pursuing justice and civil rights, many evangelical white congregations remained on the sidelines. By opting to ignore injustice in society for the sake of focusing on the salvation of individual souls, many white churches lost credibility in the black community. The power of Christian witness was diminished when the white church failed to stand with those fighting for civil rights.

The civil rights movement (rooted deeply in the black church) is an important spiritual and social movement that affected both

---

[15]Douglas A. Sweeney, *The American Evangelical Story: A History of the Movement* (Grand Rapids: Baker, 2005), 127-28.

individuals and society. The movement had an impact not only on the African American community but on all ethnic communities, including white ones. Civil rights are often seen in social and political terms. We often fail to recognize this movement as one of the most significant faith-based campaigns in American history. The failure by many in the white church to participate would lead to an understandable sense of distrust.

In his "Letter from a Birmingham Jail," Dr. Martin Luther King Jr. challenged white Christians to take a stand against injustice:

> I have been so greatly disappointed with the white church and its leadership. . . . When I was suddenly catapulted into the leadership of the bus protest in Montgomery, Alabama, a few years ago, I felt we would be supported by the white church. I felt that the ministers, priests, and rabbis of the South would be among our strongest allies. Instead, some have been outright opponents, refusing to understand the freedom movement and misrepresenting its leaders; all too many others have been more cautious than courageous and have remained silent behind the anesthetizing security of stained-glass windows. . . . In the midst of blatant injustices inflicted on the Negro, I have watched white churchmen stand on the sideline and mouth pious irrelevancies and sanctimonious trivialities. In the midst of a mighty struggle to rid our nation of racial and economic injustice, I have heard many ministers say: "Those are social issues, with which the gospel has no real concern." And I have watched many churches commit themselves to a completely otherworldly religion which makes a strange, unbiblical distinction between body and soul, between the sacred and the secular.[16]

Because of the failure of many in the white church to stand against injustice, the rift between black and white grew. These historical rifts provide obstacles for crosscultural communication and ministry even

---

[16]Martin Luther King Jr., "Letter from a Birmingham Jail," The Martin Luther King, Jr. Research and Education Institute, http://okra.stanford.edu/transcription/document_images /undecided/630416-019.pdf.

into the twenty-first century.[17] Christian witness and the unity of the
body of Christ have been damaged by a less-than-stellar racial history
in the United States.

The rich narrative of the African American Christian experience
has been largely ignored by evangelicals. The assumption of the
exceptionalism of the white American evangelical story hinders this
engagement. Despite tremendous theological affinity between the
black and evangelical churches, the historical silencing of the black
church results in a theological famine. Historical and theological
engagement between these two branches of the American church
would require new paradigms transcending the limited theological
imagination of evangelicalism.

THE THEOLOGICAL VACUUM OF
EVANGELICAL LIBERATION THEOLOGY

The expected triumph of an exceptional community prevents the
humility necessary to engage an ecclesiology that crosses racial
boundaries. An ecclesiology with a foundation in white supremacy is
unable to engage the full narrative of the American church. The
absence of lament in the American church reveals a theological
deficiency rooted in the exceptionalism and triumphalism. The white
American church is unable to lament because of deficient ecclesiology.

The Old Testament comprises multiple genres, such as poetry and
the subgenre of lament. Old Testament scholar Claus Westermann
situates the Hebrew poetic material into two broad categories: hymns
of praise and lament. Westermann asserts that "the two modes of
calling on God are praise and petition. As the two poles, they determine the nature of all speaking to God."[18] Psalms that express
worship for the good things that God has done are categorized as
praise hymns. Laments are prayers of petition arising out of need.

---

[17]This section is lightly adapted from the author's book: Soong-Chan Rah, *Many Colors: Cultural Intelligence for a Changing Church* (Chicago: Moody, 2010), 52-58.

[18]Claus Westermann, *Praise and Lament in the Psalms* (Atlanta: John Knox Press, 1981), 152.

Lament is not simply the presentation of a list of complaints, but a liturgical response to the reality of suffering that engages God in the context of pain and trouble. The hope of lament is that God would respond to the human suffering that is wholeheartedly communicated through lament.[19]

The diseased imagination of evangelicalism that arises from the assumption of triumphalism and exceptionalism results in an imbalanced emphasis on praise over and against lament. Walter Brueggemann asks this question:

> What happens when appreciation of the lament as a form of speech and faith is lost . . . ? What happens when the speech forms that redress power distribution have been silenced and eliminated? The answer, I believe, is that a theological monopoly is reinforced, docility and submissiveness are engendered, and the outcome in terms of social practice is to reinforce and consolidate the political-economic monopoly of the status quo.[20]

A triumphalistic narrative rushes to praise but silences lament. Rather than elevating one narrative over the other, both praise and lament are needed. The primacy of the triumphalistic praise narrative arises from a dominant culture resting on the assumptions of supremacy.

Brueggemann asserts the necessity for both the narrative of praise of the triumphant culture and the narrative of lament of the suffering in the theological imagination. In *Peace*, Brueggemann attempts to address the difference between *shalom* for the haves and the have-nots: "A theology of blessing [celebration] for the well-off 'haves' is very different from a theology of salvation [suffering] for the precarious 'have-nots.'"[21] The tension between the theology of celebration and the theology of suffering is the tension between the now and the

---

[19]This section is lightly adapted from the author's book: Soong-Chan Rah, *Prophetic Lament: A Call for Justice in Troubled Times* (Downers Grove, IL: InterVarsity Press, 2015).

[20]Walter Brueggemann, *The Psalms and the Life of Faith*, ed. Patrick D. Miller (Minneapolis: Fortress, 1995), Kindle loc. 1187 of 4122.

[21]Walter Brueggemann, *Peace* (St. Louis: Chalice Press, 2001), 19.

not yet. In the same way that a proper kingdom theology demands the intersection between the now and the not yet, a proper *shalom* theology dictates that there is an intersection between suffering and celebration.

The haves develop a theology of celebration. Those who live in celebration "are concerned with questions of proper management and joyous celebration." Instead of deliverance, "the well-off do not expect their faith to begin in a cry but rather, in a song. They do not expect or need intrusion, but they rejoice in stability." Praise marks the story of celebration.[22] The theology of celebration, which emerges out of the context of affluence and abundance, focuses on the proper management and stewardship of the abundant resources that God has provided. Because there is abundance, the world is viewed as generally good and accommodating to those who are living under the theology of celebration. Life is already healthy, complete, and whole. God, therefore, takes on the role of a nurturer and caregiver with more feminine attributes. In the theology of celebration, maintaining and preserving the status quo becomes a central priority. The theology of celebration is a theology of the resurrection.

The have-nots develop a theology of suffering and survival. Those who live under suffering live "their lives aware of the acute precariousness of their situation." Worship that arises out of suffering cries out for deliverance. "Their notion of themselves is that of a dependent people crying out for a vision of survival and salvation." Lament marks the story of suffering.[23] The theology of suffering emerges out of the context of scarcity and oppression and, therefore, focuses on the need for salvation and survival. Because of the reality of oppression, the world is generally considered to be evil and hostile to those who are living under the theology of suffering. Life is precarious, needing a deliverer. God, therefore, takes on the image of a warrior and

---

[22]Brueggemann, *Peace*, 28-33.
[23]Brueggemann, *Peace*, 26-28.

conqueror and assumes more masculine attributes. In the theology of suffering, fighting injustice becomes the central priority. The theology of suffering is a theology of the cross.

In examining the seemingly polar extremes presented by Brueggemann, it is essential to reflect how we can connect the two seemingly disparate theologies. In *Flesh and Stone*, Richard Sennett states the central question of our striving to understand the intersection between the theology of celebration and the theology of suffering: "How will we exit from our own bodily passivity? . . . For without a disturbed sense of ourselves, what will prompt most of us . . . to turn outward toward each other, to experience the Other?"[24] How can those of us who operate under the theology of celebration connect with those who live under the theology of suffering?[25]

American Christians who flourish under the existing system seek to maintain the existing dynamics of inequality and remain in the theology of celebration over and against the theology of suffering. Promoting one perspective over the other, however, diminishes theological discourse. The intersection of the two threads provides the opportunity to engage in the fullness of theology. Lament and praise must go hand in hand. For US evangelicals riding the fumes of a previous generation's assumptions, a triumphalistic theology of celebration and privilege rooted in a praise-only narrative is perpetuated by the absence of lament and the underlying narrative of suffering that informs lament. The theological imagination of US evangelicalism needs the prophetic disruption of lament and the voice of the suffering.

The legitimation of the voice of the suffering offers the very real possibility of justice being called out. For Brueggemann, the power of lament is that the oppressed are given the right to speak, and by

---

[24]Richard Sennett, *Flesh and Stone: The Body and the City in Western Civilization*, rev. ed. (New York: W. W. Norton and Company, 1996), 374.

[25]Previous three paragraphs lightly adapted from Soong-Chan Rah, *The Next Evangelicalism*, 143-63, and Rah, *Prophetic Lament*, 21-24.

speaking, offered the possibility of redressing injustice. "The lament form thus concerns a redistribution of power."[26] The power of lament is that the covenant relationship operates in both directions, from the powerful to the powerless as well as from the powerless to the powerful. "One loss that results from the absence of lament is the loss of *genuine covenant interaction*, since the second party to the covenant (the petitioner) has become voiceless or has a voice that is permitted to speak only praise and doxology."[27]

In *The Psalms and the Life of Faith*, Brueggemann expands the role of lament as the place of protest. The lament "shifts the calculus and *redresses the distribution of power* between the two parties, so that the petitionary party is taken seriously and the God who is addressed is newly engaged in the crisis in a way that puts God at risk."[28] "In the Old Testament, from beginning to end, the 'call to distress,' the 'cry out of the depths,' that is, the lament, is an inevitable part of what happens between God and man."[29] The lament form expressed in a worship setting gives voice to the sufferer. "The basis for the conclusion that the petitioner is taken seriously and legitimately granted power in the relation is that the speech of the petitioner is heard, valued, and transmitted as serious speech. Cultically, we may assume that such speech is taken seriously by God."[30]

This dialogue moves the theology of suffering into interaction with the theology of celebration. "In the West, God-talk is characterized by objective thinking about God. In theology God becomes an object. But in the Old Testament, talk of God is characterized by dialogical thinking."[31] A theology of celebration has the luxury of being able to objectify God. Because suffering is a distant reality, it is not necessary for the presence of God to be immanent. God can be a distant

---

[26]Brueggemann, *Psalms and the Life of Faith*, Kindle loc. 1177.
[27]Brueggemann, *Psalms and the Life of Faith,* Kindle loc. 1188.
[28]Brueggemann, *Psalms and the Life of Faith*, Kindle loc. 1177.
[29]Westermann, *Praise and Lament in the Psalms*, 261.
[30]Brueggemann, *Psalms and the Life of Faith*, Kindle loc. 1177.
[31]Westermann, *Praise and Lament in the Psalms*, 261.

abstraction whose praise is expected.[32] Lament as dialogue challenges this abstraction. A theology of suffering must acknowledge the cry of distress and suffering in lament before moving to the psalms of praise. Lament requires us to stay in the dialogue, as they offer the relentless truth of suffering.

Lament offers the very real suffering of God's people in vivid, even gory details for the world to hear. But in the process of expressing that suffering, hope is offered. "The suffering is, as it were, an affirmation that God is still there and still concerned with the fate of Israel."[33] Even if the explicit promise is not offered, the freedom to voice despair portends hope. Lament's "bitter accusations reveal profound yearning for God, even as God appears deeply untrustworthy and remote. It voices truth without which relationships cannot prosper."[34] The hope is in the relationship: not merely words spoken or promises made, but in the reality that God offers reconciliation to even his most bitter enemies (which Jerusalem has now become). Bridging the disconnect between suffering and celebration may offer the hope of authentic human relationships that offers the fullness of *shalom*.

The problem with Western ecclesiology is a self-perceived exceptionalism and triumphalism that prevents the practice of lament rooted in humility. The fullness of *shalom* is denied to a community that sees *shalom* from one angle and does not embrace the full scope of worship. Pain and suffering are not allowed to be expressed because they would interrupt the triumphalistic narrative. A theology of lament could reintroduce a worship practice that provides hope, even for those that do not realize how much they need hope.

---

[32]For example, Westermann notes that "when Western theology speaks of God's salvation or of a God who saves, God thereby becomes objectively tied to an event, and thus emerges a 'soteriology.' The Old Testament cannot pin God down to a single soteriology. It can only speak of God's saving acts within a whole series of events., and that necessarily involves some kind of verbal exchange between God and man." Westermann, *Praise and Lament in the Psalms*, 261.

[33]Adele Berlin, *Lamentations in The Old Testament Library* (Louisville, KY: Westminster John Knox, 2002), 18.

[34]Kathleen M. O'Connor, *Lamentations and the Tears of the World* (Maryknoll, NY: Orbis Books, 2003), 125.

The exceptionalistic and triumphalistic tendency of a culturally captive evangelicalism forms the diseased theological imagination. The bounded set of an evangelical theology believed to be achieved by an exceptional mind has difficulty engaging with alternative Christian narratives. The theological boundary of the creation account is transgressed by white American Christians taking the place of God in created order and asserting white supremacy and exceptionalism. A misappropriated creation account reveals a biblical anthropology that would elevate whiteness to the level of God's image.

The diseased theological imagination of the US evangelical church requires a challenge that cannot arise from within its own community. In the same way that evangelicals believe that individual salvation requires redemption to come from an external source, redemption for a diseased theological imagination will also require an external source. The interaction with an otherness that challenges the status quo would be a necessary precondition to the salvation of the soul of evangelicalism. African American Christianity is a profound and essential theological marker that has been ignored by US evangelicalism and its dysfunctional theological categories. The possibility of this intersection is the formation of a prophetic imagination that moves us beyond cultural captivity.

The pathway toward a genuine multiethnic future for the United States remains an unclear one. The venomous political dialogue and the sociological challenges of ongoing segregation contribute to a racialized problem in our society and our churches. The churches, in turn, have not supplied a theological imagination that addresses the needs of society. Instead, the historical expression of theology in the United States has provided a dysfunctional imagination that has damaged the evangelical witness. Our nation remains segregated and divided and our churches lead the way.

Evangelicals continue to cling to a bounded-set soteriology and ecclesiology that betray a sense of exceptionalism and triumphalism. The assumption of perspicuity and reasoning (exceptionalism) coupled with the strong sense of having inherited the mantel of orthodox theology, and the charge to further that exceptional theology (triumphalism), provides an obstacle for those who may display a theological affinity but not hold physical similarity to white evangelicalism. Clinging to an exceptionalistic and triumphalistic view of one's own past and future allows for the sustaining of systems that undermine unity and community in the gospel. Liberation finds no home in the evangelical worldview.

The historical development of this unique evangelical identity in the twentieth century requires a connection to a different Christian narrative that emerges from both a similar and dissimilar context. The intersection of evangelical history and theology with the narrative of African American Christianity could provide a corrective for dysfunctional narratives. By inverting the exceptionalistic assumption that nonwhites are grafted onto the tree trunk of white Christianity, and instead offering the image of multiple tributaries that contribute to the large sea of Christian faith, a new type of engagement is offered for disparate groups. Liberation may come when a cultural, captive Christianity yields to the power of a movement that embraces multiple narratives emerging from a diverse Christianity.

The ambivalence and confusion demonstrated by white American Christianity toward diversity and toward a dismantling of white Christian superiority has resulted in the ongoing inability to discern what is cultural (American exceptionalism and patriotism) from what is biblical (a call to be salt and light). In contrast, the narrative of the African American church has not been found in the center of the American Christian narrative, while Christendom is not typically an attribute of the African American church. The history of the African American church offers the possibility that a Christian community can offer cultural relevance and adaptability in the face of oppression and suffering. The lament of slave religion led to a celebration of God's work rather than an attempt to curry favor with the powers that be in the surrounding culture. The ability to incorporate both celebration and suffering, both praise and lament, should continue to be a hallmark of African American Christianity.

The theological problem of the assumption of exceptionalism of white Christians and the assertion of the inevitable triumph of white evangelicalism has derailed credible witness. The diseased theological imagination of the Western Christian mind has produced a particular gaze over creation and over humanity that places whiteness at the pinnacle. White evangelicalism could not expand community to include those of "different" and "other" peoples despite agreement on the central theological issues. The failure of the imagination to see the other as offering a positive contribution to the existing boundaries allowed white evangelicalism to continue undisturbed by the presence of African American evangelicals. Liberation was lost and captivity was reinforced.

CHAPTER THREE

IS IT TIME FOR A WOMANIST THEOLOGY OF RECONCILIATION?

CHANEQUA WALKER-BARNES

"Why am I here?" I asked myself as the conversation continued around me. The group was brainstorming names of theologians who could do some teaching on racial reconciliation at a future conference. They began throwing out names, first male faculty members at seminaries, then male seminary graduates, then white women who facilitated discussions about reconciliation. They lamented that there was no one currently present in the room who could speak on the subject with authority. Apparently, being a seminary faculty member who teaches numerous courses on race and reconciliation did not qualify me as an authority. Or was it that my invisibility superpower had triggered itself again? I shouldn't have been surprised. That thing was always switching on at the oddest times. It happened quite frequently in meetings or conferences about racial reconciliation, social justice, or community development among Christians. One of these days, I'd have to learn how to control it.

This essay was initially written for this book by invitation of the editors, but meanwhile it has also been published in Chanequa Walker-Barnes, *I Bring the Voices of My People: A Womanist Vision for Racial Reconciliation* (Grand Rapids: Eerdmans, 2019). It is now reprinted here with permission of Eerdmans.

In the past two decades, racial reconciliation has emerged as an increasingly popular topic of academic discourse in the United States and South Africa. An inherently practical discipline, the field of reconciliation studies was birthed out of the experiences of evangelical Christian ministers and laypersons whose quotidian experiences crossed traditional boundaries of race and ethnicity within the church. In the United States, the racial reconciliation movement has strong roots in the evangelical church and parachurch organizations. In 1997, for example, Promise Keepers—a predominantly white evangelical men's organization—launched a division on racial reconciliation and declared a lofty goal of eradicating racism in the church by 2000. The evangelical roots of the movement are beneficial in that the field has been first and foremost concerned with practical application. However, because of the emphasis on male headship and female submission among evangelicals, men have dominated the movement and the literature.

In the United States, reconciliation has been largely framed as a movement aimed at obliterating racial barriers between black and white men. The inaugural literature consisted primarily of autobiographical narratives of division, partnership, and friendship between black and white men, including John Perkins and Wayne Gordon, Glenn Kehrein and Raleigh Washington, and Spencer Perkins and Chris Rice. As the field of reconciliation studies has developed into an academic discipline, the masculine preponderance has continued. The leading scholars in the field include Curtiss Paul DeYoung, Allen Boesak, John Paul Lederach, Chris Rice, and Emmanuel Katongole. Women's voices and perspectives are singularly absent. It is common for the reading list on any course syllabus on reconciliation to consist of male-authored texts, augmented perhaps by one autobiographical narrative written by a female survivor of ethnic conflict in other countries. The result of this exclusively male gaze is a body of literature that examines race as a singular construct, ignoring the intersections between race, gender, and sexuality.

In this chapter, I review the historical antecedents of the racial reconciliation paradigm within the Promise Keepers movement. I describe how this legacy not only marginalizes the voices of women of color, but also results in anemic understandings of race, racism, and reconciliation. Using womanist theology as an example—with its foci on lived theology, intersectionality, power, and justice—I argue that the unique perspectives of women of color must be moved from margin to center if we truly hope to work toward reconciliation.

PROMISE KEEPERS AND THE BIRTH OF A MOVEMENT

The evangelical impact on racial reconciliation is not coincidental. In the United States, the surge in interest in racial reconciliation can be traced to movements in several evangelical organizations during the mid-1990s. To be clear, there were earlier events that set the stage. In 1970, for example, Tom Skinner delivered an address at Urbana, InterVarsity Christian Fellowship's student missions conference, in which he challenged the evangelical church to address the problem of racism.[1] What is distinguishable about the 1990s is that several national and international evangelical organizations made racial reconciliation a prominent focus. In a 1997 article for *Christianity Today*, Andrés Tapia stated,

> During the last several years, evangelicals have engaged in numerous initiatives in racial reconciliation, causing even the most jaded observers of race relations in the movement to take notice. The Southern Baptist Convention repented for its "sin of racism." The National Association of Evangelicals and the National Black Association of Evangelicals (NBEA) took significant steps toward healing their historic rift. Pentecostal denominational associations—one white, one black, which had originally split a hundred years ago—merged.[2]

The most high-profile effort, however, occurred within Promise Keepers.

---

[1]Tom Skinner, "U.S. Racism and World Evangelism" (address presented at Urbana, December 1970, Champaign-Urbana, Illinois), https://urbana.org/message/us-racial-crisis-and-world-evangelism.
[2]Andrés T. Tapia, "After the Hugs, What? The Next Step for Racial Reconciliation Will Be Harder," *Christianity Today*, February 3, 1997, 54.

In 1990, former University of Colorado football coach Bill McCartney founded Promise Keepers (PK), which called on men to commit themselves to seven promises: honoring Christ; developing friendship based on trust and mutual accountability with a few men; practicing spiritual, moral, ethical, and sexual purity; building strong marriages and families through love, protection, and biblical values; supporting the mission of the local church through prayer, active involvement, and financial support; reaching beyond racial and denominational barriers; and influencing the world in obedience to the Great Commandment (Mk 12:30-31) and the Great Commission (Mt 28:19-20). Based in Boulder, Colorado, PK quickly developed a national audience. By 1993, its Boulder conference attracted 52,000 men. In summer 1994, it held a series of six stadium rallies across the country, with hundreds of thousands of participants.[3] Two years later, it held 22 such rallies, which drew a combined total of 1,090,000 men.[4]

In 1996, PK made its sixth promise—"A Promise Keeper is committed to reaching beyond any racial and denominational barriers to demonstrate the power of biblical unity"—its primary focus.[5] PK's racial reconciliation emphasis was not simply a matter of rhetoric; the organization put substantial resources and support behind it. The commitment to diversity was born out in its hiring decisions. At its height, PK boasted a 437-member staff that was 30 percent people of color, including 16 percent African American, 13 percent Latino, and 1 percent Native American, making it arguably the most diversely staffed evangelical organization in the country.[6] In 1996, Raleigh Washington, African American pastor of Rock of Our Salvation Evangelical Free Church in Chicago, was appointed vice president of the

---

[3]Howard A. Snyder, "Will Promise Keepers Keep Their Promises?" *Christianity Today*, November 14, 1994, 20.

[4]Ted Olsen, "Racial Reconciliation Emphasis Intensified," *Christianity Today*, January 6, 1997, 67.

[5]Promise Keepers, "7 Promises," https://promisekeepers.org/promises.

[6]Olsen, "Racial Reconciliation," 67.

organization. Washington headed a newly instituted reconciliation division, which was responsible for its racial and denominational unity efforts. The division was charged with developing educational curricula, including the "Eight Biblical Principles of Reconciliation," and dispersing $1.3 million that PK had raised for churches burned by arson. A national strategic manager was appointed for each major ethnic group.[7]

At its twenty-two stadium rallies in 1996, evangelical men— possibly for the first time—heard that racial reconciliation was not only valued, but also mandated, by the gospel.[8] Most of those men, however, were white. McCartney announced a goal of diversifying the rally audiences.[9] It held a clergy summit in Atlanta that drew thirty-nine thousand clergy. The motto for the event was "Breaking Down the Walls." The audience, as with other PK events, was predominantly white, but included significantly more African Americans, Asian Americans, Latino Americans, and Native Americans than previous rallies. The speakers were also diverse, with at least one person of color featured in each session.[10] On March 6–7, 1997, PK followed up with its first African American leaders' summit in Colorado. The meeting, which gathered more than one hundred clergy, was the first of a series designed to recruit more minority participation, building up to a national gathering for prayer and repentance to be held in Washington, DC, on October 4, 1997.[11] The event, "Stand in the Gap: A Sacred Assembly of Men," was part of PK's attempt to follow up on

---

[7]Olsen, "Racial Reconciliation," 67; Promise Keepers subsequently teamed up with Moody Publishers to publish a workbook based upon its "Eight Biblical Principles of Reconciliation" (Raleigh Washington, Glen Kehrein, and Claude V. King, *Break Down the Walls Workbook: Experiencing Biblical Reconciliation and Unity in the Body of Christ* [Chicago: Moody Publishers, 1997]).

[8]Lisa Sharon Harper, *Evangelical Does Not Equal Republican . . . Or Democrat* (New York: New Press, 2008), 93.

[9]Olsen, "Racial Reconciliation," 67.

[10]"Promise Keepers and Race," *The Christian Century*, 113, no. 8 (1996): 254.

[11]The PK gathering was held just two years after the Million Man March organized by Nation of Islam leader Louis Farrakhan. It drew many comparisons to the prior march. McCartney, however, was clear to draw a distinction between the two events, saying, "We are going to D.C. not to march, but to repent" (Olsen, "Racial Reconciliation," 67).

its vow to make racial reconciliation a central part of its work. More than half a million men gathered on the National Mall, where they heard founder McCartney declare a lofty—and naive—goal of eradicating racism in the church by 2000.[12]

PK's attempt to disciple a million evangelical Christian men into the gospel of racial reconciliation was hardly a success. It was met with considerable skepticism from evangelicals of color. For example, after McCartney delivered a breakfast address at the 1995 gathering of the National Black Evangelical Association, one attendee demanded, "What is Promise Keepers going to say about the anti-affirmative action atmosphere in this country? . . . What are the men in the stadiums this summer going to hear about that? Will Promise Keepers stand up and be counted on this issue?"[13] In an article for *Christianity Today*, Latino writer Andrés Tapia asked,

> Does the white Promise Keeper wanting to hug me with reconciling fervor take into account that he may support immigration policies that make Latinos—whether U.S.-born, legal immigrant, or undocumented— feel scrutinized every time they go to the doctor or take a child to school? that [sic] many Latinos could end up on the streets once welfare reform goes into full effect at the city and neighborhood level? that crackdowns on drugs are disproportionately applied to communities of color? that English-language-only initiatives create a climate where the desire to inculcate in my daughter my language and culture is seen as un-American? The next step for racial reconciliation needs to include rethinking the social and political issues that divide and exasperate our communities.[14]

The biggest challenge to PK's racial reconciliation focus, however, came from the white men who constituted its primary audience. In the year following the Washington, DC, gathering, attendance at PK

---

[12]W. Terry Whalin, "Promise Keepers Gathers Black Leaders," *Christianity Today*, April 28, 1997, 84.

[13]Kevin A. Miller, "McCartney Preaches Reconciliation," *Christianity Today*, June 19, 1995, 43.

[14]Tapia, "After the Hugs, What?," 54.

events declined by more than 50 percent. In Emerson and Smith's pivotal book, *Divided by Faith,* McCartney attributed the decline directly to the racial reconciliation emphasis, stating, "To this day, the racial message remains a highly charged element of Promise Keepers' ministry. . . . Of the 1996 conference participants who had a complaint, nearly 40 percent reacted negatively to the reconciliation theme. I personally believe it was a major factor in the significant falloff in PK's 1997 attendance—it is simply a hard teaching for many."[15] Pretty soon thereafter, the movement that had once dominated media attention vanished from view for most Americans.

E-RACING GENDER:
THE EVANGELICAL PARADIGM

Despite its decreased prominence in the American religious landscape, PK's impact on the evangelical approach to racial reconciliation is enduring for multiple reasons. First, while other national evangelical organizations, such as the Christian Community Development Association and InterVarsity Christian Fellowship, had an explicit—and justice-oriented—focus on reconciliation, the sheer size of PK's audience far extended its influence. The target populations for CCDA and InterVarsity were highly selective; the former focused on Christians who were living and serving in marginalized communities, while the latter was a college-based movement. Both were likely considerably more receptive to the language of racial reconciliation than the tens of thousands of evangelical men who packed stadiums at each of PK's rallies. Second, none of these movements were isolated; there was considerable cross-pollination between them. For example, leaders within CCDA—including its founder John Perkins and former CEO Noel Castellanos—were frequent speakers at PK rallies. Raleigh Washington was a member of CCDA and pastored a congregation that had formed a strategic partnership

---

[15]Michael Emerson and Christian Smith, *Divided by Faith: Evangelical Religion and the Problem of Race in America* (Oxford: Oxford University Press, 2000), 67.

with a ministry founded by CCDA board member Glen Kehrein. Perkins was a mentor for Brenda Salter McNeil, a former InterVarsity staff member who delivered a powerful sermon on racial reconciliation at its Urbana 2000 convention.

To some degree, then, the theology of racial reconciliation that emerged through the PK rallies reflects the dominant evangelical paradigm. Central to this paradigm was an understanding of racism as a form of sin resulting from division based on socially constructed categories of racial identity. Critical here is the idea that separateness— particularly that separateness evident among Christians during Sunday morning worship—is the problem. The solution, then, is to- getherness. Jennifer Harvey refers to this as "the reconciliation paradigm." She states,

> On the one hand, the reconciliation paradigm seems to claim that racial identities do not innately pertain to who we are as human beings created in God's image. This version of reconciliation assumes that our separateness betrays a failure to understand our shared humanity as something that transcends our differences. The implications of this assumption seem to be that reconciliation would come if we honored the truth that at our core we are one and *the same*. On the other hand, these Christians argue that we must do better at learning about, understanding, and appreciating real differences among racial groups. This claim assumes that separateness comes from failing to value diversity enough. Reconciliation in this version becomes a matter of genuinely embracing *particularities*, or the ways in which *we are not the same*.[16]

Consistent with the evangelical emphasis on Christian identity being centrally expressed through the individual believer's personal relationship with God, the evangelical understanding of reconcili- ation focused on the following: (1) the establishment of transformed interpersonal relationships between Christians of different ethnic

---

[16]Jennifer Harvey, *Dear White Christians: For Those Still Longing for Racial Reconciliation* (Grand Rapids: Eerdmans, 2014), 28-29.

backgrounds; and (2) the establishment of racially diverse congregations. This was especially true for Promise Keepers. As Lisa Sharon Harper notes, "PK focused on individual responses to racism through personal relationship alone."[17] Thus, the sixth promise was limited to "reaching beyond . . . racial and denominational barriers," rather than dismantling structural barriers and working to ensure equity and equality.[18]

The reduction of racial reconciliation to interpersonal relationships presents a particular problem when confronted with gender. In the evangelical worldview, women are seen primarily as wives, mothers, and daughters; that is, they are extensions of men rather than human beings and leaders in their own right.[19] Male identity constitutes the basic human experience. Likewise, male racial identity constitutes the basic racial experience. Women are not seen as raced human beings; that is, they are not imagined as having experiences of race and racism that are distinct from their male counterparts. This is what enabled Bill McCartney to imagine that friendships between men of different races would singlehandedly eradicate the problem of racism, as he declared on the National Mall. In her book, *Evangelical Does Not Equal Republican . . . Or Democrat*, Lisa Sharon Harper describes her reaction on realizing that PK's website made no mention of gender in its explanation of reconciliation:

> When I first logged on to the PK Web site, I wondered how they approached gender reconciliation and was struck by one thing. None of the seven promises address men's relationship to women. In the PK statement of faith, the sixth point reads: "All believers in the Lord Jesus Christ are members of His one international, multi-ethnic, and trans-cultural body called the universal church. Its unity is displayed when

---

[17]Harper, *Evangelical Does Not Equal Republican*, 104.
[18]More recently, writings by progressive mainline Protestant clergy and academics have highlighted structural issues in racial reconciliation. Scholars such as Allan Boesak, Curtiss Paul DeYoung, and Jennifer Harvey critique the interpersonal bias in the earlier literature and call for reparations as part of racial reconciliation.
[19]Harper, *Evangelical Does Not Equal Republican*, 112-13.

we reach beyond racial and denominational lines to demonstrate the Gospel's reconciling power." Gender reconciliation is not viewed as a way God displays his reconciling power, despite the reality that one of the first biblical relationships to shatter at the Fall in Genesis 3 was the relationship between men and women.[20]

During subsequent interviews with PK leaders, Harper pressed the issue of whether the organization was concerned about shaping how men related to women, particularly those who were not their romantic partners, such as those in the workplace, in their communities, and other settings. "The men were silent," Harper says.[21] PK, it seemed, was concerned with women only insofar as they were the wives or daughters of evangelical Christian men. Otherwise, women were invisible.

So, too, women—particularly women of color—have largely been invisible in the field of reconciliation, as discussed above. Reading lists on reconciliation usually consist of exclusively male-authored texts, sometimes augmented by an autobiographical narrative written by a female survivor of ethnic conflict outside the United States. For example, one mainline denomination's racial reconciliation curriculum includes a resource list of thirteen texts on racial reconciliation and the church; of these, only one has a female author, in this case, the final of four authors on a coauthored book. The results of this exclusively male gaze are a body of literature and an approach to reconciliation that is less about ending racism than it is about ensuring that white men and men of color have equal access to male privilege.

GENDERING RACE:
THE WOMANIST PERSPECTIVE

The exclusion of women's racial experiences from dialogue on racial reconciliation is not simply a problem for women; it precludes any real understanding of the dynamics of race and racism. Race and

---

[20]Harper, *Evangelical Does Not Equal Republican*, 108-9.
[21]Harper, *Evangelical Does Not Equal Republican*, 110.

racism are far more complex than typically acknowledged in Christian racial reconciliation efforts. Nowhere is this revealed more than in the lives of women of color, whose experiences are located on the margins of the margins. In discussions where race is the primary lens through which we view identity, women of color are marginalized by virtue of their gender. When gender is the primary concern, they are marginalized by virtue of their racial identity.

Race is intertwined with gender and other categories of identity, just as racism is intertwined with sexism and other forms of systemic oppression. Indeed, the "isms" often collude in support of one another. Historically, women's bodies have been the sites on which racial boundaries have been policed and racial wars have been fought. In the United States, for example, two of the primary ways by which white supremacist patriarchy has exercised its power has been by controlling what white women could do with their bodies and by demonstrating that black women's bodies were violable. Thus, to discuss race and racism without simultaneously addressing gender and sexism is not only shortsighted; it is ineffective.

In order to develop more robust theories and practices of reconciliation, we must not only integrate the perspectives of women of color; we must center them. The nature of marginalization is that it obscures, denies, and devalues the stories and histories of targeted groups. At the same time, those who live on the bottom rungs of social hierarchies are often more keenly attuned to the interlocking systems of oppression because their survival depends on navigating them. Centering the experiences of women of color is consistent with a womanist theological perspective. The term *womanist* was coined and defined by Pulitzer Prize–winning author Alice Walker in the preface to her book *In Search of Our Mothers' Gardens*.

> **Womanist 1.** From *womanish*. (Opp. of "girlish," i.e., frivolous, irresponsible, not serious.) A black feminist or feminist of color. From the black folk expression of mothers to female children, "You acting

womanist," i.e., like a woman. Usually referring to outrageous, auda-
cious, courageous or *willful* behavior. Wanting to know more and in
greater depth than is considered "good" for one. Interested in grown-
up doings. Acting grown up. Being grown up. Interchangeable with
another black folk expression: "You trying to be grown." Responsible.
In charge. *Serious*. **2.** *Also:* A woman who loves other women, sexually
and/or nonsexually. Appreciates and prefers women's culture, women's
emotional flexibility (values tears as natural counterbalance of
laughter), and women's strength. Sometimes loves individual men,
sexually and/or nonsexually. Committed to survival and wholeness of
entire people, male *and* female. Not a separatist, except periodically,
for health. Traditionally universalist, as in: "Mama, why are we brown,
pink, and yellow, and our cousins are white, beige, and black?" Ans.:
"Well, you know the colored race is just like a flower garden, with every
color flower represented." Traditionally capable, as in: "Mama, I'm
walking to Canada and I'm taking you and a bunch of other slaves with
me." Reply: "It wouldn't be the first time." **3.** Loves music. Loves dance.
Loves the moon. *Loves* the Spirit. Loves love and food and roundness.
Loves struggle. *Loves* the Folk. Loves herself. *Regardless*. **4.** Womanist
is to feminist as purple to lavender.[22]

Womanism, broadly, can be characterized as an approach to
scholarship and activism that begins with and focuses on the needs,
histories, and experiences of black women in the US. It encompasses
both faith-centered and secular perspectives. Within the realm of
theology and ministry, womanism "minds the gap" in black liberation
theologies, which were developed primarily by black men to address
racial oppression, and Christian feminist theologies, which were developed primarily by white women to address gender oppression.
Emerging in the 1980s as a response to those schools of thought,

> womanist theology is the systematic, faith-based exploration of the
> many facets of African American women's religiosity. Womanist

---

[22]Alice Walker, *In Search of Our Mothers' Gardens* (Orlando: Harcourt Brace Jovanovich, 1983),
i-xii.

theology is based on the complex realities of black women's lives. Womanist scholars recognize and name the imagination and initiative that African American women have utilized in developing sophisticated religious responses to their lives.[23]

In other words, womanist theology approaches, interprets, and interrogates Christian Scripture and tradition from the vantage point of black women's experiences of struggle and survival. This viewpoint enables womanist theologians to attend to elements of Scripture, tradition, and contemporary practice that are frequently overlooked and neglected by other theologians. For example, a signal text for womanist scholars and preachers is the narrative of Hagar, the slave woman who is discarded after being sexually exploited by her master and mistress.[24]

It is critical to note that not all intellectual thought by black women is womanist. Indeed, some African American female theologians have critiqued the dependence on Walker's terminology and definition. In a roundtable dialogue featuring notable womanist scholars such as Emilie M. Townes and bell hooks, Cheryl Sanders, a professor of ethics and a pastor at a Holiness-Pentecostal church, deftly articulated a critique on Walker's notion of sexual flexibility.[25] In addition to this, womanist theology's hermeneutic of suspicion may seem to make it an ill-fitting conversation partner for evangelical theology, with its emphasis on the inerrancy of Scripture. However, many evangelical women of color, particularly young women, have found womanist theology to be an indispensable lens for engaging issues of faith and justice. They see no disjuncture between affirming Scripture as divinely inspired and interrogating the racist and patriarchal

---

[23]Stephanie Y. Mitchem, *Introducing Womanist Theology* (Maryknoll: Orbis Books, 2002), ix.

[24]Renita J. Weems, *Just a Sister Away: A Womanist Vision of Women's Relationships in the Bible* (Philadelphia: Innisfree Press, 1988). See also Weems's commentary about her writing process and how it was informed by the lived experience of African American women in Renita J. Weems, "Do You See What I See: Diversity in Interpretation," *Church & Society* 82, no. 1 (September 1991): 28-43.

[25]Cheryl Jeanne Sanders, "Christian Ethics and Theology in Womanist Perspectives," *Journal of Feminist Studies in Religion* 5, no. 2 (September 1989): 83-91.

cultures through which the interpretation of Scripture and the practice of the Christian faith have been filtered. Indeed, they view womanist interpretive frameworks as not only challenging, but also deepening and enriching their understandings of faith and justice.

WOMANIST GIFTS TO RACIAL RECONCILIATION

So, too, womanist theology can challenge, deepen, and enrich evangelical theologies and practices of reconciliation. Womanist theology offers at least four gifts to advance our understanding of racism and racial reconciliation: (1) it is a lived theology; (2) it is intersectional; (3) it provides an understanding of the power dynamics inherent in oppression; and (4) it is justice oriented.

Lived theology.

Womanist theology begins its analysis by understanding the lived experiences of African American women, including the ways they experience oppression and the ways they find hope and exercise agency in the midst of oppression. Womanist theology privileges black women's lives as texts, sources of authority that can tell us something about the nature of God and about the nature of human striving. Womanist theology draws from the rich well of faith traditions and spiritual practices that have enabled black women to "make a way out of no way." As Mitchem notes, womanist theology asks the questions, "Where is God in the experiences of black women? By what name should this God be called? What does it mean to live a life of faith? How should black women respond to God's call?"[26] In the case of racial reconciliation, we might say that womanist theology asks the questions, What do black women's lives reveal about the natures of the powers and principalities? How do black women understand hope, forgiveness, and reconciliation in light of their experiences of oppression? What do reconciliation and healing look like for black women? How should black women respond to God's call to be ambassadors of reconciliation?

---

[26]Mitchem, *Introducing Womanist Theology*, 23.

Womanist theology recognizes that, as the marginalized among the marginalized, the lives of black women reveal something unique about how racism works. It is one thing to ask what reconciliation looks like from the perspective of the white male whose call to reconciliation may be shaped by the sense of guilt he feels about his racial/gender privilege and his desire to appease that guilt by increasing access to that privilege for people of color. It is another thing altogether to ask what reconciliation looks like from the perspective of the black female whose quotidian experiences of gendered racism require her to bend, genuflect, and disassemble herself everyday in order to survive, and whose responsibilities as caregiver require her to teach others to do the same.

Intersectionality.

Moreover, womanist theology intrinsically employs an intersectional framework as lens through which to understand and interpret systems of power and oppression that interconnect to shape the lives of black women. It recognizes that the experiences of black women are not simply the sum of their experiences as women and their experiences as black people. Identity is not simply additive; it is multiplicative, as indicated by the algebraic equation below:

Racial/Gender Identity = Race + Gender + Race*Gender

We can extrapolate this intersectional understanding of identity to write a similar equation to demonstrate the intersectional nature of oppression:

Racial/Gender Oppression = Racism + Sexism + Racism*Sexism

In other words, black women will share some experiences with black men by virtue of their race, and they will share some experiences with all women by virtue of their femaleness. But their location at the intersection of race and gender predisposes them to experiences of gendered racism that are qualitatively and quantitatively different from those of black men (and certainly from white men), white women, and sometimes even other women of color. The same, of course, is true for all men and women of color. Of course, the equations presented above are drastically simplified for the purposes of illustration. Intersectional theory recognizes that identity and experience are not reduced to race and gender. Race and gender interact not only with each other, but also with class, sexuality, nationality, geographic origin, and disability to shape the lived experiences of black women.

Unfortunately, however, discussions of race and racism within the Christian racial reconciliation movement treat race and racism as monolithic categories, focusing almost exclusively on the experiences of black, and to lesser degree Latinx, men. Thus, many evangelicals engaged in social justice ministry can readily name forms of gendered racial oppression that happen disproportionately to black men, for example, "driving while black" as a form of racism. Fewer, however, can name or explain the forms of racism that are more common for black women and other women of color, including (1) invisibility, the experience that black women have of being ignored, silenced, and overlooked in interracial spaces, which runs counter to the problem of hypervisibility that men of color often experience; (2) colorism, a manifestation of white supremacy that privileges women of color whose skin tone, hair texture, facial features, and body type approximate whiteness; (3) sexual trauma and shaming; and (4) mammification, black women's frequent experience of being mistaken for "the help" in interracial contexts. These experiences are not ancillary to the dynamics of racism; they form its very core. Until we center them, our visions of reconciliation are anemic at best, resulting in a form of justice in which some of us, but not all of us, are free.

Racism as power.

As Jennifer Harvey deftly demonstrates in her book, *Dear White Christians*, racial reconciliation among evangelicals is characterized by its interpersonal focus. Racism is typically understood as hostility between races that results from societal separation. The dominant strategies for reconciliation, then, emphasize togetherness: fostering transformative interpersonal relationships between Christians of different ethnic backgrounds and establishing multiethnic congregations. Womanist theology helps us to understand that racism is not a problem of division; it is a problem of unjust power. Womanists carry the cultural memories of black women whose service as domestic workers for white men and women provided lots of intercultural proximity to white men and women during slavery and Jim Crow. They share kitchen table talk with female relatives who labor today as the new domestics: home care, nursing home, and hospice nursing assistants for elderly white people, and nannies for the young. They know firsthand that such proximity does not protect black women from the abuses of racism; it often renders them more susceptible.

Because power structures relationships, any approach to reconciliation that does not recognize racial differences in power is at best ineffective; at worst, it could actually reinforce racial hierarchies. Power, in this conceptualization, is not necessarily something that individuals possess; rather, it is "an intangible entity that circulates within a particular matrix of domination and to which individuals stand in varying relationships."[27] In other words, power exists beyond the individual but can be employed by individuals depending on their relationship to it. In a white supremacist context, those identified as white have more ready access to power relative to people of color.

Moreover, interpersonal power is just one of several forms of power through which oppression is mediated. Black feminist scholar Patricia Hill Collins describes systemic oppression as operating through a complex matrix of four domains of power: structural, disciplinary, hegemonic, and interpersonal.[28] Bonnie Thornton Dill and Ruth Enid Zambrana provide a concise summary of these domains:

---

[27]Patricia Hill Collins, *Black Feminist Thought: Knowledge, Consciousness, and the Politics of Empowerment,* 2nd ed. (New York: Routledge, 2000), 274.
[28]Collins, *Black Feminist Thought,* 276.

the structural domain, which consists of the institutional structures of
the society including government, the legal system, housing patterns,
economic traditions, and educational structure;

the disciplinary domain, which consists of the ideas and practices that
characterize and sustain bureaucratic hierarchies;

the hegemonic domain, which consists of the images, symbols, ideas,
and ideologies that shape social consciousness; . . . [and]

the interpersonal domain, which consists of patterns of interaction
between individuals and groups.[29]

Racism—like other forms of oppression—operates through each of
these domains. For example, it is encoded in property-tax funded educational systems that allocate higher funds per student to schools in
high-income neighborhoods, from which people of color are systematically excluded through a combination of prior housing segregation
laws, current lending practices, and disparities in intergenerational
wealth (the structural domain). It is buttressed by the gatekeepers of
these systems: the realtors who steer clients toward "the right kind" of
neighborhoods, and the mortgage brokers who influence which clients
get which interest rates (the disciplinary domain). Those individuals'
decisions are informed by societal ideals and stereotypes regarding
what constitutes a "good" or "fitting" neighborhood, such as low density
of people of color (the hegemonic domain). Finally, there are the racial
microaggressions experienced by people of color in this system on a
day-to-day basis, such as the silent stares that the new black home-
owners receive from the white residents in a community typically
characterized as friendly (the interpersonal domain).

So too, then, reconciliation, must be multisystemic. Racial reconciliation must be simultaneously concerned with overhauling the

---

[29]Bonnie Thornton Dill and Ruth Enid Zambrana, "Critical Thinking About Inequality: An
Emerging Lens," in *Emerging Intersections: Race, Class, and Gender in Theory, Policy, and Practice*,
ed. Bonnie Thornton Dill and Ruth Enid Zambrana (New Brunswick, NJ: Rutgers University
Press, 2009), 7.

social, economic, and political systems that replicate and reinforce racial oppression (structural); dismantling the bureaucratic policies and structures that maintain unjust systems (disciplinary); healing the internal and external wounds inflicted on those whose lives have been affected by racism (hegemonic); and rectifying the brokenness in relationships within and across racial boundaries.

Justice.

Womanist theology is inherently focused on justice. As Mitchem notes, womanist theology always begins with the question of ethics: "How are we to live?"[30] For womanists, the response to this question is never individualistic. Faith is not to be reduced to the strength of one's personal relationship with God or even simply the quality of one's relationships with other people. Consistent with liberation theologies broadly, womanist theology understands Christian faith as intrinsically linked to a commitment to justice that is to be lived out in one's relationships with marginalized persons as well as in one's work toward ending oppression.[31] For womanist theologians, reconciliation without justice is cheap grace. Forming relationships across racial boundaries is not reconciliation; it is merely a starting point on a journey toward establishing God's kingdom on earth as it is in heaven. For the telos of reconciliation is not simply the cessation of racial hostility; it is "the survival and wholeness of entire people, male and female."[32] It is God's *shalom*.

SUMMARY

So, is it time for a womanist theology of reconciliation? Absolutely. If anything, what the past twenty years of dialogue around racial reconciliation has demonstrated is that crosscultural relationships and multiracial congregations cannot solve the problem of racism. Womanist theology explains why that is. With its focus on the experiences of black

---

[30]Mitchem, *Introducing Womanist Theology*, 57-59.
[31]Mitchem, *Introducing Womanist Theology*, 42.
[32]Walker, *In Search of Our Mothers' Gardens*, xi.

women—which have been largely excluded from our understandings of racism—womanist theology reveals the intersection of racism with other forms of oppression to impact women of color in ways that have been excluded from dialogue and practice regarding racial reconciliation. Centering the experiences of black women forces us to reject outright the notion that reconciliation is about proximity, relationship, and feeling. It teaches us that power always structures relationship and that proximity and positive affect do not dismantle centuries-old systems, structures, policies, and practices that have been designed to maintain white supremacy and to disenfranchise people of color, especially the descendants of enslaved Africans in the United States.

Ultimately, what womanist theology does is to reveal the tragic complexity of racial oppression. It causes us to question whether racial reconciliation is even possible. This, too, is a gift, for it keeps us from being too easily satisfied with cheap grace, with prescriptions for reconciliation that demand forgiveness without justice, relationship without repentance, and hope without healing. It is precisely this complexity that points to the necessity of God's redemptive work in racial reconciliation.

PART TWO

ENGAGEMENT WITH LIBERATION THEOLOGY MOVEMENTS

CHAPTER FOUR

TOWARD A PERSPECTIVE OF "BROWN THEOLOGY"

ROBERT CHAO ROMERO

EDWIN was a p. k.(pastor's kid). His parents fled to the United States from Central America to escape the gang violence and poverty that had eclipsed El Salvador in the wake of its brutal civil war. Edwin's dad was the pastor of a Pentecostal church in Pico Union, and Edwin grew up playing piano on the church worship team. Wanting to shield Edwin from the "worldly" teachings that he might encounter at a public university, Edwin's father instead decided it was best for his son to attend a local Christian college.

Arriving in the freshman dorms, Edwin felt a little uncomfortable because none of his roommates were Latino, and they all came from privileged middle-class backgrounds. They were nice, though, and after a short while they started hanging out in the cafeteria, going to the movies, and playing soccer together.

The first year was going pretty well until one tragic day in May 2018. Edwin had been up late studying for finals when he received a phone call that would change his life forever. It was his fourteen-year-old sister Angélica. In tears, she reported to him that their mother and father had just been detained by Immigrations and

Customs Enforcement (ICE). You see, Edwin's family came to the United States as refugees because the gangs in El Salvador had targeted Edwin for recruitment, shot his uncle, and burned his grandfather's house down. Yet because his parents did not have enough money to hire an immigration lawyer, they were unable to prove to ICE that they qualified for asylum. As a result, Edwin's parents were arrested according to President Trump's controversial immigration policies.

After hearing the terrible news, Edwin fell to his knees and prayed to God for strength and the safety of his parents. A million questions raced through his mind: Would his mom and dad be safe while in custody with ICE? Could he talk to them? Did they have any legal recourse to block their deportation? When would he see them again? Who would take care of his younger sister?

After a restless and sleepless night, Edwin stumbled into his introduction to New Testament theology class the next morning. The topic of the day was salvation by grace, and class discussion was focused on Ephesians 2:8-9. To supplement their discussion, the professor read excerpts from Martin Luther's *Commentary on Galatians* and John Calvin's *Commentaries on the Epistles of Paul to the Romans*. During the break, some of Edwin's classmates started to talk about the topic of immigration. They said to Edwin, "I don't know what all the controversy is about. We need to build a wall and deport all those 'illegals' that are taking our jobs and causing crime to go up."

Edwin was stunned. He didn't know what to say or how to respond. He thought to himself, *If they believe in God's grace, how can they have such mean-spirited, anti-immigrant views on immigration? Aren't they my friends? Don't they know that they're deeply offending me? Does God's salvation have anything to do with what my family is going through and the horrible pain we are experiencing? Why doesn't our class talk about what the Bible has to say about caring for immigrants?*

I wonder if there are any Latino theologians that we can study. If there are, how come we don't learn about them at this Christian college?[1]

THE BROWN CHURCH AND BROWN THEOLOGY

Unbeknownst to Edwin and most Latinas/os in the United States, there is a five-hundred-year history of Latina/o theologians who have spoken and written about issues of race and social justice from a Christ-centered and biblical perspective. They have been Protestant and Catholic, they have been men and women, and they have written both in Latin America and the United States. In every instance of racial and social injustice in Latin America and the United States over the centuries, Latina/o theologians and church leaders have arisen to challenge the religious, socio-economic, and political status quo. Collectively, they have challenged such great evils as the Spanish Conquest and colonialism, the *sistema de castas*, Manifest Destiny, Latin American dictatorships, US imperialism in Central America, the oppression of farmworkers, and the current exploitation and marginalization of undocumented immigrants. Together, they form what may be called the *brown church*.[2] As a natural outgrowth of their prophetic advocacy efforts and praxis, they have also read their Bibles and developed a communal body of theology that may collectively be called *brown theology*. Brown theology is a vital expression of the ecclesial capital of the brown church and has been forged in the fires of five hundred years of Latina/o racial and religious struggle.

---

[1]This story of Edwin is a critical race counterstory. Counterstories share much in common with the parables of Jesus. As described by Solórzano and Yosso, critical race counterstories "draw on various forms of 'data' to recount the racialized, sexualized, and classed experiences of people of color. Such counterstories may offer both biographical and autobiographical analyses because the authors create composite characters and create them in social, historical, and political situations to discuss racism, sexism, classism, and other forms of subordination." Daniel Solórzano and Tara Yosso, "Critical Race Methodology: Counter-Storytelling as an Analytical Framework for Education Research," *Qualitative Inquiry* 8 (2002): 33. Edwin is a composite character drawn from my interaction with many Latina/o students throughout the United States over the past decade.

[2]Brown is symbolic of the cultural and biological *mestizaje*, or mixture, in Latin America. In the US context, brown is also symbolic of the historic legal and sociological racial positioning of Latinos between white and black.

As a means of introduction to brown theology, this essay offers a historical overview of three key theologians or theological movements of the brown church: Bartolomé de Las Casas, *misión integral*, and Latina/o theology. Together, these figures and movements offer a representative sampling of the brown church and its biblical ruminations on race and social justice. Though this list barely scratches the surface of the rich trove of Latina/o theologizing, it may be enough to encourage the reader to dig deeper and begin further exploration of the ecclesial capital of Latino Christianity. As a reflection of the transnational and transdenominational historical nature of the brown church, the theologians under consideration are from Latin America and the United States, and both Roman Catholic and Protestant *evangélicos*.[3] In the spirit of *teología en conjunto*, I present the concept of brown theology as a framework of communal Latina/o racial and social justice theologizing whose historical development spans from the Spanish Conquest to the present.[4]

BARTOLOMÉ DE LAS CASAS (1484–1566):
THE BIRTH OF BROWN THEOLOGY

Bartolomé de Las Casas was the central founder of the brown church and progenitor of brown theology in the Americas. He has also been credited with founding the modern concept of social justice as we know it. Las Casas was born in Seville, Spain, in 1484 and took part in the Spanish conquest of the Caribbean, most likely as a military chaplain.[5] In reward for his participation in the brutal conquest of the West Indies, he was granted special status as an

---

[3]For a more detailed discussion of brown theology, see Robert Chao Romero, *The Brown Church: Towards a History and Identity of Latina/o Social Justice Christianity* (Downers Grove, IL: Inter-Varsity Press Academic, forthcoming 2020).

[4]*Teología en conjunto*, or *de conjunto*, is a concept from Latina/o theology insisting that theologizing in the Latino context is a collaborative endeavor involving pastors, theologians, and grassroots church parishioners in egalitarian dialogue geared toward the spiritual and social uplift of the entire community. For more on *teología en conjunto*, see Miguel A. De La Torre and Edwin David Aponte, *Introducing Latino/a Theologies* (Maryknoll, NY: Orbis Books, 2001), 72, 73.

[5]Paul Vickery, *Bartolomé de Las Casas: Great Prophet of the Americas* (New York: Paulist Press, 2006), 32-33.

encomendero—one of the economic elite of the island. In the words of Las Casas himself:

> Greed increased every day and every day Indians perished in greater numbers and the clergyman Bartolomé de Las Casas . . . went about his concerns like the others, sending his share of Indians to work fields and gold mines, taking advantage of them as much as he could.[6]

On June 4, 1514, Las Casas experienced what scholars call his "first conversion."[7] While preparing a sermon for Pentecost Sunday, his conscience was stricken after reading Sirach 34:18: "The sacrifice of an offering unjustly acquired is a mockery; the gifts of the impious are unacceptable" (NJB).

Las Casas reflected on this text from the biblical Apocrypha in light of the suffering of the native peoples of the Indies and realized that he could not both follow Christ and participate in their exploitation. Las Casas speaks of this conversion experience (in the third person) in *History of the Indies*:

> He [Las Casas] spent a few days in meditation on the matter until by dint of applying his readings to this and that case he was convinced Indians were being treated unjustly and tyrannically all over the Indies. He read everything in this new light and found his opinion supported; as he used to say, from the day the darkness lifted from his eyes, he never read any book in Latin or a vulgar tongue—and he read an infinite number in forty-four years—which did not in some way provide the proof of Indian rights and Spanish injustice.[8]

Following his experience of *concientización*, or awakening of social conscience, Las Casas spent the next five decades condemning the conquest and challenging the enslavement of the native populations.

---

[6]Bartolomé de Las Casas, *A History of the Indies* (New York: Harper & Row, 1971), 208. The previous section is based on my article: Robert Chao Romero, "Immigration, Donald Trump, and American Civil Religion," *Jesus4Revolutionaries* (blog), February 25, 2016, https://www.jesus4revolutionaries.com/blog/immigration-donald-trump-and-american-civil-religion.

[7]Vickery, *Bartolomé de Las Casas*, 2, 3.

[8]Las Casas, *History of the Indies*, 208-9.

In the process, he invented social justice as we have come to know it, as well as Christian social justice theology. In the spirit of the Old Testament prophets, of which Jesus was the climax, the message of Las Casas was simple and clear: the Spanish Conquest of the Indigenous peoples of the Americas was unjust. God had given the Spaniards the opportunity to share the message of Jesus with love, and instead they exploited this divine opportunity for greed and selfish gain. The end result was genocide. If the Spaniards did not repent, there would be hell to pay.

In *A Short Account of the Destruction of the Indies*, Las Casas described in vivid detail the atrocities of the Spanish Conquest and petitioned King Philip to stop the destruction of the Indigenous peoples taking place in the name of the church:

> Meanwhile, the boldness and the unreason of those who count it as nothing to drench the Americas in human blood and to dispossess the people who are the natural masters and dwellers in those vast and marvelous kingdoms, killing a thousand million of them, and stealing treasures beyond compare, grow by the day, and, masquerading under false colours, they do everything within their power to obtain further license to continue their conquests (license that cannot be granted without infringing natural and divine law and thereby conniving at the gravest of mortal sins, worthy of the most terrible and everlasting punishment). I therefore determined to present Your Highness with this *Short Account*, which is but a brief digest of the many and various outrages and depredations which could and should be recorded.[9]

---

[9]Bartolomé de Las Casas, *A Short Account of the Destruction of the Indies* (London: Penguin Books, 1992), 7-8. Las Casas has had many critics over the centuries. Spanish nationalists of the early twentieth century argued that the abuses described by Las Casas are exaggerations, and that they contributed to the perpetuation of the "Black Legend"—a view of Spaniards as cruel, backward, and degenerate. For more on the Black Legend, see Maria DeGuzman, *Spain's Long Shadow: The Black Legend, Off-Whiteness, and Anglo-American Empire* (Minneapolis: University of Minnesota Press, 2005). On the left, Las Casas has been rightly criticized for his support of African slavery as a remedy for the enslavement of Indians. Las Casas soon recanted this position and viewed his endorsement of African slavery as one of the greatest errors of his life. He has also been critiqued for never condemning the Spanish colonial project in its entirety. Though Las Casas opposed the violent conquest of the Americas, he did not question the legal and spiritual right of the Spanish Crown to claim colonial rule over the Indigenous peoples.

Anticipating the methodology and approach of ethnic studies, Las Casas chronicled the racial violence and genocide of the Spaniards. His prophetic analysis encompassed the entirety of Latin America and included the Indigenous communities of what is now the Dominican Republic, Haiti, Cuba, Puerto Rico, Mexico, Guatemala, Peru, Venezuela, and Colombia. Spanish violence included the rape of children and women, and the indiscriminate slaughter of entire Indigenous communities. Particularly disgusting was the brutal atrocities Europeans conducted in the explicit name of Jesus and the Christian faith. The unbiblical conflation of Spanish military conquest and Christianity is described by Las Casas in the following excerpt:

> As we have said, the island of Hispaniola was the first to witness the arrival of Europeans and the first to suffer the wholesale slaughter of its people and the devastation and depopulation of the land. It all began with the Europeans taking native women and children both as servants and to satisfy their own base appetites. . . . They forced their way into native settlements, slaughtering everyone they found there, including small children, old men, pregnant women, and even women who had just given birth. . . . They spared no one, erecting especially wide gibbets on which they could string their victims up with their feet just off the ground and then burn them alive thirteen at a time, in honour of our Saviour and the twelve Apostles.[10]

Las Casas believed that the Spanish Conquest would forever sully the testimony of Christianity and asserted that the Indigenous peoples were made in the image of God and therefore children of God, equal to the Spaniards.[11] "They are our brothers, redeemed by Christ's most precious blood, no less than the wisest and most learned men in the whole world."[12] In refutation of the claim that Indians were culturally

---

[10]Las Casas, *Short Account of the Destruction*, 14-15.
[11]Bartolomé de Las Casas, *In Defense of the Indians* (DeKalb: Northern Illinois University Press, 1992), 20, 39.
[12]Las Casas, *In Defense of the Indians*, 39.

backward, Las Casas praised the sophistication of Indigenous art, architecture, and cultural production.[13]

The prophetic ministry of Bartolomé de Las Casas laid the foundations of the brown church in the Americas. Through his numerous writings, which included *A Short Account of the Destruction of the Indies, In Defense of the Indians,* and *History of the Indies,* Las Casas invented interdisciplinary social justice scholarship and theologizing, and established a model of religious protest that would go on to inspire many others throughout the colonial period and up until the twenty-first century.[14]

MISIÓN INTEGRAL: A HOLISTIC GOSPEL

Confronted with the ravages of poverty, oppression, and decades of failed programs of economic modernization, Latin American *evangélicos* of the 1960s and 1970s wrestled with constructing a movement and theology faithful to their own contextualized experience and distinct theological commitments. As Protestant evangelicals, they held firmly to belief in the centrality of Christ as Savior of the world, the Bible as the authoritative Word of God, and the Holy Spirit as the transformative and active agent in the personal lives of believers. In consonance with this characterization, theologian Emilio Antonio Nuñez of El Salvador asserts that Latin American evangelical theology is theocentric, bibliocentric, christocentric, and pneumatological.[15] As "radical evangelicals," they "sought to remain faithful to Scriptures and, at the same time, incarnated in the Latin American socio-political reality."[16] Although theologically conservative, they remained steadfastly

---

[13]Las Casas, *In Defense of the Indians,* 44

[14]In the seventeenth century, Garcilaso de la Vega el Inca, Felipe Guaman Poma de Ayala, Catarina de San Juan, and Sor Juana Inés de la Cruz followed in the prophetic footsteps of Las Casas. This diverse group of Jesus followers added Indigenous, mestizo, female, and even Asian perspectives to Latin American religious discourse and laid the second layer of foundation for the brown church. For more on the development of the brown church during the colonial period through the twentieth century, see Romero, *Brown Church.*

[15]Ruth Irene Padilla DeBorst, "Integral Mission Formation in Abya Yala (Latin America): A Study of the Centro de Studios Teológicos Interdisciplinarios (1982–2002) and Radical Evangélicos" (PhD diss., Boston University, 2016), 28.

[16]DeBorst, "Integral Mission Formation," 29-30.

committed to the outworking of the gospel through works of trans-formative justice. Moreover, despite being sympathetic to many of the concerns of liberation theology, radical evangelicals opposed the explicit adoption of Marxist ideology, the sacralization of revolution, disregard for the authority of the Bible, and any simplistic reduction of the gospel to political, sociological, or economic terms.[17]

The radical evangelical movement of Latin America was birthed out of the ministry endeavors of the Comunidad Internacional de Estudiantes Evangélicos (CIEE) and closely associated with E. René Padilla and Samuel Escobar.[18] The CIEE was formally established in Cochabamba, Bolívia, in 1958 and was the Latin American expression of the International Fellowship of Evangelical Students (IFES). The IFES was formed in 1947 in Boston by the leaders of ten evangelical student movements from throughout the world. The IFES is the worldwide representative body that emerged from InterVarsity Fellowship and InterVarsity Christian Fellowship–USA.[19]

In December 1970, Padilla and Escobar met with other Protestant church leaders and theologians in Cochabamba to discuss the formation of a distinctly Latin American evangelical theology that addressed the poverty and oppression of Latin America. Like Padilla, these leaders understood that the theological approaches and min-istry methods of North America were insufficient for the contextual needs of Latin America. They were "tired of the evangelical power centers in North America telling us how to think, who to read, and what it meant to be evangelical," and they "decided it was time to start reflecting the faith as grownups and on our own."[20] In no uncertain terms, these leaders rejected US "culture Christianity," which conflated the gospel with Western values and conformity with the

---

[17]DeBorst, "Integral Mission Formation," 128.

[18]DeBorst, "Integral Mission Formation," 77.

[19]David C. Kirkpatrick, "C. René Padilla and the Origins of Integral Mission in Post-War Latin America," *Journal of Ecclesiastical History* 67, no. 2 (April 2016): 351-71.

[20]Michael Clawson, "Misión Integral and Progressive Evangelicalism: The Latin American Influ-ence on the North American Emerging Church," *Religions* 3, no. 3 (August 2012): 791.

socioeconomic and political status quo. They decried this limited cultural expression of Christianity in which the "racist can continue to be a racist, the exploiter can continue to be an exploiter." According to Escobar, moreover, US cultural Christians were the kind of people who "oppose the violence of revolution but not the violence of war" and "condemn all the sins that well-behaved middle class people condemn but say nothing about exploitation, intrigue, and dirty political maneuvering done by great multi-national corporations around the world."[21]

In response to these extreme blind spots of western Protestant Christianity, those gathered at Cochabamba sought to reframe the gospel in a fresh way faithful both to Scripture and the distinct Latin American cultural and historical context.[22] To achieve this goal and help foster productive theological discussion, Padilla and Escobar, together with Orlando Costas, Pedro Arana, Emilio Antonio Nuñez, Orlando Gutiérrez, and Peter Savage, founded the Fraternidad Teológica Latinoamericana (FTL).[23] In subsequent decades, the FTL emerged as the leading evangelical theological organization in Latin America.[24] It also inspired numerous missional initiatives and organizations, and helped train many who have gone on to be leaders in churches and the nonprofit sector.[25]

The greatest theological contribution of FTL and radical *evangélicos* has been the framework of *misión integral*. According to the theology of *misión integral*, biblical mission must include "both proclamation and demonstration of the good news of the Reign of God through Christian teaching, presence, and social engagement for transformation."[26] Evangelism and social action are both integral to Christian mission and cannot be artificially divided, one from

---

[21]DeBorst, "Integral Mission Formation," 46.
[22]DeBorst, "Integral Mission Formation," 45, 48.
[23]Clawson, "Misión Integral," 791; DeBorst, "Integral Mission Formation," 97.
[24]Kirkpatrick, "C. René Padilla," 368.
[25]DeBorst, "Integral Mission Formation," 124.
[26]DeBorst, "Integral Mission Formation," 5.

another.[27] In 1969, Padilla, who is widely considered to be the father of integral mission, declared,

> The proclamation of the gospel (kerygma) and the demonstration of the gospel that gives itself in service (diakonía) form an indissoluble whole. One without the other is an incomplete, mutilated (mutilado) gospel and, consequently, contrary to the will of God. From this perspective, it is foolish to ask about the relative importance of evangelism and social responsibility. This would be equivalent to asking about the relative importance of the right wing and the left wing of a plane.[28]

To use another metaphor, *misión integral* declares that the gospel involves both vertical salvation (reconciliation of an individual with God through Christ) and horizontal engagement with the pressing social concerns of the day.[29] Like *harina integral* (whole wheat flour) or *arroz integral* (whole grain rice), biblical mission is all-encompassing and must entail both the verbal proclamation of the good news of Jesus and the practical expression of Christ's justice in the world.[30] Though this notion of a "holistic gospel" is somewhat common within Protestant evangelical circles today, what is much less known is that its origins lay in Latin America among radical *evangélicos* and the FTL. In fact, it has been said that the theological reintegration of evangelism and social action through *misión integral* has been "the most significant contribution which Latin American evangelicals have made internationally" to the global church.[31] Since the 1970s, the global missions paradigm of *misión integral* has spread far beyond Latin America through the International Conference on World Evangelization held in Lausanne, Switzerland, in 1974, the InterVarsity Urbana Missions Conference of 1970, and the International Fellowship

---

[27]Kirkpatrick, "C. René Padilla," 353.
[28]Kirkpatrick, "C. René Padilla," 368.
[29]Kirkpatrick, "C. René Padilla," 360.
[30]DeBorst, "Integral Mission Formation," 54.
[31]DeBorst, "Integral Mission Formation," 55.

for Mission as Transformation, Micah Global, and the Lausanne Movement.[32] Quite notably, the popular missional church movement has neglected to credit Padilla and Escobar with the central theological framework which defines their ecclesiological method and practice.

LATINA/O THEOLOGY: THE US CONTEXT

Inspired by Latin American liberation theologies, the Chicano and African American civil rights struggles, and the swell of diverse Latino communities in the United States, Latinas and Latinos began to self-theologize in the 1970s and 1980s.[33] As both Protestant and Roman Catholic, they rejected the racial paternalism and assimilationism of the broader Anglo religious community.[34] Their goal was, and is, to develop theology informed by the distinct Latina/o cultural context in the United States. According to religion scholar Edwin Aponte, Latina/o theology may be defined as

> the distinct theologies that emerge out of the social and cultural contexts of Latino/a peoples, which, nonetheless, have some shared characteristics. These common traits make Latino/a theology a communal undertaking that is scholarly, pastoral, and organically connected to grassroots communities. Latino/a theology insists on doing theology in a relevant contextual way that is both in dialogue with the received dominant theological traditions as well as questioning of them and their claims of being standard.[35]

Since the 1980s, Latina/o theology has developed in three distinct stages that theologian Oscar García-Johnson calls "founders," "builders," and "shapers."[36] Central figures in the initial development

---

[32]DeBorst, "Integral Mission Formation," 57.

[33]Justo Gonzalez, email message to author, September 1, 2015.

[34]Miguel A. De La Torre and Edwin David Aponte, *Introducing Latino/a Theologies* (Maryknoll, NY: Orbis Books, 2001), 104.

[35]Edwin David Aponte and Miguel A. De La Torre, *Handbook of Latina/o Theologies* (St. Louis: Chalice Press, 2006), 1.

[36]Oscar García-Johnson, *The Mestizo/a Community of the Spirit: A Postmodern Latino/a Ecclesiology* (Eugene, OR: Pickwick, 2009), 31-36.

of Latina/o theology, or "founders," include Methodist historical theologian Justo González, Roman Catholic pastor and theologian Virgilio Elizondo, and American Baptist missiologist Orlando Costas.[37] Allan Figueroa Deck, Orlando Espín, María Pilar Aquino, Daisy Machado, Jeanette Rodríguez, Eldin Villafañe, Elizabeth Conde-Frazier, and Ismael García are key figures of the "builders" stage.[38] "Shapers" of Latina/o theology include Oscar García-Johnson, Juan Martínez, Fernando Segovia, Harold Recinos, Ada María Isasi-Díaz, Loida I. Martell-Otero, Zaida Maldonado Pérez, Roberto Goizueta, Gastón Espinosa, Johnny Ramírez-Johnson, Miguel De La Torre, Edwin Aponte, and Alexia Salvatierra, among others.

A central tenet of Latina/o theology is *teología en conjunto*, or collaborative communal theology.[39] From a Latino perspective, theology is not a lone ranger scholastic endeavor whose aim is individualistic academic acclaim. Rather, theology is a communal endeavor springing from the firsthand experience of the grassroots Latino community itself. *Teología en conjunto* is produced from the mutual dialogue of pastors, theologians, and lay parishioners. From the start, Latina/o theology has also been ecumenical—Protestant and Catholic—as well as transdenominational—evangelical, mainline, and Pentecostal. Latina/o theology, moreover, emphasizes

---

[37]See Justo González, *Mañana: Christian Theology from a Hispanic Perspective* (Nashville: Abingdon Press, 1990), 75; Justo González, *Santa Biblia: The Bible Through Hispanic Eyes* (Nashville: Abingdon Press, 1996); Virgilio Elizondo, *Galilean Journey: The Mexican-American Promise* (Maryknoll: Orbis Books, 2005); Orlando E. Costas, *Christ Outside the Gate: Mission Beyond Christendom* (Maryknoll: Orbis Books, 1993).

[38]Allan Figueroa Deck, *The Second Wave: Hispanic Ministry and the Evangelization of Cultures* (New York: Paulist Press, 1989); Orlando Espín, "Grace and Humanness: A Latino/a Perspective," in *We Are a People! Initiatives in Hispanic American Theology*, ed. Roberto S. Goizueta (Minneapolis: Fortress, 1992) 133-64; María Pilar Aquino, "Directions and Foundations of Hispanic/Latino Theology: Toward a Mestiza Theology of Liberation," *Journal of Hispanic/Latino Theology* 1, no. 1 (1993): 5-21; Aquino, Daisy L. Machado, and Jeanette Rodriguez, eds., *A Reader in Latina Feminist Theology: Religion and Justice* (Austin: University of Texas Press, 2002); Eldin Villafañe, *The Liberating Spirit: Toward a Hispanic American Pentecostal Social Ethics* (New York: University Press of America, 1992); Elizabeth Conde-Frazier, *Hispanic Bible Institutes: A Community of Theological Construction* (Scranton, PA: University of Scranton Press, 2004); Ismael García, *Dignidad: Ethics Through Hispanic Eyes* (Nashville: Abingdon, 1997).

[39]Aponte, *Handbook*, 7.

orthopraxis, or right action. Latina/o theologians insist that, just as faith without works is dead, so is theology dead if it does not engender the social and cultural uplift of the entire Latino community.

Latina/o theology understands that all theology is contextual. Even though the Bible is God's inspired Word, there is no such thing as an entirely objective interpretation of the Bible not informed by the cultural context of the interpreter. All theologies are socially circumscribed.[40] This is not necessarily a bad thing, because it allows for meaningful and distinct cultural insights into the text of Scripture by different members of the body of Christ. Seen in this light, God-given cultural diversity only reinforces unity in the church, because it encourages us to lean on one another in order to know God more fully. At the same time, the failure to recognize the important role of ethnic culture and experience in shaping biblical interpretation can produce damaging results, because it can lead a culturally dominant community to insist that its own view of God is objective to the exclusion of all others. The end result is the tribalization of Jesus and the circumscription of God within the narrow cultural understanding of a single ethnic or racial community. This is idolatry. This is what American and European colonization did for five hundred years, and what certain pockets of Western Christianity continue to insist on.

In recognition of the value of cultural context in interpreting Scripture, Justo González has introduced the concept of "reading the Bible in Spanish," or with "Hispanic eyes."[41] By this, he does not mean reading the Bible in a Spanish translation, but rather, reading Scripture in light of the distinct and diverse historical experiences of Latinas/os in the United States. "If it is true that we bring a particular perspective to history and to theology, then we must also bring a particular perspective to the interpretation of Scripture. And, once again, it may be that this perspective will prove useful not only to us

---

[40]Loida I. Martell-Otero, Zaida Maldonado Pérez, and Elizabeth Conde-Frazier, *Latina Evangélicas: A Theological Survey from the Margins* (Eugene, OR: Cascade, 2013), 19.
[41]González, *Mañana*, 75; González, *Santa Biblia*, 28.

but also to the church at large."[42] "Hispanic eyes," moreover, according to González, "is the perspective of those who claim their Hispanic identity as part of their hermeneutical baggage, and also read the Scripture within the context of a commitment to the Latino struggle to become all that God wants us and all of the world to be—in other words, the struggle for salvation/liberation."[43] Reading the Bible through Hispanic eyes has led many Latina/o theologians to focus their reflection on the themes of marginality, poverty, *mestizaje* and *mulatez* (European, Indigenous, and African cultural mixture), exile, and communal/familial solidarity.[44] Drawing from these paradigms, Latina/o theologians have produced important analyses of the biblical significance of Galilee and the sociological framework of *lo cotidiano*.

In their reading of Scripture, Latina/o theologians have been particularly struck by the numerous biblical passages referencing Galilee. Authors such as Virgilio Elizondo have highlighted the fact that Jesus was raised in Galilee, selected his early disciples from Galilee, and performed most of his public ministry in Galilee. As noted in Scripture,

> Philip found Nathanael and told him, "We have found the one Moses wrote about in the Law, and about whom the prophets also wrote— Jesus of Nazareth, the son of Joseph." "Nazareth! Can anything good come from there?" Nathanael asked. "Come and see," said Philip. (Jn 1:45-46)

> After John was put in prison, Jesus went into Galilee, proclaiming the good news of God. "The time has come," he said. "The kingdom of God has come near. Repent and believe the good news!" As Jesus walked beside the Sea of Galilee, he saw Simon and his brother Andrew casting a net into the lake, for they were fishermen. (Mk 1:14-16)

In his pioneering book *The Galilean Journey: The Mexican-American Promise*, Elizondo argues that the Galilean roots of Jesus point to

---

[42]González, *Mañana*, 75.
[43]González, *Santa Biblia*, 28-29.
[44]González, *Santa Biblia*, 31, 57, 77, 91, 103.

God's preferential option for those of marginalized communities.[45] In Jesus' day, Galilee was a symbol of multiple rejections.[46] Whereas Jerusalem was the center of Jewish religious, economic, and political life, Galilee was looked down on as cultural backwaters—"the hood" of its day. And if Galilee in general was "the hood," then Jesus' hometown of Nazareth in Galilee was "the hood of the hood"— perhaps similar to the way popular culture (wrongly) refers to Compton, California. And so quipped Nathanael, "Nazareth! Can anything good come from there?" (Jn 1:46).

Galileans were mostly poor peasant farmers, and they spoke both Greek and Aramaic with an accent.[47] Galileans were also looked on with suspicion by their compatriots in Jerusalem because they lived in a multicultural borderlands region at the crossroads of Jewish, Roman, and Greek society.

Based on his understanding of Galilee as a marginalized socio-geographic location in the biblical narrative, Elizondo articulates the "Galilee principle": *What human beings reject, God chooses as his very own.*[48] When God became human in Jesus Christ, God chose to be embodied as a disparaged Galilean. He did not choose to be born into a rich and prestigious royal family from the capital, but to be raised and formed as a Galilean from the despised town of Nazareth. And when it came time to proclaim the good news of the arrival of the kingdom of God, Jesus began in Galilee and dedicated most of his public ministry to the marginalized community that raised him.

The Galilee principle gives great hope to Latinas/os in the United States, because we know what it is like to be despised by those from the Jerusalems of our day. When people look down on us for being from East or South Los Angeles, for being cultural mestizos, and for speaking with an accent, we say, "¿Y qué? So was our Lord." Though

---

[45]Elizondo, *Galilean Journey*, 91.

[46]Elizondo, *Galilean Journey*, 50-53.

[47]Ched Myers, *Binding the Strongman: A Political Reading of Mark's Story of Jesus* (Maryknoll, NY: Orbis Books, 2012), 49, 53; Elizondo, *Galilean Journey*, 52.

[48]Elizondo, *Galilean Journey*, 91.

the world may reject and stereotype us as uneducated, working class, undocumented immigrants, we give thanks to Jesus that he calls us his very own. We give praise, for when the good news of salvation was brought to the world, it first was preached to those like us. We also rejoice that when Jesus announced the kingdom of God, he did not select the rich and educated from influential families to lead his movement. Rather, he chose working-class fishermen, farmers, and mestizo Galileans to be his first disciples—the Latinas/os of his day. Though the gospel is for all, it first came to those like us.

Latina theologians have extended this notion of God's preferential option for the marginalized to women. Roman Catholic theologian Ada María Isasi-Díaz developed the term *mujerista* to describe a person who makes a preferential option for Latina women and their struggle for liberation.[49] Isasi-Díaz, moreover, dedicated her life to developing a "*mujerista* theology" from the perspective of Latina women.[50] *Mujeristas* celebrate and lay claim to the distinct image of God in women, and support a "process of enablement for Latina women which insists on the development of a strong sense of moral agency and clarifies the importance and value of who we are, what we think, and what we do."[51] *Mujerista* theology calls out the oppressive patriarchal and racist structures that oppress Latinas, and it promotes the process of liberation from internalized oppression.[52]

A central concept of *mujerista* theology is that of *lo cotidiano*, or the daily lived experience of Latinas.[53] *Mujerista* theology dignifies the lived experiences of Latinas in work, family, and society. Whereas majority white culture often shuns the Latina immigrant and working-class reality, *mujerista* theology privileges *lo cotidiano* as an important source of theology, wisdom, and knowledge. Though many may look

---

[49] Ada María Isasi-Díaz, *Mujerista Theology: A Theology for the Twenty-First Century* (Maryknoll, NY: Orbis Books, 2005), 60.
[50] Isasi-Díaz, *Mujerista Theology*, 1, 2.
[51] Isasi-Díaz, *Mujerista Theology*, 62.
[52] Isasi-Díaz, *Mujerista Theology*, 62, 63.
[53] Isasi-Díaz, *Mujerista Theology*, 66.

down on our mothers, *tías*, and *abuelas* for their daily commutes on
the bus; travails in agricultural, domestic, and factory work; exhausting
familial responsibilities; and faithful church participation, *mujerista*
theology declares that it is precisely in the daily rhythm and grind of
lo cotidiano that unique theological and epistemological understandings flow. As Latinas/os, we say, "Your mom may have a law
degree from Stanford, but my mom has a PhD in life from the school
of *Lo Cotidiano*." In the words of Isasi-Díaz, "Therefore, *lo cotidiano*,
the daily experience of Hispanic women, not only points to their
capacity to know but also highlights the features of their knowing.
Lo cotidiano is a way of referring to Latinas' efforts to understand and
express how and why their lives are the way they are, how and why
they function as they do."[54]

 Latina evangélicas Loida I. Martell-Otero, Zaida Maldonado-Pérez,
and Elizabeth Conde-Frazier have built on, and contextualized, these
notions of *lo cotidiano* within an evangelical and Pentecostal
framework. In their recent path-breaking work, *Latina Evangélicas:
A Theological Survey from the Margins*, Martell-Otero, Maldonado-
Perez, and Conde-Frazier contemplate a distinct Latina evangelical
identity and theology based on the perspective of Latina Protestants
in the United States.[55] In the words of Martell-Otero, "The contributors to this book are grateful for the rich theological lode provided
by such notable scholars as Ada María Isasi-Díaz, Jeannette Rodríguez,
Maria Pilar Aquino, and a host of others with whom we have
collaborated in the past; but we also recognize a need to provide a
voice that is distinctively Protestant, or evangélica."[56]

 Latina evangélica theology is distinguished by its triple emphasis
on the importance of the Holy Spirit, soteriology, and Scripture.[57]
According to *evangélicas*, the Holy Spirit empowers women and

---

[54]Isasi-Díaz, *Mujerista Theology*, 68.
[55]Martell-Otero, Maldonado-Perez, and Conde-Frazier, *Latina Evangélicas*.
[56]Martell-Otero, Maldonado-Perez, and Conde-Frazier, *Latina Evangélicas*, 18.
[57]Martell-Otero, Maldonado-Perez, and Conde-Frazier, *Latina Evangélicas*, 30, 31, 35.

legitimizes their calling in the face of patriarchal and racist social and ecclesial structures.[58] Holy Spirit personally guides and empowers Latinas in the daily struggle of *lo cotidiano*. Recognizing the feminine grammatical gender of *spirit* in the original Hebrew language of the Old Testament, Maldonado-Pérez declares poetically,

> I love the Holy Spirit. She is like the wild child of the Trinity, anywhere and everywhere moving, calling forth, and stirring things up. She is wonderfully illusive yet also fully present. She is untamable, full of possibilities and creative potential. She is the salsa beat in our daily foxtrot and the un-dos-tres-bachata in our electric slide. . . . She is life-giving breath, wind, and fire. She is the ruach elohim, the flaming divine pneuma that is always "going native" because she wants to be encountered by all. . . . Filled, inspired, and moved by the Holy Spirit, evangélicas engage life from the perspective of the One who is able to move over chaos, nothingness, and death, speaking life into death-bearing situations and being midwives to hope. The Holy Spirit emboldens us, even through the shadow of death, to fight the good fight on behalf of those gripped by despair.[59]

Latina evangélica theology may be distinguished from *mujerista* theology not only in terms of its focus on the active role of the Holy Spirit, but also insofar as it emphasizes the personal and communal salvation of Jesus in the context of *lo cotidiano*. In Christ, Latinas experience salvation as beloved daughters of God, despite their rejection by American society as *satas* (mongrels or mutts) and *sobraja* (worthless).[60] Salvation, moreover, is not just going to heaven when we die, as important as that may be, but also God's salvation experienced in the here and now, and the messiness of life—*lo cotidiano*. "The Spirit is the One who heals personally and communally (katartismos) in light of institutional injustice," and "Jesus is the divine sato jíbaro (mutt or country

---

[58]Martell-Otero, Maldonado-Perez, and Conde-Frazier, *Latina Evangélicas*, 30.
[59]Martell-Otero, Maldonado-Perez, and Conde-Frazier, *Latina Evangélicas*, 43, 44, 46, 47.
[60]Martell-Otero, Maldonado-Perez, and Conde-Frazier, *Latina Evangélicas*, 32, 87, 88.

peasant) who lives to bring life to communities crushed by death-dealing powers."[61]

In further contrast with Isasi-Díaz, who claimed that the Bible plays a minimal role among Catholic Latinas, *Latina evangélicas* assert that Scripture is central for Protestant Christian practice and belief. Within the Bible, *Latina evangélicas* find hope and wisdom for the daily realities and hardships of life, and in the Scriptures they encounter the living God who brings liberation.[62] In the words of Elizabeth Conde-Frazier, "While using the resources available to them as scholars, clergy, or laity, [Latina evangélicas] read for liberation. . . . The women read the text from the context of their lives so that they establish a dialogue between the sacred text and the text of their lives."[63]

CONCLUSION: *VOLVER*

Like Edwin of our opening vignette, thousands of Latina/o Christians are in search of a religious identity that is faithful to Jesus and appreciative of their God-given cultural heritage. In the current historic moment, in which lines have been blurred between white nationalism and evangelical Christianity, the problem has only become more acute. Latinas and Latinos are leaving the institutional church in droves because they do not see themselves, or the perspective of oppressed communities, reflected in the teaching, leadership, or congregational life of their local churches. Tragically, many are also rejecting Christianity based on the impression that it is, in its essence, a racist religion.

Unbeknownst to Edwin and most Latina/o Christians in the United States, this is not a new battle. In both Latin America and the United States, Latina/o followers of Jesus have been fighting the conflation of Christianity, racism, and colonialism for more than

---

[61]Martell-Otero, Maldonado-Perez, and Conde-Frazier, *Latina Evangélicas*, 32.
[62]Martell-Otero, Maldonado-Perez, and Conde-Frazier, *Latina Evangélicas*, 35, 36.
[63]Martell-Otero, Maldonado-Perez, and Conde-Frazier, *Latina Evangélicas*, 192, 193.

five hundred years. In the name of Jesus, the brown church has fought Spanish and Anglo colonialism, Indigenous slavery, educational segregation, abuse of farm workers, unjust exploitation and deportation of immigrants and refugees, gender inequality, and all manner of social sin. As the brown church has struggled, it has also read the Bible, prayed to God, and, *en conjunto*, articulated a communal theology of race and social justice across the centuries.

As a means of introduction to brown theology, this essay has offered a historical overview of three key theologians or theological movements of the brown church: Bartolomé de Las Casas; *misión integral*; and Latina/o theology. This list of thinkers and movements is by no means exhaustive and in fact just scratches the surface of the theological wealth of the brown church. Nonetheless, it may be enough to encourage the reader to dig deeper and engage on a lifetime of learning from the ecclesial capital of Latina/o Christians across the centuries. Even more, it is hoped that this introduction to Latina/o historical theology may encourage some to *volver*—to return to Jesús. Not the Jesus of the white colonial church, which drapes itself exclusively in *ropa anglo-sajon*, but the Cristo who has led the brown church in *misión integral* and radical personal and social transformation for more than five hundred years.

CHAPTER FIVE

JUSTICIA FAMILIAR

Misión Integral *in the United States*

ALEXIA SALVATIERRA

THE NINE-YEAR-OLD GIRL *from El Salvador is carefully making a beautiful picture in her donated coloring book in the childcare area at the volunteer legal clinic. Her mother is there to learn about applying for asylum in this country. She arrived in Los Angeles yesterday. As she colors, she cannot help telling me the story over and over again of her older brothers' beating at the hands of the police and the gang members. "There was blood everywhere," she said, "coming from his eyes and his ears and his mouth." She then adds in a whisper, "But we are going to be okay now; we are here."*

It is not likely that this child and her family will be okay. It is likely that they will be deported back to a country where an international mafia is controlling increasingly large territories. If they had legal representation, they would have a very good chance of being awarded asylum (the equivalent of refugee status, but without refugee benefits). However, the US does not provide free lawyers to asylum applicants, and the initial fee to a low-bono asylum lawyer is around $1,200. Where is God at this moment in this child's life? What is the call of the church? These are the kinds of questions that catalyze Hispanic-American theologies of liberation.

When many North American Christians hear the phrase *liberation theology*, they think first of Catholic theologians in Latin

America during the 1960s and 1970s, such as Fr. Gustavo Gutierrez, Fr. Leonardo Boff, and Fr. Jon Sobrino. In many evangelical circles in the US, these names are associated with a form of theology co-opted by Marxism. Liberation theology has been widely viewed as theology surrendered to subjectivity, captive to a leftist version of political science.

Reading liberation theology and its critics as a young evangelical campus leader in the 1970s, I was baffled by the intensity and negativity of the critique. When I read *The Power of the Poor in History*, I heard Gustavo Gutierrez accurately name the inescapable subjectivity of biblical interpretation and the need for all of the voices of the body of Christ to participate in the theological endeavor in order to overcome the distortions of their respective subjectivities:

> It must not be forgotten that the Bible has been read and communicated from the viewpoint of the dominating sectors and classes. . . . The communication of the message as reread from the point of view of the poor and oppressed, and from the point of view of militant cooperation with them in their struggles, will have the function of unmasking all intent and effort to make the gospel play the role of justifying a situation at odds with what the Bible calls "justice and right." . . . Only from the viewpoint of the poor are we going to understand the radical nature of Christ's liberation.[1]

The recognition of individual subjectivity is often linked to postmodern perspectives. However, its roots are far older. The great Protestant Reformer Martin Luther famously stood before the formal deliberative assembly of the Holy Roman Empire and said, "I cannot and I will not recant anything, for to go against conscience is neither right nor safe. Here I stand; I can do no other. God help me. Amen."[2] At least at this moment, his stance was both humble

---

[1]Gustavo Gutierrez, *The Power of the Poor in History* (Maryknoll, NY: Orbis Books, 1983), 18-19.

[2]William Jennings Bryan, ed., "Before the Diet of Worms: Martin Luther," *The World's Famous Orations*, vol. 7, *Continental Europe*, Bartleby.com Great Books Online, www.bartleby.com/268/7/8.html.

and passionate. He did not assume the capacity to see and state the truth perfectly. He rather assumed that God would help him in the midst of his human limitations to bear witness with courage and faith to the truth as he understood it. He knew that the division within the body of Christ took away a level of authority from his statements. However, he seemed to know that being ready to live and die in response to all that one has seen and heard of God is the best way to be open to God's correction in the areas where we are off-base. I have always been intrigued by Paul's comment at a certain point in his first letter to the Corinthians: "I have no command from the Lord, but I give my judgment as one who by the Lord's mercy is trustworthy" (1 Cor 7:25). The inclusion of this admission in Scripture speaks to the faith of the early church that God can communicate divine truth through human subjectivity. There is much evidence that human subjectivity affects our perspective, but the absolute God reaches people with saving truth in and through our human limitations. For this to occur, however, we must overcome the tendency to arrogance. Inaccurate claims to infallible objectivity by Christian leaders have negatively affected the capacity of many thoughtful people to hear the gospel.

There is substantial historical evidence for the claim of the liberation theologian that Scripture has often been interpreted from the perspective of the wealthy and privileged, who bring different questions to (and correspondingly receive different answers from) the Word of God. When I read *The Gospel in Solentiname*, a series of transcripts of Bible studies with Nicaraguan peasants suffering under the Somoza dictatorship and Spanish feudalism, I sense the joy of the Bible study participants at Mary's praise for the promise of economic justice to be fulfilled by her Son's birth. I understand that the immediate awareness of these promises is natural in the life of someone whose harvest was taken away by the feudal landlord, condemning her children to malnutrition.

He pulls down the mighty from their thrones and raises up the humble.
He fills the hungry with good things and he leaves the rich with nothing.

Someone asked: "That part about filling the hungry with good things?"

A young man answered "The hungry are going to eat."

And another: "The Revolution."

LAUREANO: "That is the Revolution. The rich man or the mighty is brought down and the poor person, the one who was down, is raised up."

ANDREA, Oscar's wife, asked: "That promise that the poor would have those good things, was it for then, for Mary's time, or would it happen in our time? I ask because I don't know."

One of the young people answered: "She spoke for the future, it seems to me, because we are just barely beginning to see the liberation she announces."

MARITA: "Mary sang here about equality. A society with no social classes. Everyone alike."[3]

At my campus Bible studies, these verses were by and large invisible in a study on Luke 1. Instead, we focused on how this passage supported Jesus' identity as Messiah. We would have been very uncomfortable to hear Marita's interpretation, even those of us who came from relatively poor backgrounds (personal histories that many of us were striving to overcome and forget). Yet, 1 Corinthians 1:26-29 supports the essential importance of listening to and learning from Marita's interpretation:

> Brothers and sisters, think of what you were when you were called. Not many of you were wise by human standards; not many were influential; not many were of noble birth. But God chose the foolish things of the world to shame the wise; God chose the weak things of the world to shame the strong. God chose the lowly things of this world

---

[3]Ernesto Cardenal, *The Gospel in Solentiname* (Maryknoll, NY: Orbis Books, 1975), 18-19.

and the despised things—and the things that are not—to nullify the
things that are, so that no one may boast before him.

As a young woman reading the Latin American liberation theologians, I did agree that liberation theology could be overly sweeping
in its assumptions and biased in its conclusions. However, I thought
that it was useful and worthy of a respectful hearing. I could not
understand the level of antagonism against it in the churches that I
attended. I had recently become a Christian in the Jesus Movement
and was spending my time in the Los Angeles coastal area, wandering
in and out of Calvary Chapel, the Vineyard, and other new evangelical churches; those were my new people. When I saw us react so
differently to liberation theology, I was shaken. What was wrong?

It was only years later that I grasped the big picture, when I
encountered the Latin American theological and missiological
movement known as *misión integral* (holistic mission). In 1974, René
Padilla and Samuel Escobar had led a minor mutiny at the First
International Congress on World Evangelization in Lausanne. As
evangelical pastors and professors from Latin America, they
challenged the conference leadership to recognize that First World
biblical interpretation (and the corresponding theology and visions
of mission) were not in fact objective and inerrant, but rather influenced by their sociocultural perspective and political-economic
position. They called for the contextualization of mission, listening to
the perspectives of Christians from the Global South, recognizing
their gifts and responding to the self-defined needs of their people.
They asserted that the extreme poverty and oppression experienced
by the majority of Latin Americans provided a legitimate perspective
from which to arrive at an accurate wineskin for the pure wine of the
gospel. Drs. Padilla and Escobar were ultimately successful in swaying
the language in the Lausanne Pact to include social action and social
justice as integral components of mission, as well as the recognition
of the importance of contextualization by Indigenous Christian

leaders. The story is poignant and beautiful. John Stott, the famous British Christian author whose popular text *Basic Christianity* had been critically important in the process of my personal acceptance of Christ as Lord and Savior, became their strongest ally. As a respected theological conservative and powerful evangelist, his testimony moved others to listen to the Latin America leaders. When I read the debates in the papers emerging from Lausanne, however, I began to understand the problem.

The rich young ruler went away sorrowful, having chosen not to follow Jesus because he had many possessions. We find it easier in many of our churches in the relatively privileged corners of the world to talk about sex than money. Facing the over one thousand Scripture passages calling us to social and economic justice feels very threatening to many of us. "The love of money is a root of all kinds of evil," says 1 Timothy 6:10. It is very difficult not to love all that money can make possible for us. Yet Jesus calls us: "What good will it be for someone to gain the whole world, yet forfeit their soul? Or what can anyone give in exchange for their soul?" (Mt 16:26). In order to be faithful disciples, we need to understand how to put money and all that it buys in its proper place, behind a list of more important values. Hispanic voices have gifts to bring to this predicament that Anglos need.

What we value is related to who we are—or perhaps more accurately, who we imagine ourselves to be. It is not only the historic suffering of Latin America that gives the *misión integral* movement its alternative perspective on social justice, but rather a core cultural perspective and related values across the multiplicity of Latino cultures.

In *The Power of Latino Leadership*, Juana Bordas describes Latino culture as communal and relational. "Latino power . . . has evolved from the community—it is the power of *We*—the power that people have to change their lives for the better."[4] The book *Latino Stats* by

---

[4]Juana Bordas, *The Power of Latino Leadership: Culture, Inclusion and Contribution* (San Francisco: Berret-Koehler Publishers, 2013), x.

Idelisse Malave and Esti Giordani provides a detailed overview of the Latino community in the US on multiple indices. These statistics confirm the concrete realities underlying Bordas's conclusions about culture. Hispanics rate significantly higher than other ethnic groups on family size, strength, and mutual care.[5] Latinos see the world through a family lens to a higher degree than the dominant Anglo culture. When we see the world through a family lens, we believe that the well-being of the individual is found in and through the well-being of the family. If I am an individual, dependent on my money for my safety and well-being, I must protect and defend it. I must hold on tight. When I see others as the source of my safety and well-being, then my money is secondary; it will be best used for the benefit of the whole and the strengthening of our mutual connections. I call this perspective *justicia familiar* (family justice.)

When we do not understand family justice, we easily become like the Guatemalan spider monkeys. The spider monkeys are very tasty and therefore popular with hunters, but they are also very fast and hard to catch. Savvy hunters take a figure-eight shaped gourd, place almonds in the bottom half of the gourd, and chain the gourd to a tree. The monkeys put their paws in the gourd and grab the almonds. However, the paw then becomes a fist too big to take out through the narrow part of the gourd. The monkeys stand there holding onto the almonds until the hunter captures them, unable to run away because they cannot bear to let go of the almonds, even to extract their paw from the gourd. This is a vivid image of how we can be affected by the love of money.

Family justice is a common theme in Scripture. A seminal instance is found in the story of the Jubilee in Leviticus 25. The people of God come into the promised land and they divide up the land by tribes. Each of the tribes draws its identity from its patriarch, who was one of the ten sons of Judah. Each of the tribes receives more or less

---

[5] Idelisse Malave and Esti Giordani, *Latino Stats: American Hispanics by the Numbers* (New York: The New Press, 2015), 57.

the same amount of land. We know this because the tribe of Levi does not receive land but rather receives compensation as a tithe—equal to the value of the land received by each of the other brothers' clans. More land is not awarded to the brother who is more intelligent or harder working—or more aggressive. A good parent loves all of his or her children equally and shares his or her goods with them correspondingly. This is family justice at the root. However, in the Jubilee story, it doesn't stay that way. Some brothers may be more intelligent or hard-working. Some may be more aggressive. Some may have more fertile land. One year, one of the clans cannot produce enough to feed themselves, and they have to borrow from their brother clan. However, it is very unlikely that they would be able to produce enough the following year to both feed their family and pay back their debt. The only way to pay their debt is in land. But then the next year, with less land, they are even less able to feed their family. Sooner or later, some brothers have turned over all of their land to other brothers. Then all they have left to sell is their labor. We end up, over a fifty-year period of time, with some brothers and sisters becoming indentured servants or slaves of their brothers and sisters. This situation, some siblings enslaved to other siblings, is not acceptable to the Heavenly Father who loves all his children equally. He calls for Jubilee—a reset. All of the slaves are to be freed, all of the debts canceled and all of the land redistributed back to its original owners. The people of Israel could not cease being a family; they could just be a functional family or a dysfunctional family, a healthy family or an unhealthy family, a just family or an unjust family. Some biblical commentators say that the Jubilee is not relevant for modern Christians because they believe that the Jubilee command was never observed; that baffles me, as I do not hear any other command of God invalidated just because people do not obey it.

In the New Testament, the Jubilee is reinvoked in Jesus' announcement of his mission in Luke 4:16-20. At the end of Jesus' reading of the Scripture for the day (Lk 4:21), he says, "Today this Scripture is fulfilled in your hearing." All eyes are fixed on him. I thought for many years that all eyes were fixed on him because he said that the Scripture was fulfilled. However, the passage actually says that all eyes were fixed on him before he makes that statement. All eyes are fixed on him because he has altered the reading. He has not just read Isaiah 61; he has inserted a line from Isaiah 58 that refers to the liberation of the oppressed, and he has ended the Scripture one line before its actual ending, giving emphasis to the line "the year of the Lord's favor." In the Old Testament prophetic tradition, the "year of the Lord's favor" had become a code phrase for referring to the eternal Jubilee that would come with the advent of the Messiah. The promise of the year of the Lord's favor that Jesus said was fulfilled in his advent was a promise of ongoing family justice without the need of a Jubilee year.

The earliest church understood that family justice was a consequence of the coming of the Messiah.

> All the believers were together and had everything in common. They sold property and possessions to give to anyone who had need. (Acts 2:44-45)

> All the believers were one in heart and mind. No one claimed that any of their possessions was their own, but they shared everything they had. With great power the apostles continued to testify to the resurrection of the Lord Jesus. And God's grace was so powerfully at work in them all that there were no needy persons among them. For from time to time those who owned land or houses sold them, brought the money from the sales and put it at the apostles' feet, and it was distributed to anyone who had need. (Acts 4:32-35)

They did not hold all material things in common because they were socialists or communists; those concepts and systems had not yet been invented. They shared all their goods because they were a family, living under the reign of God.

The other image for our common connection in the New Testament is the body of Christ. In 1 Corinthians 12:12-26, Paul changes the

Roman understanding of the body politic. In the body politic, a foot was worth less than a hand and a hand less than an eye. On the contrary, Paul says, the eye needs the hand and the hand the foot. Then Paul goes on to say, "God has put the body together, giving greater honor to the parts that lacked it, so that there should be no division in the body" (1 Cor 12:24-25). In order for all gifts of every part of the body to be fully honored and received, there must be an intentional counterbalancing in which the parts that have been less recognized are valued more. The early church also understood this principle. In Acts 6, the widows of the Hellenists complain that they are receiving less in the daily distribution than the widows of the Hebrews. The apostles (all Hebrew) appointed a committee consisting of all Hellenists to oversee the daily distribution (see the last names of the list of deacons). They redistributed decision-making power to give more power to those who had lacked it. In an unjust world, family justice requires an intentional counterbalancing to ensure *shalom*.

The Latino community has a cultural predilection to grasp the biblical concept of family justice. The North American Anglo community is much less likely to see and understand this truth. In the process of contextualization, the intentional switching of cultural wineskins to ensure that the full wine of the gospel is received, this beautiful and central element of the gospel can become accessible to the broader church through Latino theologians.

Over the past forty years, a wealth of *misión integral* theologians have sprung up in the United States. The Hispanic community in the United States has continued to experience discrimination and injustice, adding the burden of immigration to the struggle of working poverty. In the midst of the biculturalism that comes with migration, core Hispanic values have been surprisingly resilient among US Hispanics, and the combination of new experiences and historic values has been sparking new forms of holistic theology. The process began with the works of the Methodist pastor and scholar Justo González and Roman Catholic theologian Virgilio Elizondo, who made the case for *mestizaje* theology and other forms of contextualized theology done by Hispanic Americans. Multiple books and articles by hundreds of pastors and scholars have followed, including a wide variety of Hispanic evangelicals and Pentecostals, such as Ray Rivera of the Assemblies of God and the Latino Pastoral Action Center in New York City, and Mennonite Juan Martínez and Baptist scholar Oscar García-Johnson of Fuller Theological Seminary. In recent decades, a number of *evangélica* Latina theologians and educators have joined the chorus, such as Loida I. Martell-Otero, Zaida Maldonado Perez, and Elizabeth Conde-Frazier. These writers and teachers proclaim a holistic theology for whole gospel discipleship. They go beyond a simple focus on saving souls to an understanding of salvation and redemption that is transformative of the whole person in the whole family in the whole community in the whole world. They have popularized theology *en conjunto*—weaving the voices of theologians together to enrich and deepen their individual perspectives.

These Hispanic-American voices are serving to liberate Hispanic immigrant pastors from the shackles of loyalty to a set of wineskins bestowed by the North American missionaries of the nineteenth and early twentieth centuries, which have kept many leaders and congregations from holistic mission perspectives and practices. Two prominent examples of Hispanic Christian leaders are Lee de Leon, executive pastor of the Community Development Corporation of the ten thousand-member Assemblies of God Templo Calvario in Santa Ana, and Luis Cortez, CEO of Esperanza USA, a Philadelphia-based Baptist ministry that has coordinated the engagement of a national network of fifteen thousand Hispanic evangelical churches in ministries of community development and advocacy. They are just two of hundreds of Latino pastors, congregations, and ministries across the country who are organizing and mobilizing their churches for social action and social justice.

I teach urban transformation from a faith-rooted orientation at multiple evangelical and mainline seminaries and Christian colleges as adjunct faculty. This includes several contexts in which I teach in Spanish for immigrant Hispanic pastors and other Christian leaders. I see the potential to unleash the spiritual power of Hispanic culture for holistic mission, not only for immigrants themselves but for our nation.

The communal emphasis in Hispanic culture affects even more than just the horizontal dimension of our faith and lives. Hispanic perspectives on God also give us a deeper understanding of the Trinity. As Luis Pedraja states, "By understanding the Trinity in terms of communal relationships, those living at the margins of society cannot only find parallels with their experience but can discover a sense of belonging as part of God's community."[6] It is not only the marginalized in today's world who hunger for a sense of belonging. The economic insecurity that is an ongoing reality for almost everyone in our society, the fluidity and fragility of our positions, means that most of us need to feel that we are anchored in community at the roots of our souls. Elizabeth Conde-Frazier has written repeatedly on the understanding of the Holy Spirit in Hispanic Pentecostalism as more than the impersonal force or energy that often characterizes the dominant North American perspective on the Spirit. When the Trinity is viewed with a relational lens, the warm person of the Spirit helps us in our suffering. "Once the power of the Holy Spirit is manifested in the persons who had been suffering, their weakness is transformed into power for liberation. This power takes the form of the hope of overcoming the structures of evil in our society. It is this hope that empowers persons' gifts and persevering strength for carrying out the work of structural transformation."[7]

---

[6]Miguel A. De La Torre, ed., *Handbook of U.S. Theologies of Liberation* (St. Louis: Chalice Press, 2004), 53.

[7]De La Torre, *Handbook of U.S. Theologies of Liberation*, 43

When my daughter was in high school, she had a friend who had grown up with no religious tradition. Her friend said to me, "I am interested in finding out more about Jesus—but only if he is a Jesus who transforms the world." The understanding and practice of *misión integral*, particularly in the form of family justice, has great power to move us beyond our political divides to transform our country into a place of greater well-being for us all, including the nine-year-old girl from El Salvador who desperately needs the church to be a family that can and will protect her.

PART THREE

RETHINKING SIN

CHAPTER SIX

A BORN–AGAIN THEOLOGY OF LIBERATION

ANDREA SMITH

INCREASINGLY MORE EVANGELICALS HAVE attempted to develop theological foundations for liberating Christianity and society at large from racism and white supremacy. These attempts have largely emerged from the racial reconciliation movement within evangelicalism that began in the early 1990s. While this work has been very important, both more conservative and more liberal evangelical theological approaches to racism have generally failed to take into account the manner in which racial logics fundamentally constitute us on an individual and societal level. In this essay, I argue that an evangelical engagement with a critical ethnic studies analysis of racialization provides a helpful starting point for developing a born-again theology of liberation from white supremacy.

HISTORICAL CONTEXT

The racial reconciliation movement within Christian evangelicalism, while having prior antecedents, developed fully in the 1990s in reaction to the racial segregation within evangelical churches, as well as the historical lack of evangelical engagement against racial injustice.

Since then, there have been ebbs and flows in the racial reconciliation movement, but in the wake of the Black Lives Matter movement, evangelical engagement with racism has significantly increased.

However, this movement has also been critiqued, particularly among evangelicals of color, for its avoidance of institutional and structural forms of racism in favor of focusing on individual relationships alone. For instance, Erna Kim Hackett of InterVarsity has explained that she "stopped talking about race reconciliation and started talking about white supremacy" because white evangelicals hold a "Disney princess" theology in which "they see themselves as the princess in every story. They are Esther, never Xerxes or Haman. They are Peter, but never Judas. They are the woman anointing Jesus, never the Pharisees. They are the Jews escaping slavery, never Egypt."[1]

These critiques of racial reconciliation are important. However, the presumed response among more liberal evangelicals has now been to focus on legal and political reform as the antidote to racism. In doing so, liberals and conservatives both tend to presume that racism is an aberration that can be corrected by either better relationships or better laws. However, as many critical ethnic studies scholars have demonstrated, the world, and the individuals within it, are fundamentally constituted by the logics of white supremacy. An end to white supremacy would be an end to the world as we know it and an end to the selves we know ourselves to be. Thus, I propose that the concept of being born again provides a helpful, biblically based theological foundation for the task for liberating the world from white supremacy. While being born again is often equated with individualized approaches to salvation, read within the biblical context and in conversation with critical ethnic scholars, it is actually a radical call to end the world as we know it.

---

[1]Erna Hackett, "Why I Stopped Talking About Racial Reconciliation and Started Talking About White Supremacy," *Feisty Thought* (blog), August 23, 2017, http://feistythoughts.com/2017/08/23 /why-i-stopped-talking-about-racial-reconciliation-and-started-talking-about-white -supremacy/.

ENGAGING CRITICAL ETHNIC STUDIES

Theoretical formulations by white European thinkers are granted general applicability while those uttered from the purview of minority discourse that speak to the same questions are almost exclusively relegated to the jurisdiction of ethnographic locality.[2]

ALEXANDER G. WEHELIYE

I contend that Christian theology and scholarship will remain "provincial" as long as some major challenges continue unaddressed [such as] the perception of indigenous Christian scholars as purveyors of exotic raw intellectual material. . . . Indigenous theologians are . . . relegated to the museums of theological curiosity just like their cultures. We are then left with this: the West claiming to produce universal theology and the rest writing to articulate fundamental theology that will make [them] equal partners in the theological circles that determine what is theologically normative.[3]

TITE TIÉNOU

The first ethnic studies departments were created at San Francisco State University and UC Berkeley in 1969 when a coalition of black, Asian American, Native American, and Latino student groups coalesced under the Third World Liberation Front and led the longest student strikes in US history at both institutions. On the Berkeley campus, the California National Guard was called into quash the strike as the growing police violence against strikers escalated the protest. Eventually after academic faculty pressure to do so, the UC administration approved an interim Ethnic Studies Department on March 7, 1969. This department was soon followed by the

---

[2]Alexander G. Weheliye, *Habeas Viscus: Racializing Assemblages, Biopolitics, and Black Feminist Theories of the Human* (Durham, NC: Duke University Press, 2014), 6.
[3]Tite Tiénou, "Indigenous Theologizing from the Margins to the Center," *NAIITS Journal* 3 (2005): 116-17.

establishment of an Ethnic Studies Department at San Francisco State University on March 20, 1969. Three years later, the National Association of Ethnic Studies was founded. The history of ethnic studies emerged out of a context of struggle concerned not just with representation in the academy but also about how the university could be employed to further the aims of antiracist and anticolonial struggle. Many strikers demanded that universities admit all people of color seeking admission, and that ethnic studies departments should be under community control.[4]

However, as ethnic studies became increasingly more profession-alized in the university and more disconnected from the social justice struggles from which it emerged, it often began to focus narrowly along identity lines (Asian American studies, Native studies, etc.). Identity-based ethnic studies scholarship has done critical work that provides the foundation for looking at intersections of racism, colonialism, immigration, and slavery with the US context. However, ethnic studies often becomes mired in an identity politics that advances what Elizabeth Povinelli describes as "social difference without social significance."[5] That is to say, the work becomes about including the voices of people of color, but only as long as those voices do not fundamentally challenge any social or institutional structures, or epistemological paradigms. In this context, critical ethnic studies emerged to build intellectual and political projects that do not dismiss identity, but instead structures its work around *logics* of white supremacy, colonialism, capitalism, patriarchy, and so on in order to expand its scope. Such a shift in focus is significant in providing a space for all scholars to be part of an engagement with critical ethnic studies because these logics structure all of society, not just those who are racialized.

---

[4]Franklin Pilik, ed., *Columbia Documentary History of the Asian American Experience* (New York: Columbia University, 2002), 361-64.

[5]Elizabeth Povinelli, *The Cunning of Recognition: Indigenous Alterities and the Making of Australian Multiculturalism* (Durham, NC: Duke University Press, 2002).

The quote from Alexander Weheliye speaks to the need to develop a critical ethnic studies approach to intellectual inquiry in which ethnic studies goes beyond the positioning of communities of color as ethnographic objects of study. Rather, the theoretical analysis emerging out of critical ethnic studies is one that fundamentally challenges the epistemological frameworks of Western scholarship itself. As Denise da Silva points out in her defining text on racialization, the entire Western epistemological system is governed through logics of raciality that fundamentally shape what we even consider to be human.[6]

The quote from Tite Tiénou (professor at Trinity Evangelical Divinity School) suggests a critical ethnic studies claim about Christian evangelicalism—that evangelicalism is only willing to tolerate evangelicals of color to the extent that they can be safely incorporated within white evangelicalism—or as Povinelli might say, to the extent they add theological difference without theological consequence. While evangelical critique may not use the same terminology as those speaking in more secular critical ethnic studies venues, they are in fact critiquing settler colonialism, white supremacy, and capitalism, as well as engaging in movements to challenge them and reconstruct alternative versions of Christian evangelicalism. In essence, they are developing evangelical theologies of liberation. Thus, critical ethnic studies in conversation with Christian evangelicalism can provide a helpful place to articulate what these theologies of liberation might be. Of course, some evangelicals might reject engagement with such scholarship because it is "non-Christian," even though many such scholars may actually be Christian. But Paul Metzger's essay in this volume speaks to the need to develop a centered-set theological approach in evangelicalism that is not afraid to engage important ideas, no matter who articulates them.

---

[6]Denise Ferreira da Silva, *Toward a Global Idea of Race* (Minneapolis: University of Minnesota Press, 2007).

FROM RACISM TO RACIALIZATION

Critical ethnic studies scholars such as Sylvia Wynter, Denise Da Silva, Alexander Weheliye, and other critical race theorists have argued that raciality is not simply a result of unfortunate stereotypes from peoples of different cultural backgrounds, but the fundamental logic by which certain peoples are categorized outside the category of the human.[7] Or to quote Ruth Wilson Gilmore, "Racism, specifically, is the state-sanctioned or extralegal production and exploitation of group-differentiated vulnerability to premature death."[8] These understandings move us away from thinking about race as a noun in terms of set people groups such as African Americans, Latinos, Native peoples, and Asian Americans, to racialization as a verb that can impact different peoples across time and space. Racialization is the process by which the marker between human and nonhuman is biologized, even as who gets racialized and the markers of racialization may change over time and space.

Furthermore, by understanding racialization as a logic that structures the world, it becomes clear that legal and political institutions are not outside these logics either. First, from the perspectives of Indigenous peoples, the US legal and political system could not exist without the genocide of those peoples. The notion that Native peoples are savages and hence outside the category of the human is codified in federal jurisprudence in *Johnson v. McIntosh,* and this has never been overturned. The Supreme Court held that while Indigenous people had a right to occupancy, they could not hold title to land on the basis of the doctrine of discovery. The European nation that "discovered" land had the right to legal title. Native peoples were disqualified from being discoverers because they did not properly work.

---

[7]Sylvia Wynter, "Columbus, the Ocean Blue, and Fables That Stir the Mind: To Reinvent the Study of Letters," in *Poetics of the Americas,* ed. Bainard Cowan and Jefferson Humphries (Baton Rouge: Louisiana State University Press, 1997); Alexander G. Weheliye, *Habeas Viscus* (Durham, NC: Duke University Press, 2014); Denise Ferreira da Silva, *Toward a Global Idea of Race* (Minneapolis: University of Minnesota Press, 2007).

[8]Ruth Wilson Gilmore, *Golden Gulag* (Berkeley: University of California Press, 2007), 28.

"The tribes of Indians inhabiting this country were fierce savages, whose occupation was war, and whose subsistence was drawn chiefly from the forest. To leave them in possession of their country, was to leave the country a wilderness."[9] As they did not work, native peoples had the ontological status of things to be discovered—the status of nature, rather than the status of human who could discover. United States law is thus fundamentally based on the dehumanization of native peoples.

Critical race legal scholar Dean Spade notes that the assumption that the legal system can actually address white supremacy serves to obscure the white supremacist foundation of the system:

> The critical analysis built by many resistant social movements illuminates the limitations of a theory of law reform that aims to punish the "few bad apples" supposedly responsible for racism, sexism, ableism, xenophobia, or transphobia. It also helps us understand why, since US law has been structured from its inception to create a racialized-gendered distribution of life chances that perpetuates violence, genocide, land theft, and exploitation, we will not resolve those issues solely by appealing to law. We must also be cautious not to believe what the law says about itself since time and again the law has changed, been declared newly neutral or fair or protective, and then once more failed to transform the conditions of disparity and violence that people were resisting. . . . Law reform tactics can have a role in mobilization-focused strategies, but law reform must never constitute the sole demand. . . . If we seek transformation that is more than symbolic and that reaches those facing the most [violence], we must move beyond the politics of recognition and inclusion.[10]

Ed Dobson, who was formerly with the Moral Majority but later became disenchanted with Christian political organizing, made similar critiques of the overemphasis on legal reform, but from the position of the Christian right: "Legislation must reflect the consensus

---

[9]*Johnson v. McIntosh*, 21 U.S. 543, 590.
[10]Dean Spade, *Normal Life* (New York: South End Press, 2010), 27-28.

of the people governed, or they will just disregard the law. . . . While we work toward legislation, we must also do the more difficult task for changing people's minds and beliefs on the matter. The most effective laws *follow* moral consensus."[11] His argument is similar to that of critical ethnic studies scholars who note that the law itself is a reflection of prevailing ideologies that structure society. Thus, a change in law without a transformation of the ideologies that construct the law cannot fundamentally change society. Essentially, these analyses recognize that legal reform is not the solution to ending white supremacy, especially since the legal system itself is created through the logics of white supremacy. A critical ethnic studies lens then can be used to critically engage more conservative and liberal approaches to racial reconciliation.

LOVE, NOT LAWS

"I had to stop doing those race reconciliation events. Every time white Christians wanted to repent for their racism against Native Americans, they insisted on washing my feet—and I was having to spend too much money on pedicures."[12]

This joke by the late prominent native evangelical leader Richard Twiss speaks to the growing frustration with race reconciliation among many evangelical people of color. Race reconciliation tends to focus on symbolic performances of reconciliation without any political commitment to dismantling white supremacy. Particularly during the inception of race reconciliation, the rhetoric generally equated racism and racial prejudice, leaving out any analysis of social power.[13] As a result, racism was described primarily as a personal or

---

[11]Ed Dobson and Cal Thomas, *Blinded by Might* (Grand Rapids: Zondervan, 1999), 70.
[12]Richard Twiss, personal communication with author, January 4, 2013.
[13]Orlando Crespo, "Our Transnational Anthem," *Christianity Today*, August 2006, 32-35; Randy Frame, "Race and the Church: A Progress Report," *Christianity Today*, March 4, 1988, 16-17; Dave Geisler, "Healing America's Wounds," *Charisma*, October 1994, 33-37; Chloe George, "The Holy Spirit Melts Divisions," *Charisma*, January 2001, 58-60, 64; J. Lee Grady, "Dancing on Division," *Charisma*, November 2007, 8; Chris Hull, "Diversity Quest," *Journal of Christian Camping* 29 (January–February 1997): 10-16; Craig Keener, "Some New Testament Invitations to Ethnic

spiritual problem,[14] possibly resulting from faulty biblical analysis.[15] Its remedy lay in the changing of individual attitudes and behaviors, rather than in a fundamental reweaving of the social fabric. "Racial diversity brightens and enriches God's mural of humanity,"[16] asserted one conservative evangelical; "love—not laws,"[17] intoned another.[18]

The obvious problem with this approach can be seen in evangelical responses to abortion. Evangelical leaders don't generally say, "We don't have a problem with abortion; we have a problem with sin. Passing laws against abortion won't work. We must change the hearts of men and women in this society." For these issues, the evangelical organizations have developed an extensive array of citizen training manuals and videos offering detailed how-to information on influencing the legislative process at the local, state, and federal levels. Apparently, evangelical organizations do not trust the persuasive power of the Bible to win over the hearts and minds of America on the issues they really consider important.[19]

Reconciliation," *Evangelical Quarterly* 75 (July 2003): 195-213; Greg Lewis, *The Power of a Promise Kept* (Dallas: Word Books, 1995); Chris Lutes, "Everybody Always Stares: The Personal Side of Prejudice," *Campus Life*, March 1988, 62-66; Frederica Mathewes-Green, "Sweet Mystery of Daisy," *World*, November 4, 1995, 24; John Moore, "In the Name of Fear and Prejudice," *Moody Monthly*, January 1987, 16-18; Bob Paulson, "Encouraging Racial Harmony," *Decision*, February 2002, 31; Leanne Wiens, "Just Who Am I?" *Campus Life*, March 1988, 69-70. While Lewis addresses more interpersonal forms of racial prejudice, early Promise Keeper literature is mixed in this regard; much of it pointedly looks at structural forms of racism.

[14]Randy Frame, "Dues-Paying Time for Black Christians," *Christianity Today*, August 20, 1990, 51; Jack Gaines, "Let Forgiveness Come First," *Charisma*, November 2000, 70; Valerie Lowe, "A Cancer in the Land," *Charisma*, January 2001, 102; Nancy Stetson, "She Has a Dream, Too," *Christianity Today*, June 16, 1997, 34-36. Jack Gaines of Calvary Evangelical Baptist Church says, "Unless one deals with underlying sin, one cannot eradicate racism. . . . The only solution is found in a spiritual response to God's work of reconciliation through Christ. . . . The root issue of slavery is not skin color but sin." Since no amount of money can make up for past injustices, we must "set people free from hate and prejudice" (J. Gaines, "Let Forgiveness Come First," 70).

[15]"Loving People Who Are Different," *Alliance Witness*, February 12, 1986; William Baker, "Equal Before God," *Moody Monthly*, January 1987; Karen Mains, "Finally Listening," *Moody Monthly*, May 1994, 28.

[16]Dolphus Weary, "The Gift of Race," *Christianity Today*, April 26, 1993, 90.

[17]Ken Sidey, "Faces of Reconciliation," *World Vision* 36 (August-September 1993): 2-5. See also William Dwight McKissic, "Embracing the Spirit's Power," *Charisma*, February 2008, 20.

[18]Adrienne Gaines, "U.S. House Member Renews Call for Apology for Slavery," *Charisma*, September 2000, 40-41.

[19]Andrea Smith, "The Devil is in the Details," *Colorlines*, March 15, 2002, https://www.colorlines.com/articles/devils-details.

THE SIN OF WHITE SUPREMACY

While liberal evangelical critiques that center on the importance of addressing white supremacy on a structural level are critically important, I believe there may be an important element to what is often seen as a more conservative idea of race as a sin. That is, as critical ethnic studies scholars have noted, white supremacy fundamentally shapes subjectivity. As Frederick Moten articulates, "White supremacy is not simply the belief in white superiority; it structures belief itself."[20] The concept of sin, then, echoes this notion that one cannot simply do good because one's subjectivity is fundamentally shaped by sin. Of course, the typical evangelical articulations of sin differ from these critical black studies analyses of racialization because they often presume that one can escape one's subjectivity through a faith decision. However, a fuller exploration of what it means to be born again might lead us to an approach that would synergize an ideological/epistemological approach with a structural analysis.

Frank Wilderson argues that "the human" gains its coherence through antiblackness. That is, the human subject knows that it is human because it defines itself over and against that which is fundamentally nonhuman, that is, black. Hence, since what is human is definitionally antiblack, liberation can only occur through the dismantling of what we consider to be human.[21] Liberation thus is a refusal to be intelligible within the antiblack world order in aspiration of a different form of humanity for which we have no vocabulary. This thinking is reflected in the biblical concept of being born again: "Very truly I tell you, no one can see the kingdom of God unless they are born again" (Jn 3:3). Jesus does not say, If you have the correct doctrinal beliefs, you will see the kingdom. Rather, your humanity as you know it must come to an end and you must become a new being all together. If racialization is the logic that defines the human over and against those who are not human, then ending racism is not simply

---

[20]Frederick Moten, lecture, UC Riverside, April 8, 2014.
[21]Frank Wilderson, *Red, White and Black* (Durham, NC: Duke University Press, 2010), 23.

about changing personal beliefs or even making structural change, but creating a new sense of humanity all together. "Therefore, if anyone is in Christ, the new creation has come: The old has gone, the new is here!" (2 Cor 5:17). Humanity is so structured by whiteness that a world without oppression (which would be the kingdom of God) would be unintelligible to us. Thus, we must become new people to see the kingdom.

Many evangelicals of color (as well as many white evangelicals) have become very exasperated with what seems to be the entrenched racism of the more than 80 percent of white evangelicals who voted for Donald Trump. Given Trump's complete lack of adherence to any of the moral or social values white evangelicals claim to support, the white evangelical support of Trump seems to indicate that white evangelicals have a stronger commitment to whiteness than they do a commitment to the Bible. Liberals in particular paint these Trump supporters as irrational. Why are they voting for someone who does not support biblical principles? Why don't they see how commonsensical it is to support all peoples regardless of race? However, if we understand the nature of white supremacy in its entirety, this support of Trump and his white supremacist agenda seems to make more sense. First, many white people actually like white supremacy more than they want things like health care or better job opportunities. As critical legal scholar Cheryl Harris notes, white people have a property interest in whiteness that is of value in and of itself.[22] This is why colonial and slave economies continued after they were no longer economically profitable. And seemingly irrational conservatives support white supremacy because they correctly understand more than liberals do that an end to racism signifies an end to the world as they know and an end to their selves as they know them. Indeed, since all peoples are structured through logics of white supremacy, all of us would fundamentally change as well if racism came to an end.

---

[22]Cheryl Harris, "Whiteness as Property," in *Critical Race Theory*, ed. Kimberle Crenshaw et al. (New York: New Press, 1995).

Ending racism is not a policy change; it would end the ontological and epistemological framework of the world.

This is where evangelicals with a born-again theology of liberation should be able to step in. Instead of dismissing white people's entrenched commitment to whiteness (and all peoples' entrenched commitment to the world as it is), we should fully understand what a scary, in fact even apocalyptic, journey it is to discard everything one knows about the world and oneself and to embrace the complete unknown. But Jesus' command to be born again provides a foundation for beginning this very hard journey

BEING BORN AGAIN—THE END OF RACIALIZATION

Jesus' call for us to become new people actually coincides with the work of postcolonial scholars such as Frantz Fanon who argue that decolonization is not simply about a struggle for land and resources, but the struggle to become new peoples who do not require relationships of colonization to define ourselves.[23] This new creation is a new sense of humanity for which we currently do not have words. In fact, we can understand Jesus' life, death, and resurrection as a model for what it really means to be born again, particularly in conversation with theories of antiblackness. Lewis Gordon contends that racialization operates through two distinct but related logics. One, whiteness becomes that to which all should aspire. But two, blackness is that which all people should escape. By whiteness and blackness, Gordon does not mean people of European descent or people of African descent. He contends that there would be whiteness without Europe and blackness without Africa.[24] Essentially who gets marked as white and black can change over time. As an example, Maile Arvin notes that during conquest of the Pacific Islands, colonizers began to separate Polynesians, who they deemed as being close to whiteness, from Melanesians, who were deemed

---

[23]Frantz Fanon, *Wretched of the Earth* (New York: Grove Press, 1963).
[24]Lewis Gordon, *Bad Faith and Antiblack Racism* (Amherst, MA: Humanity Books, 1995).

close to blackness.[25] All people can be complicit in antiblackness when their struggles for liberation begin to divide who in their group is respectable and deserving of rights versus those who are disposable. An example of this tendency can be found in Martha Escobar's critical ethnic studies critique of the immigrant rights movement. She argues that the focus on immigrants as not being illegal or criminal because they are hard working essentially is a move to distance the immigrant rights movement from blackness, which gets equated with criminality and dependency. As a result, good immigrants, such as Dreamers, deserve our attention, but "bad" immigrants who have criminal convictions become disposable and undeserving of rights.[26] Thus, as Frank Wilderson contends, true liberation happens when we aspire to blackness rather than whiteness. By that he does not mean that everyone should adopt black cultural practices. Rather, liberation happens when we are willing to be seen as the worst, as that which is nonhuman. In doing so, it becomes possible to create a new human that is not constituted through whiteness. As he states, "From the coherence of civil society, the Black subject beckons with the incoherence of civil war, a war that reclaims Blackness not as a positive value, but as a politically enabling site."[27] Further, "in allowing the notion of freedom to attain the ethical purity of its ontological status, one would have to lose one's Human coordinates and become Black. Which is to say one would have to die."[28] Essentially, we can see Jesus' praxis as being grounded in blackness rather than whiteness. An all-powerful God chose to be manifested as not only a human constrained by the world, but as a colonized person living under occupation. Jesus

---

[25]Maile Arvin, "Pacifically Possessed: Scientific Production and Native Hawaiian Critique of the 'Almost White' Polynesian Race" (PhD diss., UC San Diego, 2013).

[26]Martha Escobar, *Captivity Beyond Prisons: Criminalization Experiences of Latina (Im)Migrants* (Austin: University of Texas Press, 2016).

[27]Frank B. Wilderson III, "The Prison Slave as Hegemony's (Silent) Scandal," in *Warfare in the American Homeland*, ed. Joy James (Durham, NC: Duke University Press, 2007), 33.

[28]Wilderson, "Prison Slave," 23.

refused all politics of respectability and instead associated with those who were socially marginalized and despised. To evoke the work of critical black studies scholar Jared Sexton, Jesus engaged a politics without a demand,[29] which is to say a vision that cannot be manifested through the world as it is now—through legal reform, crosscultural friendships, or a change in who is in office. As a result, his vision became illegible to even his followers and he was abandoned by most who wished to be distanced from this commitment to blackness. His resurrection stands for the promise that there can be justice, but it will not be on the terms set by a white supremacist world order. It is a world for which we cannot imagine but of which we have glimpses through Jesus' resurrection.

Building on this analysis, it could be possible to synergize the concept of being born again with the mandate to end structural forms of oppression if we think of the early church practices as a form of structural change designed to enable a change in subjectivity. That is, these early church practices implicitly recognized that one cannot simply will oneself into a sin-free existence. Rather, we must live under different structures that enable us to be different people. Thus, the early church practices of baptism were designed to initiate the less hierarchical and more egalitarian worship and living praxes necessary to enable Christians to in fact be born again.[30] And furthermore, these practices had to be ongoing because being born again is an ongoing commitment to total transformation.

As I have discussed elsewhere, many liberation movements today are deeply informed by Indigenous peoples' movements in the Americans in combination with Christian liberation theologies, and they utilize principles similar to those of the early church in creating different community structures that in turn enable participants to

---

[29]Jared Sexton, "The Vel of Slavery: Tracking the Figure of the Unsovereign," *Critical Sociology* 42 (2016).

[30]Elizabeth Schussler Fiorenza, *In Memory of Her* (New York: Crossroad, 1985).

become different people.[31] The principle undergirding these models is to challenge economic and state power by actually creating the world we want to live in now. These groups develop alternative governance systems based on principles of horizontality, mutuality, and interrelatedness rather than hierarchy, domination, and control. In beginning to create this new world, subjects are transformed. These "autonomous zones" can be differentiated from the projects of many groups in the United States that create separatist communities based on egalitarian ideals, in that people in these making-power movements do not just create autonomous zones, but they *proliferate* them.[32] A lesson learned from these organizing models is that less hierarchy does not equal fewer structures. In fact, the opposite is the case. When there are no clear structures, then informal hierarchies develop because people who have grown up under structures of white supremacy and capitalism will tend to act in conformity with those structures. As Jo Freeman famously argued in the 1970s, we end up with the tyranny of structurelessness.[33] Thus, these organizations have discovered the need to develop new structures of accountability that force them to act in ways that are not natural to them. And yet they have found that the longer they live in structures that are committed to nonhierarchy, the more they start acting differently. To end our sinful orientation to oppression, it is not sufficient to profess belief or to think ourselves into a new liberated subject position, but to live this change through the creation of collective structures that dismantle the systems of sinful oppression. To quote former coordinator of the National Assembly of Religious Women Judy Vaughn, "You don't think your way into a different way of acting; you act your way into a different way of thinking."[34]

---

[31]Andrea Smith, *Conquest: Sexual Violence and American Indian Genocide* (Cambridge, MA: South End Press, 2005).

[32]Andrea Smith, "First Nation, Empire and Gender," in Sheila Briggs and Mary McClintock Fulkerson, eds., *Oxford Handbook of Feminist Theology* (Oxford: Oxford University Press, 2011).

[33]Jo Freeman, "The Tyranny of Structurelessness," *Berkeley Journal of Sociology* 17 (1972–1973): 151-64.

[34]Judy Vaughn, personal communication, October 15, 1992.

SINNERS AND SAFE SPACES

There is no reason why churches cannot be similarly situated—cannot begin mirroring the kingdom of God through practices that make us new creatures. When Jesus stated that he came for the sinners, not the saints, Jesus is articulating the church not as a space to affirm us as we are, but as one that enables us to become something different from what we are. Certainly, many have critiqued evangelicalism for promoting prosperous churches that instantiate the status quo and affirm people within that status quo. And rightly so, because Jesus was actually a colonized person, talking to colonized peoples and thus was also providing a roadmap for decolonization. But, Jesus' command to have a church for sinners is actually also a critique of liberation movements. That is, liberation theologies have often positioned God as really being on the side of the oppressed rather than the oppressor. But these words suggest that God stands against oppression, no matter who commits it. There is no pure community before God—we are churches of sinners, and hence we need to develop church communities that engage in continual and humble self-critique and interrogation to ascertain when, even with good intentions, we may be hurting others. We do not have to be good to be loved by Christ—Christ loves us in the midst of sin. And God works through us as sinners to help us become different people.

A challenge, however, in evangelical churches creating such spaces is the tendency for evangelicalism to understand itself as a safe space from racism or other forms of oppression. Christina Hanhardt's brilliant *Safe Spaces* demonstrates that this tendency to divorce individual from social transformation is not particular to evangelical communities. Social justice organizations tend to presume that living less oppressively can be done simply by having the correct politics. This tendency is enabled by a commitment to what Hanhardt describes as "safe space." Social justice movements often focus on structures of oppression directed at them rather than structures of oppression of which they are complicit. As groups begin to organize around their common sense of oppression, the threat of oppression becomes externalized as an outside threat. Such groups then attempt to create safe spaces from oppression. However, this tends to necessarily create a racial logic in which others from outside the community are deemed to be the threats to the community. In order to enforce safety, communities become increasingly invested in the carceral system to enforce borders against perceived social threats. She states, "Safety is commonly imagined as a condition of no challenge or stakes, a state of being that might be best described as protectionist."[35]

Similarly, evangelical scholar Soong-Chan Rah argues that the concept of safe space is manifest in the notion that the church is a refuge from a sinful world. Consequently, the sins *within* the church, particularly the sins of white supremacy, go overlooked. In his book *Many Colors*, Rah asks, Why do so many churches have these dome structures in their ceilings despite the fact these structures are not cost-efficient?[36] He argued that the churches are actually supposed to resemble mini-arks symbolizing the idea that the church is essentially a life raft (similar to Noah's ark) in a world flooded by sin. The idea of the church as a refuge is the foundation for the modern suburban megachurch. According to Rah, white Christians flee urban areas to found churches in the racially homogenous suburbs. These suburban churches then develop urban mission programs to go save the communities of color they have fled. Thus, Rah notes, white evangelical churches are not a safe haven from racism, since they are fundamentally constituted through an investment in white supremacy.

Similarly, evangelical feminism began to question the presumption that churches were a safe space from abuse. If one is free from sin after being born again, what could account for the high levels of abuse within evangelical communities?[37] Evangelical feminists also rightly

---

[35]Christian Hanhardt, *Safe Space* (Durham, NC: Duke University Press, 2013), 46.
[36]Soong-Chan Rah, *Many Colors: Cultural Intelligence for a Changing Church* (Chicago: Moody Publishers, 2010), 67-70.
[37]Andrea Smith, *Native Americans and the Christian Right: The Gendered Politics of Unlikely Alliances* (Durham, NC: Duke University Press, 2008).

pointed to the obvious shortcomings in the pastoral advice often given to abused women—that they should "forgive and forget" their abusers and remain in their marriages at whatever cost to their own personal safety. In this regard, Christian wives were to take up the cross to enable the resurrection of their husbands. However, this intervention has also been critical within nonevangelical progressive circles as well. As Rita Nakashima Brock has argued, one of the problems with social justice movements is that they frequently organize around the rubric of "innocence."[38] That is, the claims of oppressed people count to the extent that they themselves are innocent of oppressive behavior. Thus, the focus on oppression at the individual level—or sin, as it were—addresses the reality that we are subjects that have been created under conditions of white supremacy, settler colonialism, patriarchy, and so forth, and we do not have to be saints to matter.

Thus, rather than see churches as safe spaces that are gatherings of saints, we should see them as dangerous places where sinners struggle together to create a world without oppression while transforming themselves in the process. Churches then do not have to be burdened with looking perfect to the rest of the world, but instead could be models of open communities, from which others can learn about their failings and struggles. In addition, if churches were to adopt some of the practices adopted by liberation movements of creating communities not based on social hierarchy and domination, they could meaningfully assist people in transitioning from their investments in racialization by providing a glimpse of what a different world could be like. People do not want to embark on a journey of either losing their whiteness or other investments in the current world order because they can only see what they would lose and not what they would gain. It should thus not be a surprise that many

---

[38]Rita Nakashima Brock, "Ending Innocence and Nurturing Willfulness," in *Violence Against Women and Children: A Christian Theological Sourcebook*, ed. Carol Adams and Marie Fortune (New York: Continuum, 1995), 71-91.

evangelicals might vote for Trump, because they fear the world as they know it is in danger, but they have no sense of another world that could be. By providing places where people can get a glimpse of what a world without racialization, otherwise known as the kingdom of God, might look like, churches can enable peoples to begin the scary journey of disinvesting in whiteness.

CONCLUSION

This essay does not mean to suggest that none of the practices adopted by those engaged in racial reconciliation, whether it be crosscultural friendships, legal reform, or something else, are not meaningful or important. There are people whose lives are on the line who need immediate assistance. But having a vision beyond the terms set by the current world order helps guide our short-term strategies so that they take us closer to where we want to be rather than farther away. I find it ironic that evangelicals who claim to believe in the God of the impossible seem to only want to adopt a politics of the possible when it comes to ending racism, sexism, and all other forms of injustice. But being content with only what seems possible is essentially heretical because it positions God as being limited by our human imagination. Jesus' life, death, and resurrection are our promise that global oppression will not have the last word, and that collectively and in conjunction with our faith in Christ, we can build a transformed world with transformed peoples who can live in that world.

CHAPTER SEVEN

THE GROANING CREATION

Animal Liberation and Evangelical Theology

SARAH WITHROW KING

CLARABELLE

Like all cows used for dairy production, Clarabelle was destined for the slaughterhouse until a nearby farmed animal sanctuary rose to her rescue. Shortly after arriving at the sanctuary, workers discovered that Clarabelle was pregnant and were thrilled that she would be able to raise a calf. But about a week before Clarabelle's due date, her behavior shifted noticeably. She lost interest in food and acted skittishly around workers.

After a search of the nearby fields, sanctuary workers discovered the source of Clarabelle's anxiety: a beautiful brown calf, carefully camouflaged in a distant stand of trees and tall grass. Clarabelle had given birth to the calf several days before, and in the following weeks sanctuary staff observed from a distance as she moved her newborn, whom they named Valentine, to a new hiding spot every day or two.

You see, like all cows used for dairy production, Clarabelle had given birth before. Cows, like other mammals, only produce milk when they have a baby to feed. As a cow between six and eight years old, Clarabelle had probably given birth to at least three, perhaps four or more, other calves in her lifetime. But, like all calves born to cows used for dairy production, Clarabelle's babies had been taken from her within a day of their birth. To make cheese, yogurt, and coffee creamer out of cow's milk, humans take the food meant for calves. So Clarabelle hid Valentine, because she did not know that this time would be different.[1]

One fall night, neighbors of the Sunshine Dairy Farm in Newbury, Massachusetts, were so disturbed by sounds emanating from the farm that many called the local police station. The following day, the local paper reported, "According to Newbury police Sgt. Patty Fisher, the noises are coming from mother cows who are lamenting the separation from their calves. The separation of mother cows from their calves is a yearly occurrence and is a normal function of a working dairy farm, Fisher said."[2]

Romans 8:22 tells us that creation is groaning, waiting for the liberation from bondage to decay. These groans aren't metaphorical or occasional; they are loud, many, and long. In the case of food production alone, we human creatures have created a system that breeds, births, raises, and kills billions of animals each year, the vast majority of whom are born, live, and die in abject misery. Every year that she lived on a dairy farm, the groans of Clarabelle's labor had been followed—less than a full day later—by the groans of the loss of her calf.

The verdant planet God created is now home to well over seven billion human beings. And though we humans share the planet with eighteen billion chickens, three million great whales, half a million elephants, and countless more animals,[3] Euro-American evangelical theologies are too rarely attentive to the nonhuman parts of God's very good creation. The consequences—to animals, to the environment, and to our fellow human beings—are disastrous. Human

---

[1] "Clarabelle and Valentine," Edgar's Mission, 2015, https://edgarsmission.org.au/animals/valentine.

[2] Dave Rogers, "Strange Noises Turn Out to Be Cows Missing Their Calves," *Newburyport News*, October 23, 2013, www.newburyportnews.com/news/local_news/strange-noises-turn-out-to-be-cows-missing-their-calves/article_d872e4da-b318-5e90-870e-51266f8eea7f.html.

[3] Literally, countless. We haven't come close to identifying all of the species of animals on land or in the sea.

activity has caused and accelerated the extinction of whole species. No longer can the woodland bison of West Virginia, the Culebra parrot of Puerto Rico, or the Rocky Mountain grasshopper—to name just a few—worship their Creator. Industrialized fishing threatens the lives and livelihoods of Indigenous coastal communities. As many humans, particularly in the Global North, have concentrated into urban areas and moved further from the rhythms of an agrarian society, many of us have lost our ability to imagine that other living beings are seen by and respond to God in their own ways.

But what if our theology, and our practice, reflected the coming and present reality of the liberation from bondage and the reconciliation of all God's creatures back to the Creator?

INVITATION

The shape and scope of an evangelical liberation theology and praxis for animals is not fixed, and the best choice we can make in any given situation is not always clear. We hope and long for the promise of eternal life in Christ, but we must have faith, since those eternal promises may not "be identified clearly and completely with one or another social reality; their liberating effect goes far beyond the foreseeable and opens up new and unexpected possibilities."[4]

My understanding of evangelical theology is rooted in the proclamation of the good news of Jesus Christ to the whole world. The good news says that "God was reconciling the world to himself in Christ, not counting people's sins against them. And he has committed to us the message of reconciliation" (2 Cor 5:19). The good news of Jesus Christ is communicated to us through an overarching narrative of the Scripture. That narrative includes the creation of the whole world; our propensity toward sin; and the redemption offered by Jesus Christ, the Creator incarnate, whose life, death, and resurrection point to the promise and inevitability of full restoration of the created both to one

---

[4]Gustavo Gutiérrez, *A Theology of Liberation* (Maryknoll, NY: Orbis Books, 1988), 97.

another and to the Creator. In Jesus, all things are possible, whether we are talking about a miraculous healing, former enemies sharing a meal, or lions lying down with lambs.

Christians follow Jesus into the extraordinary promise of life bathed in the love of an infinite God. Our understanding of God— and the actions that result from our understanding—rightfully change through time, since "evangelical theology can only exist and remain in vigorous motion when its eyes are fixed on the God of the Gospel. Again and again it must distinguish between what God made happen and will make happen, between the old and the new, without despising the one or fearing the other."[5] The shadows of the glass shift to allow us a momentary glimpse into the kingdom of God, and when those shadows darken again, we press deeper into the place where Jesus has told us to abide: in faith, hope, and love.

A theology that is liberatory pays special attention to lived experience, to concrete realities of life in a broken world, and asks how our theologies perpetuate suffering or foster flourishing. Liberation theology *is* evangelical, in that it calls for individuals and the church to be rooted in faith and therefore reshaped toward the kingdom of God.[6]

In the coming pages, we will construct a reading of Scripture that invites us to consider the place of animals in Christian faith and explore how an evangelical liberation theology might be formed. We will review some of the concrete realities surrounding human-animal relationships today and consider how we might be called to respond to those realities as individuals and as the body of Christ.

It is my hope that the exploration that follows serves as an invitation to displacement, to curiosity, to a deeper sense of God's vast love, and not to shame. I hope to provide a vision so that we can together look beyond what *is* to what *could be*.

---

[5]Karl Barth, *Evangelical Theology: An Introduction* (Grand Rapids: Eerdmans, 1963), 10.
[6]Gutiérrez, *Theology of Liberation*, 12.

WHAT DOES CHRISTIANITY
HAVE TO DO WITH ANIMALS?

From Genesis to Revelation, and from the early church to the present day, there are vivid examples of God's—and the church's—love of, care for, and delight in animal creatures.[7] William Wilberforce and other leaders of the British antislavery and anti–child labor movements were also early founders of the Royal Society for the Prevention of Cruelty to Animals, and worked to pass legislation protecting animals from various forms of cruelty. Many accounts from the lives of saints include moving tales of meaningful friendships between saints and animals, such as the story of St. Macarius, who healed a blind hyena pup: the pup's mother tried to repay Macarius's kindness by bringing him a sheep's skin. As the story goes, Macarius took the skin, but only after insisting that if the hyena was hungry, she was not to kill another creature, but should come to him for food, which she did.[8] Today, many churches include food for companion animals in their food pantry programs. Others take special care to protect and provide for wildlife who wish to make a home on church grounds. Christian college students take internships at animal welfare organizations and ask their campus dining halls to provide vegan and vegetarian food options.[9] Some pastors publicly support legislation that promotes better animal welfare, preside over pet funerals, or preach on topics that include concern for animals. Church animal welfare groups hold film screenings, book discussions, and small group studies to promote dialogue about Christianity and animal welfare in their congregations. There are many ways to care for animals, and Jesus followers are often moved to do so not in spite of their faith, but because of it.

---

[7]Of course, human beings are a kind of animal creature, different from sibling species by a matter of physiological and genetic degrees. But for our purposes, I refer to human beings as "humans" and nonhuman beings as "animals."

[8]David L. Clough, *On Animals*, volume 1, *Systematic Theology* (London: T&T Clark International, 2012), 157-58.

[9]CreatureKind helps Christian communities improve their practices related to farmed animals, including developing and implementing strategies for reduced consumption, improved sourcing, and community dialogue. Learn more at BeCreatureKind.org.

A reading of the Scripture that is attentive to animals shows that humans and animals are both created by God, worship God, and are provided for by God; humans are made in the image of God and given a particular role in that image; the whole (broken) world is in the process of being reconciled to God through Jesus Christ; and the vision of the promised kingdom is marked by peace between and flourishing of all species.

Humans and animals alike are created by and belong to God.

The creation narratives in Genesis 1 and 2 tell us that God created every living thing. When God creates sea creatures and birds, God calls them good and blesses them. When God creates land animals, God calls them good and blesses them. In the second creation account, we are given an image of God forming each and every living creature out of the ground. Each of those creatures is presented to Adam as a possible partner, and Adam names them all. A few chapters later, we learn that—because of sin—every animal and every bird and every sea creature will live in "fear and dread" of humans (Gen 9:1-3). Yet God still sees the whole of creation and it still belongs to God. Through the psalmist, the Creator declares,

> Every animal of the forest is mine. . . .
> I know every bird in the mountains,
>   and the insects in the fields are mine. (Ps 50:10-11)

> The earth is full of [God's] creatures. (Ps 104:24)

Humans and animals worship God.

"Let everything that has breath praise the LORD!," urges Psalm 150:6. The prophet Isaiah proclaims that the wild animals will honor God (Is 43:20). John sees among the angels and the elders every creature on earth singing to Jesus, "praise and honor and glory and power, for ever and ever" (Rev 5:13). The Scriptures paint a portrait not only of animals and humans responding in worship to God, but indeed the whole creation:

Praise the LORD from the earth,
>you great sea creatures and all ocean depths,

lightning and hail, snow and clouds,
>stormy winds that do his bidding,

you mountains and all hills,
>fruit trees and all cedars,

wild animals and all cattle,
>small creatures and flying birds,

kings of the earth and all nations,
>you princes and all rulers of the earth,

young men and women,
>old men and children.

Let them praise the name of the LORD,
>for his name alone is exalted;

>his splendor is above the earth and the heavens. (Ps 148:7-13)

Perhaps only someone who is intimately familiar with land and animals—as a shepherd would have been—could identify and portray in such detail how every part of God's creation responds to the Creator.

Humans and animals are provided for by God.

One of God's first provisions for the created world was a lush planet of plants to be used as food: "'And to all the beasts of the earth and all the birds in the sky and all the creatures that move along the ground— everything that has the breath of life in it—I give every green plant for food.' . . . And it was very good" (Gen 1:30-31). Other biblical writers used God's provision of and care for animals to demonstrate God's power and mercy throughout the Scriptures. God asks,

Can you . . . lead out the Bear with its cubs . . .
>and satisfy the hunger of the lions? . . .

Who provides food for the raven? . . .

Do you know when the mountain goats give birth?
>Do you watch when the doe bears her fawn? (Job 38:32, 39, 41; 39:1)

Again, the psalmist, with an intimate awareness of God's provision, calls us to

sing to the LORD with grateful praise. . . .
He provides food for the cattle,
and for the young ravens when they call. (Ps 147:7, 9)

Humans are made in the image of God.

While the creation narrative in Genesis 2 portrays animals as potential partners to humans, in Genesis 1, God says, "Let us make mankind in our image, in our likeness" (Gen 1:26). In English translations, Christ is also referred to as the image of God: "The Son is the image of the invisible God, the firstborn over all creation. For in him all things were created: things in heaven and on earth" (Col 1:15-16). Humans have not always lived up to the image endowed by the Creator in us. Fernandez posits one possible source of this failure:

We have learned to develop our identities as human beings through disconnection, rather than through connectedness and interdependence. Our way of relating to fellow human beings parallels our way of relating to other beings in the cosmos. We seek to disconnect ourselves because we want to establish our difference from other forms of life. But the difference that we seek through our acts of disconnection is an adjunct to claim our superiority. We establish our difference through disconnection because we believe deep in our hearts that it is only in disconnecting ourselves that we can claim superiority. Rather than seeing our difference and uniqueness as a reminder of our interdependence, we confuse our difference and uniqueness with superiority.[10]

When we downplay the kinship between animals and humans portrayed in Genesis 2 and center ourselves in the story of the creation and redemption of the world (anthropocentrism), there are far-reaching consequences not only for our relationship with animals and

---

[10]Eleazar S. Fernandez, *Reimagining the Human: Theological Anthropology in Response to Systemic Evil* (St. Louis: Chalice Press, 2004), 172-73.

the environment, but for our relationships with other humans as well. Liberation ethicist and pastor Christopher Carter asks us to consider whether humans are "living up to their potential as beings created in the image of God? Are they capable of re-imagining their divinely appointed role in Creation to care for nonhuman animals in a way that conforms to this image?"[11]

Humans are given a particular role in that image.

Immediately after creating and blessing humans, God tells these beings made in the image of their Creator that they are to "rule over the fish in the sea and the birds in the sky and over every living creature that moves on the earth" (Gen 1:28). And right away, God points to the lush landscape and says, "I give you every seed-bearing plant on the face of the whole earth and every tree that has fruit with seed in it. They will be yours for food" (Gen 1:29). Our first responsibility was to cultivate the plants of the land so that all God's creatures could eat. Even as the Scriptures describe sin and its consequences, including the reality of food from animal and human death, God placed limits on human use and consumption of animals, outlined in the Law. Working animals were to be given weekly rest (Ex 23:12); fields were to lie fallow, in part to allow wild animals the opportunity to eat (Ex 23:10); and it was a sin to kill an animal without giving appropriate thanks to God (Lev 17:3-7). When humans fail to obey God, the whole world suffers (Gen 7–8); when humans fail to keep God at the center of their lives, the whole world suffers (Jer 7:16-20; 12:4).

The whole (broken) world is in the process of being reconciled to God through Jesus Christ.

"For God so loved the world," John 3:16 tells us, a continuation of an old promise:

Your love, LORD, reaches to the heavens,
  your faithfulness to the skies. . . .
You, LORD, preserve both people and animals. (Ps 36:5-6)

---

[11]Christopher Carter, "Eating Oppression: Faith, Food, and Liberation" (PhD diss., Claremont School of Theology, 2015), 136.

Our Creator God stepped into the world in the form of Jesus Christ the Savior, the long-expected Messiah who was expected to liberate the Israelites from sin—and the Roman Empire. Jesus called for the people of Israel to repent from sin, and urged his disciples to be merciful peacemakers, healers who loved and prayed for their enemies. Jesus' teaching challenged the religious leaders of the day, as he seemed to prioritize relationships over regulations—healing on the Sabbath, preaching that reconciling to a brother or sister was more urgent than offering gifts at the altar, touching the unclean, or eating with Gentiles, for instance.

The inclusion of Gentiles in Jesus' missional and salvific work was not without controversy, given the great divide between the Jews and Gentiles in that time. But time and again, Jesus and his followers confirm that Jesus is the Lord of the whole world: "There is no difference between Jew and Gentile, for all have sinned and fall short of the glory of God" (Rom 3:22-23). Just as the first sinner brought sin to all, so Christ's death brought life to the whole world (Acts 3:21; Rom 5:12-21).

But even though we Christians are "free from the law of sin and death" (Rom 8:2), we still sin, and our relationships with God, with other humans, and with the rest of the created world suffer as a result. Paul's letter to the Romans tells us that "the creation waits in eager expectation for the children of God to be revealed. For the creation was subjected to frustration, not by its own choice, but by the will of the one who subjected it, in hope that the creation itself will be liberated from its bondage to decay and brought into the freedom and glory of the children of God" (Rom 8:19-21). The creation is eagerly waiting for God's beloved children to ease its suffering—to nurture rather than to destroy.

God's love extends from the highest of heights to the depths of the sea. In Jesus, the kingdom of God came near, but that kingdom is not yet fully realized. Through Jesus, "God was pleased . . . to reconcile to himself all things" (Col 1:19-20). And though we await Jesus' return knowing that the good news is "proclaimed to every creature under heaven" (Col 1:23), creation is still groaning. We are not yet fully reconciled. But we know what that reconciled creation *could* look like, how we can move toward a world, "on earth as it is in heaven" (Mt 6:10). And we know that we children of God have a part to play in the restoration of the whole creation back to its Creator.

The vision of that kingdom is marked by peace between and flourishing of all species.

Perhaps the most well-known and vivid portrayal of the peaceable kingdom promised to us through Jesus Christ is in Isaiah:

> The wolf will live with the lamb,
>> the leopard will lie down with the goat,
> the calf and the lion and the yearling together;
>> and a little child will lead them.
> The cow will feed with the bear,
>> their young will lie down together,
>> and the lion will eat straw like the ox.
> The infant will play near the cobra's den,
>> and the young child will put its hand into the viper's nest.
> They will neither harm nor destroy
>> on all my holy mountain,
> for the earth will be full of the knowledge of the LORD
>> as the waters cover the sea. (Is 11:6-9, echoed in Is 65:25-26)

This peace, and peaceful sharing of food resources between species presently hostile to one another, echoes not only the Edenic vision of God's creation but other allusions to interspecies harmony seen throughout the Scriptures.[12] The ideal is clear: a world in which humans and animals live in harmony with each another, do not fear one another, and thrive on an abundance of available plant foods. Unfortunately, the reality is far—too far—from the ideal.

---

[12]Clough, *On Animals*, 155-57. Clough points to Gen 2; 7–9; Ps 65; 66; 98; 145; 148; Eph 1; Col 1; Rev 4; 5; 21 as examples.

When I talk about the possibility of nonviolent relationships between humans and animals, I hear two frequent objections that I would like to briefly address here (I take them up in depth elsewhere).[13] The first is that the Bible is clearly *not* a handbook for veganism, evidenced in part through God's acknowledgement of the use of animals for food in Genesis 9, the system of temple sacrifices, Jesus' participation in the practice of fishing and eating fish, and the repeated New Testament exhortations to not worry so much about food rules. The second frequently raised objection, which is related, is that if we Christians take Jesus as our guide and Jesus ate meat, then clearly we do not need to trouble ourselves now with the practice of killing animals for human sustenance; in other words, there's no sense in trying to push an early adoption of Isaiah's vision.

As we will see, the scope and practice of the human use of animals looks vastly different today than it did in biblical times. Thus, our challenge is to consider how "striving to imitate the life and teachings of Jesus pushes Christians to work toward ending the oppressive human-human and human-nonhuman animal relationships that our current food system thrives on."[14] In 99 percent of cases, the practice of eating a fish or a lamb now is, in nearly every way imaginable, different than the practice of eating a fish or a lamb was in first-century Palestine. For much of the world, and particularly in the United States and Europe, eating animals is no longer a special occasion, marked by reverence and thanksgiving, where the life and death of an individual animal mattered.

Having established one possibility for a reading of the Bible that is attentive to animals, we now ask the question: Can there be a theology of liberation for animals?

---

[13]See *Vegangelical: How Caring for Animals Can Shape Your Faith* (Grand Rapids: Zondervan, 2016) and *Animals Are Not Ours (No, Really, They're Not): An Evangelical Animal Liberation Theology* (Eugene, OR: Cascade Books, 2016).

[14]Carter, "Eating Oppression," 154.

CAN THERE BE A THEOLOGY
OF LIBERATION FOR ANIMALS?

In his compelling and convicting *A Theology of Liberation*, Gustavo Gutiérrez makes clear that liberation theology is concerned with humans, with the relationship of humans to other humans and to their Creator. Humankind is "the center of creation."[15] Human economic and technological advancements that harness the earth's resources are only as good as their liberative effects for humans.[16] God is "close to human beings, a God of communion with and commitment to human beings."[17] And so, liberation theology pays particular attention to the lives, relationships, and deaths of humans, to consider how we can be liberated not only physically and spiritually from oppressive social and economic structures, but also how we can be liberated from sin.[18]

A significant part of Gutiérrez's liberatory move is to see those who have been marginalized and oppressed gain or regain their own agency. "An awareness of the need for self-liberation is essential to a correct understanding of the liberation process. It is not a matter of 'struggling for others,' which suggests paternalism and reformist objectives, but rather of becoming aware of oneself as not completely fulfilled and as living in an alienated society."[19]

So, the possibility of a theology of liberation for animals— specifically nonhuman animals, because as humans we, of course, are animals as well—is faced here with two main objections: 1) liberation theology is not for animals; and 2) attempts to articulate such a theology could never be fully realized, since the participation of animals in the process would be, at best, murky.

Writing several decades after Gutiérrez, as issues surrounding climate change have gained broader and more rapid awareness,

---

[15]Gutiérrez, *Theology of Liberation*, 87.
[16]Gutiérrez, *Theology of Liberation*, 90.
[17]Gutiérrez, *Theology of Liberation*, 106.
[18]Gutiérrez, *Theology of Liberation*, xxviii.
[19]Gutiérrez, *Theology of Liberation*, 82.

Leonardo Boff expands the reaches of liberation to include the world beyond humanity. Examining the intersections of liberation theology and ecotheology, Boff argues the value of pursuing ecological justice, not only for nonhuman creation, but for the long-term benefit of humans: "To hear these two interconnected cries and to see the same root cause that produces them is to carry out integral liberation." Boff argues that there is a proper order for the pursuit of justice and insists that right relationships between humans must be our first priority: "Once this basic level of social justice (social relationship between human beings) has been achieved, it will be possible to propose a possible ecological justice (relationship of human beings with nature)."[20] The demand for basic human-to-human justice before attending to the groaning of nonhuman creation is understandable, particularly for members of a species that have found ways to systematically treat one another like objects, means of production, or sources of sick, selfish pleasure.[21]

Boff does not diminish the task ahead of us, the enormity of the break between human and nonhuman creation, and the devastation that has caused. There will be no quick or simple fixes. Mending our relationship with the earth and her inhabitants will require much more than switching out light bulbs or making Saturday morning trips to that new organic grocery chain across town. To pursue justice for the earth and for people of the world hurt most by the earth's decay will require "a new covenant between human beings and other beings, a new gentleness toward what is created, and the fashioning of an ethic and mystique of kinship with the entire cosmic community."[22]

Boff's new covenant, with its emphasis on kinship over hierarchy, bears a striking resemblance to the worldview articulated by some

[20]Leonardo Boff, *Cry of the Earth, Cry of the Poor* (Maryknoll, NY: Orbis Books, 1997), 112.

[21]See, for example, Katie G. Cannon, *Black Womanist Ethics* (Eugene, OR: Wipf and Stock, 1988), 31, which describes how black women were *defined* as "brood-sows" or "work oxen" in the US system of slavery. The scope of this chapter prevents a more in-depth discussion of the "animalization" of people of color, but it is an important backdrop to consider as we proceed.

[22]Boff, *Cry of the Earth*, 112.

Indigenous theologies, where those tribes who have not been "evangelized" by European culture consider themselves "co-equal participants . . . standing neither above nor below anything else in God's Creation. There is no hierarchy in our cultural context, even of species, because the circle has no beginning nor ending. Hence all the created participate together, each in their own way, to preserve the wholeness of the circle."[23]

There are portraits of this creaturely togetherness in the Scriptures. The sun, moon, and stars join with sea monsters, wild animals, cattle, and flying birds to praise God in Psalm 148. In Job 12, Job reminds us that the animals, birds, plants, and fish all identify the Lord as their provider and protector. The writer of Ecclesiastes 3:19 urges us to pursue righteousness because we all have the same breath. As he prepares to send his disciples out to proclaim the gospel, Jesus imparts to them the astonishing reality that the Creator of the whole universe sees every sparrow fall and knows every hair on our heads (Mt 10:29-30). We are all cared for together, and we all suffer together when we fail to hear and follow God's word, as in Jeremiah 7:20: "Therefore this is what the Sovereign LORD says: My anger and my wrath will be poured out on this place—on man and beast, on the trees of the field and on the crops of your land—and it will burn and not be quenched."

Nearly forty years after Gutiérrez, in the year *National Geographic* says global warming "got respect,"[24] Eleazar Fernandez outlines the explicit and urgent interlocking connections between classism, sexism, racism, and abuse of creation, which he calls naturism:

> Naturism is a way of thinking and dwelling that places the human species at the top of a hierarchy in which other species are relegated to the status of others to be exploited. In the hierarchy of being, the

---

[23]Clara Sue Kidwell, Homer Noley, and George E. "Tink" Tinker, *A Native American Theology* (Maryknoll, NY: Orbis Books, 2001), 50.

[24]John Roach, "2004: The Year Global Warming Got Respect," *National Geographic*, December 29, 2004.

human being is at the top of the holy order and other objects are assigned meaning only as they serve the purposes of human beings . . . Where there is classism, sexism, and racism, there is ecocide. In the lives of the poor we can discern the interweaving of naturism and classism; in environmental racism we can discern the link between naturism and racism; in the exploitation and rape of women's bodies we can discern the interlocking of naturism and sexism.[25]

Fernandez repeatedly points out that the destruction of the earth is felt first, hardest, and longest by the poorest and most vulnerable humans. It is impossible to separate our ecological crisis from the experience of the poor, who were "living in deficit long before the elites realized that when nature goes into deficit a worse catastrophe is going to happen and affect all."[26] Liberation theology has helped Christians reshape their understanding of who they are as humans in relation to God, to one another, to themselves, and now to nonhuman creatures. We can cultivate a liberation theology for animals in part because, as Carter states, "the methodological logic of oppression does not discriminate based on species."[27]

For persons who live far removed from the rhythms and realities of the land, it can be difficult to imagine how our everyday actions impact those we cannot see. For persons who live far removed from the rhythm and realities of the land, but who benefit from its fruits, it can be painful to consider how a deeper understanding of those realities may compel us to change. But, as Gutiérrez points out, we must be willing to face new information and new challenges head-on, trusting the Holy Spirit "to expand our view—beyond our little world, our ideas and discussions, our interests, our hard times, and—why not say it?—beyond our reasons and legitimate rights."[28]

---

[25]Fernandez, *Reimagining the Human*, 160.
[26]Fernandez, *Reimagining the Human*, 161, 162.
[27]Carter, "Eating Oppression," 137.
[28]Gutiérrez, *Theology of Liberation*, xlvi.

WHAT ARE WE DOING TO ANIMALS TODAY,
AND WHAT DOES THAT MEAN FOR US?

We need to tell our children that every time we eat ham, beef-steak, and lamb stew, we are eating pig, cow, and sheep, respectively. We must help our children understand that thousands of pigs, cows, and sheep are slaughtered every day.

Eleazar Fernandez, *Reimagining the Human*

Fernandez tells his reader that he grew up in Leyte, Philippines, and that overfishing and other ecological harms have eradicated many of the species of fish and other marine life that flourished even in his own childhood.[29] He is shocked that many North American children believe that food comes from the grocery store and rightfully calls for adults to ensure that children understand that, for a human to eat flesh, an animal will die.[30] But it is not *thousands* of animals a day who are slaughtered for food, as Fernandez cites in his call for food source transparency; in the United States alone, *about one million land animals are killed for food every hour*. Globally, nearly eight million land animals per hour are killed for food. And the number of sea animals killed for food dramatically outpaces the use of land animals, though there is no accurate number available, since fish, crustaceans, and other sea lives are not counted individually; rather, they are counted by weight. Contrast that reality with the story of the miraculous catch of 153 fish in John 21, where each life, though lost, at least meant enough to be counted.

Too many of the interactions that humans have with animals are exploitive. But because "faith and life are inseparable"[31] in liberation theology, we must include our use and treatment of the nonhuman

---

[29]Fernandez, *Reimagining the Human*, 160.
[30]Fernandez, *Reimagining the Human*, 163. Companies all over the world are working to develop both plant meat (food that comes from plants, but has a similar nutritional, flavor, and texture to animal meat) and so-called clean meat, which is animal meat grown not from whole animals, but from animal cells. These exciting innovations could radically alter the scope and practices of animal agriculture. Learn more at the Good Food Institute, GFI.org.
[31]Gutiérrez, *Theology of Liberation*, xix.

world in our examination of our lives, beliefs, and actions. We have found countless creative and cruel ways to use animals for our own ends. The cleaning solution or shampoo we buy from the grocery store may have been tested on the shaved skin of a guinea pig or dripped into the eyes of a rabbit. We use metal traps that maim, or we breed and then electrocute minks and other animals anally or vaginally to use their fur in coats. High school students dissect frogs, cats, fetal pigs, sheep hearts, and other animal bits. Companies breed and sell beagle puppies to the pharmaceutical industry, where they will be poisoned. When suburban sprawl encroaches on wildlife habitats, we authorize population culls. We capture or breed animals to display for human education or entertainment. We beat other animals so they will perform in television, movies, or traveling acts. To preserve our furniture, we amputate the toes of cats. We do all these things, even though we could accomplish our ends using more humane means.

But nowhere is our abuse of animal creatures as widespread as the system of industrial animal farming (factory farming) that has been developed in the United States over the last eighty years. Factory farming supplies approximately 99 percent of the animal products we consume in the United States. Though there is increasing attention to heritage farming, those products are a tiny fraction of the current market share. Factory farming and the animal agriculture industry have radically altered the genetic make-up of animals used for food, exploited small farmers and vulnerable workers, sped the destruction of land in the Global South, fed the development of environmentally devastating monoculture, poisoned local communities, contributed to violent crime among slaughterhouse workers, and increased our appetite for animal products by pouring countless dollars into lobby and advertising campaigns. The far-reaching consequences of our current rate of animal product production and consumption are well-known, but, as Gutiérrez pointed out long before we reached our current astonishing levels of consumption, "many in the developed countries . . . are so attached—in both the East and the West—not to the past, but rather to an affluent present which they are prepared to uphold and defend under any circumstances."[32] In other words, I could never give up bacon and cheese.

One does not need to look very long or hard to find evidence of some of the grim truths and everyday cruelties that come with raising and killing animals for food on factory farms.[33] There are the routine mutilations: slicing off the beaks of baby chickens, castration, tail-docking, dehorning, and branding (all without painkillers). Lifelong confinement to tiny, crowded spaces; lack of fresh air, access to the outdoors, or a clean place to lie down; and an existence completely devoid of the opportunity to engage in God-given behaviors are all well-documented realities of factory farming. Can you imagine what it is like to be a chicken and to never be able to raise a wing? That is the life of an egg-laying hen.

Altered genetics mean animals grow very large very fast, or they produce much more milk than they would naturally. The strain of huge bodies means that chickens, cows, turkeys, and pigs often cripple under their own weight. When it is time to move from one place to another, whether that is from cage to cage or farm to truck to slaughterhouse, it is normal for human workers to beat or shock or stab animals to get them to move. Slaughter is predictably terrible, but it is just the last of a lifetime of miseries. The egg industry can only use female chickens, so all the hatched male babies are set on a conveyer belt that drops them alive into a grinder, or they are bagged up alive with hundreds of other male chicks and left to suffocate.

As Christians, we understand that our faith must inform our actions, that following Jesus means we allow ourselves to be transformed and shaped by the Holy Spirit. We seek the kingdom of God, which means we "participate in the struggle for the liberation of those

---

[32]Gutiérrez, *Theology of Liberation*, 122.

[33]To learn more about factory farming, I suggest the book or film *Eating Animals* by Jonathan Safran Foer (New York: Little, Brown and Company, 2009). A simple Netflix or Google search will also lead viewers to many informative documentaries of varying lengths, some more graphic than others.

oppressed by others."[34] Our mistreatment of animals does not happen in a vacuum. There are long-reaching effects on humans and the broader environment. Even if one rejects the claim that being attentive to nonhuman lives is an important part of Christian faith and practice, it is impossible to ignore the devastating impacts on human creatures of animal abuse generally and factory farming specifically.

The Food Empowerment Project has documented some of the dangerous conditions in which factory farm and slaughterhouse employees work.[35] While raising and killing animals is not *inherently* dangerous, the massive scale of factory farms and the speed at which slaughterhouses must operate in order to meet the high demand for animal products have created working conditions ripe for exploitation, abuse, injury, and even death. Many factory farm and slaughterhouse workers are people of color, poor, or undocumented. They are exposed to harmful particulates from carcasses, toxic gasses from animal waste, and disease from sick animals. Machinery and equipment failures result in catastrophic injuries. One group of chicken slaughterhouse workers grabbed headlines when they revealed that they wore diapers during their shifts because they were not allowed to take bathroom breaks.[36]

The work of raising and killing billions of animals for food each year is not just physically dangerous, it also poses a significant sociological risk. I met a pastor whose husband runs a small slaughterhouse. There are a limited number of kill days per week, because to stand on a kill floor, shooting animals with bolt guns, slitting their throats, or dismembering them for forty or more hours a week, every week, comes with a terrible psychological and physical toll.[37] One

---

[34]Gutiérrez, *Theology of Liberation*, 116.
[35]"Factory Farm Workers," Food Empowerment Project, www.foodispower.org/factory-farm -workers/.
[36]Peggy Lowe, "Tyson Foods Promises Better Conditions and Safety for Meat Workers," NPR, April 26, 2017, www.npr.org/sections/thesalt/2017/04/26/525736888/tyson-foods-promises -better-conditions-and-safety-for-meat-workers.
[37]"Slaughterhouse Workers," Food Empowerment Project, www.foodispower.org/slaughterhouse -workers/.

study of nearly six hundred rural counties showed that "slaughter-house employment increases total arrest rates, arrests for violent crimes, arrests for rape, and arrests for other sex offenses in comparison with other industries."[38]

In addition to being bad for humans and animals within the system, factory farming is wreaking havoc on the environment.[39] Factory farming is by no means the *only* contributor to the global climate crisis, but it is a significant one, and one that is perpetuated by and primarily benefits those who already have a great deal. Globally, factory farming contributes to deforestation, soil erosion, devastation of fish stocks and marine life, the rise of superbugs and zoonotic disease, air and water pollution, and more. Animals can be (and were for thousands of years) part of healthy ecosystems, but industrial farms devastate them.

I have used industrial animal agriculture as an example of what happens when humans disconnect themselves from one another and their fellow created beings, a disconnect borne out by "the belief that some human beings are truly human while others are not; that human beings should be removed from and master nature; and that our individual selves are defined by othering other created beings."[40]

What would it be like to extricate ourselves or throw off a system that assigns value to living creatures based on what they look like, their usefulness to those in power, the ease with which they can be physically manipulated? What would it be like to not feel trapped in a system in which the only well-known and easily accessed means of basic survival requires participation in the suffering and death of so many others? I

---

[38] Amy J. Fitzgerald, Linda Kalof, and Thomas Dietz, "Slaughterhouses and Increased Crime Rates: An Empirical Analysis of the Spillover from 'The Jungle' into the Surrounding Community," *Organization and Environment* 22 (2009): 158-84.

[39] For more information, please see Jonathan Safran Foer's outstanding *Eating Animals*. Bibi van der Zee's "Why Factory Farming Is Not Just Cruel—but Also a Threat to All Life on the Planet," the *Guardian*, Oct. 4, 2017, is also an excellent overview of the widespread environmental damage caused by factory farms. See www.theguardian.com/environment/2017/oct/04/factory-farming-destructive-wasteful-cruel-says-philip-lymbery-farmageddon-author.

[40] Carter, "Eating Oppression," 143.

have a sense that many of us long for an alternative, but do not have the means or imagination or access or agency to create and sustain it. Moreover, when our children are being gunned down, the air we breathe and the water we drink poisoned, our economic livelihoods always on the line—and when we know that nothing we do will be perfect—it can be pretty hard to muster up the energy to break out of habits and mindsets that we have inherited and lived into for generations.

But there is hope.

WHAT DOES IT MEAN TO LIVE AS A
CHRISTIAN IN RELATION TO ANIMALS?

Howard Thurman writes:

> Too often the price exacted by society for security and respectability is that the Christian movement in its formal expression must be on the side of the strong against the weak. This is a matter of tremendous significance, for it reveals to what extent a religion that was born of a people acquainted with persecution and suffering has become the cornerstone of a civilization and of nations whose very position in modern life has too often been secured by a ruthless use of power applied to weak and defenseless peoples.[41]

Liberation theology asks Christians to consider our practices in light of the concrete realities and our understanding of the Word of God. How do we accept the reign of God, the kingdom of God, in theory *and* practice?[42] When it comes to animals, what is the invitation from God? How can we claim or reclaim our heritage as beings made in the image of God for the care and flourishing of all creation? Boff suggests one important step: "Human beings live ethically when they maintain the dynamic equilibrium of all things and when, in order to preserve it, they prove capable of setting limits to their own desires."[43] Do we need to eat meat at every meal, or even every week?

---

[41]Howard Thurman, *Jesus and the Disinherited* (Boston: Beacon Press, 1976), 1-2.
[42]Gutiérrez, *Theology of Liberation*, xxxi.
[43]Boff, *Cry of the Earth*, 136.

Daisy is a cow who was used for dairy at an educational farm. When her milk production dropped, a person who had grown fond of Daisy managed to find a home for her at Pasado's Safe Haven, a farmed animal sanctuary. The sanctuary director has this to say about Daisy: "Daisy doesn't like to be alone. She's definitely a people cow, and a cow's cow. . . . She doesn't realize how big she is. She's very aware of how beautiful she is."[44] As Edgar's Mission did for Clarabelle, Pasado's Safe Haven gave Daisy an opportunity to experience life as a cow, and not as a milk- or meat-producing machine. Away from the farm, surrounded by people dedicated to their flourishing as individuals, Daisy and Clarabelle were able to express themselves, communicate their particular preferences, and make meaningful connections with humans and animals alike. Stories of rescued horses, chickens, turkeys, goats, sheep, cats, dogs, and a host of other species all shed light on these dual realities: each one of God's creations is an individual, and each one deserves to be counted.

Our christological and eschatomorphic hope—where each of God's precious creations is a part of a flourishing whole and where no one has to kill, maim, or abuse another creature just to survive—may not be realized in our lifetime. But the challenge of a liberating praxis "endeavors to transform history in the light of the reign of God. It accepts the reign now, even though knowing that it will arrive in its fullness only at the end of time."[45]

While it is not possible now to live without death, there may be actions we can take to mitigate our impact on the "others" of our time. How can we form a new kind of consciousness, one that moves beyond the ingrained status quo? The whole creation is groaning, and we followers of Jesus are being called into the reconciling work of our Savior. How will we respond?

---

[44]"VIDEO: The Moo-ving Story of Daisy the Rescued Dairy Cow," Voices of Compassion, July 26, 2017, http://cok.net/blog/2017/07/video-daisy-rescued-dairy-cow/.
[45]Gutiérrez, *Theology of Liberation*, xxx.

CHAPTER EIGHT

HOLY AND ACCEPTABLE

Liberation from Evangelical Fat Shame

J. NICOLE MORGAN

FAT PEOPLE, FAT CHRISTIANS, need to be liberated. Not from their bodies, as many may assume. Fat people need liberation from a cultural message, and far too often a theological message, that deems them second-class citizens who are lazy, dumb, unprofessional, and undisciplined. These stereotypes about fat people are found frequently in our culture, but also in our churches. Christian weight-loss studies are prevalent. Numerous books and church-based diet groups promise that if you love God enough you'll lose part of your body and become better.

Christians (for a variety of reasons) often think that being fat is a sin, or at least the symptom of a sin. This creates a culture of body shame within the church that says that a thin body is more godly than a fat body. This lie contributes toward fat Christians feeling as if they are not free to serve God in accordance with their callings and gifting. It is spiritual and emotional bondage that prohibits the full body of Christ from living into its calling to love and serve God and neighbors. Belief that God prefers us thin contributes to the breaking down of community within the people of God and our ability to speak truth and life into our greater communities. Lauren F. Winner, a historian and professor of Christian spirituality at Duke Divinity School, says,

"Although evangelicals are typically outspoken in their analysis of worldliness, weight is one area where we seem to have embraced a worldly aesthetic uncritically."[1] I could tell story after story of the way I have seen this play out in my life and in the lives of others.

This chapter will argue for a theology of liberation for fat people from fat shame within the church, specifically the evangelical church in which I was raised. I will primarily focus on the way this theology is true to how God created and equips us, no matter our size, to love God and love neighbors. I argue that fat shame in the church and the promotion of devotional diets that encourage us to get thin for God both harm individuals' ability to fully serve God and damage the church's ability to function as a healthy community that cares for its neighbors or that lives and acts as the people of God. To do this, I'll argue with a few assumed truths about the reality of life in a fat body. (1) It is possible to be fat and healthy, thin and unhealthy, and that people of any size can take steps to pursue health that will not necessarily end in thinness. (2) There is a stigma attached to fat bodies that impacts how people in charge of hiring, housing, compensation, education, entertainment venues, and so on view fat people that negatively effects the quality of life of a fat person. There are many who have argued through research and reason the existence of these truths in numerous books and articles. The research is out there, but for the sake of space, I will not examine it specifically here.

I call myself *fat*. Fat is an adjective that speaks to the amount of flesh that exists on my bones. After many years of reclaiming this word for myself, at times it feels as neutral as naming my eye color. Oppressed people have the right to name themselves. When names have been historically assigned to marginalized people, those names carry with them the worldview and intentions of the oppressors. Beyond the obvious names designed to mock fat people, the world has plenty of names for fat people that are sometimes attempts at

---

[1]Lauren F. Winner, "The Weigh and the Truth," *Christianity Today*, September 4, 2000, 57.

being polite. However, terms such as *fluffy* or *curvy* all seek to make the idea of *fat* somehow more appealing. I would like us to just accept that fat is a valid way to exist. In the same vein, medical terms for fatness are often dehumanizing and patronizing. We are called *overweight*, which assumes a correct weight. *Obese* prescribes disease to a body. *Morbidly obese* goes a step further, treating the person as if they are the walking dead.

In his famous *Pedagogy of the Oppressed*, Paulo Freire points out, "Dialogue cannot occur between those who want to name the world and those who do not wish this naming—between those who deny others the right to speak their word and those whose right to speak has been denied them. Those who have been denied their primordial right to speak their word must first reclaim this right and prevent the continuation of this dehumanizing aggression."[2] The general consensus of many fat activists is that *fat* is the preferred term. The denotation is accurate; it is the connotations that must be called out for their flaws. Those who refuse to dialogue about bodies with an understanding of *fat* as a neutral term will never be able to speak with and to those who live in fat bodies. Pastors and Christian leaders who refuse to consider the way their descriptions about the size of bodies impact those who live in fat bodies will continue to oppress those who are fat.

My theological argument is that church leaders must speak of bodies, fat or thin, in ways that acknowledge our incarnational faith. Bodies are ever present in the foundational aspects of the Christian story. Creation and incarnation are the two pivotal moments in which bodies play a central role. Yet even beyond those foundational theological moments, we see that the Holy Spirit indwells the body of believers, that all believers together make up the body of Christ—the church—and that when life on earth is over, our bodies find new life once again in eternity.

---

[2]Paulo Freire, *Pedagogy of the Oppressed*, trans. Myra Bergman Ramos (New York: Continuum, 2011), 88.

Our world has no end to the ways we have categorized and excluded bodies. We take a naturally occurring diversity and ascribe it a pecking order, assigning power to one form and relegating others to lower social classes, frequently making them less in the church as well. Much has been written about the way we have put into literal and figurative bondage our sisters and brothers because of gender, ethnicity, skin color, sexuality, and abilities. We are just beginning to understand and examine how our cultural prioritization of thinness has filtered into the church and relegated our fat sisters and brothers to second-class citizens in the kingdom of God. This favoring of thinness in the church has contributed to a culture that puts the weight of bondage onto the lives and ministry of fat people, whom God has created and called.

LIFE IN A FAT BODY

My story is the lived experience of a fat Christian woman. I have been both fat and a member of a Christian family and church for as long as I can remember. I have lived the work it took to repair the damage of fat shame in my own life. It is common to blame the media and its unrealistic images of bodies for the body shame that plagues our culture. Yet despite having limited exposure to secular media growing up in a conservative, evangelical church, I still developed the conviction that my fat body was wrong. Furthermore, I sincerely believed that my body was unbiblical and ungodly. I thought that I was unable to fully live the calling of God on my life because my body was a stumbling block to both myself and others. My pastor regularly spoke about his exercise regime as a way that he cared for his body so that he would not become "one of those fat and lazy preachers." As a teenager, one of the church groups I was involved in spent a year focusing on Luke 2:52, in which "Jesus grew in wisdom and stature, and in favor with God and man." The stature part of that verse meant that we kept up with our weight loss and our push-ups and those were marks of growing like Jesus. The weekly church bulletin listed Bible study classes that one could take; devotional diet groups like *First Place* were regular offerings in the class selection.[3] Eventually, a member of my church wrote a diet devotional. In the many years I had known her, she had never been fat.

I was taught that my body shape and size was a sin, or at least the effects of sin. It was result of eating wrong or exercising wrong. It was the result of using food instead of God for comfort. It was the evidence that I lacked self-control or discipline or understanding. Whatever the reason, my body was wrong, it was wrong in the eyes of God, and it was going to prevent me from fulfilling the ultimate goal of a biblical woman. I knew then, as a child and teenager in a Southern Baptist church, that I would be unable to be an international missionary because of my weight and the limits set by the International Mission Board. There were structural barriers in place to tell me that my body was not good enough to fully serve God or others. I more fully tell the story of how my religious community influenced and shaped the shame about my body and how I learned to see the truth in my book *Fat and Faithful*.[4]

In my early twenties, I began to question my assumptions about fatness and thinness, and I was introduced to Fat Acceptance (FA). Through learning about FA, my eyes opened to the systemic oppression of and discrimination against fat people. At first, I remember writing in my journal that I wanted to unlearn this knowledge because seeing the oppression my body faced everywhere was exhausting. I had never noticed it before, partly because I was also telling myself the same thing the rest of the world tells fat people: that I deserved the shame I felt and that I should not expect easy access to things like clothing or seating. It made sense to me at the time to find it unreasonable to expect the doctor's office to do things like stock various sizes of blood pressure cuffs in order to get

---

[3]Carole Lewis, *First Place* (Ventura, CA: Regal Books, 1998).
[4]J. Nicole Morgan, *Fat and Faithful: Learning to Love Our Bodies, Our Neighbors, and Ourselves* (Minneapolis: Fortress Press, 2018).

an accurate reading of my blood pressure. Paulo Freire speaks of this phenomenon in which the oppressed agree with their oppression, using language that fits the body-shame discussion well. He says, "Self-deprecation is another characteristic of the oppressed, which derives from their internalization of the opinion the oppressors hold of them. So often do they hear that they are good for nothing, know nothing and are incapable of learning anything—that they are sick, lazy, and unproductive—that in the end they become convinced of their own unfitness."[5] I was, as Freire says, one who had "been shaped by the death-affirming climate of oppression" and who was learning to "find through [my] struggle the way to a life-affirming humanization."[6] As I came to understand the social and political natures of fat acceptance and to see the oppression and discrimination where it exists, I became increasingly passionate about challenging these norms and pointing out their flaws. As I learned more about my own body and about the culture in which I lived, I began to believe that I was human, not a grotesque other.

My body shame started in the church. I am convinced that the fat shame that has crept from culture to church is one of the most insidious lies used to break community and destroy the capacity of Christians to live into the liberating freedom of the kingdom of God.

GLUTTONY

The common argument against fat-accepting, or fat-liberating, theology is that gluttony is a sin. I do not debate that gluttony is a sin. I do want to critique and examine the way we conflate fatness and gluttony. They are very different things. Gluttony is consumption at the expense of others.[7] When we ignore the needs of those around us and consume resources in a way that oppresses our neighbors, that is gluttony. In Judges 3, we meet King Eglon, an oppressive king. He

---

[5]Freire, *Pedagogy of the Oppressed*, 63.
[6]Freire, *Pedagogy of the Oppressed*, 68.
[7]I explore this definition of gluttony as consumption at the expense of others, as well as biblical examples of gluttony, in greater detail in my book *Fat and Faithful*.

consumes and hoards resources while the people live in poverty and hunger. He is fat, a detail included when we hear the story of his death. King Eglon is assassinated when Ehud comes in with a dagger and stabs him; the fat of King Eglon's stomach swallows the sword. He dies a gruesome death, his bowels spilling out on the floor of the bathroom. Eglon is not a bad, oppressive king because he is fat. Eglon is an oppressive king who is gluttonous; he overconsumes at the expense of those he is charged to care for. He is also fat. This does not mean that all gluttonous people will be fat, just that he is.

In Ezekiel we learn that the sin of Sodom is that they were "arrogant, overfed and unconcerned; they did not help the poor and needy" (Ezek 16:49). In Genesis 19 we see how their gluttonous behavior shows up in how they treat others. They demand that the visitors to Lot's house come out so that they can use them sexually. Lot offers his daughters instead, also viewing them as commodities to be consumed, rather than as people with dignity. This is gluttonous behavior; it values consumption over the love of neighbor. Certainly, someone in Sodom was fat; it is a naturally occurring human body type. However, we have no reason to believe that all the people of Sodom were fat. Sodom was a town of gluttons, not a town of fat people.

THE LIVED EXPERIENCE OF FAT PEOPLE

Just as white privilege and male privilege exist, so too does thin privilege. It exists in structural biases and in the attitudes and beliefs of people who view fat people as "less than." Marginalization is damaging on multiple levels, and the church should be a leader in listening to the margins. Liberation theology recognizes that we do not all have the same lived experiences, and therefore it values the lived experiences of those on the margins.

R. Marie Griffith, author of *Born Again Bodies: Flesh and Spirit in American Christianity*, recounts the stories of many women who engage in "uncontrolled bingeing and self-hatred that terminate in divine surrender" and says that the "pain trod humiliation at the heart of these stories signal a powerful despair that ought not to be trivialized."[8] These stories must be heard and understood and become a part of the way we talk about embodiment theology. "Failing to take their stories seriously, to let them stir us to understanding, intensifies the marginality and shame. . . . Opening our ears to hear them ought to sharpen our attentiveness to that same pain in the churches and communities that surround us."[9] A particular community's experience is not greater than or less than another community's experience, but it is particular. The church must listen to the voices of those who live their life in fat bodies, especially those who do so without feeling the need to change their body. The lived experience of fat people deserves a space and a voice inside a Christian incarnational theology that honors the *imago Dei* in every person. As a Christian community we will not fully understand the full beauty of the body of Christ, the image of God, until we hear all the voices that make up that body.

Fat people moving about this world encounter numerous roadblocks in day-to-day occurrences that they must navigate around in order to live life. Seating is the most common issue. There are many chairs that cause me pain as the arms press into my hips. There are some seats in which I do not fit. There are stores where I am unwelcome because the salespeople cannot imagine what business I would have there. As someone who has been fat all of her life, navigating the world and determining with a glance if I can physically enter the space is second nature to me.

Thin privilege exists; fat people are part of a marginalized and oppressed community.

What happens when we believe that our bodies are already the image of God, and that while we can care for our body, we do not need to *make* or *conquer* our body into a more holy form? Research on the way people view their bodies and the bodies of others if they

---

[8]R. Marie Griffith, "The Promised Land of Weight Loss: Law and Gospel in Christian Dieting," *Christian Century*, May 7, 1997, 450.
[9]Griffith, "Promised Land," 451.

believe that bodies are inherently sanctified or holy found that viewing one's body as sanctified is negatively correlated with body objectification and "depersonalization," or feeling disconnected from one's own body.[10] "Specifically, rating one's body as more sacred and worthy of respect was linked to feeling more satisfied about particular areas of one's body, more satisfied with one's appearance in general, and more satisfied with one's weight."[11] The study examined both non-theological views of sanctification and Christian views of sanctification and found that "the factor reflecting Christian beliefs showed much stronger correlations with the satisfaction subscales."[12] In other words, believing that our bodies are inherently sanctified is great, but believing that they are sanctified by God even further boosts our own satisfaction with our bodies. Disappointingly but unsurprisingly, the study did notice a difference in women respondents. Women, even those with sanctified views, scored lower in terms of "body awareness" about such issues as being aware when one is hungry, needs to rest, is becoming ill, and so on. The study attributes this to "the cultural objectification and pressure [women] experience. These findings further elucidate the challenges in embodiment faced by women in our culture."[13]

Another study examined the "desirable body shape" among Muslim, Jewish, and Christian men. The men were given nine outline drawings of commonly understood shapes of female humans, ranging from "very thin" (1) to "very heavy" (9) and asked to rate, among other things, which figure they found most attractive. Researchers found that for all the men, the preference was around 3 (3.36 for Muslim men, 3.15 for Jewish and Christian men).[14] The authors of the study

---

[10]Heather L. Jacobson, M. Elizabeth Lewis Hall, and Tamara L. Anderson, "Theology and the Body: Sanctification and Bodily Experiences," *Psychology of Religion and Spirituality* 5, no. 1 (February 2013): 44.

[11]Jacobson, Hall, and Anderson, "Theology and the Body," 48.

[12]Jacobson, Hall, and Anderson, "Theology and the Body," 48.

[13]Jacobson, Hall, and Anderson, "Theology and the Body," 49.

[14]Christopher J. Hallinan, "Muslim and Judaic-Christian Perceptions of Desirable Body Shape," *Perceptual and Motor Skills* 67, no. 1 (August 1988): 81.

indicate that "the gravitation by Western women to a preferred thinner figure is offered as a partial explanation. It has been suggested that such a preference may also be due to the perception by those females that Western men do prefer a thinner female image."[15] In other words, one explanation could be that women think men prefer thinner figures, so they become thinner, which in turn increases the thin preference among men.

Mary Louise Bringle, author of *The God of Thinness,* points out that "men get stroked by their wives whether they gain weight or not. In contrast, countless Christian women are motivated to diet because they fear their husbands are repulsed by fleshy thighs and protruding tummies."[16] Implicit in this explanation is an understanding of whose gaze is normative and prescriptive. If women change to please men, men have the authority to dictate the shape of a woman's body. This is problematic on numerous levels, and a theology that honors the *imago Dei* inside female bodies should not allow such a system of oppression to continue unchecked.

Another study found that we implicitly judge obesity to be immoral and use religious terms to talk about obesity (using the language of sin and virtue), regardless of our own religious affiliation.[17] The researchers found that even in academic and standard medical discourse about obesity, "Christian moral language" is used frequently to describe the body.[18] As much as Christians have adopted secular body ideals, Christian language has moralized fatness for the greater society. When we fail to understand that our bodies are holy and instead feel the need to make them holy, we start down a dangerous path that is holistically unhealthy for both the individual self and the greater body of Christ that is the church.

---

[15]Hallinan, "Muslims and Judaic-Christian Perceptions," 82.

[16]Mary Louise Bingle, in Winner, "Weigh and the Truth," 57.

[17]William James Hoverd and Chris G. Sibley, "Immoral Bodies: The Implicit Association Between Moral Discourse and the Body," *Journal for the Scientific Study Of Religion* 46, no. 3 (September 2007): 391-403.

[18]Hoverd and Sibley, "Immoral Bodies," 392.

One of the more recent popular diet devotionals is Rick Warren's *The Daniel Plan.*[19] Warren says that the goal is to make "health a form of worship [because] God made your body, Jesus died for your body, and He expects you to take care of your body."[20] This does not have to be an inherently body-shaming approach. We can work on our health to the best of our ability as a way to care for ourselves and honor God without body shaming. (Or health shaming those who will never be the world's definition of healthy.) However, the inspiration behind Warren's diet books, as reported in an interview with the *Wall Street Journal*, came to Warren while he was "doing baptisms 'the old-fashioned way'—by physically raising and lowering people into the water."[21] Warren said that as he was "lowering people, [he] literally felt the weight of America's obesity problem [and] I thought, 'good night, we're all fat!'"[22] In this moment where Christians commit their entire body to a picture of new life, Warren judged those bodies.

Warren certainly isn't the first to write a book about how God wants us thin. The modern devotional diet industry began with Charles W. Shedd's 1957 *Pray Your Weight Away*. On the inside jacket cover we find the following description:

> At one time, the Reverend Charlie W. Shedd weighed 300 pounds. For fifteen years he tried to take off the surplus blubber which made him look like a small edition of Moby Dick. . . . Then one day in despair he decided to try the spiritual approach to weight reduction. . . . From this simple beginning, the author evolved a new method of whipping his problem of obesity. . . . He gives it to you step by step, in this book. . . . He treats reducing as a spiritual problem, and suggests a technique which may provide, for those who have faith, the power to heal the disease of obesity, permanently.[23]

---

[19]Rick Warren, *The Daniel Plan* (Grand Rapids: Zondervan, 2013).

[20]Alexandre Wolfe, "Pastor Rick Warren: Fighting Obesity with Faith," *Wall Street Journal*, Jan. 17, 2014, www.wsj.com/articles/pastor-rick-warren-fighting-obesity-with-faith-1390009729.

[21]Wolfe, "Pastor Rick Warren".

[22]Wolfe, "Pastor Rick Warren".

[23]Charlie W. Shedd, *Pray Your Weight Away* (Philadelphia: J.B. Lippincott Company, 1957), inside jacket.

This jacket summary of Shedd's book sets up the expectation that true Christians ("those who have faith") will be able to replicate Shedd's weight loss. If one fails to "reduce" permanently, then perhaps that person has a spiritual problem.

Gwen Shamblin's book *The Weight Down Diet* (1997) sold nearly one million copies in three years and influenced the creation of numerous church-based weight loss groups.[24] Shamblin says there is a difference between physical hunger and spiritual hunger and that people are fat because they feed spiritual hungers with too much food.

There are far more diet devotionals on the market than I could hope to address. A couple others, like Shamblin's and Warren's, also include popular church-based weight loss support groups. Carol Showalter, the author and founder of the *3D* devotional diet group, explains the creation of her program as a direct result of weight-loss groups already meeting in the church.[25] "Weight Watchers met in the church and I had had a hard time not noticing it as I was off to Bible studies. . . . God spoke to me in a most extraordinary way: through a hand-painted sign on a Sunday School wall. The message was this: God has the answer."[26] So, she created a Christian version of Weight Watchers, 3D, teaching that Christians "can lose weight if they lead disciplined lives; disciplined eating but also disciplined prayer."[27] She took a secular program, added God's name to it, and called it good and holy.

A FAT-POSITIVE THEOLOGICAL APPROACH

These devotional diets and many like them encourage Christians to define *normal* and *holy* bodies as those that are thin, healthy, and typically abled. However, we can question these assumptions. A fat-liberation theology asks us to appreciate the diverse spectrum of human bodies as part of God's varied and beautiful creation.

---

[24]John W. Kennedy and Todd Starnes, "Gwen in the Balance," *Christianity Today*, October 23, 2000.
[25]Carol Showalter, *3D: Diet, Discipline, and Discipleship* (Brewster, MA: Paraclete Press, 2002).
[26]Winner, "Weigh and the Truth," 53.
[27]Winner, "Weigh and the Truth," 53.

Theologians who work from the margins often speak of viewing ethical questions and dilemmas from the perspective of the underside of the empire. This is no less true in terms of doing ethics and theology concerning our body size. This is not a new issue in feminist thought. Many feminist and liberation theologians talk of the body in regard to gender and race in ways that lend themselves well to fat-positive thinking, but often stop just short. It is not entirely uncommon to find casual fat prejudice in otherwise insightful discourse on embodiment theology or theological anthropology. By casual prejudice, I mean that assumptions such as "we care for our bodies so that we can be thin/healthy" that show an uncritiqued bias about body size will often show up in discussions about the body. I argue that what is happening is that there is remaining internalized shame and oppression stemming from dualistic and patriarchal beliefs that we can still conquer our body's shape, health, and mortality.

We cannot talk about a theology of the body if the only voices speaking have culturally acceptable bodies (or voices in fat bodies speaking from their own internalized oppression by believing the manipulative voice of culture and media that their bodies are wrong). A theology of the body must listen to those voices that live with other bodily experiences and the resulting social, physical, and spiritual consequences of living life in what is deemed an unhealthy or unacceptable body. In a world that prioritizes one type of body over another and supports this prioritization with the name of "health" and "honoring God," we must critique what health means and how it might hinder our discussion of encouraging people to live into their full relational embodiment as images of God. The discussion must involve the voices and lived experiences of those who live in bodies that are marginalized because of size or health.

To borrow an analogy from Miguel De La Torre in regard to introducing a counternarrative into the dominant culture, we need a new wineskin to effectively talk about liberative embodiment in regard to body size.[28] We cannot discuss fat acceptance by coming at it from a health perspective, or the wineskin will burst. This is not to say that fat people cannot be healthy, but to say that the dominant cultural assumptions about health and body size are so old that they cannot contain the wine of a message that says that there is a different way to look at health, bodies, size, and value. We need wineskins called *embodiment, incarnation,* and *imago Dei.* I even recommend a wineskin called *fat and happy.* From a theological perspective, these wineskins start with the assumption that our worth is in our being, not in our health. From a social perspective, these wineskins dismiss the faulty belief that all fat people desire to rid their body of fat. Instead, these wineskins effectively hold a wine that speaks of a full life rich in community and of stories that subvert the dominant culture by daring to be happy and loved in a fat body.

Failing to take into consideration the implications of a public or ecclesial theology that links God to thinness is detrimental. In an article that explores the effect on the Eucharist of a culture obsessed with diet and thinness, Patrick T. McCormick asks, "What does it mean to celebrate the Eucharist as *body* of Christ when our diets seem to be waging a war against our bodies (particularly against the bodies of women), when the ways in which we eat do not honor our bodies, or when our eating patterns seem indifferent to the suffering bodies of all [those] gathered at the edges of our tables?"[29] In order to partake in this sacrament that centers on the *body* of Christ, we must have a good understanding and awareness of *body.* This understanding is distorted from a hundred angles in our contemporary Western world; McCormick calls our obsession with the size and shape of our bodies "Diet America." "With its particularly undernourished perceptions of food, body, and our common tables, as well as its distorted grasp of our ties to God, creation, and our neighbors,

---

[28]Miguel A. De La Torre, *Latina/o Social Ethics* (Waco, TX: Baylor University Press, 2010), ix.
[29]Patrick T. McCormick, "How Could We Break the Lord's Bread in a Foreign Land? The Eucharist in 'Diet America,'" *Horizons* 25, no. 1 (March 1, 1998): 47.

'Diet America' places significant obstacles in the path of any Christian community seeking to understand, celebrate, and be transformed by the Eucharist."[30]

The Eucharist is not the only one of our foundational beliefs as Christians that is ultimately impacted when we have a poor understanding of our own bodies and our relationship to them. Serene Jones reminds us, "To be faithful to God is to accept and to try to embody the reality of our existence as given, beloved, differentiated, relational, embodied, free covenant partners of God."[31] Aside from damaging individuals, dualistic thinking that encourages people to conquer their bodies, or to make their bodies acceptable, impacts the larger church community, and ultimately the kingdom of God. If the thought process behind dualism is taken to the extreme, you end up with a separation not only between body and soul, but a separation at broader and deeper levels of what it means to live out the Christian faith. If we must discipline unruly bodies so that the soul may be free, then we must also discipline, punish, and disappear unruly members of our community so that the community can be free. From there, it is a short path to spiritual, physical, and mental abuse in the name of pursuing holiness.

Our public theology about how we care for our bodies has numerous rippling effects in the lives of people in our congregations. In order to have a careful public theology about our bodies, we must be cautious and thoughtful in how we read and apply Scripture that talks about our bodies, food, and gluttony. God delights in our bodily form. God created food and eating to be something more than a basic utilitarian chemistry that powers our cells. Our bodies and our eating practices exist in community and in ways that make known the kingdom of God. It is important to think about these things. It is important to know that the conclusion is not that God wants us thin or that we must be healthy in order to a part of the body of Christ.

---

[30]McCormick, "How Could We," 57.
[31]Serene Jones, "Human Beings as Creatures of God," in *Essentials of Christian Theology*, ed. William C. Placher (Louisville, KY: Westminster John Knox Press, 2003), 147.

CONCLUSION

There is much to critique in the United States' overconsuming, materialistic, self-indulged society. The evangelical church is not immune to these sins as part of that culture. However, fat people cannot be the scapegoat—the weight of these global sins is not illustrated by the weight on certain human's waistlines. US culture and churches have turned the bodies of fat people into a mocking caricature to assuage their own guilt. They desire to rid the world of fat people, perhaps hoping that if they do not have to look at excess, they will not feel its judgment in their own hearts. If fat people are why children in impoverished communities don't have food, then the average-sized people (or even the fat people who are "working on it") do not have to examine their own complicity in these structural sins at the global level. If fat people are to blame for the high cost of the healthcare system, then we can continue to neglect the poor and sick and push the thin ideal while telling ourselves that fat shame will solve problems.

Social norms that value thinness have created a dominant culture that continually reinforces thin-centric values so that we come to believe without question that to be *godly* is to be thin and beautiful. To question this assumption is to question the economic and political powers dependent on our beliefs that our bodies are wrong. These questions are met with strong opposition and a force that desires to keep us in our place striving for another body. When we tell people, especially women, to love their own bodies, it is a daring and liberative move against oppressive powers. The numerous diet devotionals that continue to roll off the presses give further evidence that United States Christians have not given up their quest for a thin, holy, and self-disciplined body. Our churches must find a way to combat the insidious dualism that is prevalent in our churches, and that way must involve the voices from the margins of the culture of body shame in which we live. We are all made in the image of God, holy and acceptable. When we accept that truth, we are closer to the freedom to live into the calling on our lives to love God and love our neighbors as ourselves.[32]

---

[32]J. Nicole Morgan, "Fat King Eglon and Scapegoating Our Guilt," *J. Nicole Morgan* (blog), September 25, 2014, https://jnicolemorgan.com/2014/09/25/kingeglon/?_wpnonce=5918db88ae&like_comment=531.

CHAPTER NINE

LIBERATION

Self and Community in Relationship

TERRY LeBLANC AND JEANINE LeBLANC

For the creation waits in eager expectation for the children of God to be revealed. For the creation was subjected to frustration, not by its own choice, but by the will of the one who subjected it, in hope that the creation itself will be liberated from its bondage to decay and brought into the freedom and glory of the children of God.

ROMANS 8:19-21

LIBERATION—freedom, if you will—has come to mean an assortment of things in the present day. Ours is a world significantly impacted by a wide range of competing social demands and diverse cultural perspectives impacting our thoughts, experiences, and feelings about freedom and the instruments of its delivery. As a result, there are identifiable clashes over what constitutes appropriate freedoms, what it means to be liberated from oppressive situations, and how we are to live in a good way together—even within the wider Christian fold.

What is more, the juxtaposition of the primacy of value assigned to either individual or community across cultures plays appreciably into decisions about what constitutes liberation and freedom; it does so in ways that carry socially transcendent weight. What is clearly an issue of sovereign individual human rights in one culture or context may demand the sublimation of those autonomous rights in another. In short, community health and well-being for some people groups may require preferencing the community's rights over that of the individual in order to ensure community survival.[1]

There are similar issues in evidence in classic Christian theologies. Some have focused on and preferenced the individual's status with and before God, while others recoil at the thought of an "individual salvation." It appears to have always been so from the earliest articulations of Christian theology—and most definitely since the arrival of post-Enlightenment and post-Reformation Christianity.

Since this issue is germane to discussions of any other theological principle, this chapter will first briefly explore the philosophical contexts of the individual and community, and then examine several other issues impacting the theological landscape we find ourselves residing within.

What compounds this situation is that Christian theology has also almost exclusively articulated its understanding of freedom in multiple sets of binaries, such as the tenuous relationship between law and grace for some Christian traditions. Depending on the theological framework in play, one permutation or another of such binaries emerges that is inevitably located along a continuum emphasizing one of them as slightly dominant over the other. Irrespective of the arrangement, however, to arrive at such a teeter-totter relationship appears to require the same specific starting point. Generally this has been described as the breach of God's law by humanity's first parents, biblically located in Genesis 3.

---

[1]Contemporary definitions of individual rights are predicated on a highly Western-influenced notion that began to see the light of day in 1946 with the UN's efforts at their articulation. Of interest is the group that was tasked with the initial responsibility for its articulation. See the UN Universal Declaration of Human Rights, www.un.org/en/documents/index.html.

In significant measure, these binaries are due to the lens through which freedom is understood. In much of current biblical and theological reflection, this lens is the contemporary social context focused through individual human rights. Yet this is neither the lens of the cultures in which the Christian Scriptures are framed nor one that is descriptive of majority-world peoples or Indigenous communities. Communal, not individual values, at least as the primary frame of reference, were, and in most cases, still are preeminent in both settings.

And so, the questions for our liberative theologies are the following: Should our understanding of the acquisition of rights as the means by which liberation is provided and assured be garnered from an ethic of individual rights and freedoms? Should this be foundational to a theology of liberation? Stated another way, are family, extended family, community and tribal values to be subsumed under individual rights and/or dominated by them? Or is there a biblically framed ethic of liberation that begins with the premise of community, and then extends outward to the individual as one among the many? Can an ethic of liberation be understood not in the individualistic sense, but as an expression of individuality (one among all) that is both differentiation from the collective and interdependence with the collective?

It is important to state a quick caveat. This reflection is not intended, in any way, to remove, limit, or undermine the uniqueness of the person, work, life, teaching, death, and resurrection of Jesus. Furthermore, we do not propose an upward lift, evolutionary-like trajectory of human beings achieving their own redemption through good, better, best behavior undertaken by them on their own behalf or under their own head of steam. Nor do we intend to suggest that something or someone other than Jesus the Christ of God is necessary for redemption. Rather, this reflection is intended to remove a roadblock to people accessing the full-orbed experience of life, and that abundantly (Jn 10:10: "I have come that they may have life, and have it to the full").

THE "WE" AND "I"

For just as each of us has one body with many members, and
these members do not all have the same function, so in Christ
we, though many, form one body, and each member belongs
to all the others.

ROMANS 12:4-5

An Indigenous philosophical understanding of communal and individual identity, the "We" and the "I," has much to offer to an ethic of liberation beyond that which is largely or solely informed by an emphasis on individual rights and freedoms. In an Indigenous context, informed by its traditional philosophy, a person conceives of the notion of freedom in different ways than those of his or her Anglo-European or Western-influenced neighbor. It is a more inclusive and wide-ranging understanding that is creatiocentric, not clearly and specifically anthropocentric. As Cordova notes of such a person,

> Instead of hierarchies she sees *differences*, which exist among equal "beings" (mountains, as well as water and air and plants and animals would be included here). The equality is based on the notion, often unstated, that everything that is, is of one process. The Native American, in other words, has a more inclusive sense of the We than others who share the sense of humans as *social* beings.[2]

As our grandfather and great-grandfather respectively said throughout the teaching years of his life, "Animals are persons too—they're just not people!" Within this perspective, communal identity, individual identity, and the wider creation context are equally important for a harmonious understanding of life and for balanced interactions with one another; the communal nature extends to and significantly includes the rest of creation.

---

[2]V. F. Cordova, "Ethics: The We and the I," in *American Indian Thought: Philosophical Essays*, ed. Anne Waters (Malden, MA: Blackwell, 2004), 177.

So while the typical human expectation of liberation would likely be limited by most peoples to a rationalization of the need for humans and groups of humans to properly and rightly express their individualism within or outside some grouping or form of community, the rest of creation has a momentous part to play. What is more, there is a significant expectation of the part(s) that humans should rightfully play within the wider creation in achieving this freedom. Contained in the writings of the most prolific of the Christian apostles is an echo of this very understanding. Paul is quite clear that he

> consider[s] that our present sufferings are not worth comparing with the glory that will be revealed in us. For the creation waits in eager expectation for the children of God to be revealed. For the creation was subjected to frustration, not by its own choice, but by the will of the one who subjected it, in hope that the creation itself will be liberated from its bondage to decay and brought into the freedom and glory of the children of God. (Rom 8:18-21)

Paul is not describing personal freedom or liberty here. Liberation in Christ is not an issue of basic human rights to freedom, equality, and personal liberty. Paul is clear that true freedom is to be experienced only within a redeemed creation where the balance enjoyed in the beginning has been restored.[3] Unless the rest of creation is understood as a full participant in this liberation, discussions about human liberty and freedom are moot. We are simply engaging in new forms of anthropocentric theological narcissism and hegemony. Liberation, therefore, involves a constellation of relationships that are inclusive of all of creation, which, in turn, reflect an integral equality of its constituent members, living well and justly.[4]

---

[3]For a discussion that has been recently advanced from within the wider theological community, but appears to borrow from Indigenous thought, see Howard A. Snyder and Joel Scandrett, *Salvation Means Creation Healed: The Ecology of Sin and Grace; Overcoming the Divorce Between Earth and Heaven* (Eugene, OR: Cascade Books, 2011).

[4]A current discussion of the implications of a wider understanding of community can be found in Randy Woodley, *Shalom and the Community of Creation: An Indigenous Vision* (Grand Rapids: Eerdmans, 2012).

As V. F. Cordova again explains,

The term *autonomy* takes on a whole different meaning in this environment. In a society of equals no one can order another about. No one can be totally dependent on another, as that would create an artificial hierarchy (the dependent and the independent) with all of its accompanying ramifications such as authoritarianism and lack of individual initiative. The autonomous person, in this environment, is one who is aware of the needs of others as well as being aware of what the individual can do for the good of the group.[5]

Autonomy here is redefined as "being aware of the needs of others and being aware of what the individual can do for the good of the group."[6] Self-determination is a consideration, but not simply for the benefit of oneself; it is for the good of the whole. What's more, doing good is not the only motive here. Instead, doing good originates within and is itself a responsibility to the group. This removes us from the typical transactional practice of relationship to one of mutuality. Furthermore, the focus is not on self as defined by vocation or contribution alone, as has characterized much of Eurocentric thought. It has wider implications.

In Indigenous relationships, for example, there is a distinct difference in how one introduces oneself and expresses one's identity as over against a more typical Euro-Canadian/American introduction.[7] The Eurocentric introduction has little if any reference to community or connectedness to the land. The other introduction, abbreviated

---

[5]Cordova, "Ethics," 178.

[6]Cordova, "Ethics," 179.

[7]This is expressed most profoundly in the difference noted in typical introductions made in the Native North American culture and those offered in the Anglo-Canadian or American culture. In the Anglo-Canadian or American culture, following your name, you're more likely to reference your vocation or contribution to your work first rather than your connections to people, place, and land. We could extend this discussion to include things like CVs, which tend to emphasize credentials first, then personal relational context if at all. The more generally observed Indigenous way of introduction (significantly abbreviated here) might resemble, "Hi, where are you from?" Response: "I am from Listuguj. My father's name is Philippe my mother's name is Eva. We are Plamu and also from the Acadian people. I now live on the land of the Cree people of Alberta with my wife, Bev. We have three children we named Jeanine, Jennifer and Matthew."

already, references connection, family, community, and the land.[8] There is no sense of self-identification—no sense that we are defined apart from relationship. The "I am" statement is absent, as it connotes a sense of being that is self-referential. In our view, the only person who has the capacity to self-define is our Creator and Restorer. Everything else in creation is defined in relationship with the Creator and with the rest of the creation.

In the anatomical language Paul also uses so adeptly, the eye is neither understandable, nor can it survive or express freedom, apart from the body. Yet the body needs the eye to be the body and experience all the freedom that only a functional whole can provide. Thus, Paul clearly places human beings in the context of the wider body of creation that Indigenous North Americans have frequently called "Mother Earth." It is she who has given us birth through the resources she provided—resources that nurtured and sustained our human mothers during our gestation. And, it is she—Mother Earth—who continues to provide for us today through and as part of her created body. We cannot live apart from her.

Not unlike the biblical portrayal of individual and communal freedom expressed above, Indigenous people consistently understand the individual as both uniquely functioning within the collective, but also as interdependent within the collective. And so, instead of Descartes's assertion, "I think, therefore I am," Indigenous people might understand being as "We are, therefore I am."[9] Within this understanding, there is an emphasis on both the "we" and the "I" as interdependent. Returning to the metaphor Paul uses, Burkhart suggests,

---

[8]This way of being is part of widely accepted Indigenous protocols. See L. Little Bear, "Naturalizing Indigenous Knowledge," Synthesis Paper, University of Saskatchewan, Aboriginal Education Research Centre, Saskatoon, and First Nations and Adult Higher Education Consortium, Calgary, Alberta, 2009. Also see the Aboriginal Education Research Centre, www.aerc.usask.ca; the First Nations Adult and Higher Education Consortium, www.fnahec.org; and the Canadian Community on Learning, www.ccl-cca.ca.

[9]Brian Yazzie Burkhart, "What Coyote and Thales Can Teach Us: An Outline of American Indian Epistemology," in Waters, *American Indian Thought*, 25.

The hand may not have the same experiences as the foot, but this hardly matters if we understand them not as feet and hands but as this body. If it is through the body, or the people, that understanding arises, then no one part need shape this understanding. All the experiences of all the parts should be brought into the process of understanding.[10]

Burkhart continues, "The combination of defining the human as a social being and denying any hierarchical systems, and a recognition of humans as a part of the greater whole, leads to a complete ethical system."[11] The functional whole, therefore, expresses liberation and experiences freedom when it comprises individual parts functioning together for the good of the whole. For Indigenous people, this often implies responsibility for one's actions toward others, which is a part of being autonomous, but is also a part of being an individual functioning for the sake of the communal good.[12] One component of expressing freedom, in a biblical sense, as well as for Indigenous people, therefore, might mean that an individual part functions for the sake of the proper functioning of the whole, not simply because we exist as autonomous individuals entitled to "individual rights."

Liberation, freedom if you will, in both cases seems to denote responsibility as an individual working as part of a functional whole. There is a responsibility to be other-aware, *to anticipate the needs of others*, combined with a need to be self-aware, *for the sake of others*. Instead of the Hobbesian idea that human beings, due to "the war of each against all," just want to fulfill their personal desires and are only invested in self-interest, we find the ideas of responsibility and interdependence, one to the other. The actions of the individual matter for the "good of the whole." The actions of the individual are not just self-serving.

At this point we need to ask some questions of ourselves. How does the social, ethical, and legal ethos of the majority society understand

---

[10]Burkhart, "Coyote and Thales," 25.
[11]Burkhart, "Coyote and Thales," 26.
[12]Cordova, "Ethics," 179, 180.

the "I" and the "we" in light of an ethic of liberation that leads to freedom? How do Indigenous peoples typically understand the "I" and "we" in view of freedom? What are their respective foundations in philosophy? How do these understandings influence our biblically framed theologies of freedom or its hermeneutic?

The social, ethical, and legal ethos of the majority society seems to understand the "I" as an assertion of the need for individual rights, often pursuing individualistic goals to the exclusion and detriment of communal ones. The individual is, in significant ways, sovereign. What makes this challenging to a more inclusive ethic of liberation is that this understanding mutes any notion of responsibility to the community since "traditional European-Western concepts of sovereignty provide no place for groups in the state."[13] This is largely true because European-Western concepts of the "I" are often based on the theories of philosophers such as Thomas Hobbes and John Locke, who, according to Boldt and Long, "emphasized the role of the individual in his relationship to the sovereign state. Western liberal political theorists have continued this emphasis on the relationship between the individual and the state." This concept not only permeates most of European-Western life, as Boldt and Long make clear, it can also be identified as "the most influential philosophy of freedom in modern Western society."[14]

Due to the permeation of this philosophy, any ethic of liberation and freedom within Western influenced societies has often been built simply on the concept of individualism, inherited from its philosophical proponents, and which espouses, "I am more free to pursue my individual goals over and against the group." This has the potential to lead to the self-fulfilling prophecy of Locke that "[the] primary purpose in life is to fulfill your desires, and if anyone or anything gets in your way, then it is a constraint. . . . Freedom means being free

---

[13]Menno Boldt and J. Anthony Long, eds., *The Quest for Justice: Aboriginal Peoples and Aboriginal Rights* (Toronto: University of Toronto Press, 1985), 550.
[14]Boldt and Long, *Quest for Justice*, 550.

from constraints that get in the way of fulfilling what you desire."[15] With respect to an ethic of liberation and freedom, therefore, individuals who understand the "I" in this fashion often express an entitlement to individual rights, but not necessarily for the sake of the group.

Many Indigenous people, on the other hand, have historically viewed individual rights in a much different light. For them, as per the discussion above, individuals can no more assert self-referential autonomy than the finger can say to the hand, "I divorce thee!" To do so incontrovertibly leads to the death of the finger. In part, this understanding is due to the fact that

> in Indian tribal society individual self-interest was inextricably intertwined with tribal interests; that is, the general good and the individual good were taken to be virtually identical. Laslett's "onion skin" analogy aptly illustrates the mythical quality of individuality in traditional Indian society. To apprehend the individual in tribal Indian society, he says, we would have to peel off a succession of group-oriented and derived attitudes as layers of onionskin. The individual turns out to be a succession of metaphorical layers of group attitudes, which ends up with nothing remaining.[16]

An ethic of liberation and freedom built solely on an assertion of individual rights, therefore, would not be likely to emerge from Native North American or other Indigenous contexts still connected to traditional ways of being and thinking, because

> Indians traditionally defined themselves communally in terms of a "spiritual compact" rather than a social contract. The "tribal will" constituted a vital spiritual principle which for most tribes gained expression in sharing and cooperation rather than private property and competition. . . . Indigenous Americans, just as did the Greeks, found their codes of conduct on the premise that humans are naturally

---

[15]John Locke, *Second Treatise of Government*, 35.
[16]Boldt and Long, *Quest for Justice*, 541.

social beings. Humans exist in the state of the "We." . . . From an
indigenous perspective, Westerners are also a conglomeration of the
"We." The West simply seeks to deny this fact about human existence.[17]

Here, as she stands outside of the group and labels it as such, Cordova
can only make the assumption that Westerners are simply a
"conglomeration of the 'I.'" Western thought is based on a deeply
rooted philosophy of individualism, a philosophy fed by contributors such as Locke, Hobbes, and Descartes in the early going,
followed on by contemporary philosophers like Craig Biddle.[18] They
do not see themselves as "we" in other than the conglomerate sense.
This, as we have said above, is a trend clearly evidenced in behavior
patterns that express the entrenched notions of entitlement and
individual rights. Biddle, in his argument that individualism has "the
facts on its side," argues,

> Groups, insofar as they exist, are nothing more than individuals who
> have come together to interact for some purpose. This is an observable
> fact about the way the world is. It is not a matter of personal opinion
> or social convention, and it is not rationally debatable. It is a perceptual-
> level, metaphysically given fact.[19]

In contrast to the deeply philosophical approach used by Westerners
to argue for one over the other, concepts and experiences of liberation, freedom, and identity did not emerge from defined principles
or theories for Indigenous people. These were not concepts to be
learned and studied apart from their lived context. Boldt and Long
note, for example,

> In European thought the Enlightenment concept of egalitarianism
> emerged as a reaction and response to excesses resulting from the

---

[17]Cordova, "Ethics," 175.

[18]In what seems a straw-man argument about individualism versus collectivism, Biddle argues in
favor of the former, appearing to interpret the latter as a mild form of communism at best. This
is intriguing, since many American authors struggle to understand communal identity and
individual identity in other than this way. See Craig Biddle, "Individualism vs. Collectivism:
Our Future, Our Choice," *The Objective Standard*, Spring 2012.

[19]Biddle, "Individualism vs. Collectivism," 2.

hierarchical doctrine of sovereignty. Egalitarianism was imposed on, and interacted with, the hierarchical concept of sovereign authority to produce more humane political structures. In traditional Indian society, however, the idea of egalitarianism did not emerge as a reaction to the excesses of hierarchical authority. Equality was derived from the Creator's founding prescription. The creation myth held that, from the beginning, all members of the tribe shared and participated equally in all privileges and responsibilities.[20]

Moreover, Indigenous people contribute not only to a fuller sense of the "we" and the "I," but also to a sense of community and individual as arbiter and interpreter of a liberative freedom, which is neither dictator nor passive recipient of such freedoms. Community and individuals function freely as a group, not by "a derived, delegated, or transferred right, but one that came into existence with the group itself."[21]

This has clear implications for theology, whether a theology of liberation, salvation, of the eschaton, or of the church. Given the metaphors of the church used by the biblical authors, for example, it is really quite impossible to imagine the church as a conglomeration of individuals. What we find instead is the description of an integrated, interconnected, and interdependent whole, where individual parts and their functions are clearly identified, but not as standalone fragments of a whole.[22] Whether the metaphor is of bricks and mortar (1 Cor 3; Eph 2), a body (1 Cor 12), or a bride (Eph 5; Rev 19), we are presented an interconnected, interrelated, and interdependent whole. Western theologies, very much rooted in the philosophy of individualism, in contrast, emphasize individual distinction quite clearly. This is equally true when we consider the nature of sin.

---

[20]Boldt and Long, *Quest for Justice*, 542.

[21]Boldt and Long, *Quest for Justice*, 551.

[22]Take, for example, the penchant to define salvation in strictly individual terms within the evangelical traditions of the church as over against what appear as more inclusive understandings in biblical accounts such as the Philippian jailor and Joshua crossing over Jordan.

In his book *The Wounded Heart of God*, Andrew Park suggests a helpful corrective to the Western notion of sin as individual transgression and responsibility. He suggests that the church might be further ahead to understand sin in light of the Korean concept of Han—collective responsibility, collective impact.[23] The collective ownership of sin creates a very different response than that of the individual saying, "I have sinned." In the Hebrew Scriptures and in the New Testament, sin was inevitably articulated as "we." Paul, for example, held the whole Corinthian church responsible for the behavior of one of its members and their response to it, not simply the individual who had transgressed. The prophet included himself or herself in any statement or confession of sin so as to ensure he or she was not separated from the community and its complicity. Collective responsibility has become foreign to the Western church, framed as it is, in societies embedded in the social liberal doctrine of personal autonomy. Western theologies reflected in the songs sung on a given day of worship reflect this. All too often they are self-absorbed. They frame one-on-one relationships with God in the journey toward eternity.

It should be clear from the above that a theology predicated on the notion of the autonomous individual will differ in significant ways from one that is predicated on the notion of individuals within and forming community. Using a foundational "I" will impact theological constructions in significantly different ways from one that is substantially the "we" as we have discussed above. Our questions, then, are, From what foundation can and should we build a biblical theology of liberation or freedom? How is our theological context to be understood—as individually or communally defined, or something that blends the philosophical drivers of each?

---

[23]Andrew Sung Park, *The Wounded Heart of God: The Asian Concept of Han and the Christian Doctrine of Sin* (Nashville: Abingdon, 1993).

RETHINKING OUR THEOLOGICAL BEGINNINGS

The universe is made of stories, not of atoms.

MURIEL RUKEYSER

Most of us would affirm, at least at some level, that life is mostly about relationship—about the interconnectedness, interrelatedness, and interdependence of all things we see and experience. Contemporary science unpacks this more and more each day. Yet our theologies do not often make the same point clear. We have emphasized the relationship between God and human beings, and increasingly, through the twentieth and now twenty-first centuries, the relationship between human beings and other human beings. And we have done so in more than modes of living and compassionate ways of being. But our theologies are still not, strictly speaking, holistically relational.

Why do we say Western theologies are not holistically relational— that they are compartmentalized and anthropocentric? It appears to us that there are at least a few interconnected reasons.

First, the biblical departure point for most Western Christian theology has been and largely continues to be Genesis 3 and its description of the sin of our first parents. Elsewhere I write,

> Western theology, in the firm grip of Augustine's articulation of sin and sin's nature, has inevitably commenced its theological under-takings with the "fall." Scraping the bottom of the sin barrel, then turning it over to see what lies beneath, has occupied much of Western Christian thought through the centuries.[24]

Unfortunately, Genesis 3, read as if it were the beginning of the story, does not make overly clear that right relationship and the relatedness of all things in creation is the Creator's focus. We are left to imply this in some reverse fashion from the brokenness of the relational associations inherent in this text. The story in Genesis 3,

---

[24]Terry LeBlanc, "Mission: An Indigenous Perspective," *Direction* 43, no. 2 (Fall 2014): 152-65, www.directionjournal.org/43/2/mission-indigenous-perspective.html.

essentially described is, "Oops, we messed up. Woe to us; we are now lost and separated from God." While we may say this is a reasonable conclusion in Christian theology, this idea neither describes nor addresses itself to the nature of the intended relationships inherent within Godself or the rest of creation. We must interpolate these. Nor does this point of departure adequately account for all that was lost. We are introduced only obliquely to the reality that it has been whole at some juncture.

Stated another way, rather than focusing on the nature and significance of the tree of life (the first tree specifically named in the Genesis narrative), Western theologians have framed their theologies by reflecting on the tree of the knowledge of good and evil, or rather the consequences of the consumption of its fruit.[25]

Many years ago now, Edward Sapir and Benjamin Whorff put forward a principle that can be captured succinctly in the phrase "Words create worlds."[26] In this short phrase is embedded the notion that what you look for is in fact what you find; what you seek appears before you. In an effort to thoroughly describe humanity's plight, Christian theology has painted a word picture both aspired to and achieved countless times in its history. LeBlanc observes, "We know the consequences, not only for the theology of the West, but also for Western missiology: mission work became, literally and figuratively, a witch-hunt for heathen and savage, occasionally seasoned with grace for early adopters."[27] Perhaps our theological starting points—and the language that defines them—does determine the trajectory of our lived theology after all. LeBlanc goes on to say,

> It is precisely this mission theology that made it possible for missionaries and monarchs, popes and priests, vicars and viceroys, to declare that we lacked humanity and souls—to assert, as did missionaries of

---

[25]LeBlanc, "Mission."

[26]For a fuller discussion of this, see Paul Kay and Willett Kempton, "What Is the Sapir-Whorf Hypothesis?," *American Anthropologist* 86 (1984): 65-79.

[27]Terry LeBlanc, "Walking in Reconciled Relationships," *Consensus* 37, no. 1 (2016).

the seventeenth century, "These heathen must first be civilized so that they might then become fit receptacles of the Gospel of Jesus Christ." Is it not altogether curious that a people who believed in the omnipresence of God could announce his absence from what they deemed to be a godless heathen land and people? Were it not for the horrendous acts perpetrated in the name of Jesus which this thinking allowed, we might simply note the theological contradiction: the theist believing the deist's truth![28]

It is difficult to be holistically relational when what you see and describe in the creation around you is viewed largely or only through a tainted lens. Today that lens is often simultaneously individually egocentric and collectively ethnocentric—the challenge of the "I" and the "we."

BINARY THEOLOGIES

If the biblical theological starting point is concerning, the philosophical framework used to appropriate the Christian narrative of beginnings is equally disconcerting. Honesty would lead us to conclude that Genesis 3 has been both source and support for a hermeneutic deeply rooted in the binary of "either/or." It goes something like this: sin enters God's realm through the enticement of the nonhuman physical and material creation; only human beings are spiritual and redeemable; creation must therefore be shunned as evil, as evidenced in the fact that it has enticed sin; humanity must pursue the path of redemption in a hostile world, finding only temporary relief here while we await the future hope of spiritual redemption.[29] Augustine was deeply engaged in this type of dualist self-debate, something that spilled over into his theological masterworks. The same might be said to be true of many foundational thinkers of the

---

[28]LeBlanc, "Mission." The quote in this paragraph is from Chrestien LeClercq, *New Relations in Gaspesia*, trans. and ed. W. F. Ganong, 2nd ed. (Toronto: The Champlain Society, 1910 [1691]).

[29]This is altogether curious since human beings were part of the material creation and, arguably, the means by which the whole of creation was subject to decay. Does this portend the dualism it is both the victim and support for?

faith throughout the years.[30] The outcome is that sin is defined in strict legal and moral terms.

This discussion—dare we say argument—over law and morality has dominated much historical discourse and continues in the present. Contemporary Christian theology—often expressed very much according to individual perception, experience, and preference has continued the same discussions begun in the days of Augustine and Pelagius. Whether in the writing of such influential figures as Brian McLaren in the progressive evangelicalism movement, pushing back against the "constitutional" interpretation of Scripture and calling for a "New kind of Christianity,"[31] or the almost pendular-swing counter-movement exemplified in the works of neo-Calvinists such as John Piper, D. A. Carson, and other members of the Gospel Coalition,[32] calling for a return to the pristine days of "biblical manhood," law and morality have been at the center of theological, missional, and ecclesial debate.

For McLaren and others associated with faith-inspired justice movements, creating a more just society, one that addresses a particular set of perceptions and values, one that is described by a clear pushback against a legally and morally framed gospel, is the answer to right relationship and right relatedness. Unfortunately, at least in some situations, right relationship with God is the price paid for arriving at this place of what can be a clearly human-centered relational justice. According to Bart Campolo, for example, "progressive Christians turn into atheists."[33] In a 2017 interview with Campolo, Sam Hailes observes,

---

[30]This list would, of course, include Aquinas, Calvin, Knox and others.

[31]See Brian McLaren, *A Generous Orthodoxy* (Grand Rapids: Youth Specialties, 2004), and *A New Kind of Christianity: Ten Questions That Are Transforming the Faith* (New York: HarperCollins, 2010).

[32]See "A Conversation with Tim Keller, John Piper, and D. A. Carson," The Gospel Coalition, 2008, https://resources.thegospelcoalition.org/library/a-conversation-with-tim-keller-john-piper -and-d-a-carson-1-of-6.

[33]Sam Hailes, "Bart Campolo Says Progressive Christians Turn into Atheists. Maybe He's Right," *PremierChristianity*, September 25, 2017, www.premierchristianity.com/Blog/Bart-Campolo -says-progressive-Christians-turn-into-atheists.-Maybe-he-s-right.

Campolo doesn't think he's a special case. On the contrary, he believes the current world of "progressive Christianity" (what he calls "the ragged edge" of Christianity) is heading towards full-blown unbelief. Speaking during the Wild Goose Festival (the American version of Greenbelt) Bart was clear: "What I know is if there's 1,000 people at Wild Goose today, then in 10 years from now three or four hundred of those people won't be in the game anymore."[34]

It would seem that not all progressive theologies—or at least their outcomes—hold the answer to the full-orbed set of relationships we are looking for in a liberative Christian theology since at least some are no longer articulating a theology, Christian or not, but a new form of individually expressed humanism in faith's clothing. They may simply be yet another articulation of either/or thinking that suggests a polar opposite reaction to a perceived set of relational injustices. This way of theologizing is about defining right behavior, not right relationship and relatedness, and pays no heed to how the rest of creation might inform the response to and then adjust our understanding of right relationship.

Yet theologies that purport to be a response to progressive evangelical theologies are not necessarily helpful either since they also focus first on the state of the individual, not the community. John Piper (inadvertently or intentionally?) sets up a pendular response to the current shifts in church life and thinking when he says,

> The critical question for our generation—and for every generation—is this: If you could have heaven, with no sickness, and with all the friends you ever had on earth, and all the food you ever liked, and all the leisure activities you ever enjoyed, and all the natural beauties you ever saw, all the physical pleasures you ever tasted, and no human conflict or any natural disasters, could you be satisfied with heaven, if Christ were not there?[35]

---

[34]Hailes, "Bart Campolo."
[35]John Piper, *God Is the Gospel: Meditations on God's Love as the Gift of Himself* (Wheaton, IL: Crossway), 15.

This idea that heaven without Christ is possible, never mind desirable, is absurd and implicitly conflates the notion of God's intention for right relationship with the maintenance, by the individual, of legal and moral principles, instead of simultaneously living in right relationship with God in Christ and the other aspects of creation mentioned. In this admittedly strange description, God seems to serve in the primary role of provider of stuff and circumstance for human pleasure and satisfaction, which will only be fully appreciated with Christ present. Yet the description seems vaguely deistic and the focus unnecessarily egocentric and nonholistic. Neither does this fiction invite us to clearly reject the absurdity and enter into right relationship. Instead, stated behind the scenes, we are to engage in right behavior—this time from the standpoint of maintaining a legal, moral, and material certitude. Once again, the anthropocentric nature of this theological response fails to ask questions about or be informed by the rest of creation of which the human community is but a part.

Neither of the above appears to have assisted us toward right relationship. In fact, it can be argued that each has done quite the opposite—one in a progressive libertine anthropocentric frame invites us to relax our understanding of law and morality so that we might have justice—a justice that at some level appears to create the opportunity for the theology itself to be moot as the theologian vacates the landscape where God is present. The other, in what we might describe as a more regressive, legalistic, but still nonetheless human-centered frame, suggests law and morality simply need to be tightened yet again, and in so doing create an alienating status between human beings and other human beings and the rest of creation in favor of appeasing God with our behavior.

Pro and con, Augustine's theology, and that which has been built on it, has framed this theological landscape for a very long time.[36]

---

[36]It is intriguing that not a few in the conservative evangelical community who uphold Augustine's theology of original sin would disavow virtually all else in Catholic theology.

This is not to reopen the Pelagian debate or, as Tillich might have done,[37] suggest that sin is strictly existentially relational and that it therefore differs from that described in the biblical narrative.[38] Nor would I hope that we would, through our questioning of Augustine's perception of reality, be perceived through the lens of Tillich's question: "How far can we extend our theological horizons before our theology ceases to be Christian?"[39] But we desperately need a theological framework that does not sacrifice the intention of God for relationship in favor of a legal or moral debate. Given the nature of the fractures in the church we see around us, we need a focus that moves us outside the traditional debate.

Sin, defined in terms of the breaking of a specific law or a morality rooted in a specific biblical text, which, in turn, is often a function of interpretation, seems incapable of creating an experience of having been liberated from a condition, itself created by this paradox. Somehow, in our contemporary theological environment, we have managed to live in this uneasy tension—desiring right relationship within the body of Christ, but unable to bring it into existence because of differing legal and moral perspectives. We are seeking community, yet for the same reasons, remaining unaware of its existence all around us within creation.

TOWARD RIGHT RELATIONSHIP, RIGHT RELATEDNESS

In parallel with the biblical narrative, Indigenous creation stories make clear that human beings were intended for right relationship with their Creator and other spiritual powers, right relationship with one another, and right relationship and relatedness to the rest of

---

[37]See Paul Tillich, *The Shaking of the Foundations* (London: Penguin, 1962), 49.

[38]As Ray Aldred would allude to, this appears to be a rather classic Western foible—to disassociate or diminish the narrative and the tradition in which the narrative resides, in favor of contemporary experience and interpretation. Aldred, "The Resurrection of Story," *Journal of NAIITS: An Indigenous Learning Community* 2 (2004): 5-14.

[39]See Jeremy Bouma's discussion in "The Gospel According to Paul Tillich: On the Human Condition," *Theology*, August 24, 2011, 1.

creation, of which they are part.[40] Much as the biblical narrative describes the moon relating suitably to night and the sun to day, all of creation is set within a framework of right relatedness and right relationship—each maintained in correct interaction with the other through a treaty.[41]

Indigenous people have viewed creation as primarily and innately relational because "the entirety of it is primarily and ontologically spiritual."[42] For those who look carefully, the same perspective is true in the biblical account of creation. The Spirit brooding over the chaos brings forth life as a deeply spiritual and relational act. The creation emerges into an interdependent covenant of relationship, the very essence of Godself.[43] Germane to this discussion is that restored relationship, the very essence of liberation, must happen within the multiple spheres that have been impacted by the collapse of the harmony of God.[44] According to Paul in Romans 8:18-26, it is inconceivable for it to be otherwise. This restoration is also at the heart of the liberative gospel of Jesus—a message that promises the renewal of all things to their intended, created state.

Some years ago, Philip Hughes, echoing the epistle of James, stated, "What we believe is not to be found in what we say or write—it is found in what we do. Therein is the heart of our belief."[45] If we are honest about our collective observations of human nature, few,

---

[40]See, for example, David Adam Leeming in his two-volume set *Creation Myths of the World: An Encyclopedia*, 2nd ed. (Santa Barbara, CA: ABC-CLIO, 2010).

[41]We use *treaty* here to signify that this is not a legal framework but one that describes a covenant of relationship. See, for example, the work of Larry Shelton in *Cross and Covenant: Interpreting the Atonement for 21st Century Mission* (Tyrone, GA: Paternoster, 2006).

[42]Terry LeBlanc, "Recovering the Real Beginning: Genesis 1, 2," in *Ministry Matters*, Fall 2009, 1.

[43]We must realize that the very breath of God has been imparted to the whole of creation, such that it became *nephesh hayah*, "a living soul" (Gen 1:28-31). While humanity has been given the gift of divine image and likeness (whatever that might fully mean), the rest of creation is nonetheless possessed of a spiritual nature instilled by the creative acts of the Spirit of God, who brooded over chaos and brought forth all of life, not just human.

[44]See also Randy Woodley, *Shalom and the Community of Creation: An Indigenous Vision* (Grand Rapids: Eerdmans, 2012).

[45]Phillip Hughes, "The Use of Actual Beliefs in Contextualizing Theology," *East Asia Journal of Theology* 2 (1984): 255.

if any of us, would differ with James's words and Hughes's assertions. Unless what we say comports with what we do, we are likely to consider others, and to be ourselves considered, hypocrites. And so we must ask ourselves, Do our lived theologies of liberation clearly articulate what we actually believe about the "I" and the "we"—about the focus of the gospel as liberation into right relationship for all of God's creation? Perhaps they do, and yet we continue nonetheless to live as a conglomerate of the "I," choosing or rejecting the fullness of God's community of creation in almost whimsical fashion at times. Or perhaps we have moved into an understanding that "I am because we are" and "we are because God is." That is a theology that is truly liberative.

In this chapter we have invited you, the reader, to consider that a full theology of liberation requires a shift from the I-centered individualist frames resident at each end of the current theological continuum to one that is more holistic—that is focused through the lens of "we" and is inclusive of the rest of creation of which we are part.[46] If God, who is a nondependent relationship of three, has created all else to be in right relationship and relatedness with God's self and the rest of creation, including one another in the human community, then perhaps we need to take a better look at the nature of sin and how it is that God liberates us from its effects.

The Scripture declares that the whole world is a prisoner of sin, "so that what was promised, being given through faith in Jesus Christ, might be given to those who believe" (Gal 3:22).

---

[46]As the rest of the creation around us makes more than abundantly clear, we maintain the focus of the "I" in liberation at the expense of the rest—and not just human. As I, Terry, have often said to my students in my Creation Theology class, we must think long and hard on when the last time was that human beings did more for the rest of creation than it daily does for us. The answer, of course, is obvious.

PART FOUR

THEOLOGICAL RESOURCES FROM THE MARGINS

LEAN IN TO
LIBERATING LOVE

The Birth of Evangelical Theology of Liberation at
Gordon-Conwell's Center for Urban Ministerial Education

PETER GOODWIN HELTZEL, PABLO A. JIMÉNEZ,
AND EMMETT G. PRICE III

What does the LORD require of you? To act justly,
and to love mercy and to walk humbly with your God.

MICAH 6:8

EVANGELICAL THEOLOGY OF LIBERATION was born in Boston, home of the American Revolution. This theology originated two hundred years after that revolution, with the 1976 founding of the Center for Urban Ministerial Education (CUME) at Gordon-Conwell Theological Seminary. CUME's first director, Eldin Villafañe, wrote a manifesto for the Spirit-led movement of justice, love, and *shalom* titled *The Liberating Spirit*.[1] "Led by the Spirit" to follow Jesus in loving and serving the city, CUME provides a prophetic pathway for the renewal of evangelical theology, missiology, and ethics in the new millennium (Rom 8:14).

---

[1] Eldin Villafañe, *The Liberating Spirit: Toward a Hispanic American Pentecostal Social Ethic* (Grand Rapids: Eerdmans, 1993); *El Espíritu Liberador: Hacia una ética social pentecostal hispanoamericana* (Grand Rapids: Nueva Creación/Eerdmans Company, 1996).

Given the racial discord and ethnic divisions of the difficult days in which we live, and as committed evangelical theological educators and devoted members of the Gordon-Conwell family, we coauthor this chapter on evangelical theology as an act of *intercultural liberation*. The authors all have direct connections to Gordon-Conwell either as former students or current professors. We draw on deep and different wells of cultural tradition—African American, Puerto Rican, and Scottish-German-Southern—as we collectively seek to recover Jesus Christ's liberating message of good news to the poor and freedom to the oppressed (Lk 4:18-19).

Our thesis is simple: evangelical liberation theology was born as a theological movement at the Center for Urban Ministerial Education, Gordon-Conwell Theological Seminary. From its beginning in 1976, CUME had a collective commitment to Jesus and justice, bringing the personal and social together in a Spirit-led mission of prophetic liberation and urban transformation. Led by the Spirit, Eldin Villafañe was the founding director of CUME, a prophetic intercultural urban theological center with over four hundred students representing forty denominations and twenty-five distinct nationalities. After defining evangelical theology of liberation and discussing evangelicalism's struggle with social sin, we highlight the prophetic ministries of evangelical leaders of deep faith and moral courage such as Eldin Villafañe, Michael E. Haynes, and Dean Borgman who were instrumental in the development of the emerging evangelical theology of liberation in the United States.

CHRIST THE LIBERATOR HAS COME

In his "The Liberator Has Come" address at InterVarsity's Urbana Mission Conference in 1971, Tom Skinner (1942–1994) said, "Any gospel that does not talk about delivering to man a personal Savior who will free him from the personal bondage of sin and grant him eternal life and does not at the same time speak to the issue of enslavement, the issue of injustice, the issue of inequality, any gospel that does not want to go where people are hungry and poverty-stricken and set them free in the name of Jesus Christ—is not the gospel."[2] For Skinner, the gospel's declaration of deliverance from sin is both personal and political. Skinner's call for Jesus *and* justice was clear and compelling, but it has taken many evangelicals decades to catch up with his call to follow Christ the Liberator.[3] While some conservative evangelicals resisted Skinner's specific call to follow Jesus on the pathway of prophetic discipleship through evangelism, racial justice, and reconciliation, there was a holy remnant of prophetic evangelicals who stepped up to the plate.[4]

On November 25, 1973, "The Chicago Declaration of Evangelical Social Concern" (also known as the *Chicago Declaration*) was issued by a broad array of prophetic evangelicals who called on "our fellow evangelical Christians to demonstrate repentance in a Christian discipleship that confronts the social and political injustice of our nation."[5] Organized by Canadian evangelical Ron Sider, the "Thanksgiving Gathering" was held at the YMCA Hotel on South Wabash Street in

---

[2]Tom Skinner, "The Liberator Has Come," address at Urbana 1970 Missions Conference, December 1970, Urbana, IL, originally titled "US Racism and World Evangelism?" www.youtube.com /watch?v=bvKQx4ycTmA.

[3]Tom Skinner, *Black and Free* (Grand Rapids: Zondervan, 1968) and *How Black Is the Gospel?* (Philadelphia: Lippincott, 1970). On Tom Skinner's legacy of liberation in the evangelical movement, see Edward Gilbreath, "A Prophet out of Harlem: Willing to Tell the Hard Truth, Evangelist Tom Skinner Inspired a Generation of Leaders," *Christianity Today*, September 16, 1996, 36-43. See David R. Swartz's brilliant analysis of the faith-rooted organizing strategies that prophetic evangelicals used to broaden the evangelical movement: "The Chicago Declaration and a United Progressive," *Moral Minority: The Evangelical Left in an Age of Conservatism* (Philadelphia: University of Pennsylvania, 2012), 170-86.

[4]For a fuller treatment of the prophetic evangelical movement see Peter Goodwin Heltzel, "Prophetic Evangelicals: Toward a Politics of Hope," in *The Sleeping Giant Has Awoken: The New Politics of Religion in America*, ed. Jeffrey W. Robbins and Neal Magee (New York: Continuum, 2008), 25-40; Peter Heltzel and Robin Rogers. "The New Evangelical Politics," *Society* 45, no. 5 (September 2008): 412-15. In *Jesus and Justice*, Heltzel points to John Perkins (Christian Community Development Association) and Jim Wallis (Sojourners) as two examples of vibrant prophetic evangelical movements today. Peter Goodwin Heltzel, *Jesus and Justice: Evangelicals, Race, and American Politics* (New Haven, CT: Yale University Press, 2009), 160-218.

[5]Ronald J. Sider, ed., *The Chicago Declaration* (Carol Stream, IL: Creation House, 1974); Marjorie Hyer, "Social and Political Activism Is Aim of Evangelical Group," *Washington Post*, November 30, 1973, D12.

Chicago and included black evangelicals William Panell and John Perkins, Latinx leaders like Peruvian theologian Samuel Escobar, women leaders like Sharon Gallagher and Nancy Hardesty, as well as white leaders like Carl F. H. Henry and Stephen Charles Mott, Gordon-Conwell's first social ethicist. Mott's book *A Passion for Jesus, A Passion for Justice* was a groundbreaking manifesto for faith-rooted social action.[6]

With the same passion for Jesus and justice as the *Chicago Declaration* signatories, a growing community of prophetic evangelicals in Boston began working for a more transformative evangelicalism, including Efraín Agosto, Dean Borgman, Pamela Cole, Ira Frazier, Douglas Hall, Michael E. Haynes, Bruce Jackson, Rafe Kelley, Loida Martell-Otello, Eugene Neville, Pablo Polischuk, Wesley Roberts, Garth M. Rosell, Aída Besançon Spencer, William David Spencer, Eldin Villafañe, Bruce Wall, and many others. Black, brown and white, these prophetic evangelicals crossed what W. E. B. Du Bois called the "color line," in order to collaborate on something bigger for the glory of God.[7] Believing that our evangelistic proclamation and our merciful demonstration of the gospel in our life together go hand in hand, these prophetic evangelicals were part of the emerging evangelical theology of liberation.[8]

TEOLOGÍA EVANGÉLICA DE LA LIBERACIÓN: ELDIN VILLAFAÑE'S *LIBERATING SPIRIT*

Eldin Villafañe's groundbreaking book *Liberating Spirit* unveils a *teología evangélica de la liberación*. While classical Pentecostal theology emphasized the Holy Spirit as the "Purifying Spirit," Eldin Villafañe

---

[6]Esther Byle Bruland and Stephen Charles Mott, *A Passion for Jesus, A Passion for Justice* (Valley Forge, PA: Judson Press, 1983). Becoming a handbook for faith-rooted organizers in the 1980s, this book popularized *Biblical Ethics and Social Change*, 2nd ed. (New York: Oxford University Press, 2011 [1982]).

[7]The term *color line* was first published in 1881 in an article titled "The Color Line" in *North American Review* but made popular in W. E. B. Du Bois's *The Souls of Black Folk* (New York: New American Library, Inc., 1903), 19.

[8]Carl F. H. Henry, *A Plea for Evangelical Demonstration* (Grand Rapids: Baker Book House, 1971).

argues for the biblical conception of the Holy Spirit as the *El Espíritu liberador* ("liberating Spirit"). For Villafañe, the holiness of the Holy Spirit is closer to social justice than personal purity. Unlike *dikaiosynē* in Greek, which can be translated as "justice" or "righteousness" in English, *justicia* in Spanish can mean both. *Justicia* opens up a broader scope of God's justice that includes liberation, restoration, and *shalom*. Villafañe's theology of the liberating Spirit is a bold call to the world Christian movement to live into its prophetic destiny today.[9]

Eldin Villafañe's theology of liberating Spirit was a synthesis of social ethics, biblical theology, and Puerto Rican Pentecostalism. In *Individualism and Social Ethics: An Evangelical Syncretism*, Dennis P. Hollinger identified individualism as the primary problem in evangelical theology and ethics. Identifying the inadequacy of the individualist ethic of evangelicals, Hollinger called them to a broader social ethic that intentionally includes deeper reflection and engagement with our communal and institutional realities.[10] The *individualist vision* of many conservative evangelicals in the twentieth century was predicated on the idea that the conversion of individuals would lead toward the transformation of the culture. The cultivation of a Christlike personal character was the primary strategy for social transformation. In contrast to the individualist vision of conservative evangelical ethics, Eldin Villafañe offers an *integral vision* of Spirit-led social ethics that accounts for Christ's transforming presence in all spheres of life: individual, spiritual, social, and cosmic.

Villafañe's vision of the liberating Spirit is based on the gospel. The word *evangélico* in Spanish is the preferred term that Latin American Protestants use to refer to themselves. While meaning "gospel" or "Protestant," the term does not have the ideological

---

[9]Eldin Villafañe, "Justice," in *The Liberating Spirit: Toward an Hispanic American Pentecostal Social Ethic* (Grand Rapids: Eerdmans, 1993), 214-15. For a concise pneumatology of justice, see Peter Goodwin Heltzel, "The Holy Spirit of Justice," in *The Justice Project*, ed. Brian McClaren, Elisa Padilla, and Ashley Bunting Seeber (Grand Rapids: Baker, 2008), 44-50.

[10]Dennis P. Hollinger, *Individualism and Social Ethics: An Evangelical Syncretism* (Lanham, MD: University Press of America, 1983).

implications that *evangelical* has in English.[11] However, conservative politicians are increasingly courting Latin American Protestants, addressing wedge issues similar to the ones that have polarized the Christian community in the United States. In this sense, we must recognize that the term *evangelical* is beginning to be politicized throughout the Americas.

Villafañe's commitment to a distinctively Protestant, or *evangelical*, theology of liberation was influenced by Orlando Costas, whose *Christ Outside the Gates: Mission Beyond Christendom* (1982) was a missional manifesto for *teología evangélica de la liberación*.[12] Costas served as a missionary in Central America, teaching at the Seminario Bíblico Latinoamericano or SBL (Latin American Biblical Seminary) in San José, Costa Rica; collaborating with Instituto de Evangelismo A Fondo or INDEF (Institute for In-depth Evangelism); and the Centro Evangélico Latinoamericano de Estudios Pastorales or CELEP (Evangelical Latin American Center for Pastoral Studies). His experience as a missiologist in Central America led him to develop a fruitful dialogue between evangelicalism and Latin American liberation theology.

While conducting the research for his PhD at the Free University of Amsterdam and serving as a research fellow at Selly Oaks College in 1975, Orlando Costas received a call from a Puerto Rican Pentecostal pastor Raymond Rivera, director of the Hispanic Council of the Reformed Church in America (RCA), to come and consult in a Latinx church-planting project in New York City. As a result of the trip to the United States, Costas (born in Ponce, Puerto Rico) became interested in renewing evangelical theology and missiology in the United States. In 1980 Costas would accept a teaching position at Eastern Baptist

---

[11]For a theological analysis of *evangélico* and its role in the formation of Latinx identity, see Juan F. Martínez, "Stepchildren of the Empire: The Formation of a Latino *Evangélico* Identity," in *Evangelicals and Empire,* ed. Bruce Ellis Benson and Peter Goodwin Heltzel (Grand Rapids: Brazos Press, 2008), 141-51.

[12]Orlando Costa, *Christ Outside the Gates: Mission Beyond Christendom* (Maryknoll, NY: Orbis, 1982).

Theological Seminary (now Palmer School of Theology at Eastern University) in Philadelphia.[13] When we read Villafañe's theology of liberating Spirit through the institutional history of CUME, the evangelical theology of liberation was growing in community in Boston before it took strong institutional form at Eastern Baptist Theological Seminary in the 1980s through Costas's collaboration with Tony Campolo, the founder of the Red Letter Christian Movement, and Ron Sider, "whose book *Rich Christians in an Age of Hunger* was the most significant literary product of the prophetic evangelical movement that emerged with strength in the 1970s."[14]

"As a Puerto Rican Pentecostal, I have lived and ministered in the city almost all my life. I have been called a 'Pentecostal Liberationist.' Some have thought than an oxymoron. But in reality, the label makes sense when it is set within a theological understanding of the Holy Spirit as Liberating Spirit," writes Eldin Villafañe in "The Jeremiah Paradigm for the City."[15] While Roman Catholic theologians in Latin American were talking about the "preferential option of the poor," the Puerto Rican diaspora was poor. "If liberation theology opted for the poor, it would appear that the poor in the last generation has opted for Pentecostalism," writes Amos Yong.[16] Prophetic Pentecostalism was not a theology *for* the marginalized, it was a theology *from* the marginalized.

Eldin Villafañe's prophetic Puerto Rican Pentecostal theology was birthed in barrios of the Bronx, where storefront Hispanic Pentecostal

---

[13]Orlando Costa, "A Personal Word," *Christ Outside the Gates*, xiii. Raymond Rivera, "The Reformed Church in America and the Hispanic Council," in *Liberty to the Captives* (Grand Rapids: Eerdmans, 2012), 75-80.

[14]David P. Gushee, "Shalom," in *Prophetic Evangelicals: Envisioning a Just and Peaceable Kingdom*, ed. Bruce Ellis Benson, Malinda Elizabeth Berry, and Peter Goodwin Heltzel, Prophetic Christianity (Grand Rapids: Eerdmans, 2012), 62.

[15]Villafañe, "The Jeremiah Paradigm for the City," introduction to *Seek the Peace of the City: Reflections on Urban Ministry* (Grand Rapids: Eerdmans, 1995), 1-3.

[16]Amos Yong, "Jubilee, Pentecost, and Liberation," chapter 14 in this book, in the section "The Preferential Option *for* the Poor: Global and Evangelical Developments," 310. See Yong's discussion of the nuances between the Catholic conception of the "preferential option of the poor" and evangelical Jesus-centered approaches to the poor.

Churches provided a matrix for a new movement of God's Spirit. Committing his life to Christ at ten years old, Villafañe was baptized by water at twelve years old at a Pentecostal Church in East Harlem (called *El Barrio*). After bringing the Pentecostal fire to Puerto Rico from the Azusa Street Mission and Revival Los Angeles, Juan Lugo shared his Pentecostal passion in New York City as well. In 1928, Lugo sent Thomas Alvarez from Puerto Rico to plant La Iglesia Misionera Pentecostal in Brooklyn. In 1931, Lugo founded "La Sinagoga" Church in El Barrio. A Pentecostal revival broke out in Puerto Rico, called *El Avivamiento del 33*, renewing churches and adding members and challenges to Protestant denominations like the Christian Church (Disciples of Christ) in the United States and Canada. In 1933, a group of Christians were meeting in Calle Comerío Christian Church, and the Holy Spirit descended on them. The Spirit ignited a renewal movement that would inspire the Disciples movement in Puerto Rico and plant churches in New York City, like La Hermosa at Duke Ellington Circle at the intersection of Fifth Avenue and Central Park North.[17] Baptized in El Barrio, Villafañe carried the Pentecostal fire into a dynamic youth ministry.

With a call to preach, he was given a license by the Assemblies of God in 1970 and installed as minister of education at Iglesia Cristiana Juan 3:16, Bronx, pastored by Ricardo Tañon, who became a spiritual father to him.[18] While a lion in the pulpit, Tañon was a lamb on the streets, always taking time to feed the hungry, help the homeless, and pray with a drug addict. Growing up in New York City and having to struggle for survival, Villafañe found it easy to fight for social justice with a spiritual presence to encourage people in their struggle for survival.

---

[17]Pablo A. Jiménez, "Hispanics in the Movement," in *The Encyclopedia of the Stone-Campbell Movement*, ed. Douglas A. Foster, Paul M. Blowers, Anthony L. Dunnavant, and D. Newell Williams (Grand Rapids: Eerdmans, 2004), 395-99.

[18]Eldin Villafañe, "Salsa Christianity: Reflections on the Latino Church in the Barrio," in *A Prayer for the City: Further Reflections on Urban Ministry* (Austin: Asociación para la Educación Teológica Hispana, 2001), 63-68.

Then the largest Latinx church in the United States, Iglesia Cristiana Juan 3:16 was the epicenter of Puerto Rican diaspora community for the members of the church. Villafañe led a Christian education program with a Sunday school that had close to two thousand members. While Puerto Ricans came to America looking for status and success, these proved to be a challenge to achieve. However, in Iglesia Cristiana Juan 3:16 young Puerto Ricans had the opportunity to be recognized and respected leaders in the life of the congregation. They worshiped, learned, found jobs, fell in love, had children, and made a new life together in the United States.

In addition to Ricardo Tañon, "Mama Leo" was another one of Villafañe's prophetic Pentecostal mentors in New York City. In the mid-1930s, Leoncia Rosado was the cofounding pastor of the Iglesia Cristiana Damasco in the South Bronx. Born on April 11, 1912, "Mama Leo," as she was affectionately known, was baptized in the Spirit in 1933 during *El Avivamiento del 33* revival in Puerto Rico. She copastored the Iglesia Cristiana Damasco with her husband Francisco Rosado.[19] In 1957, she received a vision to start a drug treatment center for those suffering from addictions in New York City. Going on to help establish treatment centers in cities around world, Mama Leo "inspired *a grassroots theology of women's liberation.*"[20] Inspired by Mama Leo, Eddie Villafañe (Eldin Villafañe's brother) started *Way Out Ministries*, a rehabilitation ministry for drug addicts and gang members in New York City. Puerto Rican Pentecostalism was intentional about meeting the needs of those who were suffering and struggling in their communities.

Leaning into liberating love, evangelical theology of liberation gives priority to the perspective of the poor in our theologizing. Villafañe cut his teeth reading Gustavo Gutiérrez, a Catholic theologian in Peru, who introduced liberation theology in Latin America

---

[19]Villafañe, *Liberating Spirit*, 94-96.
[20]Samuel Cruz, *Masked Africanisms: Puerto Rican Pentecostalism* (Dubuque, IA: Kendall/Hunt Publishing Company, 2005), 80.

in 1971. In the United States, James Cone wrote *A Black Theology of Liberation* in 1970, calling Christians in the United States to confess and repent of its greatest sin of racism. Down at Duke Divinity, Frederick Herzog, a Reformed theologian in the United Church of Christ, wrote liberation theology from an antiracist white perspective.[21]

As a prophetic bilingual and bicultural theologian, Villafañe developed insightful theological perspectives that broke new ground. Being bilingual led him to read Gutierrez in dialogue with Protestant Latin American theologians such as Orlando Costas, Samuel Escobar, and C. René Padilla. As a Boston University graduate who lived in Boston and New York City, he also dialogued with African American theologians such as James H. Cone and Cornel West. Being evangelical, Villafañe was able to examine these varied theological perspective from a prophetic pentecostal point of view. All this led Eldin Villafañe to be the first theologian to stress the role of pneumatology in liberation theology. Before his writings, both Latin American and African American liberation theologies stressed the role of Jesus as Liberator. Villafañe assumed Jesus' liberating role, but then stressed the role of the Holy Spirit in a way never heard before. These new perspectives were possible because Villafañe broke barriers: The linguistic barrier (English-Spanish), the continental barrier (North America-South America), the ethnic barrier (Latinx-African American-Anglo European), and the theological barrier (Catholic-Mainline Protestant-Evangelical-Pentecostal). Such a theological feat was only possible through the illumination of the Liberating Spirit of God.

Shaped by liberation theology's understanding of sin as both personal and institutional, Villafañe began to think through how the Holy Spirit was involved in the church and the city. As he constructed a *teología evangélica de la liberación*, Villafañe argued that "the

---

[21]See James Cone, *A Black Theology of Liberation*, 2nd ed. (Maryknoll, NY: Orbis Books, 1986); Gustavo Gutiérrez, *A Theology of Liberation: History, Politics, and Salvation*, trans. Sister Caridad Inda and John Eagleson, rev. 15th anniversary ed. (Maryknoll, NY: Orbis, 1988 [1971]); Frederick Herzog, "Theology of Liberation," *Continuum* 7:4 (Winter 1970): 515-24, and *Liberation Theology: Liberation Theology in the Light of the Fourth Gospel* (New York: Seabury Press, 1972).

Pentecostal church must see itself not just as the community of the Spirit *in* the world, but rather as the community of the Spirit *for* the world, but not *of* the world—a sign of the promise and presence of the Spirit's historical project, the Reign of God."[22] As a "community of Spirit *for* the world," the church was conceived as a Spirit-led movement for justice, liberation, and love.

Inspired by James Cone's call to confront racism, Villafañe argued that the church's confrontation of social sins like racism was an integral part of embodying its mission:

> The Hispanic Pentecostal church must see itself not only as a locus for personal liberation, but also as a locus for social liberation. . . . *The church's mission includes engaging in power encounters with sinful and evil structures.*[23]

Liberation theology was not just an abstract idea, but a communal practice. Given the structural racism that actively oppressed black and brown people in Boston, Philadelphia, New York, and cities around America, Villafañe's vision of liberating Spirit spoke and continues to speak deeply to evangelicals, Pentecostals, and charismatics of color who long for individual *and* social liberation.

EVANGELICAL THEOLOGY OF LIBERATION
IN AN AGE OF GLOBAL CITIES

"Every city is both Jerusalem and Babylon; it can be a place of refuge, but it is also the place of refugees, displaced families and persecuted minorities. . . . *Jesus' special concern for the poor and marginalized* is a call for us all to enter the world's cities, especially the slums," writes Scott M. Sunquist.[24] Because Jesus had a "special concern for the poor and marginalized," we need to follow in his footsteps in transformational mission.

---

[22]Villafañe, *Liberating Spirit*, 222.

[23]Villafañe, "The Challenge to Confront Structural Sin and Evil," *Liberating Spirit*, 201.

[24]Scott W. Sunquist, "Urban Community: Mission and the City," in *Understanding Christian Mission: Participation in Suffering and Glory* (Grand Rapids: Baker, 2013), 341, 344.

Villafañe's *teología evangélica de la liberación* is the frame for our own evangelical theology of liberation (as opposed to a more natural rendering in English: "evangelical liberation theology"). We are evangelical (gospel) theologians first, but we are evangelical theologians *of liberation* because of God's delivering love for the least and the lost (Mt 25). As David P. Gushee and Glen Stassen argue, God's love is not sentimental affection but a "delivering love" that sets people free from their oppressions.[25] Since sin is individual and institutional, we need a stout-hearted love prepared to prophetically engage sinful systems for the long haul. "Evil is both individual/personal and societal in nature, it must be attacked by a combination of strategies rather than merely one. . . . A combination of regeneration and nonviolent reform would seem to provide the best hope for combating sin and evil in our world. This would call for emphasis on evangelism, personal ethics, and social ethics," writes Millard J. Erickson.[26] Jesus saves us from both personal and social sin, so we need to follow Jesus and embody God's reign through our life as a community at church, at home, in the work place, in the public square, and in the community of creation.

Following Jesus who loved the poor, evangelical theologians of liberation proclaim and embody Christ's righteous reign through joining the liberating Spirit in seeking justice, embodying love, and walking humbly with our Lord (Mic 6:8). Just as Jesus called his disciples to join him on a journey toward love, we are called to be discipled by Jesus in the context of the church. On the basis of our loving relationship with God, we are called to testify to the hope within through evangelism (1 Pet 3:15). Accounting for *the hope within* means to testify to the reality of God's love as demonstrated through our personal character and our participation in God's reign of justice and shalom. Led by the liberating Spirit, we follow Christ in the ministry of transformation

---

[25]David P. Gushee and Glen Stassen, "The Greatest Commandment: Love," in *Kingdom Ethics*, 2nd ed. (Grand Rapids: Eerdmans, 2016), 107-25.

[26]Erickson distinguishes himself among evangelical systematic theologians with his thoughtful discussion of "The Social Dimension of Sin," in *Christian Theology*, 3rd ed. (Grand Rapids: Baker, 2013 [1983]), 599, 584-99.

of individuals, cultures, and the community of creation. Evangelical theologians of liberation *lean into liberating love* through prophetic embodied testimony to Jesus Christ our Messiah, faith-rooted solidarity for justice with love, and stout-hearted reconciliation with God, others, and the community of creation through the power of the liberating Spirit.

Evangelical theology of liberation blends a clear understanding of the personal, social, and cosmic implications of the gospel with the basic tenets of Protestantism, such as the authority of Scripture; the central role of Christ as Lord and Savior; and salvation by grace through faith, not by works. Jesus saves us from both personal and social sin. Therefore, the gospel is not only for individuals. Societies should also repent from their sins, convert, and live according to the values of God's new creation.

Evangelical theology of liberation provides a transformative framework for moving the evangelical movement from our multicultural fragmentation toward authentic intercultural solidarity. With the transformation of missiology into intercultural studies in the theological academy, we have a strategic window of opportunity for theological, educational, and social innovation. Intercultural solidarity is crosscultural connectivity for the common good embodied in the *beloved community*, Martin Luther King Jr.'s metaphor for Jesus' teaching of the kingdom. Dr. King argues that beloved community is the "creation of a society where all men can live together as brothers, where every man will respect the dignity and the worth of human personality."[27] Creating a society built on dignity, gender equity, and neighbor love is a daunting task in our age of global cities. This

---

[27]Martin Luther King Jr., "The American Dream" (1961), in *A Testament of Hope: The Essential Writings and Speeches of Martin Luther King, Jr.*, ed. James Melvin Washington (San Francisco: Harper Collins, 1986), 215. For some of the key writings on King's notion of beloved community, see Lewis V. Baldwin, *Toward the Beloved Community: Martin Luther King, Jr. and South Africa* (Cleveland: Pilgrim Press, 1995); Ralph Luker, "The Kingdom of God and the Beloved Community in the Thought of Martin Luther King, Jr.," in *Ideas and the Civil Rights Movement*, ed. Ted Ownby (Jackson: University Press of Mississippi, 2001), 39-54; Charles Marsh, *The Beloved Community: How Faith Shapes Social Justice, from the Civil Rights Movement to Today* (New York: Basic Books, 2005), especially chapter 1, and Peter Goodwin Heltzel, "Martin Luther King Jr.'s Theology of the Cross," *Jesus and Justice*, 46-71.

universal ideal must seek local embodiment. Since the city is the primary place people gather in community, we can deepen the King's call to beloved community and see it more aptly named as a search for the *beloved city*.[28]

THE UNEASY CONSCIENCE OF EVANGELICALISM

"What the Blacks and whites could not pull off, took the leadership of a courageous Puerto Rican prophet from New York City," said Michael E. Haynes, senior pastor of Twelfth Baptist Church (1964–2004) in the Roxbury neighborhood of Boston. The church was founded in 1840, the oldest direct descendant of the African Baptist Church, which was founded on Beacon Hill in 1805. A civil rights activist who helped to organize Marin Luther King Jr.'s rally in Boston Common on April 23, 1965, Haynes was a prophetic evangelical activist for racial justice and school desegregation. He was an early advocate and a generous supporter of CUME. In September 1976, CUME opened its doors at the Martin Luther King Jr. House of Twelfth Baptist Church, with Villafañe as the founding director. When accepting God's call to lead CUME in 1976, Villafañe proclaimed he was excited "to establish and begin a new program with the people of the inner city, my people."[29] His passionate commitment for the establishment of a seminary for "the people of the inner city, my people," provided the tipping point for the bold establishment of CUME, which was a long time coming. *Why did it take seven years to found an urban campus since a pledge was made to do so in 1969?*

Since the historic merger between Gordon Divinity School and Conwell School of Theology at Temple University in 1969, Gordon-Conwell Theological Seminary's first president, Harold John Ockenga, tried to discern how to best carry on the mighty river of prophetic

---

[28]See Peter Goodwin Heltzel's argument for a theology of beloved city based in the prophetic black tradition in "Building the Beloved City: Howard Thurman and Martin Luther King, Jr.," in *Resurrection City* (Grand Rapids: Eerdmans, 2012), 90-121.

[29]*The Center for Urban Ministerial Education: An Evaluation 1986–87* (Contextualized Urban Education), Gordon-Conwell Theological Seminary, 3.

urban ministry that flowed through two streams: Russell Herman Conwell's Temple College, founded in inner city Philadelphia in 1884, and Adoniram Judson Gordon's Boston Missionary Training Institute, founded in 1889 in the Fenway neighborhood of Boston. Both Baptist ministers who embodied the prophetic spirit of Roger Williams (1603–1683) and William Carey (1761–1834), Conwell and Gordon shared a commitment to a prophetic Christ-centered missional witness in the city.

Moved to tears during the ecumenical memorial service held in Boston for Martin Luther King Jr. in April 1968, Ockenga struggled to discern a way ahead to overcome the racial antagonism in the evangelical movement. Inspired by Billy Graham's courageous speaking out against segregation, Ockenga saw Graham's integrated crusades as an important example of evangelicals working for racial reconciliation.

During a crusade in Jackson, Mississippi, in 1952, Graham said, "There is no scriptural basis for segregation. It may be there are places where such is desirable to both races, but certainly not in the church. . . . The audience may be segregated, but there is no segregation at the altar. The men and women who come down to accept Christ stand as individuals. *And it touches my heart when I see white stand shoulder to shoulder with black at the cross.*"[30] Graham stopped segregating his crusades by cutting the crimson cord at a crusade in Chattanooga, Tennessee, in 1953. The tearing of the veil of separation between blacks and whites in the evangelistic crusades marked an important recovery of the egalitarian ideal of many antebellum revivals, an ideal that was buried during D. L. Moody's segregated revivals in the age of Jim Crow. From 1953 on, Graham understood

---

[30]United Press International, "Billy Graham Hits State Liquor System, Scores Segregation in the Church," *Jackson (Mississippi) Daily News*, July 9, 1952. Emphasis is ours. This paragraph and the next are adapted with permission from Peter Goodwin Heltzel's *Jesus and Justice*, 82-83. For the definitive biography of Billy Graham, see Grant Wacker, *American's Pastor: Billy Graham and the Shaping of the Nation* (Cambridge, MA: Harvard University Press, 2014).

his integrated crusades as his primary gospel witness for racial justice and reconciliation.[31]

While Billy Graham's integrating evangelistic crusades in the 1950s was an important step ahead for an evangelical movement seeking to come to terms with race, it was only the first step on the journey toward racial reconciliation. The individualist ethic of evangelicalism was based on the presupposition that if people converted to Christ, they will become moral people and work for a moral future. But this does not adequately account for the structural inequities in the United States, including racism, one of America's original and ongoing sins. Carl F. H. Henry's *The Uneasy Conscience of Modern Fundamentalism*, published in 1947, was a wake-up call, encouraging evangelicals to come out from their cultural hibernation and begin to actively engage in social transformation.[32] Henry called on evangelicals to confront specific political issues of the day, including "aggressive warfare, *racial hatred and intolerance*, the liquor traffic, and exploitation of labor and management."[33] Henry's clarion call to evangelicals to embody a publicly engaged faith that addressed "racial hatred and intolerance" was to be applauded, but his own lengthy book *Personal Ethics* reinforced the trajectory of individualist ethics within evangelical theology.

While the evangelical movement led by Billy Graham, Carl F. H. Henry, and Harold John Ockenga grew rapidly in the postwar boom in the 1950s, it struggled with its deepest theological and moral commitments during the revolutionary 1960s. With the rise of the civil rights movement, the feminist movement, the antiwar movement, and the student movement, the white male leaders of the evangelical

---

[31]David L. Chappell, *A Stone of Hope: Prophetic Religion and the Death of Jim Crow* (Chapel Hill: University of North Carolina Press, 2004), 96-97, 140-44; for helpful overviews of evangelical participation in the civil rights movement, see Curtis J. Evans, "Evangelicals and the Civil Rights Movement," (master's thesis, Gordon-Conwell Theological Seminary, 1999); Evans, "White Evangelical Protestant Responses to the Civil Rights Movement," *Harvard Theological Review* 102 (2009); Michael D. Hammond, "Conscience in Crisis: Neo-Evangelicals and Race in the 1950s" (master's thesis, Wheaton College, 2002).

[32]Carl F. H. Henry, *The Uneasy Conscience of Modern Fundamentalism*, 3rd ed. (Grand Rapids: Eerdmans, 1982).

[33]Henry, *Uneasy Conscience*, 17.

movement were presented with an opportunity to begin to listen and learn from women, young people, and people of color. While Vernon C. Grounds of Denver Seminary (Conservative Baptist Theological Seminary) rose to the occasion in his book *A Revolutionary Gospel* (1969), Ground's prophetic testimony proved to be the exception to the rule among white evangelical seminaries.[34]

On accepting the presidency of Gordon-Conwell Theological Seminary in 1969, Harold John Ockenga wrote,

> Although I have recently accepted the Presidency of Gordon College and Gordon-Conwell Theological Seminary, engagement in Christian education is not new to me. . . . My transition from the pastorate to Christian education is due to the desperate need of our youth in America today. *The hot spot of our sociological scene is the student revolution which is taking place on our campuses.* This has manifested itself in riots, violence, drug addiction, destruction of buildings, and insurrection against authority. The object of the student radicals is to overthrow our present system of education, and ultimately, the form of government in the U.S.A.[35]

President Ockenga's argument that the "student radicals" sought to "overthrow our present system of education" and "form of government in the U.S.A.," demonstrates that he fundamentally misunderstood the student's deep and abiding educational concerns. When you view photographs of the student protests at Conwell School of Theology and Temple University in the 1960s, the students are holding up signs that read, "We want Puerto Rican Programs" and "We want Afro-American Studies." Students of color in Philadelphia did not want riots and rebellions. They were focused community organizers and made their demands clear: they wanted professors, courses, and books that spoke to their lived experiences and concerns as young people from diverse cultural traditions. Given the legacy of white

---

[34]Vernon C. Grounds, *Revolution and the Christian Faith* (Philadelphia: J. B. Lippincott, 1971).
[35]Harold John Ockenga, *No Other Lord* (Wenham, MA: Gordon Publications, 1969), v. Emphasis is ours.

supremacy, colonialism, and Eurocentric curriculums at Temple University in Philadelphia and other universities, the students of color wanted to study the theology, history, literature, music, theatre, dance, and cultures of Africa, Asia, and Latin America and their diasporas within the Americas.

PURITANS, PROPERTY, AND PROPHETIC LAMENT

In 1969, President Ockenga was tone deaf to the cries of students of color. Ockenga's aggressive repudiation of the student movement and its ideals of access to education for people of all cultures, so that they could learn from those cultures, also unveils his cultural commitment to the myth of Manifest Destiny. "The Puritans believed that the Anglo-Saxon race was divinely mandated to guide history to its end and usher in the millennium," writes South African missiologist David J. Bosch.[36] We can illustrate how the myth of Anglo-Saxonism and a Western conception of property functioned in the Puritan theology and practice of colonial New England through telling the story of the colonization of the North Shore of Boston.

After arriving on the *Arbella* in 1630, Jonathan Winthrop became governor of Massachusetts Bay Colony. Puritan lawyer Winthrop came to the "New World" with a legal strategy: (1) should he be able to neutralize Native Americans and resolve conflict among the colonials who had landed in Gloucester, he was assured by the authorities in England that he could have legal rights to the land; (2) he would need to identify one of the local chiefs of a tribe in order to get them to sign a deed to transfer the ownership of the land to him and the new British colony.

In 1634, Winthrop sent his son John Winthrop the Younger to purchase the North Shore of Boston from Sagamore (chief) Masconomet of the Agawam. When Chief Masconomet gave gifts of the earth to Winthrop the Younger and received a gift of twenty pounds of silver

---

[36]David J. Bosch, "Mission and Manifest Destiny," in *Transforming Mission: Paradigm Shifts in Theology of Mission*, American Society of Missiology Series (Maryknoll, NY: Orbis, 1991), 300.

back from him, they agreed to share God's land together, both Indigenous people and white people of European descent living in harmony in the community of creation.

Masconomet had lived on that land of the North Shore for years. When he woke up in the morning, he would walk through the dunes to the beach and feel the soul of the universe as the waves came in. His tribe spent the summers close to the beach, but when the temperature dropped and the snow started to fall, they would migrate further inland and settle down close to Boxford, Massachusetts, taking warm cover for a long, cold New England winter. They knew the rhythm of land because they lived it every day and every year.

When Jonathan Winthrop arrived with a call from God to "settle" the "New World," he brought with him the British legal concept of *property ownership* with which Masconomet and his tribe were not familiar. As a result of this misunderstanding, Chief Masconomet surrendered the land rights to a swath of land north of Boston, including the current towns of Andover, Beverly, Boxford, Hamilton, Ipswich, Marblehead, Middleton, Gloucester, Rockport, Rowley, Topsfield, Salem, and Wenham. Soon after John Winthrop the Younger closed the land deal, Chief Masconomet died and was buried in 1658 on Sagamore Hill, two miles from the Hamilton Campus of Gordon-Conwell Theological Seminary.

In his sermon "A Modell of Christian Charity" (1630), Winthrop wrote,

> God Almightie in his most holy and wise providnce hath soe disposed of the Condicion of mankind, as in all times some must be rich and some poore, some highe and eminent in power and dignitie; others meane and in subieccion. . . . Now the onely way to avoyde this shipwracke and to provide for our posterity is to followe the Counsell of Micah, to do Justly, to love mercy, to walke humbly with our God.[37]

---

[37]John Winthrop, "A Modell of Christian Charity" (1630), in *Political Thought in America: An Anthology*, ed. Michael E. Levy (Chicago: The Dorsey Press, 1988), 7, 11-12.

While Winthrop called on the Puritans to follow the Hebrew prophet's call to justice, love, and walking humbly with God, his Calvinist call to be a city on the hill was based on a social hierarchy sanctioned by the sovereign God. It is easy for a white man who is governor of Massachusetts, and would rather talk to other governors of colonies than his own assembled freemen, to say some must be rich and some poor, some high and with power and dignity, while others must remain in subjugation. Using God to support a social hierarchy only helps those on the top of the hierarchy.

If anything, the Puritans were earnest, with their passionate prayers, biblical preaching, and their bold belief in achieving a truly Christian commonwealth in the Americas. While Puritans sought to purify the church, it had a shadow side of social sin. In 1637, Winthrop banned Anne Hutchinson from the Massachusetts Bay Colony because of her antinomian theology.

Just as Israel invaded Canaan, the Puritans invaded the Americas. Flowing through the dynamic interaction of bodies, laws, and institutions, white supremacy as an ideology and institutional reality is often perpetuated by Christians using the stories of Scripture (the exodus story; Jesus's death on a cross) to sanction racist cultural myths (the Anglo-Saxon ideal; Manifest Destiny) that continue to legitimize and perpetuate white male power. "John Winthrop's 'Model of Christian Charity' . . . delineates the behavior and demeanor that he expects the Puritans to exhibit . . . as if he is admonishing them to follow their divine Anglo-Saxon instincts," writes Kelly Brown Douglas, who argues that the Puritan's theological mistake was the idea that Anglo-Saxon blood made one chosen.[38] In this early episode in New England history, John Winthrop and John Winthrop the Younger used the exodus story to sanction the myth of Manifest Destiny in order to steal the land from the Indigenous people and build their wealth and power in the New World. In theological terms, they were engaged in social sin.

---

[38]Kelly Brown Douglas, *Stand Your Ground: Black Bodies and the Justice of God* (Maryknoll, NY: Orbis, 2015), 26.

Given the Indigenous genocide, the enslavement of African Americans, the subjugation of women, economic exploitation through slavery and land deals, and environmental devastation of the land, we as evangelical theologians of liberation confess, lament, and repent of five social sins: (1) racism, (2) sexism, (3) militarism, (4) economic inequity, and (5) environmental devastation.[39] The book of Lamentations (Lam 5:20) ends with the questions, "Why do you always forget us? Why do you forsake us so long?" and calls on the Lord for restoration. "The book of Lamentations ends in a minor key. Musical pieces that end in a minor key often signal that issues have not quite been resolved—they leave you hanging. The book is an unfinished story," writes Soong-Chan Rah in *Prophetic Lament*.[40] In his chapter "Evangelical Liberation Theologies" in this volume, Rah argues that evangelicalism is captive "to Western, white culture." The Jeremiah of prophetic evangelicalism, Rah calls our congregations to read and pray the book of Lamentations, which is a "necessary corrective to the triumphalism and exceptionalism of the American evangelical church."[41] This call resonates with African Americans and people of color living in the white-led evangelical world, and they cry out with the psalmist, "How long, Lord?" (Ps 13:1).

When Israel cries out for liberation from their enslavement in Egypt, God hears their cries (Ex 3:9). Our God loves all people, hearing their cry and working for their redemption, liberation, and restoration. Heeding Soong-Chan Rah's call to lament, evangelicals of all colors and theological perspectives are invited to join us in confessing, lamenting, and repenting of our sins, including the sins of racism, sexism, environmental devastation, militarism, and economic inequity.

---

[39]For a biblical, historical, and theological argument for why confession, lament, and forgiveness of sins is an essential aspect of the evangelical church, see Mae Elise Cannon, Lisa Sharon Harper, Troy Jackson, and Soong-Chan Rah, *Forgive Us: Confessions of a Compromised Faith* (Grand Rapids: Zondervan, 2014).

[40]Soong-Chan Rah, *Prophetic Lament* (Downers Grove, IL: InterVarsity Press, 2015), 190.

[41]Rah, *Prophetic Lament*, 198.

Lamentation with the least, the lost, and the left behind is the beginning of an evangelical theology of liberation. Since sin is both personal and social, liberation should have a personal and social dimension, as well as spiritual and ecological dimensions, as we seek to embody a holistic ethic of transformational love. A failure to repent for the totality of our social sins leaves a gaping lacuna in our desire— and thus ability—to fully be free of our complicity in these social sins. Evangelicalism's cultural captivity means that it continues to live with an "uneasy conscience" that on occasion can inspire something fundamentally new for the flourishing of all.

We begin with confessing and lamenting the sin of racism. As Patrick T. Smith writes,

> As Christians, we cannot be blind to the ongoing intergenerational negative effects of American slavery, Jim Crow laws, sharecropping, peonage or the so-called Black Codes that were informed by racism. Nor can we simply ascribe the deep inequities that exist between whites and communities of color, *generally speaking,* in education, criminal justice and health care systems in the United States *only* to narratives of personal irresponsibility. Too much historical, sociological and theological data for such reductionistic explanations of these complex social realities suggest otherwise. We mustn't speak of personal responsibility without a corresponding social responsibility to remedy the collective intentional agency of society that enabled and supported policies and practices that are harmful to human flourishing.[42]

Race signifies power relations associated with skin color. Racism is more than personal prejudice (e.g., when whites say "I have a black friend" to indicate they are not racist). Since racism is "prejudice *plus* power,"[43] Patrick T. Smith argues that Christians need

---

[42]Patrick T. Smith, "Love of Neighbor and Its Challenge to Racial Reconciliation," *Contact Magazine, Issue Theme: Racial Reconciliation* (Gordon-Conwell Theological Seminary) 44, no. 1 (Summer 2017): 13.

[43]A definition of racism from Crossroads Anti-Racism Organizing and Training (http://crossroads antiracism.org/). For a thoughtful treatment of Christian theology and the problem of racism,

to take both personal and social responsibility in our ministries of reconciliation, faith-rooted organizing, and public advocacy to confront social sins in our society. Smith's "*shalom* ethics" offers a promising and prophetic trajectory for Christian social ethics in the new millennium.

THE CENTER FOR URBAN MINISTERIAL EDUCATION (CUME): THE BIRTH OF THE EVANGELICAL THEOLOGY OF LIBERATION AT GORDON-CONWELL

The Center for Urban Ministerial Education (CUME) is an urban theological educational center. Its classes are designed contextually to actively address ministry in the city while incorporating the needs of urban pastors and Christian leaders in its course offerings. The goal is to collectively "seek the peace and prosperity of the city" (Jer 29:7). This pioneering contextualized urban theological education center in Boston serves a multilingual and multicultural constituency. Seminary courses are offered to pastors and church leaders in six languages: English, Spanish, Portuguese (for Brazilians), Khmer for Cambodian students, Creole and French (for Haitians), and American Sign Language. The center serves over five hundred matriculated students per year, representing 150 distinct churches, fifty denominations, two hundred ministers and twenty-five nationalities. It offers diploma and degree programs—MA in urban ministries, MA in youth ministry, MDiv in urban ministries, and the doctor of ministry degree program (e.g., Ministry in Complex Urban Settings and The Public Ministry of the Hispanic American Church). As we reflect on CUME's history, we divide it into two phases: (1) institution building (1976–1996) and (2) global expansion. The third phase is breaking forth.

---

see Drew G. I. Hart, *Trouble I've Seen: Changing the Way the Church Views Racism* (Harrisburg, PA: Herald Press, 2016).

Phase one: Institution building.

Eldin Villafañe pioneered and was the founding director (1976–1990) of CUME; he accepted the call to lead it while completing his PhD in social ethics at Boston University. Stephen Mott was originally hired in February of 1970 to direct the urban theological program in Philadelphia, but three months later, at the May 1970 faculty meeting, "the faculty expressed a desire to *phase out Philadelphia* and to have an urban center in Boston no matter what happened in the other city."[44] Dean Borgman, Doug Hall, and Stephen Mott were the committee that searched for Villafañe. Borgman tracked him down in his dorm room at Boston University and invited him to join the Gordon-Conwell team. Together Borgman, Hall, and Mott provided a "covering" for Villafañe, who was appointed as assistant professor of Christianity and society and director of CUME in 1975.

Villafañe's vision of prophetic urban ministry was inspired by Jeremiah's call "seek the *shalom* of the city" (Jer 29:7, adapted). In this passage, the prophet Jeremiah, who was in Jerusalem, sent a prophecy to the elders of Israel who were in exile in Babylon, encouraging them to "build houses and settle down; plant gardens and eat what they produce. Marry and have sons and daughters; find wives for your sons and give your daughters in marriage, so that they too may have sons and daughters. Increase in number there; do not decrease. Also, seek the *shalom* of the city to which I have carried you into exile. Pray to the LORD for it, for in its *shalom* there will be *shalom* for you" (Jer 29:5-7, adapted). In this passage, Jeremiah, the singing prophet, calls on Israel to stay planted where they are. Let God's love and light immerse them for sustainable and flourishing growth in the years ahead. To "seek the peace and prosperity of the city" was the pathway to realize contextual theological education in Boston, basing the curriculum and course offerings on the concrete needs of urban

---

[44]Stephen Charles Mott, "The History of Planning of an Urban Program at Gordon-Conwell Theological Seminary," the Center for Urban Ministerial Education: An Evaluation—Contextual Urban Theological Education, Gordon Conwell, 77. Emphasis is ours.

pastors and Christian leaders who were equipped in Bible, theology, and prophetic urban planning.

While offering certificates on the Bible institute model helped to recruit hundreds of students, Villafañe had to work closely with administration in Hamilton to develop a degree. In 1980, a master of religion degree was established at CUME. Villafañe worked closely with President Robert E. Colley and Academic Dean Garth M. Rosell. "Wise, courageous and compassionate, Garth Rosell is a Spirit-filled man who had my back with Boston and the administration of the Seminary. Garth was also one of our most generous and steady donors through the years because he understood our evangelistic mission in the city," said Villafañe.[45] While Gordon-Conwell granted CUME's degree, Villafañe and his team were given freedom when it came to the curriculum.

Using an action-reflection model of contextual education, the CUME curriculum began with the *hermeneutical advantage of the poor*: "CUME is committed to empower the 'Poor.' The program is primarily directed to those who have been denied access by traditional seminaries to theological training largely because of social-economic reasons."[46] With tuition rising and the economy working against them, poor people of color struggled with finding an accessible and affordable theological education. Riding the wave of the Quiet Revival in Boston, CUME grew quickly to become a shining example of urban contextual theological education.

In September 1983, Efraín Agosto became the assistant director for administration at the Center for Urban Ministerial Education. The year 1983 was paradigmatic within the evangelical movement because it was the year that evangelicals decided that mission entailed evangelism *and* social transformation. The International Congress on

---

[45]Phone interview with Eldin Villafañe, conducted by Peter Goodwin Heltzel, December 3, 2018.
[46]Center for Urban Ministerial Education: Uniqueness of CUME, June 10, 1986, *The Center for Urban Ministerial Education: An Evaluation 1986–87* (Contextualized Urban Education), Gordon-Conwell Theological Seminary, 56.

World Evangelization was held at Lausanne, Switzerland, July 16–25, 1974. There was a diverse group of evangelicals from around the world, including 2,474 participants from 150 countries (50 percent from the majority world). Argentinian René C. Padilla, Peruvian theologian Samuel Escobar, and members of the evangelical group Latin American Theological Fellowship persuaded North Atlantic evangelicals to see evangelism and justice as part of one integral mission (misión integral).[47]

While evangelism and social concern were affirmed at Lausanne, their relationship was not clarified. Historian Darren Dochuk argues that there was a "Latin turn" in American evangelicalism at Lausanne 1974.[48] Evangelicals were trying to determine the relationship between evangelism and social action. At Wheaton College in 1983, the problem was solved. The Wheaton 1983 statement argued, "The mission of the church includes both the proclamation of the Gospel and its demonstration. We must therefore evangelize, respond to immediate human needs, and press for social transformation" (paragraph 26).[49] Also in 1983, Howard Snyder wrote Liberating the Church, the first evangelical liberationist ecclesiology, calling the evangelical church to follow Jesus on the journey toward justice.[50]

Completing his MDiv at Gordon-Conwell in 1982, Agosto spent a middler urban year working with Stephen Mott, chair of the Urban Year Committee. In 1985 Agosto began his PhD studies in New Testament at Boston University, exploring the apostle Paul's use of

---

[47]See Alexia Salvatierra's chapter "Justicia Familiar" in this volume for a fuller discussion of misión integral. René C. Padilla, Mission Between the Times: Essays on the Kingdom, rev. ed. (Carlisle, UK: Langham Monographs, 2010 [1985]); Samuel Escobar, "Evangelism and Man's Search for Freedom: Justice and Fulfillment," in Let the Earth Hear His Voice, ed. J. D. Douglas (Minneapolis: World Wide Publications, 1975).

[48]Darren Dochuk, "Lausanne '74 and American Evangelicalism's Latin Turn," in Turning Points in the History of American Evangelicalism, ed. Heath W. Carter and Laura Rominger Porter (Grand Rapids: Eerdmans, 2017), 247-81. See Al Tizon's discussion of the transformation of evangelical missiology after Lausanne 1974 in Transformation After Lausanne: Radical Evangelical Mission in Global-Local Perspective (Eugene, OR: Wipf and Stock, 2008).

[49]René C. Padilla, "Evangelism and Social Responsibility: From Wheaton '66 to Wheaton '83," Transformation 2 (1985): 27-33.

[50]Howard Snyder, Liberating the Church (Downers Grove, IL: InterVarsity Press, 1983).

Greco-Roman conventions of commendation as he planted churches and developed missional teams around Greece and Asia Minor. In 1987 Agosto became the associate director of CUME, being mentored by Villafañe in many roles and duties as a seminary administrator.

From 1990 to 1995, Agosto would serve as the director of the Center and adjunct instructor of New Testament at Gordon-Conwell Theological Seminary. Agosto and Villafañe worked collaboratively to expand CUME's course offerings and establish many new degrees, including a nonresidential MDiv. Ira Frazier designed a mentoring ministry program in 1989 that started during Agosto's tenure. A new MA in Christian education (MACE) replaced the earlier master of religious education (MRE) degree. Seeking to approach Christian education in the urban context, the MACE was reconfigured as the MA in urban ministry (MAUM), CUME's signature degree. Through the passionate and persistent leadership of Dean Borgman, a MA in youth ministry (MAYM) was established in 1995. During Agosto's directorship (1994–1995), the CUME director title became dean in 1994 because President Robert Cooley wanted CUME to be the urban campus of Gordon-Conwell, and the director should be campus dean. Seeing the amazing success at CUME, Hartford Seminary called Agosto and offered him a tenure-track teaching job in New Testament Studies and the opportunity to direct their Hispanic Ministries Program.

With his Spirit-led, strategic, and rock-steady leadership, Agosto expanded the academic programs of CUME, encouraged faculty publication, and began theological education for the deaf (TED). Lorraine C. Anderson, coordinator of Student Advisement and Academic Services, began teaching courses in American Sign Language at CUME, liberating persons with disabilities. Disability theology is the practice of reflection on the embodied experience of disability, or embodied difference. With the rise of the international disability rights movement, largely predicated on the social model of disability (disability as a social construction) in the past century, disability and impairment have become essential terms to begin to outline claims for justice in this movement. CUME branched out in order to liberate people oppressed in all kinds of different ways, maturing a strong and vibrant seminary in the city.

Phase two: CUME's global expansion.

The second phase of global expansion at CUME was from 1997 to 2019. While CUME had always offered courses to African American and Latinx students in Boston, Alvin Padilla expanded the outreach of CUME globally, offering courses and degrees to students in the Caribbean, Africa, Asia, Latin America, and the Pacific Islands. Attentive to the explosive growth of Christianity in the majority world, Aída Besançon Spencer and William David Spencer gathered a group of evangelical theologians to think about God, given the movement of the liberating Spirit in the world Christian movement.[51]

Alvin Padilla was also instrumental in the acquisition of the current facilities in Boston, which was a monumental accomplishment. When some administrators and trustees wanted to sell the CUME building at South Huntington Avenue, Padilla fought the good fight to keep it open by raising money. Padilla also entered into a partnership with the Church of God of Prophecy, working alongside Hector Ortiz to offer master degree–level courses for that denomination in different parts of the world. This partnership was the spark that gave Gordon-Conwell's Hispanic Ministries Program its current structure.

Padilla focused on leadership development during his tenure as the dean of CUME. Working with Dean Borgman and Ana Reid, the Youth Resource Center research assistant at CUME (1997–1998), Padilla offered resources and leadership to the Urban Youth Street-workers Program. Committed to building a new generation of evangelical leaders of deep faith and moral courage, Padilla developed young leaders like Juan C. Morales, who Padilla recruited as an office

---

[51]Aida Besancon Spencer and William David Spencer, eds. *The Global God: Multicultural Evangelical Views of God* (Grand Rapids: Baker, 1998).

manager in 1997. Graduating with his master of arts in urban ministry from CUME in 2001, Morales went on to serve as the assistant registrar of the Boston Campus and assistant director of the Hispanic Ministries Program. Padilla developed a doctor of ministry track in Spanish, called Liderazgo Cristiano (Christian leadership), for Gordon-Conwell. Wanting to develop a postcolonial historiography at CUME, Padilla recruited David A. Currie to teach world Christianity by comparing Western Christianity to Asian Christianity, with a special focus on Christianity in China.

Padilla's administrative leadership at CUME was Spirit led and Christ centered with a heart for global mission. While it serves the African and African American communities (in English) with renewed zeal, CUME has continued to offer courses for Latinx students (in Spanish), Haitian (in French-based Haitian Creole), and in Brazilian Portuguese. Padilla demonstrated the same passion after leaving CUME to lead the Hispanic Ministries Program at Gordon-Conwell (2010–2016).

In addition to the Center for Urban Ministerial Education's ongoing vigorous theological education efforts in Boston, CUME has developed one and inspired another vibrant expression of intercultural theology of liberation at Gordon-Conwell: the Hispanic Ministries Program and the Institute for the Study of the Black Christian Experience, which are offering new educational avenues for liberative intercultural theological education where students can become prophetic leaders who are formed and filled by the Holy Spirit to fulfill their deepest callings. When evangelicals of color and antiracist white evangelicals begin to collaborate in the Holy Spirit, we have the possibility of deep reconciliation so we can begin the reparative work that will lead to a more healthy and whole evangelical church and world.

THE HISPANIC MINISTRIES PROGRAM AT GORDON-CONWELL THEOLOGICAL SEMINARY

The majority of evangelicals in the United States will soon be Latinx. The Latinx community is projected to be 130 million by 2040. Yet in 2009, in the Association of Theological Schools only 4 percent of seminary students were Latinx. Building on the prophetic legacy of Spirit-led urban ministry at CUME, Gordon-Conwell Theological Seminary continued to serve the Spanish speaking church by developing a specific Hispanic Ministries Program at Gordon-Conwell (Programa de Ministerios Hispanos del Seminario Teológico Gordon-Conwell) under the leadership of Alvin Padilla (2010–2016).

In January 2017, Pablo A. Jiménez was called to serve as associate dean for the Hispanic Ministries Program in Massachusetts, North Carolina, Florida, South Texas, and Puerto Rico. "By the end of this century, the majority of evangelicals in America will be of Hispanic descent. So Gordon-Conwell is not investing just in the Hispanic community, Gordon-Conwell is investing in the future of American Evangelicalism," said Samuel Rodriguez, president of the National Hispanic Leadership Conference, as Gordon-Conwell launched its new Hispanic Ministries program in 2010.[52]

Led by the Spirit, Puerto Rican Pentecostalism points to a prophetic intercultural future for the world Christian movement. Villafañe, Agosto, Padilla, and Jiménez sought a third way through their triple consciousness as Puerto Ricans (Spanish, African, and Latinx). "Of all Hispanics, the Puerto Rican American is perhaps the most representative of *mestizaje* in the U.S.A. The *mestizaje* of Puerto Ricans is threefold: Spaniard, Amerindian, and African," writes Villafañe.[53] Latinx Christians have a hybrid identity. They exist in a liminal space between several worlds, Spanish and English, white, brown, and indigenous. Given the divides between conservatives and liberals, peoples of color and whites, Latinx Christians can provide a hybrid dialogical model for reconciling some of our differences. Triple consciousness provides a theoretical and theological path to break

---

[52]Lisa Wangsness, "Seminary Launches Program for Hispanic Ministers: Offers Program for Growing Group," *Boston Sunday Globe*, September 12, 2010, Metro B5, continued from page B1.
[53]Villafañe, *Liberating Spirit*, 58.

the black-white, conservative-liberal binary that continues to plague the evangelical movement.

To be Puerto Rican in Boston is to inhabit a liminal space between black and white, between the island and the mainland. Describing the prophetic possibility of Latinx Christian leaders, Juan Martínez writes, "They have a clear sense of being part of a minoritized community, these leaders will naturally develop a *polycentric identity*. They will implicitly know how to deal with people of different cultures and will tend to have good intercultural skills, learned through life experience."[54] As transnationals, Puerto Ricans in the United States often move back and forth between two or three places that nurture their "polycentric identity" in different ways.[55]

The rising strength of the Latinx community could cause a rift and divisive posture with African Americans. In the third millennium, we cannot afford repeating this form of systemic racism, as the white establishment has strategically used a divide-and-conquer strategy among people of color for decades.

THE INSTITUTE FOR THE STUDY OF THE BLACK CHRISTIAN EXPERIENCE

In the fall of 2016, the Institute for the Study of the Black Christian Experience (ISBCE) was launched at Gordon-Conwell by Patrick T. Smith and Emmett G. Price III, with Price serving as the founding executive director.[56] A CUME graduate and former student of Villafañe, Price envisioned a new postcolonial historiography of the world Christian movement, offering an important trajectory for the practice

---

[54] Juan Francisco Martinez, *The Story of Latino Protestants in the United States* (Grand Rapids: Eerdmans, 2014), 214-15. Emphasis is ours.

[55] On transnational identity, see Linda Basch, Nina Glick Schiller, and Christina Szanton, *Nations Unbound: Transnational Projects, Postcolonial Predicaments, and Deterritorialized Nation-States* (New York: Gordon and Breach, 1994).

[56] African American theologian and ethicist Patrick T. Smith taught philosophical theology and ethics at Gordon-Conwell 2008–2018. When he was installed as assistant professor of theology and philosophy, Smith delivered a lecture in 2008 titled, "Some Ministerial Musings of an Aspiring Christian Philosopher," *Africanus Journal* 2 (2010): 5-12.

of prophetic intercultural evangelical ministry and mission today. The growth of the world Christian movement has shifted dramatically to the Global South.

"Over the last 1,000 years, Europe had more Christians than any other continent. By 2018 Africa had the most Christians: 599 million, vs. 597 million in Latin America, and 550 million in Europe," write Johnson, Zurlo, Hickman, and Crossing.[57] These data points challenge us to be more cognizant of the changing demographics of global Christianity. One of the ways that white Western evangelicals can be more self-critical is to begin to question their own paternalistic tendency when relating to leaders of color. Since African Christians are courageous leaders and will increasingly be leaders in theological education, it is vitally important that we nurture Christian leaders in America who understand the historical and theological contributions of Africans and the African diaspora to the world Christian movement.[58]

Focused on the global black Christian experience, the ISBCE traces the migration of Afro-diasporic Christianity from the Bible through the middle passage into the twenty-first century. "The word *Diaspora* refers to the dispersion of peoples from their traditional homelands, and was used as early as 1964 to address the experiences of the Jewish Diaspora. In the 1960s, scholars and activists began referring to the African Diaspora to describe the numerous African-derived cultures and communities around the globe that now exist outside the continent and their varied interrelationships with each other."[59] Through

---

[57]Todd M. Johnson, Gina A. Zurlo, Albert W. Hickman, and Peter F. Crossing (Center for the Study of Global Christianity, Gordon-Conwell Theological Seminary), "Christianity 2018: More African Christians and Counting Martyrs," *International Bulletin of Mission Research* 43 (2018): 20.

[58]For some thoughtful volumes on the history of the African diaspora in the Black Atlantic, see Justo L. Gonzalez and Ondina E. Gonzalez, *Christianity in Latin America: A History* (New York: Cambridge University Press, 2007); Armando Lampe, ed., *Christianity in the Caribbean: Essays on Church History* (Kingston, Jamaica: University of the West Indies Press, 2000); and Lamin Sanneh, *West African Christianity: The Religious Impact* (Maryknoll, NY: Orbis Books, 1996).

[59]"National Museum of African American History and Culture: A Peoples Journey, A Nation's Story." Opened in September 2016, the National Museum of African American History and

the transatlantic slave trade, Africans were bought and sold as commodities, producing great profits in Europe and in the Americas. "The first Africans arrived in Boston in February of 1638. They were brought as slaves, having been purchased at Providence Isle, a Puritan colony off of the coast of Central America. By 1705, there were over 400 slaves in Boston as well as the beginnings of a free black community, which settled on Beacon Hill and in the North End," writes Garth M. Rosell.[60] Shortly after General George Washington and the colonial militias were victorious in the American War of Independence, there was an influx of enslaved West Africans. As the slave population in Boston began to grow, so did faith-rooted opposition against slavery. For example, in 1832 ardent abolitionist William Lloyd Garrison founded the New England Anti-Slavery Society in the African Meeting House (1806), the oldest black church building in the United States.[61] With time, brave activists like Garrison, Charles Finney, Jonathan Blanchard, and William Wilberforce were able to successfully abolish the slave trade. From slavery to liberation, centering the black narrative is a game changer in evangelical theological education.

Guided by the desire to share with the global church the powerful testimony, rich heritage, and dynamic distinctives of the collective (diasporic) black Christian experience, the ISBCE has a deep commitment to engage in the theological formation of seminarians, pastors, and faith-rooted organizers; encourage and support research and scholarship by ISBCE faculty, scholars, and fellows; stimulate interactive dialogue locally, regionally, nationally, and internationally; and offer educational opportunities through lectures, forums, and symposia. Active on all four Gordon-Conwell campuses through course offerings, digital gatherings, research opportunities, and a

Culture serves as a place for all people to explore the African American experience through an African American lens. *National Museum of African American History and Culture: Official Guide to the Smithsonian* (Washington DC: Smithsonian Institute, 2016).

[60]Garth M. Rosell, *Exploring New England's Spiritual Heritage* (South Hamilton, MA: Gordon-Conwell Theological Seminary, 2013), 8.

[61]Rosell, *Exploring*, 8.

doctoral track, the ISBCE is reviving a concerted effort to not only recruit, retain, and matriculate black seminarians but also students who are not black, yet committed to the study of the black Christian experience as well as race relations and racial reconciliation.

Historian Prathia Hall defines the black church as "the institution that has most consistently and effectively mediated the struggles of African American people for survival and freedom."[62] Drawing from the deepest wells of their faith, black Christians have found the black church to be a site of survival amid a white supremacist regime that seeks to oppress them. While learning from and drawing wisdom from black church studies, ISBCE has strategically chosen a broader framing of black Christian experience in order to investigate the lived theology of black folks in the world Christian movement, as we seek "to advance Christ's Kingdom in every sphere of life by equipping Church leaders to think theologically, engage globally and live biblically."[63]

From John Wesley to Jonathan Edwards, Protestants have always emphasized the importance of Christian spiritual experience as we seek to follow Jesus Christ on the path of discipleship. Yet white evangelical theologians, historians, and ethicists have not always considered the black spiritual experience. "A crucial consequence of the inbreaking of the age to come is the giving of a new, deeper, richer experience of the Holy Spirit to the people of God," writes John Jefferson Davis.[64] When read through Davis's work, our experience of the Holy Spirit through contemplative activity becomes the basis for faith-rooted activism in the world. By focusing its research on the black Christian experience, the ISBCE unveils the prophetic

---

[62]Prathia Hall, "The African American Church at the Crossroad: Facing the Moral Challenge of Gender," 1. This unpublished essay was shared with Peter Goodwin Heltzel when he served as a teaching assistant in Dr. Hall's seminar, The African American Religious Experience, during the fall of 2000 at Boston University School of Theology. For a brief introduction to the history of the black church in the United States, see Albert J. Raboteau, *Canaan Land: A Religious History of African Americans* (Oxford: Oxford University Press, 2009).

[63]Gordon-Conwell Theological Seminary vision statement, www.gordonconwell.edu/about /Mission-and-Purpose.cfm.

[64]John Jefferson Davis, *Meditation and Communion with God: Contemplating Scripture in an Age of Distraction* (Downers Grove, IL: InterVarsity Press, 2012), 37.

legacy and eschatological possibility of African Christianity as a source of renewal.

One of the unique approaches to teaching, research, and scholarship used within the institute is a contextualized model borrowing heavily from the field of ethnomusicology. Price argues that music was one of the principle ways that black Christians have theologized in North America. For a people who were stolen, enslaved, and considered property, making music was one way they could worship our God, crying out for love and liberation. Richard Lints argues that the slave spiritual incorporates "both direct biblical themes (often recounting narratives of salvation history) and an emphasis on personal experience."[65] From the slave songs to the spirituals to gospel music, black Christians hold the biblical vision together with the quest for liberation.

Known as the "Prince of Preachers," Methodist minister and gospel music composer Charles Albert Tindley was a widely influential black pastor in Philadelphia. He was noted for his influence on all sides of town, as well as in the areas of commerce and politics. He was most known, though, for his fluidity between the preached word and the sung word. "Tindley's alignment to the systematic theology of the United Methodist Church is reflected in both song and sermon. It allowed him to effectively transition back and forth between the two mediums, particularly in those moments when he 'sang the sermon.'"[66] Tindley's singing preaching gives us an example of crosscultural contextual homiletics.

Price analyzes Charles Albert Tindley's hymn "Stand by Me" to illustrate the double meaning inherent in black Christian music. Tindley composed this hymn during the Progressive Era. "Known for its prolific muckrakers, Jim and Jane Crow laws, and daunting Philadelphian political machine, this was no age for the weak at heart.

---

[65]Richard Lints, *The Fabric of Theology: A Prolegomena to Evangelical Theology* (Grand Rapids: Eerdmans, 1993), 47, 48.

[66]Emmett G. Price III, "Singing the Sermon: Where Musicology Meets Homiletics," *Yale Journal of Music & Religion* 1 (2015): 65.

The persecution Tindley encountered was not mere spiritual warfare, but the maiming of the body by systemic oppression in many forms. His summoning the God of Paul and Silas still rings forth a century later, as the hymn speaks poignantly to the concerns of the Black Lives Matter and Me Too movements," writes Price.[67]

> When my foes in battle array
>
> Undertake to stop my way,
>
> Thou Who saved Paul and Silas,
>
> Stand by me (stand by me).

While Paul and Silas were stuck in jail, they sang and praised the Lord, and the walls started to shake, the prison cell bars broke, and the prisoners were set free (Acts 16:25-34). While everyone was on the run, the prison guard woke up and drew his sword to commit suicide. Paul rebuked him and told him, "God loves you." Then the prison guard asked Paul, "What must I do to be saved?" When we are under attack by the powers and principalities, God will "stand by me [us]" until the end.

Viewing the black Christian experience as a struggle for liberation opens up a new vantage point for viewing the world Christian movement. "The theme of liberation expressed in story form is the essence of black religion," writes James H. Cone, the founder of black liberation theology.[68] While its theme is liberation, black music is fundamentally unity music, pulling people together from the trans-formative depths of the black soul in America.

> Black music is *unity music*. It unites the joy and the sorrow, the love and the hate, the hope and the despair of black people; and it moves the people toward the direction of total liberation. It shapes and defines black existence and creates cultural structures for black expression. Black music is unifying because it confronts the individual with the

---

[67]Emmett G. Price, III, "Stand by Me," *Image: Art, Faith, Mystery* 96 (n.d.): 26.
[68]James H. Cone, *God of the Oppressed* (New York: Seabury Press, 1975), 61.

truth of black existence and affirms that black being is possible only in a communal context.[69]

Concerned about white theologian's silence on racism, Cone argued that "black religious experience must become one of the important ingredients in the development of Black Theology."[70] Affirming black religious experience as an important source of theology opens up a broader array of resources, including music, to shape evangelical theology in the third millennium.

Holding together the sorrow songs of the slaves and the joyful ecstasy of John Coltrane's anthem *A Love Supreme*, black music as "unity music" expresses a longing for the beloved community, which we can achieve if we only have ears to hear and the courage to make it a reality. Coltrane's *A Love Supreme* is an anthem to liberation love. Price writes,

> Coltrane provides the greatest example of one who used the *spiritual ethos* within black music to bridge and unify the youth and the elders, the poor and wealthy, the religious and the spiritual, the southern and the northern, and numerous other groups that are supposedly disparate. Coltrane's influence expanded far beyond the music known as "jazz" and even further beyond music itself. When chastised by the critics for playing "anti-jazz" or playing angry music, Coltrane always responded that his music was an attempt to fix what he found wrong within society. Musicians from the concert world, the rock world, the folk world, and beyond were enamored by his unique, intense, honest, and sincere sound. Coltrane accomplished what most have not been bold enough to endeavor—to allow spirituality to be present, front and center in his music as its own entity separate from any system of religion. Coltrane knew and proved that spirituality mattered in black music.[71]

---

[69]James H. Cone, *The Spirituals and the Blues* (Maryknoll: Orbis Press, 1991 [1972]), 5.

[70]James H. Cone, "Epilogue: An Interpretation of the Debate Among Black Theologians," in *Black Theology: A Documentary History, 1966–1979*, ed. Gayraud S. Wilmore and James H. Cone (Maryknoll, NY: Orbis Books, 1979), 618; see also Preston Williams, "The Black Experience and Black Religion," *Theology Today* 26 (1969): 246-61.

[71]Emmett G. Price III, *John Coltrane & Black America's Quest for Freedom: Spirituality and the Music* (New York: Oxford University Press, 2010), 171.

Just as the Hebrew prophet Joel promised that the Holy Spirit would fall on "all flesh," as it did on Pentecost, Coltrane's *A Love Supreme* offered spiritual witness to God's unswerving and unrelenting covenantal love. Drawing on "the spiritual ethos within black music," Coltrane's musical vision is crystalized in the album, a prayerful cry to everyone to lean in to love. Coltrane and the band chant, "A love supreme . . . a love supreme . . . a love supreme," and were inspired to hope for a better tomorrow, across the lines of race, religion, class, age, ableism, gender, and nationality.[72]

The lens of *A Love Supreme* illuminates the black Christian experience, working synergistically with the Latinx Christian experience. "If Christian preaching is indeed the theological interpretation of life, the aim of Hispanic preaching must then be the theological interpretation of Latino and Latina experience," write Justo L. González and Pablo A. Jiménez.[73] As we preach the big idea of the biblical text in Christ-centered preaching, the preacher is also offering a theological interpretation of cultural experience. For the Hispanic theologian, preaching includes the "theological interpretation of Latino and Latina experience."

When we view the black Christian experience through the African diaspora, we begin to witness the black encounter with brown folks in the origins of jazz music. Eldin Villafañe also entered in dialogue with musical improvisation in two seminal articles. First, in "Hispanic and African-American Racial Reconciliation: A 'Latin Jazz' Note,"[74] Villafañe suggests that a "jazz-approach" to evangelical theology that includes an ethic of improvisation provides an important pathway ahead for liberative theology and practice. Second, in Villafañe's article "Salsa Christianity: Reflections on the Latino Church in the Barrio," he finds a point of contact between this musical genre and the Latino church,

---

[72]See Peter Goodwin Heltzel's theological analysis in "A Love Supreme," *Resurrection City*, 145-71.

[73]Justo L. González and Pablo A. Jiménez, *Púlpito: An Introduction to Hispanic Preaching* (Nashville: Abingdon Press, 2005), 13, 14.

[74]Villafañe, *Seek the Peace*, 57-63.

representing a mixture of traditions from different ethnic groups.[75] A jazz-inflected theology of migratory mission is an inspiring trajectory for evangelicalism's prophetic, intercultural, gender-just future.

It is in the music where we see the common cultural roots in the Afro-Latinx matrix. A jazz approach to liberation offers an *improvisational possibility* of a strong cultural and political coalition forged between the Latinx community and the African American community.[76] "Improvisation is innovation through collaboration."[77] When we have the courage to collaborate across the lines of race, we open the space of grace for the Spirit to liberate us, so we can all go forth and fulfill our prophetic missions in Christ Jesus in the power of the Holy Spirit. A fusion of black, brown, and antiracist white movements for racial reconciliation, justice, and peace is motivated by love for God and all God's children, pointing to a prophetic, intercultural future for Christianity in our age of global cities.

GRATITUDE FOR THE KEEPERS OF THE VISION, HOPEFUL ABOUT THE FUTURE

In 2019, we give thanks to our God for these fifty years of blessing at Gordon-Conwell Theological Seminary since the merger of Conwell School of Theology and Gordon Divinity School in 1969. As we reflect on the past five decades, we celebrate the contributions to theological education that the Center for Urban Theological Education (GCTS Boston) has made throughout the years. Contextualized Urban Theological Education is a prophetic paradigm for theological education in our age of global cities.

---

[75]Eldin Villafañe, "Salsa Christianity: Reflections on the Latino Church in the Barrio," in *A Prayer for the City: Further Reflections on Urban Ministry* (Austin: Asociación para la Educación Teológica Hispana, 2001), 35-51. This chapter is based on Villafañe's keynote address at an Urban Ministry Symposium at Harvard Divinity School, Cambridge, Massachusets, on October 15, 1998.

[76]Eldin Villafañe, "Hispanic and African-American Racial Reconciliation: A 'Latin Jazz' Note," in *Seek the Peace of the City*, 57-63.

[77]Peter Goodwin Heltzel, *Revolutionary Spirit: Introduction to Constructive Theology* (Grand Rapids: Eerdmans, forthcoming).

The story of CUME at Gordon-Conwell is best understood as a story of the liberating Spirit. CUME is the fruit. Eldin Villafañe's prophetic vision, and core group of courageous leaders included the following: Michael E. Haynes, senior pastor of Twelfth Baptist Church; Harold John Ockenga, first president of Gordon-Conwell Theological Seminary; Efraín Agosto, the second dean of CUME; Alvin Padilla, the third dean of CUME; Douglas Hall, president of Emmanuel Gospel Center; Mark G. Harden, the fourth dean of CUME; Seong Hyun Park, the fifth dean of CUME; Stephen Charles Mott, Emeritus Professor of Social Ethics; Dean Borgman, Emeritus Charles E. Culpeper Professor of Youth Ministry; and many others. We stand on the shoulders of these keepers of the fire.

We celebrate these keepers of the CUME vision, for without them, we would have never seen the possibility of living into Jesus' charge that we "will do even greater things than these" (Jn 14:12). By looking at the past, we can gain a better understanding of the origins of the evangelical theology of liberation, but we are also realistic about resistance to the vision of "seeking the *shalom* of the city," both inside and outside the evangelical movement. Since "God is love" (1 Jn 4:8), we call on fellow Spirit-led, Christ-centered liberationists to join us in the journey toward God's *shalom*. Will you join us?

CHAPTER ELEVEN

TOWARD AN INDIAN LIBERATION THEOLOGY FOR THE *SHUDRA* AND DALIT

RAJKUMAR BOAZ JOHNSON

QUEST FOR MEANING

My search for the meaning of life began quite early. I was not raised in the lap of luxury. I grew up in one of the slums of New Delhi and saw poverty and excrement all around me. High-caste Hindus took poor outcastes into slavery: sexual slavery, carpet industry slavery, and so forth. To escape this reality, my parents sent me to a Hindu grammar school, far removed from the slum. At this school, I was trained in Sanskrit and the monistic Hindu texts of the Upanishads. I learned the skills of *jnana marga*, the "way of Hindu Gnostic Knowledge." (A kindergarten version of it may be seen in yoga classes popular today in the West).

When I walked to this school from the slum, I faced a dilemma—I encountered two different realities. One was the reality of poverty and injustice among my low caste (*Shudra*) and outcaste (Dalit) neighbors and friends. The other was the reality of high-caste Hindu learning. At school, when I asked the question, "How do these realities come together?," my gurus told me that the greatest goal of learning was the realization that life is *shunyata*, nothingness, and the "apparent life" was an illusion, *maya*. On the one hand, I was learning the reality of sciences and literature, yet on the other hand, in my *jnana marga* classes, I was taught that life was *maya*, an illusion. *If humanity and the universe were nothing,* shunyata, *then what is reality?* I asked myself. The question took on another dimension when I related it to the inhumanity and suffering I saw when I returned home daily. I was told by my guru that human beings, who were living a life in this realm of *maya,* must suffer the consequences of their karma. My questions took another shape: Should I then just overlook all that I was learning, in the arts and the sciences, because people will suffer the consequences of their karma anyway? Was the goal of life, then, just to enable the high-caste "haves" to enjoy the results of learning, while outcaste "have-nots" must suffer the consequences of their karma? These were among the plethora of questions that formed my quest for answers to the question of the meaning of life and learning.

In my quest for answers, I went to Ramakrishna Ashram, the institution established by Swami Vivekananda, the guru who brought Hinduism to the United States during the Chicago World Fair in 1893. Yet, the Upanishadic answers left me quite dissatisfied. I began a deep search for answers in different world religions—Buddhism, Sikhism, Islam, and so on. These centers of worship and learning were all around me. Eventually, I encountered the writings of Pandita Ramabai, a high-caste Hindu woman, who died in 1922. Before she died, she had done amazing things in India. She had rescued temple prostitutes. She had rescued young girls who were forced into prostitution in the harems of Bombay. She had rescued young widows who were treated as untouchables in society. She also rescued little female infants who were about to be killed. "These were not human beings who were merely suffering the consequences of their karma," she surmised. I found out that she had done all this, after she had dramatically encountered the Jesus of John 4, who transformed the life of the outcaste Samaritan woman and her whole community. This same Jesus had transformed the lives of many other outcaste men, women, and children.

QUEST FOR THEOLOGY

In my twenties, I began studying at a seminary in India to formulate a theology for ministry in India. However, I realized quickly that Indian Christian theology was not meant for 80 percent of Indians, who are low caste and outcaste. Two philosophical frameworks have dominated the development of Indian Christian theologies. First, there was the colonial framework, espoused by those theologians who are trained in Western methodology. This still is the majority paradigm in both mainline and evangelically oriented seminaries. Second, there is the Brahmanical framework, which is espoused by a powerful group of theologians who came from the dominant priestly caste of Hindu society. These two are the frameworks of most models of Indian biblical interpretation and Christian theology. This is the case, although more than 90 percent of the people come from low-caste or outcaste backgrounds, such as *Shudra* and *Atishudra* families. Just 10 percent of the church comes from high-caste families. Yet the interpretive and theological framework of the church is led by the minority group of high-caste leaders and theologians. In more recent times, the lowest rung of society, the *Atishudras*, or the untouchables, have taken the lead from what is going on in Indian society, at large, and have come up with Dalit interpretive thought and Dalit theology.

DALIT THEOLOGIES

The Dalits are the untouchables of India, *Atishudras*. The Hindu Brahmanical texts define these people as lower than human beings. Dalit intellectuals have realized that the consciousness of their people was shaped by Vedic and puranic myths, which served the interests of the dominant castes and classes. A consciousness based on ancient history had to be formed to strengthen a Dalit existential identity.

Dalit theologies began emerging in the 1980s and the 1990s. They expressed discontinuity with traditional Indian Christian theologies, which have mainly been articulated by upper-caste theologians. Arvind Nirmal, one of the pioneers of Dalit theologies, expresses it best. He suggests that the core of Dalit theology will be formed from the existential experience of the Dalits: "It will be produced on their own Dalit experiences, their own sufferings, their own aspirations, their own hopes. It will narrate the story of their pathos and their socio-economic injustices they have been subjected to throughout their history. . . . This also will mean that a Christian Dalit theology will be a counter theology."[1]

Maria Arul Raja, another prominent Dalit theologian, claims that Dalit theology must take as its basis "the wretched condition violently imposed on the Dalits [that] forces them to seek an immediate apocalyptic intervention from the unseen God." This desire for an "apocalyptic intervention" must form the basis of Dalit theology. "The method of the Dalit reading of the Bible is oriented towards concrete historical commitment transforming the present reality into a new liberative one."[2] The method of interpretation is oriented to liberation and praxis.

It becomes clear that Dalit biblical interpretation and Dalit theology are refreshing new developments in Indian society. Unfortunately, these liberation theologies, while pointing out the issues of oppressions against the Dalits, have not been very successful in proposing fresh theologies. There remains a quest for a movement toward coming up with genuine interpretive methods and theologies that arise from the stories and the narratives of the Dalit people.

SHUDRA THEOLOGIES

Over the centuries, there have arisen low-caste, or *Shudra*, leaders who have spoken up against the colonial nature of Hinduism and the enslaving nature of high-caste Hinduism. These include the fourteenth-century Namdev (1270–1350); fifteenth-century liberationists like Kabir (1398–1448) and Ravidas (ca. 1450–1520); seventeenth-century

---

[1]Arvind Nirmal, "Towards a Christian Dalit Theology," in *A Reader in Dalit Theology* (Madras: Gurukul, 1990), 59.

[2]Maria Arul Rajah, "Towards a Dalit Reading of the Bible: Some Hermeneutical Reflections," *Jeevadhara* 26 (1996): 31.

liberationists like Tukaram (1608–1649); nineteenth-century liberationists like Jotirao Phule (1827–1890); and twentieth-century liberationists like B. R. Ambedkar (1891–1956) and Periyar E.V. Ramasamy (1879–1973). I will not be able to cover all these *Shudra* and Dalit (Ambedkar) liberationists. That will require a book-length work. I will focus on two thinkers: a fifteenth-century reformer, Kabir, and a woman liberationist of the late nineteenth and early twentieth centuries, Pandita Ramabai.

KABIR'S LIBERATIVE *SHABAD* (WORD)

Kabir (1398–1448) was a fifteenth-century low-caste reformer.[3] He was raised in the weaver caste. His poems are very popular among the low-caste people. In these poems, Kabir scoffs at the destructive worldview set by the Vedas, the Upanishads, and the Puranas. In several poems, Kabir derides the Aryan Brahmanical scriptures. Following is my translation of some of Kabir's Ramainis. These are the "Essential Encounter Words" (*Shabad)* of the low-caste and outcaste people groups.

Ramaini 30

O brother, you follow the six Darshanas (of Hinduism) and mislead by their hypocrisies. These hypocrisies destroy the meaning of soul and life.

The four Vedas and their clever teachings are nothing but dumb (*mowna*) . . .

Ramaini 31

All that the Smriti legends do is make known three qualities:

The ways of sinfulness and virtue are seen.

The recitation of the Smriti and Vedas only led to disputing.

Ramaini 32

The Vedas and the Puranas are the mirror of the blind.

---

[3]Vinay Dhawadker, *Kabir: The Weaver's Songs*, Penguin Global, 2003, 2-3.

Does the spoon know the flavor the food?

As the donkey laden with sandalwood,

So the fool does not know the sweet fragrance par excellence.

Says Kabir, "They (the Hindus) may search even the heavens, but do not find it because of their pridefulness."

The beginning Ramainis give a clear sense of Kabir's understanding of God. It is very different from the Hindu understanding of God. This is the God of the low-caste (*Shudra*) and the outcaste (Dalit) peoples groups. He is the Word, the *Shabad*.

Kabir conceives the picture of God as being the Uncreated Lord (*Angad Dev*). He contrasts this theology of God with the ten avatars of Hinduism and the hundreds of deities that emerge from these ten avatars. The Uncreated One, the *Shabad*, in Kabir's thought is not an impersonal principle, the *Brahman*, but rather the Love Song (*Rag*). According to Kabir, when one encounters the Love Song, one experiences salvation (*tar*). This *Angad Dev*, the Uncreated Lord, creates the universe by his *Shabad*, his Word. This is quite similar to the biblical image of the creation by the *Memra* of God.

In this poem, Kabir brings the transcendent image of God and the immanent image of God together. God is the Lord of the Universe, the *Jagat Sai*. Yet, he is also the Beloved (*Piyu*). It is interesting to observe that Kabir brings together the biblical idea of the *Memra*, as it is presented in the Torah and the Prophets and the Writings, all together. It is interesting to observe that the ancient Jewish Targums sought to show the transcendence of God and the immanence of God in their use of the concept of the *Memra* of God. Similarly, Kabir shows that the transcendent, *Shabad*, or the Word, is also the immanent, *Piyu*, or the Beloved. This fusion of the transcendent, *Memra*, into the immanent, *Piyu*, in the thought of Kabir is the liberation encounter moment.

Ramaini 4

In the First (*pratham*) the Guru expressed the *Shabad*.

The witness is that he is the Maker Creator (*karta Sirjanhara*)

Karma has led the world astray

Maya has bound the world to the worship of Shakti

He showed them wondrous works, and taught them the *Shabad*, the Word.

Then love arose to him, and he gave the Ramainis (Essential Encounter Words)

The worshipers of *sugun* and *nirgun* (gods of the Hindus) did not understand their true meaning.

But whoever realized them became pure (*nirmal*).

Whoever did not encounter them became like insects.

Sakhi: O wise one, sing with knowledge

O foolish one, you do not know the song

Beginning and end (*Adi Ant*)

Creation and De-creation (*Utpati Parlai*)

He has clearly Worded (*Shabad*).

In Ramaini 6, he explains further the incarnational revelation of this God, as the Purush, the God-Man, and the Sacrificial One, quite similar to Phule's proposal of the sacrificial king, Baliraja.

Ramaini 6

How may I explain his form or outline?

There is no one like him

He is neither Om, nor is he Veda

What may I say of the secret of his being?

He is neither stars, nor sun, nor moon.

He is not born of the sperm of a father.

He is neither waters, nor dry land, nor stillness, nor wind.

Who may name him or command him?

There is no day, no night.

One may say anything about his tribe or caste.

Sakhi: This Consciousness Word arose out of the void;

O brother he was the Light.

That Purush is the BaliHari (the Sacrificial God).

He is the Self-existent one—*the Shabad,* the Word.

The liberative theme of the *Shabad* is seen in several other songs of Kabir. Kabir says, "Listen to the Word, the Truth, which is the liberative essence. He speaks the Word; and he himself is the Creator."[4] This *Shabad* dispels ignorance, which has been the fate of the low-caste and outcaste people. It enables them to fight for themselves.[5] Kabir goes on to urge the low-caste and outcaste to deeply receive this *liberative Word,* from which the universe came into being. This liberative Word is the Guru. It will free them. It is beyond the Hindu texts. However, "from the liberative Word the world was formed. That liberative Word reveals all. Kabir says: 'But, who knows whence the Liberative Word comes.'"[6] This liberative Word is the primal Word, and it is readily available to the lowest of low-caste people.[7]

Kabir gives the low-caste and the outcaste people groups the basis of liberation. For him the only God is the BaliHari, the sacrificial God. This is the God of the low-caste and the outcaste people groups. This self-revelation of God is the creative *Shabad,* the Word of God; it is also the liberative *Shabad.* To the low-caste and outcaste people, this concept of the *Shabad* is a radically transformational and freeing

---

[4]Rabindranath Tagore, trans. *One Hundred Poems of Kabir* (London: Cheswick Press, 1914), song 46, 33.
[5]Tagore, song 49, 35.
[6]Tagore, song 57, 40.
[7]Tagore, song 99, 61.

concept. They no longer need to depend on the high caste Brahmins to do their religious rituals. They no longer need to fear the lack of access to God and religious texts. The liberative Word is itself freely available to them and gives them freedom.

I have traveled to several low-caste and outcaste villages where I have seen this liberative Word. The people sing the *Shabads* of Kabir. They get transformed by the liberative Word and gain an inexplicable freedom from high-caste dominion over them.

PANDITA RAMABAI:
A LIBERATIVE BIBLE TRANSLATION

Pandita Ramabai is a much later, yet similar example of the liberative Word. This time it is the written liberative Word.

In 1989, the Hindu-led government issued a commemorative stamp on the life of a woman named Pandita Ramabai, perhaps the most important model of liberation in India. The official brochure with the stamp reads as follows:

Pandita Ramabai (1858–1920): Pandita Ramabai, the youngest daughter of Anant Shastri, was a social reformer, a champion for the emancipation of women, and a pioneer in education. Left totally alone by the time she was 23, Ramabai acquired a great reputation as a Sanskrit scholar.

Deeply impressed by her prowess, the Sanskrit scholars of Calcutta University conferred on her the titles of "Saraswati" and "Pandita." She rebelled against the caste system and married a shudra advocate, but was widowed at 23, having a baby girl. In 1882, she established the Arya Mahila Samaj for the cause of women's education in Pune and different parts of Western India. This led to the formation of the Sharda Sadan in 1889—which school completes a hundred years this year—a school which blossomed into an umbrella organization called Pandita Ramabai Mukti Mission, 40 miles outside Pune.

In 1896, during a severe famine Ramabai toured the villages of Maharashtra with a caravan of bullock carts and rescued thousands of outcaste children, child widows, orphans, and other destitute women and brought them to the shelter of Mukti and Sharada

Sadan. A learned woman knowing seven languages, she translated the Bible into her mother tongue—Marathi—from the original Hebrew and Greek. Her work continues today, a memorial to her life and path.[8]

Two issues that Ramabai confronted at a very early age in her life were gender bias against women in Hindu society and racial bias against the *Shudras*, the untouchable caste, and the Dalits. These two issues form the background of the development of her biblical theology and her work. She wrote,

> There were two things on which all those books, the Dharma Shastras, the sacred epics, the Puranas . . . were agreed: women of high and low caste, as a class, were bad, very bad, worse than demons, and that they could not get Moksha (salvation) as men. The only hope of their getting this much-desired liberation from Karma and its results, that is, countless millions of births and deaths and untold suffering, was the worship of their husbands. The husband is said to be the woman's god; there is no other god for her. This god may be the worst sinner and a great criminal; still HE IS HER GOD, and she must worship him. She can have no hope of getting admission into Svarga, (heaven), the abode of the gods, without his pleasure; and if she pleases him in all things, she will have the privilege of going to Svarga as his slave, there to serve him and be one of his wives among the thousands of the Svarga harlots who are presented to him by the gods in exchange for his wife's merit. . . . The woman is allowed to go into higher existence thus far but to attain Moksha or liberation, she must perform such great religious acts as will obtain for her the merit by which she will be reincarnated as a high caste man, in order to study Vedas and the Vedanta, and thereby get the knowledge of the true Brahma and be amalgamated in it.[9]

Commenting on the important issue of race and caste, she continued,

---

[8]"Pandita Ramabai," iStampGallery.com, August 29, 2015, www.istampgallery.com/pandita -ramabai/.
[9]Pandita Ramabai, *A Testimony: Of Our Inexhaustible Treasure* (Kedgaon, MA: Mukti, 1907), 6.

The same rules are applicable to the Shudras, the untouchables. The Shudras must not study the Veda and must not perform the same religious act, which a Brahman has a right to perform. The Shudra who hears the Veda repeated must be punished by having his ears filled with liquefied lead. . . . His only hope of getting liberation is in serving the three high castes as their lifelong slave.[10]

In a book titled *The High Caste Hindu Woman*, which she published in 1887, Ramabai makes some very incisive comments about Hinduism and its treatment of women. She realized that as long as Indian women are subjected to the codes of conduct expected of them in the Hindu texts, they will never be free. This began a quest for a text that would become the grounds of female liberation in India. Secularization of the codes of Manu would not cut it. In my opinion this is what fueled her biblical theology. It became the heart of her quest for a biblical theology for the Indian woman.

She wrote in *The High Caste Woman*, "A Brahman of a High clan will marry ten, eleven, twenty. . . . The illustrious Brahman need not bother with the care and support of many wives, for the parents pledge themselves to maintain the daughter all her life."[11] She observed regarding female infanticide,

> Opium is generally used to keep the crying child quiet, and a small pill of this drug is sufficient to accomplish the cruel task; a skillful pressure on the neck, which is known as "putting nail to the throat" answers the purpose. There are several other nameless methods that may be employed in sacrificing the innocents on the unholy altar of the caste and clan system.[12]

Therefore, she deemed it

> of first importance to prepare the way for the spread of the gospel by throwing open the locked doors of Indian *zenanas*, which cannot be

---

[10]Ramabai, *A Testimony*, 7.
[11]Ramabai, *A Testimony*, 13.
[12]Ramabai, *A Testimony*, 14.

done safely without giving suitable education to the women, whereby they will be able to bear the dazzling light of the outer world and the perilous blasts of social persecution . . . millions of heart-rending cries are daily rising from within the stony walls of Indian *zenana*; thousands of child widows are dying annually without a ray of hope to cheer their hearts. . . . Will you not, all who read this book, think of these, my countrywomen, and rise by a common impulse to free them from life- long slavery?[13]

After Ramabai rescued hundreds of girls from sexual, emotional, and physical enslavement of various kinds, she sought to give them a text that would keep them free. The obvious answer to her was the Bible. Yet when she began reading the text of the Marathi Bible—her native language and the language of the girls she rescued—she was horrified to find words and ideas borrowed from high-caste Hinduism. Therefore, in her Bible translation work, Ramabai distanced herself from anything that would enslave women and low-caste or outcaste peoples groups.

A good example is in Ramabai's scorn for the Hindu text *Manush-astra*. She quotes from it, "Though destitute of virtue, or seeking pleasure elsewhere, or devoid of good qualities, yet a husband must be constantly worshipped as a God by a faithful wife. . . . A faithful wife, who desires to dwell after death with her husband, must never do anything that might displease him who took her hand, whether he be dead or alive" (*Manushastra* V, 147-56).[14] The *Code of Vishnu* adds, "A woman after the death of her husband should either lead a virtuous life or ascend the funeral pile of her husband" (*Vishnu* xx.2).[15]

Ramabai sought to avoid terms of divinity that were intended to subject women and the untouchables to a demeaning state. *Ishvar, Parameshvar, Bhav, Bhavsagar, Bhagwan,* and so forth were Brahmanic terms. The theologies of God that emerged from these names

---

[13]Ramabai, *A Testimony*, 118-19.
[14]Ramabai, *A Testimony*, 33.
[15]Ramabai, *A Testimony*, 41.

of the divine were completely out of reach for women and *Shudras*. For this reason Ramabai preferred to transliterate the Hebrew names for God. For example, she considered that the name YHWH, the "one who is, who was, and who is to come," would give women and untouchables a great amount of encouragement and power. This God does not change according to the whims and fancies of the Brahmanical texts that brought women and *Shudras* under the subjection of the Brahmins. This God is a being who elevates the status of the subaltern.

Throughout the Old Testament and the New Testament, Ramabai chose to translate the word *sāmayim* ("heaven") with the word *Akash*. This is the word she used in Genesis 1:1: *Pra-rambhi Devane Akashe Ani Prithvi hi asthithvath anli*. Her translation of Psalm 19:1 reads, *Akashe Devacha mehima vernithath*—"the heavens declare the glory of God." The literal translation of Ramabai's Marathi would be the "skies." This translation is in contrast to other Indian translations that use the word *swarg*. She wrote,

> The word *swarg* denotes the abode of the gods where Indra, the king of the Hindu gods is supposed to reign. The place is described to be full of sensual pleasure, where a man goes to enjoy the pleasure brought by *apavarga*, merit. He is supposed to be fortunate, and lives a life of unmixed pleasure, enjoying the company of hundreds and thousands of celestial harlots called *apsaras*. After all this *karma* is spent, he is cast down to the earth, and is reincarnated in some good high-caste family. Where he has all the chances of re-attaining *swarga* by his *apavarga*. (This is also the state of) *Nirvana*, which is attained by the *jnana*, knowledge of *Brahman, Bhagavad-Gita* 9:20, 21.[16]

It seems clear that Ramabai has again avoided antifeminine terms. The term *swarg* suggests a man-oriented heaven. Women are denigrated to the role of those who ingratiate the sexual desires and needs of men. This was the kind of situation from which she had rescued

---

[16]Ramabai, *A Testimony*, 211.

the temple prostitutes who became an essential part of the Mukti Ashram. These young ladies were taken by high-caste Hindus into the temple precincts, as soon as they got their first menstruation. They were then trained to become temple priestesses, who gave men sexual-spiritual pleasures. This also became the picture of the Hindu *swarga*. Therefore, Ramabai very vigorously sought the disuse of terms like *swarga*. Instead, she sought the simple use of pre-Vedic-oriented vernacular, which simply presented the place of afterlife, heaven, as the place of the presence of God.

The narrative of the creation of woman is a classical text as to who a woman is (Gen 2:18). The English Bible translates it in the following: "The Lord God said . . . I will make a helper suitable for him" (NIV); " . . . helper as his partner" (NRSV); " . . . an help meet for him" (KJV). In many senses this translation has defined the attitude regarding womanhood, in Western as well as Eastern societies. Is a woman merely a suitable helper for men? Or is she something else? Unfortunately, this attitude in the Indian context compounds the attitude against women already present in the Hindu society. The Hindi translation puts this in similar words to the English translations of the Bible: "I will make him a helper who will be suitable for him, *us se mel khaye*." The Hebrew phrase used here is *ezer kenegdo*, "an *ezer* before him." In the third section of the Hebrew Bible, this word is always used to describe God himself: for example, "you are the helper [*ezer*] of the fatherless" (Ps 10:14); "we wait in hope for the Lord; he is our help [*ezer*]" (Ps 33:20).

In this crucial text, Ramabai seeks to underline the strong sense of womanhood portrayed in the Bible. She moves away from the Hindi, Marathi, and English translations. She describes this woman as "a companion in his image, a Creator helper, *misathi tyacha pratiru-pacha sahay nirman karin*." It seems very clear that in describing the creation of the woman in such strong categories, Ramabai captures the strong sense of the Hebrew and conveys it to the Marathi readership. In doing so she gives several generations of the women in

India self-worth, which will keep them from being ensnared into human trafficking. The main liberator in the works of Ramabai is the Word of God, just like in the poetry of Kabir.

LIBERATION MOTIFS IN THE THOUGHTS OF KABIR AND PANDITA RAMABAI

In analyzing the works of low-caste, outcaste, and women reformers like E. V. Ramaswamy, Phule, and especially Kabir and Ramabai, it has become clear to me that there are certain common motifs in their quest for liberation.

Each of them sees the root cause of injustice against the low-caste, outcaste, and especially women, as the polytheism brought into India by the Aryans.

Each of them looks for a messianic figure that predates the colonial rule of the Aryans, who invaded India around 1500 BC. For example, Phule seeks to resurrect the pre-Aryan king Baliraja, the King Bali, as the messianic figure.

Each of them sees the core solution as a concept of the kingdom of God as distinct from the Ramarajya concept or VishnuRajya concept of Aryan Brahmanism. Phule, for instance, seeks to resurrect the concept of Balirajye (kingdom of Bali) of low-caste communities.

Each of them sought to focus on a liberation motif. This liberation motif finds its focus in the concept of the liberation Word. In Kabir, for example, the liberation Word is the *Shabad*. This is the *Shabad* of the *Khalak*, the Word of the Creator God, who is responsible for creation and subsequent acts of liberation.

MEMRA LIBERATION MOMENTS IN THE ARAMAIC TARGUMS, AND IN THE TRANSLATION OF RAMABAI

In the rest of this essay I would like to show how the Aramaic translation of the Old Testament, and the New Testament as well, address the injustices the people of those times faced in the context of the religions of the surrounding people, and how the story of the Bible seeks to liberate people of low classes and women.

I will focus on the theme of the *Memra,* the Word of God in the Aramaic Bible and in the New Testament. This liberation motif, found in Ramabai's translation of the Bible, and most crucially in the *ragas* (liberative poems) of Kabir, forms the central thought of translations of the Aramaic Bible. These translations were done around two hundred years before the time of Jesus and become the basis of the Logos theology of the New Testament.

The book of John begins with the words:

> In the beginning was the Word [Greek: Logos], and the Word was with God, and the Word was God. He was with God in the beginning. Through him all things were made; without him nothing was made that has been made. In him was life, and that life was the light of all mankind. The light shines in the darkness, and the darkness has not overcome it. . . . The Word became flesh and made his dwelling among us. We have seen his glory, the glory of the one and only Son, who came from the Father, full of grace and truth. (Jn 1:1-5, 14)

The Gospel of John is essentially showing that Jesus the Messiah is the liberative Jewish *Memra* of YHWH. Several studies have done a comparative analysis of the Gospel of John and Jewish Targums to show the relationship between the Logos of John and the *Memra of YHWH* of the Targums.[17] I am of the opinion that, just like Kabir and Ramabai, the translators of the Targums saw the motif of the *Memra* as a distinctly liberative motif. Other Indian languages choose to translate the Greek *Logos* with the word *vachan.* This is a weak word. Ramabai, in contrast, chooses to use the strong Kabir term, *Shabad:* "In the beginning was the *Shabad,* the *Shabad* was with God, and the *Shabad*

---

[17]See, e.g., Daniel Boyarin, "The Gospel of the Memra: Jewish Binitarianism and the Prologue to John," *The Harvard Theological Review* 94, No. 3 (July 2001): 243-84; F. McNamara, "Logos of the Fourth Gospel and Memra of the Palestinian Targum (Exo 12:42)," *The Expository Times* (1968): 115-17; L. Sabourin, "The MEMRA of God in the Targums," *Biblical Theology Bulletin* (1976): 79-85; P. Borgen, "Observations on the Targumic Character of the Prologue of John," *New Testament Studies* 16 (1970): 288-95.

was God."[18] This was the liberative Word, which has the power to create and liberatively transform the world.

The book of Genesis in the Aramaic Targum begins like this: "Right at the beginning of the creation of the universe, when the state of the universe seemed to be utterly hopeless, when everything was without form and void, and darkness was over the face of the deep, the *Memra* of the LORD said, 'Let there be light,' and there was light, according to the decree of His *Memra*" (Targum Neofiti, Gen 1:3).[19] The *Memra* of the Lord was not just the creative Word. It is primarily portrayed as the liberative Word. The *Memra* of the Lord was therefore responsible for the liberation of the universe. This same *Memra* of the Lord is portrayed as the source of the rest of creation, and thereafter liberation, when injustice and such happens in history.

This liberation model is espoused in the Gospel of John, which attributed creation to Jesus the Logos, the Word of God. This is indeed the *Shabad*, the Creator-Liberator incarnation of God, as seen in both Kabir and Ramabai.

The next time *Memra* of the Lord breaks through into biblical history is in Genesis 6, when the sons of God see the daughters of men and forcibly take them. Pandita Ramabai sees these sons of God as high-caste human beings who regard themselves as divine beings. They have sexual intercourse with common women as a part of a religious rite. This was quite common in Hindu society, as was true in the ancient Near Eastern religions. Noah's flood, both in the Targums and Ramabai, is seen a divine response to sexually oriented religions that unjustly abused women.

It may be noted that this was a real happening in Ramabai's time. Hindu priests and high-caste men would regularly take low-caste and outcaste girls and force sexual intercourse with them as a religious ritual. These girls were called *devadasis*, which means slaves of the

---

[18]I am using Pandita Ramabai's Marathi translation of the Bible, Mukti Mission Press, Kedgaon, 1924.

[19]All Targum quotations have been translated by the author.

gods. Ramabai rescued hundreds of *devadasis* and gave them refuge in her *Mukti* house, which means house of liberation.

The next crucial time the *Memra* of the Lord breaks through into biblical history in the Targums is in Genesis 18:20: "The outcry against Sodom and Gomorrah is so great and their sin is grievous." The Hebrew word translated as "outcry," *za'aqah*, is always used to describe the cries of help of women who are raped, and the cries of slaves who are abused. In Exodus 2:23, it describes the enslavement and rape of the Hebrew people in Egypt. In Genesis 18 the outcry of or the cries of the pain of people raped comes up before God, and the *Memra* of the Lord comes to liberate them and bring about justice in Sodom and Gomorrah. Pandita Ramabai uses the strong Marathi word *Aroli* to give the sense that God hears the cries of enslaved, persecuted, and raped people in both Genesis 18:20 and Exodus 2:23. The *Word of the Lord*, in both the Targums and the translation of Ramabai, always hears the cries of the enslaved, persecuted, and raped people, and descends to set things right.

On several occasions I have heard these liberated women singing songs and psalms. They weep for joy when they sing these songs of liberation. Whenever I hear them, even today, I weep uncontrollably.

The *Memra* of the LORD appears to non-Hebrew people, as well, and prevents them from doing unjust things. This is the case in Genesis 20, where the *Memra* of the Lord appears to Abimelech the king of Gerar and prevents him from raping Sara, even though Abram her husband had put her in a position to be raped. The Targums make it clear that the *Memra*, the Word of the Lord, does not discriminate between Jews and non-Jews. The liberative *Memra* is nondiscriminatory. He reveals himself to both Jews and non-Jews. Pandita Ramabai describes the character of Abimelech as one who has a "clean heart" (Gen 20:5, 6). In her estimation, this highest character may be bestowed on all human beings and thus become the basis of liberation and peacebuilding in societies across the world.

In Ramabai's liberation thought, she saw it as her goal to liberate the high-caste enslavers as well. She sought to liberate their minds, souls, and actions through the liberative *Shabad*. In her thought this was a crucial aspect of her women's liberation movement.

In Genesis 21, when Sarah unjustly drives her African slave girl and her son out into the wilderness, in the Aramaic Targum it was the *Memra* of the Lord who appeared to her and liberated the lad and then blessed him and all his future generations. Ramabai stresses that liberation happens when the *Shabad* of God intrinsically encounters the *Shabad* of those who are persecuted and unjustly treated. In this case the *Shabad* of God encounters the *Shabad* of the lad. This is a crucial liberative principle: liberation happens when the *Shabad* of the persecuted reaches the *Shabad* of the Lord. The latter *Shabad* then descends to liberate and transform the persecuted.

According to the Targums, this same *Memra*, or Word of the Lord revealed himself to Moses in the burning bush. Targum Neofiti, Exodus 3:4, 8: "The *Memra* of the Lord called to him from the midst of the bush and said, 'Moses, Moses.' And Moses answered in the language of the temple and said, 'Here I am. . . . And I have been revealed in My *Memra* to deliver them from the hand of Egypt.'" The *Memra* of the LORD then says to Moses, "I have indeed seen the pain of My people in Egypt, and I have heard their outcry from their oppression, for their servitude has been revealed before Me. And I have been revealed in My *Memra* to deliver them from the hand of Egypt" (Targum Neofiti 3:7, 8).

"I have surely seen the affliction of my people who are in Egypt and have heard their cry because of their taskmasters. I know their sufferings, and I have come down to deliver them out of the hand of the Egyptians" (Ex 3:7-8). The *Memra* of the Lord, according to the Targums, always sees the pains of the enslaved and persecuted, hears the shrill cries of the raped, and then seeks to liberate them. Both the Targums and Ramabai make it clear that true liberation happens because the liberator *Shabad* himself suffers the deepest forms of suffering endured by sufferers.

Pandita Ramabai translates the angel of the Lord as the divine messenger, the Word of the LORD. In Exodus 3:7-8, she is very careful in choosing strong words in Marathi to describe this liberative God. The Marathi word for "outcry" is a strong word, *aroli*, which describes the shrieking cries of those severely persecuted and the raped. Both the Targums and Ramabai seek to underline that this *Memra* of the Lord is not a distant God. Rather, he suffers with the suffering. Therefore, liberation of the suffering and the persecuted is a deep and thick form of liberation. It is not the thin and superficial liberation that political liberation movements bring about.

These Targum translations make it clear that the *Memra* of the Lord always appears to bring about justice in very unjust and violent situations. Each of the prophets call out to the people to turn from their unjust ways and hear the voice of the *Memra* of the Lord. So Isaiah the prophet cries out, "Return to the Torah. Be cleansed from your sins; remove the evil of your deeds from before My *Memra*; keep yourselves from doing evil" (Targum Onkelos, Is 1:16). Or, "Listen to My *Memra*, O islands, and kingdoms will increase strength. Let them come near, then they may speak as one, "We are brought near for judgment" (Targum Onkelos, Is 41:1). When Jeremiah is reluctant to go out and prophesy, because he was just a lad, and because he is scared of the opposition, the Lord says to him, "They will not overcome you, for My *Memra* is at your help, says the LORD" (Targum Onkelos, Jer 1:9).

In these Memra of the Lord texts, Pandita Ramabai uses words like *dushtpan*, which describes human evil as deep and phenomenological systemic problem. Thus the deep cleansing can only happen by the deep and phenomenological work of the *Shabad*, the Word of the Lord.

The *Memra* of the Lord is also a distinct motif of liberative hope in the prophets. This *Memra*, which calls for justice, will come on the people to provide hope. So, the prophet Jeremiah says, "And it will come about, just as My *Memra* rejoiced over them to uproot and to tear up and to break down and to destroy and to cause harm, so My *Memra* will rejoice over them to build and to establish, says the Lord" (Targum Onkelos, Jer 31:28). This *Memra* will cause a new and just society, a new ethic, a completely transformed world to come into being. Similarly, the prophet Ezekiel proclaims, "For, behold, I will reveal Myself to you, and in My *Memra* I will turn back to bring about good for you, and you will be tilled and sown" (Targum Onkelos, Ezek 36:9). The *Memra* of the Lord will cause a new just society to come into being, where unjust things against the weak, and especially women, will not happen.

The Targums translate the word of the prophets as the *Memra* of the LORD. The Septuagint translates this as the *Logos* of the LORD. Ramabai translates this phrase as *Yehovache Shabad.* Two things may be noted here:

One, while other Indian translations translate YHWH as *Parameshwar*, Ramabai refuses to use this term for YHWH. *Parameshwar* applies to the highest deity of the Vaishnavite sect of high-caste Hinduism. This is the God who enslaves low-caste and outcaste people, and especially women, to slavery. Ramabai chooses to use the term *Yehovah* to describe the liberating God of the Bible.

Two, Ramabai chooses to stay faithful to the biblical idea of the liberating Word of the Lord. This liberation happens through the supernatural *vachan* the decree of the *Yehovah,* and the *Shabad* of the Lord. This is the constant message of the prophets. Liberation does not happen by human will or actions. Rather, liberation happens by the *Yehovache vachan*, the supernatural decree of the Lord and the *Shabad* of the Yehovah.

MEMRA IN THE GOSPEL OF JOHN

The New Testament claims that this *Memra* of the Lord is Jesus the Messiah. He liberates society from a range of injustices pointed out in the Hebrew Bible and especially underlined in the Aramaic translation of the Bible.

The basic thesis of the book of John is that Jesus, the *Memra* of God, is the *Ego Eimi,* the I AM who revealed himself to Moses in the wilderness. This *Memra* of the Lord broke through into liberation moments in history. Now, in a final way, he again breaks through into history as Jesus the Son of David, the Son of Abraham. This Jesus does seven miracles, each of which was a liberation miracle. In the book of John, Jesus proclaims himself to be the Everlasting I AM seven times. Each of these is a liberation moment of the Word of the Lord, and each of the miracles is done to correct a situation of systemic injustice.

In John 2:1-11, Jesus the *Memra* of God turns the water into wine. This was done at the wedding ceremony of a poor couple in Cana of Galilee. The ancient Jewish wedding ceremony consisted of participation in four cups of wine. Of these, the third cup was the most important. Without this third cup of wine, the couple could not have been pronounced as one. This is the basis of liberation from cruel Roman soldiers, who raped virgins in villages like Cana of Galilee. The miracle of Genesis 2, where a man and woman became one, could not have happened. So Jesus, the *Memra* of the Lord, did the supernatural miracle of turning the water into wine, so that the supernatural miracle of the man and the woman becoming one would happen. This miracle of turning the water into wine was an act of liberation of the poor couple, who could not afford more wine to complete their marriage rite.

Ramabai saw the centrality of this miracle and vowed to marry to faithful men widows and temple prostitutes whom she had rescued. Hindu men, especially high-caste Hindu men, would never do this. Much in contrast, in Ramabai's home, the wedding ceremonies were celebrated as liberation moments.

In John 4:46-54, Jesus the *Memra* of God heals the son of a Gentile person. Jewish rabbis do not associate with Gentiles. They are considered to be unclean. This miracle is more than a physical healing event. It is dealing with the injustice of the attitude toward Gentiles.

It is interesting that this miracle follows the miracle of the social healing of a Samaritan woman—a woman who was raped and abused by five men. The *Memra*, Logos, *Shabad* of God in these situations brings about gender, economic, and social liberation.

In John 5:1-15, Jesus the *Memra* of God heals a paralytic at the pool of Bethesda. Obviously, this poor paralyzed person had no place in society. But Jesus' miracle gave him wholeness and a place in society. This is true liberation.

The Samaritans of India are the *Shudra* and the Dalit women. These were the women Ramabai rescued. It may be noted that just as the Samaritan woman was the cause of a liberative revival in the Samaritan village, so were the Ramabai girls. The early 1900s saw a huge revival take place in the state of Maharashtra and all over India. It began with the Ramabai-liberated girls. They saw visions. They laid hands on low-caste and outcaste people in the villages of India. These villages were liberated through a great word of the *Shabad* of God, through these liberated girls.

In John 6:5-14, Jesus the *Memra* of God feeds the five thousand-plus people. These were people who could not afford a Passover feast, the symbol of liberation. But Jesus the *Memra* of the Lord provided this crucial ritual, so that liberation would become a reality for them. Following this, in John 6:35, 48, 51, Jesus the *Memra* of the Lord proclaims that he is the I AM who revealed himself to Moses in the burning bush. These were both liberation moments in the wilderness.

In John 6:35, Jesus the *Memra* of God declares, "I am the bread of life," thus reminding people that he is the same *Memra* who provided bread, the manna to the fleeing slaves in the wilderness (Deut 8:3). Ramabai uses the term *bhakari* to describe the unleavened bread eaten by the low-caste people groups of India. In using this term, Ramabai is seeking to show that the *Memra* of God comes from the low-caste sections of society, to liberate them from the bondage of the high-caste people.

In John 10:7, 9, Jesus declares "I am the gate for the sheep," and John 10: 11, 14, Jesus declares, "I am the good shepherd." He saved the exodus community from slavery at the cruel hands of the Egyptian Pharaoh, and as Jesus the *Memra* of the Lord, he continues to do the same. The *Memra* of the Lord is the everlasting great shepherd. In biblical times, the shepherd was regarded as a low-class person. The Egyptians did not want to associate with the children of Israel since they were shepherds, and this was "detestable" to them (Gen 43:32). In India, shepherds are regarded with the same kind of disdain by the high-caste Brahmins. They have to live outside the villages of high-caste people groups.

Ramabai seeks to address this caste injustice head-on in her translation. The shepherd caste is called by various names—*dhangar, gadaria, medpal,* and so on. These are all *Shudras,* or slave castes, who have been enslaved by the high-caste people groups for hundreds of years. The *Changla Medpal,* or the Good Shepherd, is therefore a revolt against the caste norms of Hinduism. How can God be called the Good Shepherd? Ramabai's translation sees this as a liberation motif. If the *Shabad,* the Word of God can be called the *Changla Medpal;* this is the central motif of the liberation of all low and slave castes who have been enslaved to the high-caste Hindus for hundreds of years.

In my travels to Ramabai country, I have noticed that it is always these low-caste and outcaste men who have married Ramabai girls. The high caste, even the so-called high-caste Christians, refuse to marry the Ramabai girls. This is sad!

John 9:1-7 deals with the issue of blindness squarely. In Hinduism, a person is handicapped because she or he has done much evil in the last life. Therefore, the person is facing the consequences of her or his karma. This was the question that Jesus is asked: "Rabbi, who sinned, this man or his parents?" In Hinduism, when a person is handicapped, that person is supposed to endure the punishment of karma. Ramabai faces this issue squarely when Jesus the *Memra* of God heals a man blind from birth. Jesus touches the untouchable (Jn 9:6). He asks the untouchable to go and wash in the pool, where only the high-caste people could go near (Jn 9:7). He washed, and he was healed. He saw. It is fascinating that the dispute was not about his liberation healing, but, according to the laws of the Pharisees, should he have done this on Sabbath? These laws, called the *halakhoth*, are the same as the laws of the high-caste Brahmins of Hinduism. Ramabai in her translation brings out the full ramifications of this healing miracle. The *Shabad* Word of the Lord, liberates physically, socially, and in the religious realm. Then Jesus says, "I am the light of the world" (Jn 9:5). The word for "light" in Ramabai's translation is not the common word. Ramabai's term, *Ujer*, is the uncreated light, the first cause of all light. This light liberates people from all forms of darkness—social, economic, spiritual, and so on. This "Uncreated light" now becomes the domain of the liberated Ramabai girls.

John 11:1-45 in Ramabai's translation is a powerful liberation story of victory over death among the poor and slave castes of India. The story is formed in a small village, very similar to the villages of the *Shudra* and slave people groups. Death is a common thing among these people groups. Mourning is a common happening on a regular basis. Of course, there is no hope after death, because the high-caste priests will tell them that they would become a lower caste or outcaste in the next life, given that they did not perform their low-caste or outcaste karma well. Further, it is only the high-caste priests who may perform the death rituals, for which they would charge the low-caste and outcaste people very exorbitant fees. This religious fee would often cause the low-caste and outcaste people to go into huge debt, followed by slavery. In the light of this background, the words of Jesus, "Lazarus, come out," are very striking. In Ramabai's translation, these were the liberative *Shabad* of Jesus (Jn 11:43). Following this, Ramabai describes Jesus using a liberative phrase, "*Mokle Kera*, Free him." Ramabai seeks to describe this as not just a physical resurrection. That would not have been enough. It is a physical, social, economic, and spiritual resurrection and liberation.

This Jesus, the *Shabad* of God, then says, "I am the resurrection and the life." (Jn 11:25). To the poor, low-caste, and outcaste people groups of India, this is a huge liberation motif.

The final I AM *Shabad* of Jesus is John 14:6—"I am the way and the truth and the life." In the translation of Ramabai, this is a final liberative motif for the slave castes and the untouchable castes of India. Path, truth, and life are in the sole possession of the high-caste people groups of India. Yet, when this *Shabad* Word of God says, "I am the way and the truth and the life," it takes it out of the hands of the domineering and despotic hands of the high-caste Brahmins. It puts these essential liberative states of being in the reach of the slave and outcaste people groups.

CONCLUSION

In contrast to the traditional high-caste Brahmin theologians of India, like Brahmabandab Upadhyaya and Appaswamy, and in contrast to Indian liberation theologians, like M. M. Thomas, Arvind Nirmal, and Maria Arul Raj, both Kabir and Ramabai clearly seek to take a different and more powerful route. They seek to focus on the reality of God breaking through into history as the *Shabad*, the Word of God. Kabir gave the *Shudras*, the slaves, and the outcastes, the sung, liberative Word, the *Shabad*. Pandita Ramabai gave the *Shudras* and the *Atishudras* the written liberative *Shabad*. This was in their own language—not in the high-caste language of the Aryan enslavers. This *Shabad* of God has the power to transform and liberate humans who have faced much injustice in society. This concept of the liberation *Shabad* vitalizes the thoughts of other *Shudra*, slave castes, and Dalit thinkers like Periyar E. V. Ramaswamy and Phule. I have suggested that this Indian liberation concept of *Shabad* is the same as the Targumic concept of the *Memra*. That was aspiration of the enslaved and persecuted people of God for the liberated Word for about four hundred years before the time of Jesus. Finally, the New Testament claims, the living liberative Word, Jesus the Messiah, became incarnate to liberate them.

According to Ramabai and Kabir, *Shabad* is the liberative Word because it is first and foremost the creative Word. Because it is the creative Word of God, it breaks through into history wherever injustice and the resultant de-creation happens. In Ramabai's translation, this is seen in the response to the outcry in Sodom and Gomorrah (Gen 18; 19); in the cries of Hagar, the black slave girl (Gen21); in the cries of the slaves in Egypt (Ex 2); and so on. This liberative *Shabad* finally breaks through into history in the person of Jesus the Messiah. He proclaims and does miracles to show the transforming and liberative power of God.

The final word of this *Shabad/Memra/Logos* is, "It is finished" (Jn 19:30)! It must be noted that Targum Neofiti translates Genesis 1:1 as "In the beginning the *Memra* of God, with wisdom and understanding, created and 'finished' the heavens and the earth." This finishing work of the *Memra* of the Lord creates and liberates, till there is a new heaven and new earth, and the *Shabad* of the Lord "will wipe every tear from their eyes. There will be no more death or mourning or crying or pain, for the old order of things has passed away" (Rev 21:4).

This is the liberation theology of the *Memra* Word of the Lord in the Targums.

This is the liberation theology of the *Shabad* Word of God in Kabir.

This is the liberation theology of the *Shabad* Word of the Lord in Pandita Ramabai.

CHAPTER TWELVE

STRANGE FREEDOM

Liberation for the Sake of Others

MAE ELISE CANNON

ALL PEOPLE are in need of liberation. Liberation may be a quest for physical (or material) freedom through endeavors toward political independence and self-governance. Or one's journey toward freedom could be a quest to move beyond self-doubt into a place of personal acceptance and inner peace. Whatever an individual or community needs to be free from, all of us are in need of experiencing deliverance and being set free.

Liberation is not a foreign concept to evangelical traditions and theology. Even Jesus spoke of his own teachings as leading to liberation: "If you hold to my teaching, you are really my disciples. Then you will know the truth, and the truth will set you free" (Jn 8:31-32). Prior to the times of the New Testament, in the Hebrew Scriptures, God is described as the one who liberates. Teachings of liberation permeate throughout the Pentateuch, the Wisdom Literature, and the writings of the Prophets. One of the most famous stories of liberation in history is the story of the Israelites and how Moses led God's people out of slavery in Egypt and toward the promised land. For God commanded Moses, "Leave this place, you and the people you brought up out of Egypt, and go up to the land I promised on oath to Abraham, Isaac, and Jacob" (Ex 33:1). Leviticus, the book of the law, describes the Year of Jubilee as one where God commanded, "Consecrate the fiftieth year and proclaim liberty throughout the land to all of its inhabitants" (Lev 25:10). Liberty and freedom was an expressed goal of the Year of Jubilee. Psalm 119 speaks of how obedience to the decrees of God lead to liberation, "I will walk about in freedom, for I have sought out your precepts" (Ps 119:45).

Christians throughout history have proclaimed a message of *evangelion* (good news): that the person of Christ came to set the captives free from both personal sin and depravity and the physical yokes of oppression.[1] God is the one who brings freedom—freedom from sin (Acts 13:39) and from the powers of evil that manifest themselves in material poverty and physical limitations. Jesus' ministry on earth was not limited to the care of the soul, but also addressed physical and material needs and a concern his followers' corporal condition as flourishing members of society with material freedom. We see Christ's care exemplified in the work of his ministry as he healed the sick (Mt 4:23), blessed the poor (Lk 6:20), fed the hungry (Jn 6:11), comforted the sorrowful (Mt 5:4), and walked alongside those who were excluded from society (Mk 2:15). The good news of Christ sheds profound wisdom on the question of theological freedom both in the spiritual and the material world. Consider also Jesus' response to the woman who was crippled for eighteen years: to the woman bent over by her infirmity, Jesus said, "Woman, you are set free from your infirmity." On touching her, she straightened up and praised God (Lk 13:12). Christ had set her free.

Historically, evangelicals have been known for preaching about these particular types of liberation—freedom from individual sin in pursuit of righteousness and freedom from individual struggles or limitations. However, white evangelicals have largely ignored responding to systemic issues of injustice or affirming theologies of

---

[1]As an evangelical pastor, I make the theological assumption that the person of Christ draws people into relationship with himself and offers atonement for sin (Rom 3:22-23), while also proclaiming the kingdom of God on earth by staking claims of freedom and justice (Lk 4:18-19).

liberation that apply to people groups and communities. I write extensively about this false binary in my first book *Social Justice Handbook*, as it manifested itself in the early twentieth-century divisions between Christian groups: while liberal Protestant Christians who engaged in the social gospel movement focused more on addressing issues of systemic injustice like racism and poverty, conservative evangelical Christians focused more on one's individual relationship with God and the pursuit of personal righteousness. "Evangelicals continued to uphold orthodox Christian beliefs rooted in systematic theology and Scripture. The necessity of faith in Christ for salvation continues to be a core [tenet] of the evangelical faith. However, though twentieth century evangelicals held strongly to traditional doctrine, they largely neglected to respond to the needs of the poor, as taught by the gospel of Christ."[2] Evangelicals, in the context of the church, during the twentieth century (and through today) have a tendency to be less engaged in social political issues and also, in large part, have ignored contemporary movements of liberation. There is much to learn about these different types of liberation through the black theological tradition.

LEARNING FROM BLACK LIBERATION THEOLOGIANS: EXISTENTIAL AND SOCIAL FREEDOM

Cornel West, philosopher, thinker, and civil rights activist, argues that prophetic Christianity is composed of two inseparable notions of freedom: existential freedom and social freedom. West says, "Existential freedom is an effect of the divine gift of grace which promises to sustain persons through and finally deliver them from the bondage to death, disease, and despair."[3] Existential freedom is embodied in Jesus' message in the Sermon on the Mount (Mt 5; Lk 6), where Christ speaks of comfort, satisfaction, and eternal reward. Social freedom,

---

[2]Mae Elise Cannon, *Social Justice Handbook: Small Steps for a Better World*. Downers Grove, IL: InterVarsity Press, 2009), 61.
[3]Cornel West, *Prophesy Deliverance! An Afro-American Revolutionary Christianity* (Louisville, KY: John Knox Press, 2002), 18.

for West, is inextricably linked to the existential state of one's being, and is the "aim of Christian political practice, a praxis that flows from the divine gift of grace."[4] The relationship between the internal struggles of the soul and the external realities of the material world is complex and must be understood without minimizing the devastating effects of constraints in either existential or social freedom.

In dissecting these complexities, it is valuable to consider the perspective of two prophetic black Christian voices for freedom: Howard Thurman and Martin Luther King Jr. While never ignoring the quest for material freedom, Thurman places emphasis on existential freedom and the internal peace of one's soul when the reality of being known, called, and loved by God becomes clear. King, on the other hand, asserts that social and existential freedom are inseparable ideals that cannot be sought or experienced apart from the other. For King, freedom exists as an absolute, or not at all. Both Thurman's emphasis on the centeredness that comes from being known and King's relentless reminder that freedom cannot be objectified are necessary in divulging a holistic theology of liberation. The good news of the gospel of Christ reveals a theology of liberation that constitutes both spiritual provision and material deliverance. When absolute freedom comes and liberation is realized, peace (*shalom*) is achieved both transcendentally in one's spirit and palpably on the earth through social justice and the reconciliation of individuals and communities. However, in the interim of waiting for such material liberation, the freedom of one's soul that comes from faith in Christ sustains, uplifts, and motivates in continual pursuit of justice while waiting in hope and expectation for deliverance to come.

Howard Thurman, philosopher, theologian, and educator, placed emphasis on the spiritual release, comfort, and anchoring that comes from knowing one is cared for by God. Thurman specifically asks the question of how the gospel of Christ relates to those "with their backs

---

[4]West, *Prophesy Deliverance!*, 18.

against the wall," who have been oppressed and overlooked. Thurman's theology of freedom places an emphasis on personal freedom as a discipline and internal structure that allows for "the living of one's life with confidence that transcends discouragement and despair."[5] This inner confidence is not dependent on the realities of the external or material world, but rather transcends social circumstances. This transcendentalism is never achieved apart from the terror of oppression that marked Thurman's reality and the history of America where "never before in human history have so many and so much been exploited by so few so fast."[6] For Thurman, existential freedom is emphasized and experienced by being known by God and being called by one's name. He identifies the effects of being called by name and says that an awareness of oneself as a child of God "tends to stabilize the ego and results in new courage, fearlessness, and power."[7] For those who hear and obey the word of God, they will be called by a new name and experience a freedom that transcends the harsh realities of this world.

For Thurman, one comes to understand the love of God when one is called by name and begins to have a true sense of personal identity. This spiritual liberation occurs when one is known and called by name. When a person is oppressed and is not seen or acknowledged for their soul and identity, Thurman describes it this way:

> It is a strange freedom to be adrift in the world of men without a sense of anchor anywhere. Always there is the need of mooring, the need for the firm grip on something that is rooted and will not give. . . . The very spirit of a man tends to panic from the desolation of going nameless up and down the streets of others minds where no salutation greets and no friendly recognition makes secure. It is a strange freedom to be in the world of men.[8]

---

[5]Howard Thurman, "Freedom Is a Discipline," in *The Inward Journey* (Richmond, VA: Friends United Press, 1961), 63.

[6]Charles H. Long, "Howard Thurman and the Meaning of Religion in America," in *The Human Search: Howard Thurman and the Quest for Freedom; Proceedings from the Second Annual Thurman Convention* (New York: Peter Lang, 1988), 139.

[7]Howard Thurman, *Jesus and the Disinherited* (Richmond, VA: Friends United Press, 1981), 50.

[8]Howard Thurman, "A Strange Freedom," in *The Inward Journey*, 37.

The naming of an individual, the recognition of personhood, soul, and giftedness, is a critical component of existential freedom for Thurman. He describes the name as a "private banner" under which a person has free will, the freedom of determination, and the ability to choose how one is going to react and respond to the world.[9] This naming allows us to experience a centeredness with God allowing us to transcend being alone and to achieve a "realization of the importance of our selves [*sic*]."[10] The emphasis on individual identity and realization is an important contribution of Thurman's theological perspective. For the extent to which one understands the love of God is the degree to which "he is unconquerable from within and without."[11]

The power that results from this type of existential freedom or peace in the soul is identified by Thurman as a *strange freedom*.[12] This strange freedom, rooted in relationship with Christ, is willing to endure cruelty, the realities of occupation, the limitation of mobility, the lack of access to material resources, limited economic opportunities, and other such impositions on one's ability to prosper; yet all the while strange freedom holds onto hope. The paradox of existential freedom is the power that one possesses over the external world, when one's internal being is in right relationship with God: when a person is seen, known, and belongs. The power of belonging is so strong it enables people to withstand and overcome physical trials and the experience of unfreedom in the material world. For Thurman, one can lose one's physical freedom, but not existential freedom. No matter what the physical circumstances, the condition of one's soul is dependent first and foremost on that individual's relationship with God and understanding of one's self-worth in relation to their Creator.

Thurman writes of Jesus' example, saying he "recognized with authentic realism that anyone who permits another to determine the

---

9 Thurman, "Strange Freedom," 38.
10 Long, "Howard Thurman and the Meaning of Religion," 139.
11 Thurman, *Jesus and the Disinherited*, 56.
12 Thurman, "Strange Freedom," 37.

quality of his inner life gives into the hands of the other the keys to his destiny."[13] Similarly, Jesus declared the soul, when secure in him, is safe from destruction. Jesus' words state, "Do not be afraid of those who kill the body but cannot kill the soul. Rather, be afraid of the One who can destroy both soul and body in hell" (Mt 10:28). Under these circumstances, the threat of violence no longer has power—even if it results in death—for death is not the worst thing in the world. Thurman writes, "There *are* some things that are worse than death. To deny one's own integrity of personality in the presence of the human challenge is one of those things."[14] Cornel West describes this phenomenon using the example of the black experience in America. He sees the music of black people—spirituals, blues, jazz—as a sort of expression of the soul and an acknowledgement of self. West writes, "The spirituals embody the creativity of courageous human beings who engaged the world of pain and trouble with faith, hope, and spirit—and a kind of existential freedom even in slavery."[15] Even men and women who were considered chattel and were limited in almost every capacity of material freedom sang of the freedom of their souls in spirituals such as *Oh, Freedom*: "And before I be a slave, I'll be buried in my grave. And go home to my Lord and be free." Such is a strange freedom.

STRANGE FREEDOM FOUND IN
PRISONS AND INCARCERATION

This strange freedom can be witnessed around the world in different communities of faith. Interestingly, one of the places where evangelicals most engage in ideas about liberation is in the context of prison ministry. Evangelicals, like Charles Colson—who was formerly himself incarcerated—have invested significant time and resources to take the word of Christ into the prison system. Colson later founded

---

[13]Thurman, *Jesus and the Disinherited*, 28.
[14]Thurman, *Jesus and the Disinherited*, 51.
[15]Cornel West, "The Spirituals as Lyrical Poetry," in *The Cornel West Reader* (New York: Civitas Books, 1999), 464.

International Prison Fellowship, whose mission is to "engage the Christian community to pursue justice and healing in response to crime to the end that offenders are transformed, relationships are reconciled, and communities are restored."[16] While Colson's emphasis in large part emphasized the individual conversion of the incarcerated inmate, the mission of International Prison Fellowship has developed into something much more holistic.

For inmates who have chosen to follow Christ, they describe a sort of existential freedom that exists in the absence of material freedom. For example, Don Smarto, former director of the Billy Graham Center's Institute for Prison Ministry, speaks of the testimony of Don Holt, a former inmate who wrote his testimony, "Free at Last." In the evangelical book *Setting the Captives Free!*, Don Smarto writes, "Don Holt's testimony is an example of what prison ministry is all about: a person living in crime and brutality who really becomes a new creature in Christ."[17]

Louisiana State Penitentiary at Angola provides another example of the collision of ideas about existential and material freedom. Within the prison, there is a Christian community of committed Christ followers who have dedicated their lives (even if the remainder of their days will be spent behind bars) to building up the body of Christ by being witnesses of the gospel. Many of these men have committed serious crimes that have resulted in their physical imprisonment. However, the message of redemption that is promised through Jesus Christ extends even to the worst of sinners. Revelation 1:5-6 says of Jesus, "To him who loves us and freed us from sins by his blood . . . to him be glory and power for ever and ever." The testimony and living witness of these men forces one to ask questions of the gospel: Does the liberating message of freedom in Christ extend even to the soul of a convicted felon? Does this freedom extend even

---

[16]Taken from Prison Fellowship International, "Who We Are," https://pfi.org/who-we-are/.

[17]Don Smarto, *Setting the Captives Free! Relevant Ideas in Criminal Justice and Prison Ministry* (Grand Rapids: Baker Books, 1993), 141.

to a person who has taken the life of another human being? What I experienced in meeting many of the men in the Christian community at Angola, several of whom now serve as inmate chaplains and ministers, was a faith and freedom more profound and real than that of many individuals and communities that live in the "free world." One person's observation: "Because of the personal faith in Jesus amongst these inmates, there is more freedom behind the walls of this prison than in my own church community." These men, as Thurman has suggested, know their identity and worth and have heard their Creator call them by name. They have (at times) transcended discouragement and despair and are living lives of purpose while their physical bodies remain in captivity; they exemplify an existential freedom that cannot be contained.

Cornel West offers a valuable reminder that existential freedom includes ideas of love, death, suffering, pain, joy, and friendship; however, this does not mean individuals and communities should not be concerned with the avid pursuit of liberation within social circumstances.[18] There has sometimes been the tendency among liberal theologians to emphasize liberation of the material to the exclusion of the existential. Martin Luther King Jr., a prophetic Christian voice and civil rights hero, takes a more integrated approach and asserts, like West, that social and existential freedom cannot be obtained independently of the other. King's framework is more dialectical and embodies an inclusive theology of both existential and social liberation. He works out in more concrete ways the social and political implications of Thurman's *Jesus and the Disinherited*. King believed the will, the soul, could never be removed from the physical realities surrounding one's personhood:

> The very phrase, freedom of the will, abstracts freedom from the person to make it an object; and an object almost by definition is not

---

[18]Cornel West, "The Making of an American Radical Democrat of African Descent," in *The Cornel West Reader*, 13.

free. Freedom cannot thus be abstracted from the person, who is always subject as well as object and who himself does the abstracting. So I am speaking of the freedom of man, the whole man, and not one faculty called the will.[19]

King advocated for an *absolute freedom* of both will and person, placing emphasis on social liberation expressed in the ability to weigh alternatives, make decisions, take responsibility, and face consequences.[20] These corporal realities of life—what a person is able to do, to be, and to become—are what declare to the world that someone is free.

Evangelicals have tended to struggle with King's notions of absolute freedom, because of the lack of emphasis on personal salvation and the pursuit of personal righteousness. Nonetheless, while Jesus emphasized freedom of the soul and the pursuit of personal and corporate righteousness, his ministry also encapsulated a message of "set[ting] the oppressed free" (Lk 4:18-19). Material freedom, deliverance from oppression, and the pursuit of justice are all important theological themes that are present throughout the Old and New Testaments. Oppression, the absence of justice, is the use of power to subjugate an individual or group of people.[21]

Social freedom exists when communities are reconciled and there is no oppression. We see a picture of this in Leviticus 25: consider the biblical instructions to the Israelites about the Year of Jubilee. The Jubilee was constructed on seven-year cycles, following Sabbath principles to teach and remind the people of Israel that the land, and everything in it, belonged to God. The marks of Jubilee were the freeing of slaves, debts being wiped clean, the return of land to its original owners, and the land lying fallow in a state of rest. The Jubilee, as described in Leviticus 25:42, "is God's comprehensive unilateral

---

[19]Martin Luther King Jr., "The Ethical Demands for Integration," in *A Testament of Hope: The Essential Writings and Speeches of Martin Luther King, Jr.,* ed. James M. Washington (New York: HarperCollins, 1986), 120.

[20]King, "Ethical Demands for Integration," 120.

[21]Cannon, *Social Justice Handbook,* 25.

restructuring of the community's assets" and was to remind the people "that they were an exodus people who must never return to a system of slavery."[22] Jesus began his ministry by using language of the Jubilee and declaring "the year of the Lord's favor" (Lk 4:19). King's ministry emphasized Christ's promise to set the captives free, both in the existential realm, and also in regard to their social circumstances. For King, "true peace is not merely the absence of tension: it is the presence of justice."[23] For King, freedom exists not only when a state of existential peace is achieved, but also when justice is expressed in the material realm.

King's ministry was in the throes of unrest occurring during the civil rights movement. Blacks all over the United States, especially in the South, were subjugated to brutal treatment, the enforcement of racist Jim Crow laws, the psychological implications of segregation, and other impositions on their social liberty. In direct response to the oppression of African Americans, King declared unequivocally that absolute freedom was being pursued through means of peaceful nonviolent protest:

> What the Negro wants—and will not stop until he gets—is absolute and unqualified freedom and equality here in this land of his birth, and not in Africa or in some imaginary state. The Negro will no longer be tolerant of anything less than his due right and heritage.[24]

King, like Thurman, emphasized how the personal identity of an individual is important. However, King viewed the lack of physical freedom as the denial of self and stated "the very character of the life of man demands freedom."[25] King emphasized that existential freedom cannot be obtained apart from material freedom, because the presence of one aspect of freedom necessitates the existence of the other. King described freedom as the "chosen fulfillment of our destined nature."[26]

---

[22]Shane Claiborne, *Irresistible Revolution* (Grand Rapids: Zondervan, 2006), 171.
[23]Martin Luther King Jr. quoted in Stephen Oates, *Let the Trumpet Sound* (New York: Harper Collins, 1993), 84.
[24]King, "Ethical Demands for Integration," 119.
[25]King, "Ethical Demands for Integration," 119.
[26]King, "Ethical Demands for Integration," 120.

In order to be whole, in order to be complete, in order to be human, one must not only have freedom over the mind, soul, and will; a person must also have the opportunity to experience civic freedom within a society where material oppression does not exist and is not imposed on any individuals or group within that society. King asserted his vision and theology of freedom in these words:

> We have come to the day when a piece of freedom is not enough for us as human beings nor for the nation of which we are part. We have been given pieces, but unlike bread, a slice of which does diminish hunger, a piece of liberty no longer suffices. Freedom is like life. You cannot be given life in installments. You cannot be given breath but no body, nor a heart but no blood vessels. Freedom is one thing—you either have it all, or you are not free.[27]

CONTEMPORARY STRUGGLES FOR LIBERATION

Abstract notions of theologies of freedom can get lost in rhetoric and philosophical discourse. How do ideas of existential and social freedom impact our considerations of the world today? History is wrought with stories of contemporary struggles for liberation around the globe—from the black toil for freedom and autonomy in the United States; to Jewish realities of genocide and grotesque global anti-Semitism; to the present-day struggles between Palestinians seeking to "shake off" the physical bonds of occupation in East Jerusalem, the West Bank, and Gaza; and many other examples of people groups seeking liberation and freedom.

Jewish liberation theology.

Liberation has been at the heart of Jewish theology since the very beginning. The story of Moses and the Jewish people being liberated from slavery at the hands of Pharaoh in Egypt by the faithfulness of God is one that is foundational in Jewish theological tradition. Exodus 13:3 reads, "Then Moses said to the people, "Commemorate this day,

---

[27]Martin Luther King Jr., "An Address Before the National Press Club," in *Testament of Hope*, 104.

the day you came out of Egypt, out of the land of slavery, because the LORD brought you out of it with a mighty hand." The story of the exodus, as mentioned above, has been foundational in Christian and evangelical understandings of liberation.

Maimonides, a Sephardic Jewish philosopher who was one of the most prominent Torah scholars of the Middle Ages, highlighted the Jewish themes of liberation in his work.[28] Ralph Lerner's book *Maimonides' Empire of the Light* emphasizes how Maimonides viewed the primary task of the Torah as being one of liberation. Obedience to the law led to perfection. Maimonides offers his work, according to Lerner, as "an act of liberation or, perhaps better put, as a means by which a single virtuous man can liberate himself."[29]

Contemporary Jewish historian and liberation theologian Marc Ellis further expands on the idea that Jewish theology has long been rooted in a "paradigm of liberation that forms the heart of the Jewish experience."[30] However, Ellis, somewhat controversially, calls on the Jewish people to not only be satisfied with the liberation of their own people, but to call for the liberation of others as well. He asserts that the policies of Israel vis-à-vis the occupation "increasingly resemble those historically used to oppress our own [Jewish] people." Ellis continues, "But fidelity to our own values and history is ultimately connected to the struggles for liberation of others; the brokenness of our past is betrayed, our political empowerment made suspect, when others become our victims."[31] Ellis asserts that the oppression of the Palestinian people at the hands of the state of Israel must end in order for Jews to be truly liberated themselves. In this quest for emancipation, Ellis seeks to define a Jewish theology of liberation. He concludes the first edition of *Toward a Jewish Theology of Liberation* with the following:

---

[28]J. Litvin, "Maimonides (1135–1205)," *Jewish Quarterly* 2 (1955): 7-9.
[29]Ralph Lerner, *Maimonides' Empire of Light* (Chicago: University of Chicago Press, 2000), 74-75.
[30]Marc H. Ellis, *Toward a Jewish Theology of Liberation: The Uprising and the Future* (Maryknoll, NY: Orbis Books, 1989), 1.
[31]Ellis, *Toward a Jewish Theology*, 2.

The hope of liberation, however, remains always before us, and five thousand years of history, with its chapters of Holocaust and empowerment, provide a unique foundation on which to build a future. . . . A Jewish theology of liberation seeks to join with others in rediscovering the prophetic voice with the hope that we can become what we are called to be.[32]

Palestinian liberation theology.

Palestinian liberation theology, on the other hand, has focused more on social and material freedom, marking 1948 and the establishment of the state of Israel as *Nakba*, or the great catastrophe that led to the displacement of more than three-quarters of a million Arab residents of the former Ottoman territory of Palestine. Palestinians today mark 1967 as one of the most significant years in their quest for self-determination, because that was the year that the military control or occupation of East Jerusalem, the West Bank, and Gaza began.

In 1989, Naim Stifan Ateek published a book called *Justice and Only Justice*. That same year, Ateek founded an organization in Jerusalem called *Sabeel* (meaning "the Way" in Arabic) as an Ecumenical Liberation Theology Center. Many consider Ateek to be the founder of Palestinian liberation theology. American feminist scholar and Catholic theologian Rosemary Radford Ruether wrote in her foreword to *Justice and Only Justice*,

> Father Naim Ateek's presentation of Palestinian liberation theology is written in an extraordinary spirit that unites justice and love. One finds in this testimony to his faith as a Palestinian Christian both the dignified claims of truth and righteousness against injustice and the peacemaking extension of the hand of forgiveness to those who have injured the Palestinians, once the wrongs are acknowledged. It is a liberation theology that comes, first and foremost, from the heart and mind of a pastor, who lives in the midst of the tragedy of one

---

[32]Ellis, *Toward a Jewish Theology*, 122.

victimized people suffering at the hands of another historically victimized people.[33]

The Palestinian Christian context, from within which Naim Ateek's
liberation theology was born, must daily ask what it means to practice
a contextual theology that responds both to the needs of their souls
and to the harsh circumstances of living under military occupation. A
part of the daily reality of Palestinians living in the occupied Palestinian territories is the use of the military weight of Israel to exert
control and power. While the state of Israel has the right to exist, and
to defend itself, its rights should not extend to placing limitations on
the freedom of others through the imposition of economic disad-
vantage and the experience of "oppression, exploitation, and dependency" on the Palestinians.[34] Community infrastructures in Palestine,
such as the healthcare and education systems, are inhibited by the
realities of occupation. The result is substandard healthcare and a state
system of education that must rely on external sources of funding because the state support is not sustainable.[35] In the words of Mitri Raheb,
a pastor and leader in Bethlehem, "I am a Palestinian living under Israeli occupation. My captor daily seeks ways to make life harder for me.
He encircles my people with barbed wire; he builds walls around us,
and his army sets many boundaries around us. He succeeds in keeping
thousands of us in camps and prisons."[36] Palestinians living today in
the occupied territories understand what it means to live in the absence
of material freedom. In addition to the pursuit of social liberation,
Christian Palestinians must also wrestle with how their identity is
shaped by the existential certainties of their faith.

Although Thurman places an emphasis on individual identity and
the hope that is found in existential freedom, he does not neglect

---

[33]Rosemary Radford Ruether, foreword to *Justice and Only Justice: A Palestinian Theology of Liberation* by Naim Stifan Ateek (New York: Orbis, 1989), xi.
[34]Mitri Raheb, *I Am a Palestinian Christian* (Minneapolis: Fortress Press, 1995), 29.
[35]Raheb, *I Am a Palestinian Christian*, 31.
[36]Raheb, *I Am a Palestinian Christian*, 112.

acknowledging the harsh realities of physical oppression. He argues that until one has personally experienced severe limits on his or her own material freedom, one is not able to understand the deleterious effects of subjugation and what it might take to overcome it: "It ill behooves the man who is not forced to live in a ghetto to tell those who must how to transcend its limitations."[37] Thurman reminds those who are powerful and liberated of their own limitations to understand the realities and constraints of oppression. He criticizes their paternalistic condescension and the assumption that the poor should simply work their way out of their oppressive circumstances. Nonetheless, Thurman reminds his readers of the positive aspects of existential freedom, and the hope that transcends an individual's or community's limitations in the physical realm. Jean Zaru, a Palestinian woman who is known for her involvement in human rights issues, writes of this actuality, "Despite the current Israeli government's determination, no amount of its violence could subjugate the will of a people, or destroy their spirit as they struggle for their freedom, dignity, and their right to sovereignty on their own land."[38]

Although the Palestinian people experience physical oppression and are in active pursuit of material freedom, a person's spirit and personal will cannot be contained. Rather, the Christian community in Palestine possesses a hope that exemplifies the strange freedom that Thurman describes. Zaru writes of this hope, "Sometimes we try to look for hope in what seems to be a hopeless situation. But if there is hope after such a brutal death of the resurrected Jesus Christ, then there surely is no situation devoid of hope and promise."[39]

This hope and promise makes it clear that individuals and communities can experience liberation of the soul apart from material freedom. Within societal circumstances filled with despair, extreme poverty, and

---

[37]Thurman, *Jesus and the Disinherited*, 56.
[38]Jean Zaru, "Theologising, Truth and Peacemaking in the Palestinian Experience," in *Speaking the Truth: Zionism, Israel and Occupation*, ed. Michael Prior (Northampton, MA: Olive Branch Press, 2005), 171.
[39]Zaru, "Theologising, Truth and Peacemaking," 171.

lack of physical freedom, an existential transcendence manifests itself in hope, joy, and even love of one's enemies. This existential freedom exists in such a way that people may then be motivated to peacefully pursue racial equality, cultural reform, and social justice while eagerly anticipating the emergence of the kingdom of God.

Considering the Palestinian problem in light of King's dialectical theology of freedom, it becomes clear that existential freedom does not limit, but rather enhances the pursuit of social freedom. Political and social freedom in the state of Israel, for both Israelis and Palestinians, is a complicated question. I have chosen specifically to look at the perspective of the Palestinian people, because they have less immediate access to resources and have less power than their Israeli counterparts in their immediate relationship to one another. This does not mean that I do not support the right of Israel to exist and the legitimate security needs of the state. Nor does it mean that I am not sensitive to the power differentials and fears of Jewish Israelis who live under threats of violence from neighboring Arab states. Nonetheless, in the current situation, and the occupation of East Jerusalem, the West Bank, and Gaza, the Palestinians are a community that has been disinherited. Mitri Raheb writes of this imbalance of power, "The Palestinian problem is the problem of a perverted relationship. It is a problem of unjust division of power, a problem of an unjust system that protects oppression and exploitation. It is the problem of law perverted to support the interests of the powerful and to satisfy their expansionist plans."[40]

King's theology of freedom would cry out on behalf of the Palestinian people and demand that absolute freedom be expressed not only toward the Israeli community, but also for Arab Palestinians living in the land. It is important to note that this is a biblical notion of freedom as well. In the Scriptures, the people of Israel were freed from captivity and then were called by God to extend the same kind of deliverance and compassion that he showed them to others around

---

[40]Raheb, *I Am a Palestinian Christian*, 27.

them who had need.[41] King advocated for a form of peaceful protest that would overturn the tides of oppression. The existential freedom that exists from faith in Christ and right relationship with God motivates and compels one toward pursuit of full freedom. According to King, "When oppressed people rise up against oppression there is no stopping point short of full freedom. Realism compels us to admit that the struggle will continue until freedom is a reality for all the oppressed peoples of the world."[42]

Cornel West refers to a "guttural cry that erupts from the depths of the souls of each of us" in the quest for both existential meaning and the political struggle for freedom.[43] Existential freedom compels and empowers people to fight for social freedom by releasing them from despair and propelling them toward hope. Absolute freedom, the existence of both existential and material freedom, is manifested in the *shalom* of God, a complete and absolute state of justice. *Shalom* brings wholeness, completeness, safety, tranquility, and restoration to creation—the way God intended things to be.[44] The Christian theologian Nicholas Wolterstorff describes shalom this way:

> Shalom is the state of flourishing in all dimensions of one's existence: in one's relation to God, in one's relation to one's fellow human beings, in one's relation to nature, and in one's relation to oneself. Evidently justice has something to do with the fact that God's love for each and every one of God's human creatures takes the form of God desiring the shalom of each and every one.[45]

In pursuit of shalom, existential freedom transcends material freedom, while crying out for release from physical captivity and the extension of social liberation to all.

---

[41] Cannon, *Social Justice Handbook*, 42.
[42] Martin Luther King Jr., "Nonviolence and Racial Justice," in *Testament of Hope*, 7.
[43] Cornel West, "Introduction: To Be Human, Modern, and American," in *Cornel West Reader*, 11.
[44] Cannon, *Social Justice Handbook*, 25-26.
[45] Nicholas Wolterstorff, "The Contours of Justice: An Ancient Call for Shalom," in *God and the Victim: Theological Reflections on Evil, Victimization, Justice, and Forgiveness,* ed. Lisa Barnes Lampman and Michelle D. Shattuck (Grand Rapids: Eerdmans, 1999), 113.

The holistic gospel and the promise of the kingdom of God demands one seek the work of redemption for the internal soul; and from that place of strange freedom, one is motivated in the external world to work toward the end of oppression and injustice. If justice is not obtained, or if one loses their life along the way, the soul has still tasted strange freedom while waiting in anticipation for the chains to be broken and the captives to be set free. Cornel West calls all people along the journey to become advocates of freedom who fuse intellectual engagement, political transformation, and the existential struggle in the active fight for social and existential freedom.[46] As one seeks to understand the relationship between existential and social freedom, a theology of freedom emerges that calls Christ followers to be "freedom fighters" in pursuit of an existential peace that drives advocacy and action while demanding justice and material deliverance.

The work ahead of us has never seemed more extreme. The divisions within the United States under the Trump Administration have reached catastrophic proportions. In 2018, more Americans would rather marry someone of a different religious tradition than from a different political party. White evangelicals have supported the current administration, while evangelicals of color (and a very small minority of white evangelicals) are crying out against bans on immigration (being enforced disproportionately against Arabs and Muslims), racist rhetoric being spewed via Twitter from the president himself, and a societal climate that seems to have emboldened bigotry, anti-Semitism, racism, and hatred. For example, according to a report published by the Anti-Defamation League, anti-Semitic incidents rose 60 percent in 2017.[47] Oppression runs rampant; the need for liberation is desperate.

---

[46]Cornel West, "The Indispensability Yet Insufficiency of Marxist Theory," in *Cornel West Reader*, 215.

[47]Anti-Defamation League, "Anti-Semitic Incidents Surged Nearly 60% in 2017, According to New ADL Report," February 27, 2018, www.adl.org/news/press-releases/anti-semitic-incidents -surged-nearly-60-in-2017-according-to-new-adl-report.

In addition to the US context, the terrors of oppression that Thurman describes continue to exist around the world. The powerful oppress the weak by limiting access to resources, hoarding material possessions, imprisoning the innocent, and further subjugating the disinherited. The body of Christ must have a holistic understanding of both existential and material freedom in order to be an advocate on behalf of oppressed people around the world. Resting on the truth that justice and righteousness are the foundations of God's throne, evangelicals—alongside of so many others—must commit to being advocates of freedom, and to diligently pursuing liberation for all people by being voices for the voiceless and advocates for the disinherited, so that all may one day be free.

PART FIVE

RETHINKING OUR EVANGELICAL HERITAGE

LIBERATING BARABBAS

And the Things That Make for Peace

DREW G. I. HART

INTRODUCTION

Next to Jesus, Barabbas might be the most misunderstood person in the Bible. Readers of Scripture frequently sever both Barabbas and Jesus from their first-century sociopolitical context, which distorts their meaning and challenge for the church today. Mainstream Christianity continues to convert Jesus into a status quo religious mascot who provides no hope to people suffering from oppression or seeking God's liberating intervention. This Jesus has been westernized, whitened, and domesticated when compared to the first-century poor Palestinian Jew who preached good news to the poor and came to "set the oppressed free" while living under Roman occupation (Luke 4:18-19). For many people raised in mainstream American Christian communities, the idea of a liberative Jesus is not only strange but it feels misguided. For some, that has nothing to do with Christianity. In American evangelicalism, salvation is often personal and individualistic, spiritual with little social implications, and it primarily focuses its adherents on escaping hell and going to heaven. However, the mainstream American Christian portrait of Jesus is often not consistent with the Jesus of Matthew, Mark, Luke, and John. The American church must carefully examine Jesus in the biblical accounts, which is the most authoritative witness to the person and character of our resurrected Messiah. For this chapter I will examine one dimension of Jesus' story through a reconsideration of the person named Barabbas in Scripture. This chapter will demonstrate that the gospel portrait of Barabbas is not there to serve merely as an atonement theology metaphor, where a rebellious people release a sinful murderer in place of a sinless Savior. Much more than that, their highlighting of Barabbas in the Jesus story provides actual sociopolitical analysis. A fresh look at Barabbas, I contend, also reveals Jesus as a nonviolent liberator responding to the earthly conditions of poor and oppressed people. Participating in the delivering presence of this living Messiah leads disciples of Jesus into empathetic joining and intimate presence with the oppressed, while committed to struggling for liberation and the things that make for peace in the way of Jesus.

Mainstream Christianity holds mental projections of Barabbas that are unscriptural yet taken for granted. Speaking to congregations or young people in the classroom, I have asked whether they have ever looked carefully at Barabbas in Scripture. Without fail, most people say no. Apparently, Barabbas is not a popular biblical figure to engage in contemplative reflection or to do a close reading on. People will sooner study the prayer of Jabez than examine and strengthen their faith and life in Christ by making sense of why Barabbas is present in Jesus' story. This lack of careful consideration, however, has not halted stereotypes and ideological manipulations of Barabbas in mainstream thought.

Widespread sentiments and ideas persist about Barabbas that dehumanize him or turn him into an evangelical foil to Jesus' innocence. I too once perceived Barabbas through the ableist stereotype of a psycho serial killer who went town by town randomly killing innocent people. In Sunday school class, he was presented as the epitome of sinful and fallen humanity rebelling against God, harming oneself and others. Most striking, though, was the perception that his murders were random. There was no logical rationale provided for why he was so violent and dangerous. Nothing provoked his action.

Another popular stereotype depicts him as a brutish barbarian. A Google search of Barabbas will result in many images coming straight from movies. Many of these images dehumanize Barabbas as an animalistic brute. Sometimes Barabbas has a cocked eye, other times he is drooling from the mouth. Frequently his facial features were of a stereotype of a crazed man lacking social cues and civility. One particular movie clip has Barabbas laughing uncontrollably while bound in chains, suggesting again that his atypical mental state led him to this destination. Taken collectively, the messaging is clear: Barabbas is an evil and dangerous animalistic brute and is a madman lacking logical thinking. Scripture might not be the primary source for these Barabbas portraits, but they are powerful controlling images nonetheless.

In mainstream evangelical theology, Barabbas usually has a more sophisticated role, yet this approach still ignores the sociopolitical focus provided in Scripture. Evangelicals often understand Barabbas as Jesus' foil, which is right. It is how the two are related to one another that needs reexamination. In this framing, the primary subject that matters most is Jesus' innocence (referring to his sinless life) versus Barabbas's sinfulness as a murderer (referring to his guilty status under God's law). The dominant atonement theology for mainstream evangelicalism is not Christus victor, in which Christ is demonstrated to be victorious over sin, death, Satan, the rulers and authorities, and the evil forces of this world that keep humanity in captivity.[1] Many evangelicals prefer the penal substitutionary atonement model, emphasizing that Jesus took the place that humanity deserved. This theological approach is often understood as having its origins in Anselm's satisfaction theory and as a further development of Calvin's

---

[1] Some scholars have argued that Christus victor is the most dominant and ancient atonement metaphor in Scripture.

own atonement theory.[2] The kind of atonement theology adopted matters in this case because the penal substitution model provides the rails of interpretation that direct how Barabbas is understood for many evangelicals. Barabbas, in this model, represents all of sinful and guilty humanity that deserves the punishment of death; instead, Jesus takes his (and our) place on the cross as a substitution.[3] This atonement model does not demand one ignore the sociopolitical cues in the text, but it tends to have that result. Jesus' taking our place on the cross is interpreted as an individual transaction with God providing spiritual salvation, with no liberative consequences for sociopolitical conditions. Ultimately, Jesus' substitution provides Christians with salvation from hell and an escape to a spiritual heaven. In this model, Jesus' salvation has little to do with social arrangements on earth. Barabbas, in this theological framework, is a sophisticated way to dramatize Jesus' substitutionary atonement for sinful and guilty humanity.

I suggest that Barabbas needs reconsideration. Popular stereotypes of Barabbas portray him as an animalistic brute, a pyscho serial killer, and a dangerous murderer randomly taking life without reason. American evangelical theology is often more sophisticated. Often drawing from an individualistic and otherworldly framework coupled with commitments to a substitutionary atonement model, Barabbas is used to bolster this theological system. However, in the process, the sociopolitical focus surrounding Barabbas (and Jesus) that is actually recorded in the Bible continues to be ignored. The result is that Barabbas's presence in Scripture continues to be distorted, domesticated, and misdirected away from what Scripture is suggesting to us. In doing so, Jesus also continues to be distorted, domesticated, and misdirected away from how the biblical narrative reveals his liberative significance.

---

[2]James K. Beilby and Paul R. Eddy, *The Nature of the Atonement: Four Views* (Downers Grove, IL: InterVarsity Press, 2006).

[3]David Mathis, "Barabbas and Me," Desiring God, April 5, 2012, www.desiringgod.org/articles /barabbas-and-me.

Getting familiar with some historical background helps illuminate often-missed features of the Jesus narratives. Such familiarization prepares readers to reconsider Barabbas based on biblical accounts. A reconsideration of Barabbas also helps to better understand Jesus. Following those steps, this chapter will conclude by articulating how empathizing with Barabbas aids us in living Jesus-shaped empathetic solidarity through intimate joining and liberative struggle with communities facing oppression, poverty, and death-dealing violence.

REVOLUTION WAS IN THE AIR

Revolution was in the air well before, and well after, Jesus and Barabbas walked the earth. Getting a glimpse of this history will help contextualize the life and words of these two men. Barabbas and Jesus responded to the death-dealing threats that overshadowed their people's lives every day. Likewise, when these Gospel accounts of Jesus were recorded, imperial dangers continued to exist. When scholars consider the dating of the Gospels, a big concern is whether they were written before, during, or after the Jewish-Roman War. The war was the culmination of Jewish resistance that had persisted for generations. In reality, the anti-imperial spirit traces all the way back to the exodus story in Hebrew Scripture, followed by life under Babylon, Assyria, and Persia. For our purpose it will suffice to take snapshots, beginning with the Maccabees.

By the time of Jesus, the Maccabees were larger-than-life legends. In 164 BC, while under the rule of Syria, the Maccabees led a surprisingly successful revolt. As an act of religious and sociopolitical resistance to overreaching foreign powers, the Jews cast out their oppressors. It began while taking a stand against an imposition on their religious practices and a takeover of the temple. Not all Jews were willing to accept this imposition, so a revolution was born. However, once the freedom struggle started unrolling, the goal of complete political independence became the new goal. Their victory ushered in the Hasmonean dynasty and created a new Jewish holiday,

Hanukkah. This dynasty would continue ruling for about one hundred years, formally ending in 63 BC. After the dynasty ended, the Maccabean revolution and reign would continue to shape Jewish radical political imagination and subversive dreams of a messianic revolt. The Maccabees fostered Jewish loyalty to the Torah, a willingness to accept martyrdom ("take up your cross"), uncompromising resistance when foreign powers crossed a line, and violent revolutionary action, believing God would intervene on their behalf. It would be mistaken to understand such sociopolitical action as merely secular revolution, like the revolts derived from the Enlightenment in the West. Not so. They sought to participate in God's liberation as demonstrated through the Maccabees as well as the Exodus. Salvation for them had a thicker and more holistic meaning than most Western theologies (especially compared to evangelicalism).[4]

In 63 BC, the Roman Empire took over, causing the end of the Hasmonian Dynasty. The empire appointed puppet kings in their place, but they were a hollow shell compared to true independence under God's rule. There would be numerous clashes with the Romans moving forward. Sporadic revolts and acts of Jewish resistance would reoccur in different regions. The mass poverty and economic exploitation that people experienced resulted in the emergence of the *lestai* brigands or bandits. Facing impoverishment, these revolutionaries strategically and defiantly robbed the wealthy of their riches throughout the first-century. Hyperindividualism might lead some to think of stealing as only an individualistic act of immorality. However, when society and the weight of its institutions are stacked against you, and when law and order is organized around your community's exploitation and slow death, then these responses are often seen more as defiant acts of resistance to a society that puts its foot on your throat and calls it benevolence. Such was the case for these bandits living under the empire and experiencing devastating poverty.

---

[4]N. T. Wright, *The New Testament and the People of God* (Minneapolis: Fortress, 1992), 158-69.

There were many acts of resistance around Jesus' lifetime as well. In fact, Galilee was fertile soil for revolutionaries to be born. Around AD 6, Judas of Galilee led an infamous revolt against Rome. In that struggle he was encouraging Jews to not participate in the census and to not pay taxes to the empire. While the Gospel of Luke tries hard not to sound anti-imperial, if you read between the lines of Jesus' birth story, one can see the sociopolitical occupation and exploitation of the people in full manifestation as Mary and Joseph head to Jerusalem for the census. Historically we know of other acts of Jewish resistance during the time of Jesus. There were multiple acts of Jewish resistance, as well as imperial backlash, under the governing watch of Pilate between AD 26 and 36. Often, revolts turned into bloody massacres. In 48 AD, twenty thousand Jews were murdered under Cumanus during a revolt. New resistance groups would continue to emerge throughout the first century. In the middle of that century, the Sicarii, or "the dagger-men," emerge. They became a serious Jewish resistance movement seeking liberation.

The Jewish sect that is most associated with seeking liberation from Roman oppression are the Zealots. Despite the name recognition of this group, there is scholarly debate about whether the Zealots actually existed during the time of Jesus. It has been argued that the usage of the term *Zealot* is anachronistic in the Gospel accounts. For our purposes, it matters very little if the formal group called the Zealots had formed during the time of Jesus, since it is clear the revolutionary spirit that would eventually lead to the formation of the Zealots was already in place. When the Gospel writers use the term *Zealot* to describe a disciple of Jesus, we can get the point, even if that term was not used quite that way until the Gospel accounts were written a few decades later.

That aside, revolutionary zeal culminated in the forming of the Zealots, who, alongside other groups like the Sicarii, fought against Rome in the Jewish-Roman War beginning in AD 66. Were they freedom fighters? Yes, but they were also acting by faith that God would deliver Israel from their enemies like God had done in the past. They were zealous for God and ready to cooperate with God for Israel's liberation. Unfortunately, the Jews were completely put down and slaughtered in Jerusalem by the Roman forces. They were also defeated because of internal fighting and battling between competing revolutionary Jewish sects. By AD 70, it was all over. It was a bloody and horrifying loss. The temple was completely destroyed. About six thousand Jews were crucified as a public spectacle to show everyone else what happens when people resist Rome.[5]

While the Jewish-Roman War occurred after Jesus' lifetime, it is important to note that the Gospel narratives record Jesus as predicting its coming. Jesus suggests that it happens because the people do not choose his way. Revolution was in the air long before Jesus or Barabbas lived, it repeatedly occurred while they lived, and those movements would coalesce into a much larger war with Rome after they lived. This historical context and sociopolitical backdrop is vital to understanding the Gospel accounts, and what the writers want us to know about who Barabbas was (as well as Jesus).

LIBERATING BARABBAS

Despite the mainstream images that suggest Barabbas was a foaming at the mouth, cock-eyed, serial killer, and in spirt of the evangelical temptation to force his meaning to fit this man exclusively into a penal substitution model of atonement, scripture has a different emphasis. The scriptural record will be our primary authority for reflecting on the meaning of Barabbas. The task for us is to take seriously how Barabbas is described by the Gospel writers. Keep track of this concern moving forward: Is there a specific characteristic or description of Barabbas that is central to the biblical accounts? Next, does our knowledge of the historical background enhance our reading and interpretation? What might the original audience have heard and

---

[5]Wright, *New Testament and the People of God*, 170-81.

understood when these words were originally written? Soon we will discover that Barabbas, as described in the Bible, was a revolutionary and liberating figure.

Every Gospel writer has something to say about Barabbas. This is not an insignificant observation. There are only a handful of biblical units that are in Matthew, Mark, Luke, and John. Yet, at the end of the Gospel accounts, Barabbas shows up every single time. Barabbas is important. Contrast it to Jesus' birth. The biggest Christian celebration in the United States is easily Christmas, but there are only two Gospel writers that even write anything about the birth of Jesus. Even then, they do so differently with varying purposes. Barabbas, on the other hand, consistently emerges right before Jesus is crucified.

The Gospel of Mark, thought by most scholars to be the oldest Gospel account, is definitive about Barabbas's revolutionary involvement.[6] In Mark 14, Jesus holds the Last Supper with his disciples and goes to Gethsemane, where he is betrayed. He is condemned by the Jerusalem establishment and then condemned by Pilate. It is in the context of Pilate questioning and condemning Jesus that Barabbas makes his first appearance in the story. The Gospel of Mark writes, "Now a man called Barabbas was in prison with the rebels who had committed murder during the insurrection" (Mk 15:7 NSRV).[7] Barabbas, translated as "son of the father," was arrested as an insurrectionist. This means that he resisted the imperial forces that crushed his community. Barabbas, however, was not a lone ranger in this work; he was participating in a broader insurrection. His acts of murder can only be understood in light of this insurrection. He was not killing people randomly but was participating in Jewish revolt. Ultimately, in Mark 15:11-15, we are told that Pilate provides a customary option of release for Jesus, but the leaders convince the

---

[6]David A. DeSilva, *An Introduction to the New Testament: Contexts, Methods & Ministry Formation* (Downers Grove, IL: IVP Academic, 2014), 161-67.
[7]Michael David Coogan et al., *The New Oxford Annotated Bible* (New York: Oxford University Press, 2001), Mark 15:7.

crowds to choose Barabbas for release. He was a political prisoner of a well-known insurrection, according to the story, and was now being released. Barabbas was an insurrectionist and freedom fighter who was not opposed to utilizing religious violence to gain victory. Gospel of Mark scholar Ched Meyers explains Barabbas's place in this account:

> Mark describes Barabbas in a manner that had concrete historical signification: as a Sicarius terrorist . . . there was constant insurrectionary activity in Jerusalem during this period. What Mark calls "murder" . . . would have been characteristic of the modus operandi of the Sicarii . . . or "dagger men," who were infamous for their stealth in political assassination. Thus Mark's narrative concern here is to dramatize the choice. Jesus and Barabbas each represent fundamentally different kinds of revolutionary practice, violent and nonviolent, both of which have led to a common fate: prison and impending execution.[8]

In the Gospel of Luke, Barabbas appears during Pilate's examination of Jesus. Pilate is concerned with particular charges brought against Jesus. We will explore these charges later, but for now it suffices to say that Jesus is found innocent of the charges. Luke portrays Pilate as the most sympathetic. Right as he is about to have Jesus beaten and released, the people respond, "'Away with this fellow! Release Barabbas for us!' (This was a man who had been put in prison for an insurrection that had taken place in the city, and for murder)" (Lk 23:18-19 NSRV). Barabbas is only mentioned one more time in Luke's account. It is a repeat of the sociopolitical identity and activity of Barabbas who is now being freed by Pilate: "He released the man they asked for, the one who had been put in prison for insurrection and murder, and he handed Jesus over as they wished" (Lk 23:25 NRSV).

---

[8]Ched Myers, *Binding the Strong Man: A Political Reading of Mark's Story of Jesus* (Maryknoll, NY: Orbis Books, 1988), 380.

We will consider Matthew's narration of Barabbas later, but right now we turn to John's account. Some might be tempted to interpret the Gospel of John as hovering above temporal and earthly concerns. This is because it has an explicitly theological portrait compared to the more subtle theological narratives of the Synoptic Gospels; nonetheless, the apolitical stereotype is a poor reading. Even the Johannine account turns the focus on Barabbas's political act of resistance rather than to dramatize his sinful and guilty status before God. Right before Barabbas's introduction, we find Pilate engaging the Jerusalem establishment leaders. He mocks them by encouraging them to execute justice for themselves, when he knows good and well that Rome does not permit them to execute their own law and justice. They must admit their helplessness in the situation: "We are not permitted to put anyone to death" (Jn 18:31 NSRV). Then comes an exchange between Jesus and Pilate. John portrays Jesus as more defiant with Pilate than the other Gospel writers. The primary concern for Pilate is whether Jesus considers himself a king. Jesus does not answer the question. By the end of the exchange Pilate is asking Jesus about truth. This initiates Pilate's referencing the custom of releasing someone for Passover. He mockingly says to the crowd, "Do you want me to release for you the King of the Jews?" The people respond resolutely: "They shouted in reply, 'Not this man, but Barabbas!' Now Barabbas was a bandit" (Jn 18:39-40 NRSV).

Some translations say that Barabbas had taken part "in an insurrection." That is an excellent dynamic equivalent of ideas, though the NRSV provides a more literal translation with "bandit" from *lestai*. But *lestai* does connote "insurrectionist" based on how it was used at that time.[9] There is no mention of Barabbas other than this one time. One might have expected an explication of Jesus as a spotless lamb in relation to Barabbas's sinfulness. We have none of that. For the Gospel of John, Barabbas's sociopolitical act of resistance is what matter's for his Jesus story.

9Coogan et al., *The New Oxford Annotated Bible*, 178.

It is fair now to begin deconstructing false depictions of Barabbas. He is not a killer out of one's worst nightmare, he is not an animalistic brute, a random and crazed serial murderer, nor is he thoughtless and merely acting out of lower instincts. Neither is Barabbas merely a foil to Jesus' sinless life (though that is certainly closer than the previous options); instead, he was a Jew who sought to engage in religious insurrection as a freedom fighter, believing his resistance aligned with how God had acted on Israel's behalf in the past. We must think of Barabbas more like Nat Turner or Thomas Müntzer (both men are historical figures who engaged in religious revolt) and less like the Joker or the Zodiac Killer. We should interpret him as frustrated and angry that oppressors occupied his land, mocked his God, and exploited his people. He dreamed of a restored Israel standing tall next to its neighbors. He wanted peace to be established, and was willing to risk his life in its pursuit. This sociopolitical portrait of Barabbas has been narrated repeatedly. To dilute, domesticate, or misdirect this simple and clearly stated aspect of Barabbas is not only problematic, but it affects our understanding about an essential dimension of who Jesus was and is today.

Ironically, Jesus' disciples responded in a similar fashion as Barabbas. Jesus routinely said revolutionary things, expressing concern for the poor and oppressed. The disciples eventually recognize that Jesus is the Messiah. Our twenty-first-century sensibilities miss Jesus' first-century sociopolitical relevance, which emboldened the disciples toward revolutionary struggle. Remember the response of Jesus' disciples when he is arrested: all four Gospel writers portray the disciples as ready for insurrection. During Jesus' arrest, the disciples ask, "Lord, should we strike with the sword?" (Lk 22:49 NRSV). According to Matthew 26:47-56, Mark 14:43-52, and Luke 22:47-53, an unnamed disciple cuts off the ear of a servant of the chief priest. The Gospel of John, however, snitches on Peter as the one who tries to kick off the rebellion (Jn 18:10). It is clear that the disciples have their own revolutionary aspirations. These radical commitments are the result of witnessing the teachings and ministry enacted in Jesus' life.

One can finally make sense of the charges leveled against Jesus in Luke's account. Most evangelical theologies are focused on Jesus' innocence, which is language found in the Gospel of Luke. However, when many evangelicals refer to Jesus' innocence, they usually mean Jesus' sinless life. A careful reading of the charges placed against Jesus in Luke demonstrate that the concern is not whether Jesus lived a sinless and perfect life, but whether he is guilty of the political charges made against him. In Luke 22:52, as Jesus is about to be arrested, Luke states, "Then Jesus said to the chief priests, the officers of the temple police, and the elders who had come for him, "Have you come out with swords and clubs as if I were a bandit?" (NRSV). The NIV translates this as "Am I leading a rebellion, that you have come with swords and clubs?" The response to Jesus is something that would only be expected of a political revolutionary. It is interesting that Jesus does not exactly answer his own question. Jesus is not involved in a revolution in the traditional sense, but he has inaugurated the kingdom of God, a new social order on earth, that is revolutionary and threatens the foundations of the old order.

The charges leveled against Jesus before Pilate are sociopolitical acts against the empire. Here is the first charge: "We found this man subverting our nation, forbidding us to pay the tribute tax to Caesar and claiming that he himself is Christ, a king" (Lk 23:2 NET). This was false on the surface but true on a deeper level. Pilate asks for himself, "Are you the king of the Jews?" However, he continues to see him as innocent of this charge. "But they persisted in saying, 'He incites the people by teaching throughout all Judea. It started in Galilee and ended up here!'" (Lk 23:5 NET). Jesus is then sent to Herod, where he is mocked and then sent back to Pilate. Again, for Pilate, the issue is whether he is innocent or guilty of the charge put before him. Therefore, Pilates says, "You brought me this man as one who was misleading the people. When I examined him before you, I

did not find this man guilty of anything you accused him of doing"
(Lk 23:14 NET). The concern is not whether or not Jesus had a sinless
life (whether true or not); the focus is on his innocence in relation to
the sociopolitical charges brought against him. Is he a threat to the
present social order?

JESUS BARABBAS OR JESUS THE CHRIST?

Matthew's account of Barabbas will help us pull these various arguments together to consider the often-ignored sociopolitical meaning
of Jesus. In Matthew 26, Jesus is betrayed by Judas and then approached
by a crowd carrying swords and clubs. Here "one of those with Jesus
put his hand on his sword, drew it, and struck the slave of the high
priest" according to Matthew (Mt 26:51 NRSV). Jesus, however, does
not recognize religious violence as compatible with the reign of God
he is inaugurating. In John's account, Jesus explains to Pilate, "If my
kingdom were from this world, my followers would be fighting to
keep me from being handed over to the Jews" (Jn 18:36 NRSV). In
Matthew 26:52, Jesus says to his disciples, "Put your sword back into
its place; for all who take the sword will perish by the sword" (NRSV).
Religious violence is incompatible with the way of Jesus and it leads
to destruction. At other times, Jesus directly suggests that the destruction from the Jewish-Roman War will fall on Jerusalem for the
path they have chosen.

Once again, Jesus asks them why they have come so heavily armed
to arrest him, "as though I were a bandit?" (Mt 26:55 NRSV). Jesus is
taken to the Jewish establishment leaders and charges are leveled
against him. Matthew's emphasis is less explicitly concerned with the
anti-imperial implications of Jesus we saw in Luke, but still attuned
to sociopolitical concerns. The central focus is whether Jesus is God's
anointed Messiah of Israel. They pressure Jesus, saying, "I put you
under oath before the living God, tell us if you are the Messiah, the
Son of God" (Mt 26:63 NRSV). Jesus doesn't answer the question, but
instead quotes from Daniel 7:13 and Psalm 110:1, implying that he is.

It is on the charge of claiming to be the Messiah and king that they seek his execution.

During Jesus' interrogation before Pilate, Barabbas is introduced in Matthew for the first time. Matthew provides a longer unit with Barabbas but is focused more on his relation to Jesus. We are told immediately that Barrabas is "a notorious prisoner." Yet Matthew narrates Barabbas's presence more provocatively than just ending there. Among the oldest manuscripts of Matthew, we are told that Barabbas is "called Jesus Barabbas." However, later scribes omitted *Jesus* as part of Barabbas's name. Now some contemporary translations have left out *Jesus* as part of Barabbas's name as well, like the King James translation, in contrast to the NRSV, NET, and the latest NIV translation, which include it. Omitting *Jesus* from Barabbas's name probably was an attempt to honor Jesus. However, omitting *Jesus* from Barabbas's name leaves out some of the rhetorical punch:

> Now at the festival the governor was accustomed to release a prisoner for the crowd, anyone whom they wanted. At that time they had a notorious prisoner, called Jesus Barabbas. So after they had gathered, Pilate said to them, "Whom do you want me to release for you, Jesus Barabbas or Jesus who is called the Messiah?" . . . Now the chief priests and the elders persuaded the crowds to ask for Barabbas and to have Jesus killed. The governor again said to them, "Which of the two do you want me to release for you?" And they said, "Barabbas." Pilate said to them, "Then what should I do with Jesus who is called the Messiah?" All of them said, "Let him be crucified!" . . . So he released Barabbas for them; and after flogging Jesus, he handed him over to be crucified. (Mt 27:15-17, 20-22, 26 NRSV)

The contrast between Jesus Barabbas and Jesus the Messiah leaves us with a choice between two revolutionaries, offering two paths to liberation. Barabbas already had a proven track record. Like the disciples, he was tired of his people being humiliated, he was tired of the excruciating poverty, and he was tired of witnessing Roman brutality against his people. Plus Barabbas had already put his own life on the line before. He was notorious for his revolutionary activity. It was Passover weekend, and he fit the Maccabean mold more than Jesus did.

That said, Jesus was no status quo religionist. Jesus courageously came to Jerusalem and defiantly clashed with the establishment rulers and authorities. In fact, he called them a "den of thieves" (Mt 21:13 KJV) for their participation in the concentrated exploitation of the people. Jesus also hungered for a just and righteous world. We know he preached a radical message to the poor, condemned the wealthy, and invited people to new life organized around himself. Preaching the kingdom of God was subversive. However, his revolutionary reign did not justify religious violence. His path meant enduring suffering as the faithful consequence that comes with accepting God's intervening liberation. The visible manifestation of Jesus' way is demonstrated in the reality that he would sooner be crucified than crucify his enemies. No matter how radical Jesus was, one can imagine why not everyone would be convinced that God's victory would unfold through a crucified Christ.

Jesus' message was revolutionary good news for the poor. Jesus, in Luke, offers his messianic manifesto in Luke 4:18-19:

> The Spirit of the Lord is upon me,
>   because he has anointed me
>   to bring good news to the poor.
> He has sent me to proclaim release to the captives
>   and recovery of sight to the blind,
> to let the oppressed go free,
>   to proclaim the year of the Lord's favor. (NRSV)

Throughout Luke–Acts, we are told stories about several wealthy people. Some voluntarily lay down their riches, while others are unwilling to share in common life on behalf of the poor: examples include the rich young ruler, Zacchaeus, Barnabas, and Ananias and Sapphira. In the Gospel narratives, Jesus is shown to privilege the least, the last, and the lost in his upside-down kingdom. It is surprising how ethnic outsiders and Samaritans, vulnerable women, lepers, and the poor hungry masses are prioritized in Jesus' new order made visible on the earth. Other books have tackled this subject more thoroughly, but for now we can say that the politics of Jesus were revolutionary.[10]

We ought not miss the liberative and revolutionary relevance of Jesus and Barabbas. Each offers something concrete for the here and now, and each is a Jew with a holistic understanding of liberation that would never split the spiritual apart from the social. A common mistake at this juncture would be to suggest that Barabbas was for an earthly kingdom and that Jesus had an exclusively spiritual kingdom in mind. That is scriptural malpractice and the text never suggests that. In fact, Jesus' teachings and ministry do not make sense within a spiritual-only framework. Jesus explicitly teaches his disciples to pray that the kingdom come on earth as it is heaven. Denominational or ecclesial doctrine ought not override Jesus' own teaching. Both Jesus and Barabbas have implications for how we organize life on earth.

We get a hint of this holistic meaning of liberation when we take the name of Jesus literally. Jesus is "Joshua" or "Yeshua," "the one who saves." Both of these men are given names that identify them as the one who saves. This is not a thin, watered-down salvation only good for individuals, having merely spiritual implications, or only able to spare us from hell so we can escape to heaven. This is salvation in the tradition of God's intervening in the life of Israel. This salvation is thicker and holistic. This is divine deliverance that saves us from anything that holds us captive. When each of them are identified as Jesus, we are confronted with a choice between what kind of liberator we will trust and follow in our own lives. Who can save us? Will we have faith in God's Messiah when violence seems to make the world go

---

[10]Obery M. Hendricks, *The Politics of Jesus: Rediscovering the True Revolutionary Nature of the Teachings of Jesus and How They Have Been Corrupted* (New York: Doubleday, 2006); John Howard Yoder, *The Politics of Jesus: Vicit Agnus Noster* (Grand Rapids: Eerdmans, 1994).

round? Or will we take up the way of Barabbas, which makes more sense to us. Violence, the logic goes, only listens to more forceful violence. Who can save you? Who will you follow? Who will be your liberator? You have to feel the lure of violent resistance before you really understand the liberating way of Jesus.

That is why Jesus should not be contrasted to Barabbas carelessly. They are not opposed to one another in all things. Jesus empathizes with every Barabbas of the world. His own disciples had the spirit of Barabbas in them, because they cared about the oppression of the people and wanted to join in God's liberating intervention. Very little separated Jesus' disciples from Barabbas. Jesus intimately understands Barabbas and empathetically journeys in solidarity with his oppressed community. Jesus opposes religious violence as a fruitful path to liberation and peace, but he also identified with and for the most vulnerable of society through his joined presence among them, and sought deliverance from whatever bound the people in his ministry.

Jesus' response to those who chose religious violence as the means for liberation, instead of *shalom*-shaped liberation on earth, was not condemnation but lament. Jesus empathized with the revolutionaries and desired they become peacemakers in his way in their society. The coming loss of life and the destruction of Jerusalem from the Jewish-Roman War pained Jesus tremendously to the point of deep empathetic lament:

> Now when Jesus approached and saw the city, he wept over it, saying, "If you had only known on this day, even you, the things that make for peace! But now they are hidden from your eyes. For the days will come upon you when your enemies will build an embankment against you and surround you and close in on you from every side. They will demolish you—you and your children within your walls— and they will not leave within you one stone on top of another, because you did not recognize the time of your visitation from God." (Lk 19:41-44 NET)

The temptation for those who want to justify religious violence is to spiritualize or avoid Jesus' radical message so that it has no earthly demand on our lives. On the other hand, the temptation of doctrinal pacifists is to apathetically condemn oppressed people's revolutionary methods from the sidelines. The distance from the oppressed, the condemnation of the oppressed, and the apathy toward the oppressed are all out of alignment with the way of Jesus. That is not participating in God's choosing the vulnerable, weak, and oppressed of our world as sites of divine vocation and deliverance (1 Cor 1:18-31). Only when we empathize with our Barabbas in our society through actual joining of life, sharing intimately in suffering, and taking up our cross in the struggle for God's dream of a new society, can we grasp the things that make for peace that Jesus calls us to live.

The things that make for peace will never be found on the sidelines, they will not be found through condemning how others deal with oppression that do not affect you, but they do demand empathetic solidarity and liberative struggle that intimately joins people living on the underside of the empire. There we find both Barabbas and Jesus caught in the whirlwinds of the establishment and under the punitive control of the empire. Each desires liberation and peace.

CONCLUSION

Barabbas has been (intentionally?) mischaracterized and misunderstood in many Christian communities. He has been dehumanized, used as an ideological tool to fit into elaborate theological systems, and Scripture's portrayal of him is ignored. The four Gospels are consistent; Barabbas was a political prisoner held for his participation in a Jewish insurrection against oppressors. Barabbas sought liberation and freedom. His understanding was not unique, since God's liberation is embedded into the story of Israel's journey with God found in the Hebrew Scriptures. Ignoring the long history of Jewish resistance inevitably leaves readers missing key aspects of the Jesus story as well (of which we have only scratched the surface). However, not only have we missed the revolutionary figure that Barabbas was, but in renarrating his story for other purposes, the church developed one more trick to disregard the revolutionary vocation of Jesus. Once again, the church can continue on as the church of the status quo, of the establishment, of the empire, without recognizing the obvious contradictions with the life and teachings of Jesus.

Barabbas's presence in the Gospel story leaves us wrestling with the sociopolitical implications of Jesus' Messiahship. If he is the anointed king, and if he claimed that the new society was here, near, and among them while injustice and oppression persisted, what does that mean for his disciples? It has been argued here that Jesus rejected religious violence as God's liberation, but he did not reject the oppressed and their desire for liberation. The entire New Testament repeatedly invites us to follow Jesus, to walk in his footsteps, to become his disciples, to share in his life, death, and resurrection, and to obey his teachings. The big secret that has been kept from most of the church is not only that this is what being a Christian is, but that the way of Jesus reveals the revolutionary "things that make for peace." Jesus is liberation and is the way of liberation. And his way includes empathetic solidarity that joins oppressed and vulnerable people in intimate struggle against that which comes to steal, kill, and destroy life. We are all invited to participate in the liberative things that make for peace.

The things that make for peace are not self-evident or taken-for-granted church doctrines. The things that make for peace are the exercise of faith in God's liberation and peacemaking, even in the midst of a social order organized around the strategic and systemic use of violence. The things that make for peace include the practice of empathetic solidarity that joins the crucified of the world through presence. The things that make for peace confront and clash with the establishment and the dens of exploitation and are willing to accept the consequences for such faithful resistance. The things that make for peace lead us to visibly embody the radical story of Jesus before our neighbors, manifesting God's reign on the underside of the empire. And strangely, it is a revolutionary named Barabbas that helps us see the things that make for peace once more. When we liberate Barabbas, we see Jesus anew and are graced with the opportunity of experiencing God's deliverance from status quo religion. When we liberate Barabbas, the doors of the church are opened as we are invited to encounter afresh the revolutionary Messiah, who is able to save, deliver, and liberate all of us from every captivity and stronghold, and he continues to invite each of us into divine liberative struggle in the way of Jesus.

CHAPTER FOURTEEN

JUBILEE, PENTECOST, AND LIBERATION

The Preferential Option of the Poor on the Apostolic Way

AMOS YONG

RECENT TRENDS IN LIBERATION theology show remarkable diversification compared with the perceived Marxist underpinnings of the first generation's efforts. In the meanwhile, although it was said that liberation theologians opted for the poor, it was also noted that the poor were opting for Pentecostalism.[1] This chapter considers how pentecostal spirituality,[2] which has served the poor across the majority world, can *both* gain further theological traction and specification *and* expand evangelical thinking on this topic. The chapter will do this via sustained engagement with the "many tongues" of liberation theology in the present global context, as refracted through the apostolic witness, particularly of the third Gospel and its sequel volume.[3] The

---

This essay was initially written for this book by invitation of the editors, but meanwhile it appeared as chap. 8 in Amos Yong, *The Hermeneutical Spirit: Theological Interpretation and the Scriptural Imagination for the 21st Century* (Eugene, OR: Cascade Books, 2017). It is now reprinted here with permission of Cascade Books/Wipf & Stock.

[1] A saying that goes back decades; for one version, see Donald E. Miller and Tetsunao Yamamori, *Global Pentecostalism: The New Face of Christian Social Engagement* (Berkeley: University of California Press, 2007), 215.

[2] I do not capitalize *pentecostal* when used adjectivally, only when used as nouns—e.g., Pentecostalism and Pentecostals—referring to members of the group.

[3] Most immediately in the background of this essay is my book, *The Future of Evangelical Theology: Soundings from the Asian American Diaspora* (Downers Grove: IVP Academic, 2014), esp. chs. 5–6.

argument, unfolded in the three sections that follow, begins with contemporary liberationist impulses in global and evangelical theological discourses, continues with developments of pentecostal liberationist thought, and concludes with scriptural reflections, focused particularly on Luke–Acts.

THE PREFERENTIAL OPTION *FOR* THE POOR: GLOBAL AND EVANGELICAL DEVELOPMENTS

Liberation theology burst onto the scene not too long after the Latin American Catholic Bishops' conference in Medellin, Colombia, in 1968. In the first decade-plus after Medellin, the dominant liberation voices (e.g., Gutierrez, Bonino, Segundo, and the Boff brothers) drew from a wide range of critical theories, most prominently neo-Marxist social analysis, and brought such into dialogue especially with the tradition of Roman Catholic social thought (these were mostly Catholic theologians) vis-à-vis the contexts of poverty widespread across the Latin American hemisphere. The point about liberation was that the gospel was historically, politically, economically, and socially relevant, and this also impacted the nature and mission of the church as the people of God and the body of Christ. Methodologically, liberation theology emphasized the hermeneutical starting point of solidarity with the poor: the Scriptures and the Christian tradition were received from those perspectives and in relationship to those realities and the challenges identified therein, and the goal was not armchair speculation but—here consistent with Marx's own commitments—to change the world.

Within two decades, reactions came in hard and fast, not only from the Roman Catholic magisterium—with concerns about the role of Marxist analyses and implications of such for mobilizing uncritical participation in class struggles, even to the point of violence[4]—but

---

[4]See the Congregation for the Doctrine of the Faith, "Instruction on Certain Aspects of the 'Theology of Liberation,'" August 6, 1984, at www.vatican.va/roman_curia/congregations/cfaith /documents/rc_con_cfaith_doc_19840806_theology-liberation_en.html; cf. Rohan M. Curnow, "Which Preferential Option for the Poor? A History of the Doctrine's Bifurcation," *Modern Theology* 31 (2015): 27-59.

also from evangelical quarters. Like the Roman Catholic hierarchy, evangelicals, among others, also perceived that Marxist tools would precipitate revolutionary violence, so even if liberationists were rightly and justifiably driven by motivations regarding the alleviation of poverty, liberation theology ought to be approached very reservedly.[5] So although the liberationist option for the poor was recognized by some evangelicals to have biblical moorings, the concern was that as a hermeneutical principle it would compromise evangelical convictions about allowing Scripture to interpret itself, thus subjecting the message of the Bible to biased perspectival lenses or other ideological commitments.[6] Within these main lines of the evangelical theological tradition, then, liberation theology, even if useful thematically, could not provide the primary framework even to engage the concerns of Latin America and the challenges of global poverty; instead, liberationist perspectives could make their contribution only when resituated within a more biblically oriented paradigm, such as that provided by contextual theological approaches.[7]

Part of the challenge was that the emerging postcolonial world since the 1960s inspired theological thinking from those outside the traditional theological orbit of the Euro-American West. Hence one way to read the tradition of liberation theology is as an expression of non-Western experiences, frustrations, and aspirations. Evangelical theology at large, however, has been ill-equipped to grapple seriously with such hermeneutical and methodological pluralism. So even when evangelicals labor to propose a holistic theology that is Jesus centered, oriented to the poor and marginalized, directed toward the reign of God, and communally engaged[8]—each of which themes are

---

[5]Raymond C. Hundley, *Radical Liberation Theology: An Evangelical Response* (Wilmore, KY: Bristol Books & OMS International, 1987); Paul C. McGlasson, *Another Gospel: A Confrontation with Liberation Theology* (Grand Rapids: Baker Books, 1994).

[6]Emilio A. Núñez C., *Liberation Theology*, trans. Paul E. Sywulka (Chicago: Moody Press, 1985).

[7]See Sharon E. Heaney, *Contextual Theology for Latin America: Liberation Themes in Evangelical Perspective* (Colorado Springs, CO: Paternoster Press, 2008).

[8]E.g., Priscilla Pope-Levison, *Evangelization from a Liberation Perspective*, American University Studies Series VII, Theology and Religion 69 (New York: Peter Lang, 1991).

central to liberation theologies—these have remained marginal to rather than received by the center of the evangelical theological tradition. The result is that when contemporary evangelical thinkers have embraced the liberationist vision, such has to be parried under a *postconservative* label rather than being defensible as belonging to the heart of evangelical thought and action.[9]

The present ferment in liberation theology shows no signs of abatement on the global stage, but even further complexification. A number of trajectories are worth noting. First, liberation theology is needed not only for so-called Third or underdeveloped World contexts but also in the "First" and "Second" World regions, wherever there are marginalized groups;[10] in fact, on that score, even the Western world needs liberation from its own oppressiveness (its tendencies toward exploitation and victimization of those less fortunate). Second, and along this same line of inquiry, there are now urban liberation theologies focused particularly on the slums and ghettos of the cosmopolitan centers of the world, arguably all developed environments but stratified socioeconomically and in many other ways;[11] here, because of the systemic networks that constitute twenty-first century global cities, liberation must operate in multiple directions, addressing different and many layers of systems that generate urban flows. Third, liberation theology in the last two decades faces fundamentally different circumstances than before 1989–1991, and can therefore no longer merely oppose capitalism with socialism, but has to envision global capitalism not as a monolithic whole but as a set of dynamic and constructed systems that is thereby also open to piecemeal

---

[9]For instance, João B. Chaves, *Evangelicals and Liberation Revisited: An Inquiry into the Possibility of an Evangelical-Liberationist Theology* (Eugene, OR: Wipf & Stock, 2013).

[10]Part 4 of Jacques Van Nieuwenhove and Berma Klein Goldewijk, eds., *Popular Religion, Liberation and Contextual Theology: Papers from a Congress (January 3–7, 1990, Nijmegen, the Netherlands) Dedicated to Arnulf Camps OFM* (Kampen: Uitgeversmaatschappij J. H. Kok, 1991), is on Eastern Europe with two chapters on Czechoslovakia and Hungary and calls attention to liberation theologies among the Roma across the continent and among Native North Americans as operative, ostensibly, in the so-called First World.

[11]Representative here is Chris Shannahan, *Voices from the Borderland: Re-imagining Cross-Cultural Urban Theology in the Twenty-First Century* (2010; reprint, New York: Routledge, 2014).

democratization, transformation, and redemption; this means that socioeconomic theory itself needs to be updated in order to engage neoliberal capitalism with global poverty in its many twenty-first century guises.[12] The point is that liberation theology in the twenty-first century is pluriform not only in its regional, ethnic, and cultural diversity but also in its interdisciplinarity and in its multiple layeredness moving between and within the grassroots and the theoretical elite.[13] The constant refrain, however, is the preferential option *for* the poor, albeit increasingly the mantra, is being developed along multiple registers and availing itself of a myriad of analytical tools.[14]

What hope is there for an evangelical theology of liberation in this ever more diverse and convoluted phenomenon? A traditionalist evangelical hermeneutic that simply insists on scriptural priority too easily dismisses or ignores liberationist claims that might be uncomfortable. A range of holistic missiological models are emerging within evangelical circuits that seek to incorporate liberationist perspectives, but inevitably these are elements sanitized of intercultural, transethnic, or racialized features in order to be compatible with the traditional evangelical imagination.

It is here that I suggest we look at an evangelical spirituality—that of modern Pentecostalism—for resources with which to engage liberationist concerns. If liberation theology opted for the poor, it would appear that the poor in the last generation has opted for Pentecostalism.[15] As Harvey Cox, Philip Jenkins, and many other observers have noted,

---

[12]Leading the discussion here is Ivan Petrella; see Petrella, *The Future of Liberation Theology* (Burlington, VT: Ashgate, 2004), "Liberation Theology: A Programmatic Statement," in *Latin American Liberation Theology: The Next Generation*, ed. Ivan Petrella (Maryknoll, NY: Orbis Books, 2005), 147-72, and *Beyond Liberation Theology: A Polemic* (London: SCM Press, 2008).

[13]Thia Cooper, ed., *The Reemergence of Liberation Theologies: Models for the Twenty-First Century* (New York: Palgrave Macmillan, 2013).

[14]See further Daniel G. Groody, ed., *The Option for the Poor in Christian Theology* (Notre Dame, IN: University of Notre Dame Press, 2007), and Daniel G. Groody and Gustavo Gutiérrez, eds., *The Preferential Option for the Poor Beyond Theology* (Notre Dame, IN: University of Notre Dame Press, 2014).

[15]E.g., R. Andrew Chesnut, *Born Again in Brazil: The Pentecostal Boom and the Pathogens of Poverty* (New Brunswick, NJ: Rutgers University Press, 1997), and Andre Corten, *Pentecostalism in Brazil: Emotion of the Poor and Theological Romanticism* (New York: Palgrave Macmillan, 1999),

world Christianity has been growing largely due to the vibrancy of pentecostal and charismatic renewal movements across the Global South.[16] My claim in the next section is that pentecostal spirituality can assist evangelical theology precisely because its "many tongues" sensibility provides theological and not just pragmatic justification for attending to the voices of the poor and many others in a pluralistic and needy world.

THE PREFERENTIAL OPTION *OF* THE POOR: LIBERATIONIST ROUTES IN GLOBAL PENTECOSTALISM

Let's not naively think that classical forms of Pentecostalism, the kind that is closest to evangelicalism in various respects, has been enthusiastic about liberation theology from the beginning. In many ways, traditional pentecostal thinkers, especially within white pentecostal movements and churches, would not object to the evangelical prioritization of Scripture and even subordination of perceived liberationist ideological constructs within that biblical frame. Even within the African American pentecostal community, dispensationalist and premillennialist eschatology, traditionalist demonology, and rigid holiness stances impede whatever impulses might be present toward liberationist initiatives and projects, and this is the case even though black Pentecostals are often much more sociopolitically alert and even engaged than their white counterparts.[17] We can only proceed, then, fully cognizant that there are significant hurdles to be overcome in any efforts to craft a liberation theological platform from pentecostal sources.

Yet granting the above, there has also been a substantive compulsion toward dialogue with liberation theology from the pentecostal

---

are representative of global Pentecostalism at the grassroots, even if they are focused on the Brazilian context.

[16]Harvey G. Cox, *Fire from Heaven: The Rise of Pentecostal Spirituality and the Reshaping of Religion in the 21st Century* (Reading, MA: Addison-Wesley, 1995), and Philip Jenkins, *The Next Christendom: The Coming of Global Christianity*, 3rd ed. (Oxford: Oxford University Press, 2011).

[17]E.g., Frederick L. Ware, "On the Compatibility/Incompatibility of Pentecostal Premillennialism with Black Liberation Theology," in *Afro-Pentecostalism: Black Pentecostal and Charismatic Christianity in History and Culture*, ed. Estrelda Alexander and Amos Yong, Religion, Race, and Ethnicity Series (New York: New York University Press, 2011), 191-206.

sector.[18] In the following I attempt to summarize particularly those who have attempted book-length contributions at this interface, and focus especially on the diversity of pentecostal voices across the majority world.

We begin with Latin American contributions, not least because the impact of Medellin has been felt even within the emerging pentecostal academy. The 1990s featured two substantive contributions: by Hispanic American social ethicist Eldin Villafañe and by Puerto Rican theologian Samuel Solivan.[19] The approach of the former (Villafañe) sought to triangulate around Hispanic American social realities, its religious dimensions (including the interwoven narrative of Roman Catholicism in Hispanic American life), and the urban pentecostal experience within those communities, but promoted a congruence amid this plurality through the work of the Spirit that enabled these various voices to speak toward a spirituality of social justice without insisting that they all said the same thing. The latter (Solivan) attempted a parallel strategy of harmonizing (without homogenizing) the many Hispanic American hermeneutical sensitivities, but entwined these around the felt presence of the Spirit, identified in terms of suffering, thus opening up to considerations of the mutuality between human anguish and divine pathos (*orthopathos* in the latter case). The goal in each case was to register Hispanic pentecostal hermeneutical and methodological approaches to the Christian tradition and to push liberative pathways forward.

It was quickly becoming recognized that pentecostal spirituality provided an alternative paradigm for liberation theology that, while consonant with the main thrusts of classical liberationist approaches,

---

[18]See, for example, an academic engagement between the two: Miroslav Volf, "Materiality of Salvation: An Investigation in the Soteriologies of Liberation and Pentecostal Theologies," *Journal of Ecumenical Studies* 26 (1989): 447-67.

[19]Eldin Villafañe, *The Liberating Spirit: Toward a Hispanic American Pentecostal Social Ethics* (New York: University Press of America, 1992), and Samuel Solivan, *Spirit, Pathos and Liberation: Toward an Hispanic Pentecostal Theology*, Journal of Pentecostal Theology Supplement 14 (Sheffield, UK: Sheffield Academic Press, 1998).

could not be reduced to sociotheoretical or Marxist frameworks.[20] In the meanwhile, Hispanic and Latin American pentecostal theologians have pressed on. Peruvian pentecostal mission theologian Darío López Rodriguez has proffered a biblical and even Lukan liberation theology, even as Hispanic systematic theologian Sammy Alfaro has recommended a spirit-christological vision that connects the struggle of Jesus amid the Roman imperialism of his day with the struggles of Hispanic immigrants with the American empire of the current era.[21] The former provides grassroots pentecostal readings of the biblical text, while the latter mines pentecostal *coritos* and *hymnos* for liberative purposes. This next generation of Latin American pentecostal scholars, as it were, unveils how the voices of the pentecostal poor read for and sing about the liberation of the gospel by the power of the Spirit.[22]

Asian pentecostal theology is a bit less developed along the liberation axis than their Latin American counterparts. Korean American pentecostal systematician Koo Dong Yun has written books about Spirit baptism and pneumatology in interreligious perspective, but framed neither in liberative terms.[23] Yet along the way, he has also begun to propound an Asian pentecostal liberation theology in conversation with Minjung sources advocating that pentecostal perspectives lift up the affective and emotive aspects of the indigenous Korean Minjung (or the poor) spirituality, and connect these to biblical

---

[20]See the observations of nonpentecostal observers like Richard Schaull and Waldo Cesar, *Pentecostalism and the Future of the Christian Churches: Promises, Limitations, Challenges* (Grand Rapids: Eerdmans, 2000), and Manfred K. Bahmann, *A Preference for the Poor: Latin American Liberation Theology from a Protestant Perspective* (Lanham, MD: University Press of America, 2005), esp. ch. 12.

[21]Darío López Rodriguez, *The Liberating Mission of Jesus: The Message of the Gospel of Luke*, trans. Stefanie E. Israel and Richard E. Waldrop (Eugene, OR: Pickwick Publications, 2012), and Sammy Alfaro, *Divino Compañero: Toward a Hispanic Pentecostal Christology* (Eugene, OR: Pickwick Publications, 2010).

[22]See also the range of proposals in Néstor Medina and Sammy Alfaro, eds., *Pentecostals and Charismatics in Latin America and Latino Communities* (New York: Palgrave Macmillan, 2015).

[23]Koo Dong Yun, *Baptism in the Holy Spirit: An Ecumenical Theology of Spirit Baptism* (Lanham, MD: University Press of America, 2003), and *The Holy Spirit and Ch'i (Qi): A Chiological Approach to Pneumatology* (Eugene, OR: Pickwick Publications, 2012).

themes of the Spirit's converting, sanctifying, and saving work.[24] If this more East Asian vantage point connects to the Minjung poor, then South Asian theologian Shaibu Abraham starts with the Indian context to formulate a liberation theological option from this vantage point.[25] Yet the latter does not reengage Indian Pentecostal sources (reliant primarily on Shaul and Cesar's work—see above), which leaves much space for next steps in this discussion. Pointing the way forward here would be Indian Pentecostals engaging with Dalit traditions, although a full-fledged Dalit pentecostal liberation theology still is on the horizon.[26] Yet the point is that Asian Pentecostalism is vast, and the available resources are strewn across various spectra, so the emergence of organically Asian commitments is just a matter of time.[27]

On the African front, the liberation accents are more on development and socioeconomic treks, and the literature is being

---

[24]Koo Dong Yun, "Pentecostalism from Below: Minjung Liberation and Asian Pentecostal Theology," in *The Spirit in the World: Emerging Pentecostal Theologies in Global Contexts*, ed. Veli-Matti Kärkkäinen (Grand Rapids: Eerdmans, 2009), 89-114. More traditionally pentecostal, and in that sense more consistent with conservative evangelical approaches, is Bae Hyoen Sung, in his response to efforts to bring pentecostal thought more fully in line with Minjung theology; this is elaborated by Korean Presbyterian theologian Lee Hong Jung, "Minjung and Pentecostal movements in Korea," both in *Pentecostals After a Century: Global Perspectives on a Movement in Transition*, ed. Allan H. Anderson and Walter J. Hollenweger, Journal of Pentecostal Theology Supplement series 15 (Sheffield, UK: Sheffield Academic Press, 1999), 161-63 (Bae) and 138-60 (Lee).

[25]Shaibu Abraham, *Pentecostal Theology of Liberation: Holy Spirit and Holiness in the Society*, Christian Heritage Rediscovered 6 (New Delhi: Christian World Imprints, 2014).

[26]An initial foray is Paulson Pulikottil, "Ramankutty Paul: A Dalit Contribution to Pentecostalism," in *Asian and Pentecostal: The Charismatic Face of Christianity in Asia*, ed. Allan Anderson and Edmond Tang (London: Regnum International: Asia Pacific Theological Seminary Press, 2005), 245-57. More recent developments include V. V. Thomas, *Dalit Pentecostalism: Spirituality of the Empowered Poor* (Bangalore: Asian Trading Corp., 2008), and Yabbaju (Jabez) Rapada, *Dalit Pentecostalism: A Study of the Indian Pentecostal Church of God* (Lexington, KY: Emeth Press, 2013). M. Stephen is an Indian pentecostal ethicist, but his work circles around rather than engages liberation discourse explicitly; see Stephen's *A Christian Theology in the Indian Context* (Delhi: ISPCK, 2001), ch. 23, which includes discussion of subaltern, Dalit, tribal, women's, and ecotheology, which can resource Indian pentecostal liberationist efforts.

[27]Simon Chan's *Grassroots Asian Theology: Thinking the Faith from the Ground Up* (Downers Grove, IL: IVP Academic, 2014) features distinctive pentecostal resonances, but does not embrace liberation theological verbiage or agendas; more promising for the latter trajectory are the chapters by Finny Philip, Ekaputra Tupamahu, and Iap Sian-Chin, among others, in *Global Renewal Christianity: The Past, Present, and Future of Spirit-Empowered Movements*, vol. 1, *Asia and Oceania*, ed. Vinson H. Synan and Amos Yong (Lake Mary, FL: Charisma House, 2015).

produced by those studying pentecostal activities as much as by those crafting pentecostal ideas or doctrines in relationship to their practices.[28] While the focus here is surely not on liberation as understood in the Medellin tradition, what is being described and categorized in this related field of literature concerns liberative developments within pentecostal churches, communities, and movements, especially in the sub-Saharan region. African theologians like David Ngong are attempting to articulate liberative soteriological visions for African societies in dialogue with pentecostal spirituality, but African pentecostal theologians themselves have yet to produce full-blown liberation theological treatises.[29] Two instances in the wider Afro-pentecostal diaspora, however, deserve mention at this juncture.

First, Nimi Wariboko, Redeemed Christian Church of God missionary and Walter Muelder Professor of Social Ethics at the Boston University School of Theology (since 2015), has been at work on what might be called a pentecostal or charismatic theology of economics. With a background on Wall Street and a commitment to thinking through the Nigerian pentecostal experience for a global pentecostal theology and social ethics,[30] Wariboko's contributions related to liberative initiatives include at least the following: reflections on pentecostal spirituality for ecclesial public life; extensions of charismatic piety and practice sensibilities for urban formation; and reappropriations of pentecostal-charismatic entrepreneurship for engaging

---

[28]For instance: Robert Mbe Akoko, *"Ask and You Shall Be Given": Pentecostalism and the Economic Crisis in Cameroon*, African Studies Collection 2 (Leiden: African Studies Centre, 2007); Jaako Lounela, *Mission and Development: Finnish Pentecostal, Lutheran and Orthodox Mission Agencies in Development Work in Kenya 1948–1989* (Abo: Abo Akademi University Press, 2007); Dena Freeman, ed., *Pentecostalism and Development: Churches, NGOs and Social Change in Africa* (New York: Palgrave Macmillan, 2010).

[29]David Tonghou Ngong, *The Holy Spirit and Salvation in African Christian Theology: Imagining a More Hopeful Future for Africa*, Bible and Theology in Africa 8 (New York: Peter Lang, 2010); see also Samuel Zalanga and Amos Yong, "What Empire? Which Multitude? Pentecostalism and Social Liberation in North America and Sub-Saharan Africa," in *Evangelicals and Empire: Christian Alternatives to the Political Status Quo*, ed. Bruce Ellis Benson and Peter Goodwin Heltzel (Grand Rapids: Brazos Press, 2008), 237-51.

[30]E.g., Nimi Wariboko, *Nigerian Pentecostalism* (Rochester, NY: University of Rochester Press, 2014).

with the volatility of the global market.[31] Obviously Wariboko is not writing liberation theology in its traditional or classical style. Yet it would be a mistake to ignore his contributions toward what might be considered a distinctive pentecostal modality of formulating a liberative theological praxis, one that is just at home in, albeit resisting and subverting variously, the neoliberal global economy in its destructive guises. Wariboko's major contribution in this direction, one that emphasizes cultivation of what he calls the *pentecostal principle* that creatively innovates so as to always be able to begin again, is applicable to liberative theological projects, since the challenge is always how to imagine a more just and shalomic alternative to the sociopolitical status quo. So if the poor have opted for Pentecostalism since the rise of liberation theology, arguably more recently the poor have been opting for specifically prosperity forms of pentecostal spirituality, those more conducive to being operationalized in the unpredictable market economy,[32] and it is here that Wariboko's socioeconomic praxis can potentially intervene to engage and temper, if not redirect, glocal systems.

On the British front, in some respects twice removed from the Afro-pentecostal diaspora because of mediations through the Caribbean, Robert Beckford has been long at work on a Dread pentecostal and liberation theology.[33] On multiple fronts—such as theology of cultural transformation, political theology, theology of social transformation[34]—Beckford has consistently pressed through

---

[31]Respectively, Nimi Wariboko, *The Pentecostal Principle: Ethical Methodology in New Spirit* (Grand Rapids: Eerdmans, 2012); *The Charismatic City and the Public Resurgence of Religion: A Pentecostal Social Ethics of Cosmopolitan Urban Life* (New York: Palgrave Macmillan, 2014); and *Economics in Spirit and Truth: A Moral Philosophy of Finance* (New York: Palgrave Macmillan, 2014).

[32]As documented in Katherine Attanasi and Amos Yong, eds., *Pentecostalism and Prosperity: The Socioeconomics of the Global Charismatic Movement*, Christianities of the World 1 (New York: Palgrave Macmillan, 2012).

[33]The following summarizes an earlier discussion of Beckford's work in Yong, "Justice Deprived, Justice Demanded: Afropentecostalisms and the Task of World Pentecostal Theology Today," *Journal of Pentecostal Theology* 15 (2006): 127-47, esp. 134-40.

[34]E.g., Robert Beckford, *Jesus Is Dread: Black Theology and Black Culture in Britain* (London: Darton, Longman, and Todd, 1999); *Dread and Pentecostal: A Political Theology for the Black Church*

the black pentecostal experience, especially in dialogue with Jamaican ideological and cultural resources, to explore the possibilities of an authentic pentecostal vision for the British public square. If Beckford's focus on race is unique and practically singlehanded within the global pentecostal theological landscape, its implications for liberation theology are palpable. One might argue that Beckford's is the most obvious sustained contribution to liberation theology from a pentecostal perspective, even as the radicality of his proposals, particularly due to its Dread credentials, means that its reception within pentecostal circles, even among pentecostal academia, is gradual at best and contested (even if not so much in print).

The preceding survey of pentecostal contributions to liberation theology reflect their crosscultural, transnational, and interdisciplinary character. Western contributions are emerging precisely on the heels of their majority world colleagues, and these efforts engage with the full range of sociopolitical issues related to the liberation of the poor and oppressed, including but not limited to race and ethnicity, class, gender, globalization, and ecology and creation care.[35] If liberation theology opted for the poor and the poor opted for Pentecostalism, then pentecostal scholars, theologians, and academics are slowly but surely also reflecting on the prospects for a pentecostal liberation theology from out of these realities on the ground.

DIVINE PREFERENCES AND OPTIONS?
APOSTOLIC LIBERATION TODAY

In this final section, then, I'd like to build constructively toward what might be called a pentecostal-evangelical theology of liberation and do so in ways that address the pluralism inherent in the many levels of the conversation. My argument will suggest that the preferential

---

in Britain (London: SPCK, 2000); *God of the Rahtid: Redeeming Rage* (London: Darton, Longman, and Todd, 2001); and *Jesus Dub: Theology, Music and Social Change* (New York: Routledge, 2006).
[35]Michael Wilkinson and Steven M. Studebaker, eds., *A Liberating Spirit: Pentecostals and Social Action in North America*, Pentecostals, Peacemaking & Social Justice series (Eugene, OR: Pickwick Publications, 2010).

option *of* the poor is one that empowers their voices toward liberative ends. We will briefly unpack this thesis hermeneutically and develop the normative arguments, both via scriptural engagements within the corpus of Acts–Luke.[36]

I begin with Acts 2, not only because I am adopting a modern pentecostal perspective that derives its name from the Day of Pentecost narrative, but because the Pentecost event is arguably the other side of Easter and locates the situatedness of all followers of Jesus as Messiah. What I mean is that all Christian reflection proceeds not just after Easter (the resurrection and, relatedly, ascension) but also after Pentecost. As such, a proper Christian hermeneutical stance and posture is not only incarnational—after and through Jesus' life, death, and resurrection—but also pentecostal: informed primordially and in the life of each believer by the gracious gift and outpouring of the Spirit "on all people" (Acts 2:17).[37]

There are two interrelated consequences to this claim: one more theological and the other more methodological. Christian theology in general is trinitarian, but an authentic and robust trinitarianism links incarnation and Pentecost, Christology and pneumatology in ways that foreground the import of the Acts narrative. For our purposes in this essay, Christian (and evangelical, and pentecostal) liberation theology thereby also ought to be trinitarian and begins to achieve this aspiration when pneumatology is intrinsic rather than incidental to the theological enterprise.[38] This leads to the second,

---

[36]The reasons for my saying Acts–Luke in contrast to the usual Luke–Acts is that, as will be unfolded in the next few paragraphs, I begin with Acts 2 and work backward from there through Luke's two volumes; see for instance my *Who Is the Holy Spirit? A Walk with the Apostles* (Brewster, MA: Paraclete Press, 2011).

[37]I have done a good deal of work on the Acts narrative, starting with a Day of Pentecost hermeneutic that reads not only Acts but also Luke from the apostolic experience of the Spirit; see, e.g., Yong, "The Science, Sighs, and Signs of Interpretation: An Asian American Post-Pentecostal-al Hermeneutics in a Multi-, Inter-, and Trans-cultural World," in *Constructive Pneumatological Hermeneutics in Pentecostal Christianity*, ed. L. William Oliverio Jr. and Kenneth J. Archer (New York: Palgrave Macmillan, 2017), 177-95.

[38]This thesis is argued extensively—some might say in an exhausting manner—in my *Spirit-Word-Community: Theological Hermeneutics in Trinitarian Perspective*, New Critical Thinking in Religion, Theology and Biblical Studies Series (Burlington, VT: Ashgate Publishing Ltd., 2002).

methodological claim: that the Acts narrative should be read not just historically, as it has been traditionally, but theologically, so that the content of pneumatology in the Day of Pentecost outpouring has hermeneutical force. For the purposes of Christian—and evangelical and pentecostal—liberation theology, Acts 2 provides hermeneutical warrant for thinking about how many tongues opens up to many liberative beliefs and practices.[39]

The Acts 2 narrative identifies the witness of and to the "wonders of God" (Acts 2:11) that arises exactly through the many languages spoken around the Mediterranean world. In other words, the witness of the gospel emerges *through* the cacophony, bewilderment, and perplexity of the plurality of tongues. Whether such is a miracle of speech or of hearing—it is recorded of the crowd that "each one heard their own language being spoken" (Acts 2:6), leading them to ask, "How is it that each of us hears them in our native language?" (Acts 2:8)—is immaterial, since Luke's communicative intent is that God's redemptive purposes are achieved via the multivocity of the known world's cultures and languages, not apart from such.[40]

The result, it ought to be noted, is the formation of a new community (that of the three thousand who were baptized on that day; Acts 2:41), a new political economy ("All who believed were together and had everything in common. They sold property and possessions to give to anyone who had need"; Acts 2:44-45), and in effect, a new liberative way of life.[41] There is plenty of argument about how to

---

[39]This is an extension of my prior theses regarding many tongues many modalities of interfaith engagement, many tongues many political practices, and many tongues many disciplinary modes of inquiry argued respectively in my *Hospitality and the Other: Pentecost, Christian Practices, and the Neighbor*, Faith Meets Faith series (Maryknoll, NY: Orbis Books, 2008); *In the Days of Caesar: Pentecostalism and Political Theology—The Cadbury Lectures 2009*, Sacra Doctrina: Christian Theology for a Postmodern Age series (Grand Rapids: Eerdmans, 2010); and *The Spirit of Creation: Modern Science and Divine Action in the Pentecostal-Charismatic Imagination*, Pentecostal Manifestos 4 (Grand Rapids: Eerdmans, 2011).

[40]See Michael Welker, *God the Spirit*, trans. John F. Hoffmyer (Minneapolis: Fortress Press, 1994), ch. 5.

[41]Other of my essays touch on these themes, albeit without accentuating the liberation theological thrust: Yong, "Salvation, Society, and the Spirit: Pentecostal Contextualization and Political Theology from Cleveland to Birmingham, from Springfield to Seoul," *Pax Pneuma: The Journal*

understand Luke's admittedly idealized description of this nascent messianic community, how such relates to modern and late-modern forms of collectivities, and how long or short it persisted and why it did not have much staying power, despite being of divine provenance. Any thorough response exceeds the scope of this essay, but suffice to say for the moment that the redemptive outpouring of the Spirit at Pentecost had concrete liberative consequences. The implications for contemporary liberation theology of whatever guise—remember that the Day of Pentecost belongs to all followers of Jesus as Christ, not to pentecostal believers only—have yet to be realized.

As important is the interconnectedness between Acts and the Gospel of Luke. Clearly, the many tongues of Pentecost (Acts 2:1-21) spawned a liberative community (Acts 2:41-47) through the proclamation about Jesus (Acts 2:22-40). More specifically, the Spirit-inspired and empowered work among the apostolic community followed the paradigm of the Spirit-led and anointed Jesus of Nazareth. Thus when Luke writes of Peter's message to the Cornelius household, "God anointed Jesus of Nazareth with the Holy Spirit and power, and . . . he went around doing good and healing all who were under the power of the devil, because God [the Holy Spirit] was with him" (Acts 10:38), this calls attention to how the first of these two Lukan volumes provides the prototype of the Spirit-filled life.

The Day of Pentecost event and its outcomes are further clarified when we turn to the Gospel narrative. If Acts 1:8—"But you will receive power when the Holy Spirit comes on you; and you will be my witnesses in Jerusalem, in all Judea and Samaria, and to the ends of the earth"—provides the outline for the apostolic community in book

---

of Pentecostals & Charismatics for Peace & Justice 5 (2009): 22-34; "Glocalization and the Gift-Giving Spirit: Informality and Shalom Beyond the Political Economy of Exchange," *Journal of Youngsan Theology* 25 (2012): 7-29; and "Informality, Illegality, and Improvisation: Theological Reflections on Money, Migration, and Ministry in Chinatown, NYC, and Beyond," in *New Overtures: Asian North American Theology in the 21st Century—Essays in Honor of Fumitaka Matsuoka*, ed. Eleazar S. Fernandez (Upland, CA: Sopher Press, 2012), 248-68, originally published in the *Journal of Race, Ethnicity, and Religion* 3 (2012), www.raceandreligion.com/JRER /Volume_3_%282012%29.html.

two, then Luke 4:14-21 provides the table of contents for the life and ministry of Jesus in the first volume:

> Jesus returned to Galilee in the power of the Spirit, and news about him spread through the whole countryside. . . . He went to Nazareth, where he had been brought up, and on the Sabbath day he went into the synagogue, as was his custom. He stood up to read, and the scroll of the prophet Isaiah was handed to him. Unrolling it, he found the place where it is written:
>
> *"The Spirit of the Lord is on me,*
> *   because he has anointed me*
> *   to proclaim good news to the poor.*
> *He has sent me to proclaim freedom for the prisoners*
> *   and recovery of sight for the blind,*
> *to set the oppressed free,*
> *   to proclaim the year of the Lord's favor."*
>
> Then he rolled up the scroll, gave it back to the attendant and sat down. The eyes of everyone in the synagogue were fastened on him. He began by saying to them, "Today this scripture is fulfilled in your hearing."[42]

More particularly, the Isaianic quotation (italicized above, from Is 61:1-2) provides the basic template for the ministry and message of Jesus unfolded in the remainder of the Gospel account, all accomplished via the work of the Holy Spirit.[43] Thus we see Jesus evangelizing, healing, and delivering people, those who are poor not only in the socioeconomic sense alone, but in terms of their being marginalized outside of the centers of imperial power, in the power of the Spirit.[44]

---

[42]This passage is central to the thesis of pentecostal New Testament scholar Holly Bears, *The Followers of Jesus as the Servant: Luke's Model from Isaiah for the Disciples in Luke–Acts*, Library of New Testament Studies 535 (New York: Bloomsbury/T&T Clark, 2015), esp. ch. 5.

[43]Michael Prior, *Jesus the Liberator: Nazareth Liberation Theology (Luke 4.16-30)* (Sheffield, UK: Sheffield Academic Press, 1995).

[44]See Joel B. Green, "Good News to Whom? Jesus and the 'Poor' in the Gospel of Luke," in *Jesus of Nazareth: Lord and Christ—Essays on the Historical Jesus and New Testament Christology*, ed. Joel B. Green and Max Turner (Grand Rapids: Eerdmans: Paternoster Press, 1994), 59-74.

Yet Jesus' efforts were directed ultimately to heralding—not just proclaiming but inaugurating—"the year of the Lord's favor." In Isaianic terms, such amounted to the messianic installation of the Day of the Lord announced by the prophets, which in turn relied on the Pentateuchal message regarding the liberative Year of Jubilee.[45] Thus when Jesus heals the sick, or cleanses lepers, or delivers the oppressed widow, he is not only speaking about the coming reign of God but instantiating its presence by the power of the Spirit: "the kingdom of God is in your midst" (Lk 17:21).[46] From this vantage point, then, Jesus is not just a liberation theologian in the abstract, but one who charismatically embodies the liberative good news.

It is thus no wonder that the poor, those most in need of liberation from the yoke of imperial Rome, flocked to Jesus (see Lk 7:22b), and it is also therefore not unexpected that those variously oppressed from the countryside flocked to join the apostolic community in Jerusalem (Acts 5:16).[47] Jesus' ministry of empowerment for the poor in Luke is followed by his pouring out of the Spirit in Acts 2:33, so that they (the poor) are given their own voice and, surely through that vocality, enabled to also further herald and inaugurate the redemptive and liberative message of Jubilee in the first-century imperial context. The Spirit-empowered ministry of the apostolic community was not identical with that of Jesus (in Luke) but there are fundamental continuities amid the differences. For our purposes, Jesus' ministry of liberation of the poor in the Gospel was transformed into the liberative ministry in Acts by many who were themselves poor (fishermen, widows, and others), but all by the power of the Spirit.

---

[45]Sharon H. Ringe, *Jesus, Liberation, and the Biblical Jubilee: Images for Ethics and Christology,* Overtures in Biblical Theology 19 (Philadelphia: Fortress Press, 1985).

[46]Thus did Baptist charismatic New Testament scholar Howard M. Ervin write, *Healing: Sign of the Kingdom* (Grand Rapids: Baker Academic, 2002).

[47]See also Richard B. Harms, *Paradigms from Luke–Acts for Multicultural Communities,* American University Studies Series VII Theology and Religion 216 (New York: Peter Lang, 2001), ch. 3 on "Good News to the Poor (Luke 4:18)" as explicating the central thrust of this Lukan mission paradigm; Harms presents an evangelical-Catholic-liberationist paradigm as an Episcopal priest who works with Hispanic communities in Puerto Rico, Texas, and California.

Central to this essay is that liberation theology's preferential option *for* the poor is one side to—and the other side of— pentecostal theology's preferential option *of* the poor. If the former focuses on identification and repair of systems and structures of oppression, the latter enables faithful perseverance against the life-destroying principalities and powers. It is within such a complementary framework, then, that I have suggested the Day of Pentecost narratives provide theological legitimation not only for the many voices, but also for the many tongues of the poor. Pentecostal theology thus asserts a liberative theology, spirituality, and praxis *of* the poor via its multivocality.[48] Its contribution to evangelical theology then is to underwrite the plurivocity of liberative witnesses and testimonies, not only from the majority world but wherever people find themselves marginalized and oppressed by dominant cultures.[49]

More generally, and here beyond the evangelical horizon toward the wider ecumenical frontiers, pentecostal perspectives provide pneumatological resources for revitalizing liberation theology, at least in terms of empowering the impoverished in faithful witness *in* the world. If at this intersection the role of pneumatology has already been recognized,[50] the contemporary pentecostal contribution seeks to renew such tasks within a global context of many tongues and many cultures. As the Spirit indeed gives many gifts (1 Cor 12:4), then the gift of the Spirit empowers many witnesses to the liberative gospel

---

[48]Cheryl Bridges Johns, *Pentecostal Formation: A Pedagogy among the Oppressed* (Sheffield, UK: Sheffield Academic Press, 1993), chs. 4-5.

[49]The perennial question of course has to do with how to discern among the many voices; the christological criterion is always indispensable—see my *Spirit of Love: A Trinitarian Theology of Grace* (Waco, TX: Baylor University Press, 2012), esp. ch. 9, and *The Missiological Spirit: Christian Mission Theology for the Third Millennium Global Context* (Eugene, OR: Cascade Books, 2014), part 4—but oftentimes, the Spirit empowers prophetic witness unrecognized at the time; for the challenges and opportunities pertaining to the latter, see Johnny Bernard Hill, *Prophetic Rage: A Postcolonial Theology of Liberation* (Grand Rapids: Eerdmans, 2013).

[50]E.g., José Comblin, *The Holy Spirit and Liberation*, trans. Paul Burns (Maryknoll, NY: Orbis Books, 1989); Tae Wha Yoo, *The Spirit of Liberation: Jürgen Moltmann's Trinitarian Pneumatology*, Studies in Reformed Theology 2 (Zoetermeer, The Netherlands: Uitgeverij Meinema, 2003).

of Jesus Christ. It is perhaps the charism of pentecostal spirituality to the church catholic that it renews liberation theology indeed from the underside of history as the poor are enabled to speak and act in the power of the Spirit.[51]

[51]I am grateful to PhD and ThM students in my informal seminar in "Mission and Theology in the Spirit," especially Christopher The, for the careful reading and vigorous discussion of the paper and response to it. Thanks also to Andy Smith for her editorial work on shortening the previous version of this chapter for inclusion in this volume (the longer version can be found in my *The Hermeneutical Spirit: Theological Interpretation and the Scriptural Imagination for the 21st Century* [Eugene, OR: Cascade, 2017], ch. 9). All errors of fact and interpretation remain my own responsibility.

CHAPTER FIFTEEN

SACRAMENTAL THEOLOGY

DOMINIQUE DUBOIS GILLIARD

As evangelicals who deeply value Scripture, we know that we are called to seek the kingdom first, but have we truly reckoned with how this is connected to liberation? When we pray the Lord's Prayer, have we considered what God's will being done "on earth as it is in heaven" means for people living under the weight of physical, not just spiritual, oppression? Historically, evangelicalism has not. Traditionally, most evangelicals have exclusively understood liberation as a spiritual issue, strictly a matter of the heart and mind. Liberation has therefore been articulated as an internal personal struggle with individual, rather than social, implications. Consequently, liberation has solely been expressed as a gift that is freely given by God when someone accepts Jesus Christ in their heart as personal Lord and Savior. This inadequate understanding of liberation has distorted evangelical theology and ethics.

Liberation undoubtedly hinges on the salvific, sacrificial offering of Jesus. On the cross, Christ poured himself out as an atoning offering for the sins of the world, freeing us from the shackles of sin and death. Nevertheless, the liberation that Christ birthed and offers us is not just spiritual, nor is spiritual liberation the exclusive concern of God or the gospel. Biblically speaking, we are spiritually liberated in order to recalibrate our lives—to be empowered by the Holy Spirit to partner with God in the work of holistic liberation and restoration within the confines of our fallen (material) world.

God has a vested interest in liberation, both material and spiritual. God is at work in the world reconciling all things; God was in Christ reconciling the world to Godself. Jesus said that he came to proclaim the year of the Lord's favor: to bring good news to the poor, proclaim release to the captives, recovery of sight to the blind, and liberation to the oppressed. Liberation is God's primary concern.

Too many evangelicals believe that *liberation* and *social justice* are tantamount to *the social gospel*. These individuals fear that doing justice will distract us from fulfilling the great commission. This anxiety prohibits evangelicals from fully realizing our ethical responsibility to partner with God in the world in both word and deed. Due to apprehension about the possibility of threatening the primacy of proselytizing and preaching of the gospel, evangelicals have largely strayed from justice, opting instead for acts of compassion and mercy.

Furthermore, many evangelicals reject the concept of structural sin. This leaves no categories for thinking through the implications of corporate sin, institutional injustice, and systemic bias. This void prevents most evangelicals from constructively partaking in crucial dialogues about the state of our nation, like those concerning income inequality, police brutality, and mass incarceration. Moreover, it stunts our biblical interpretation, particularly of passages where Scripture clearly illustrates that sin and injustice are decimating communities in ways that are beyond the realm of individual responsibility (e.g., Mic 6:9-16; Is 58; Acts 6:1-6; Jas 5:1-6). The inability to theologically unpack systemic sin and the evil it manifests fosters a type of psychosclerosis that inhibits evangelical ethics.

Few ministers have articulated the holistic nature of God's liberation better than Dr. Martin Luther King Jr. said, "The gospel at its best deals with the whole man [*sic*], not only his soul but his body, not only his spiritual well-being, but his material well-being. Any religion that professes to be concerned about the souls of men and is not concerned about the slums that damn them, the economic conditions that strangle them and the social conditions that cripple them is a spiritually moribund religion awaiting burial."[1] Unlike many preachers, King had a theology that was never otherworldly or overly concerned with spiritual liberation at the expense of taking seriously the physical circumstances of oppression. King always elucidated the connection between orthodoxy and orthopraxy, right belief and right action. In his 1968 "I've Been to the Mountaintop" speech, King said, "It's all right to talk about 'streets flowing with milk and honey,' but God has commanded us to be concerned about the slums down here, and his children who can't eat three square meals a day. It's all right to talk about the new Jerusalem, but one day, God's preacher must talk about the new New York, the new Atlanta, the new Philadelphia, the new Los Angeles, the new Memphis, Tennessee."[2] King's theology was deeply influenced by Howard Thurman, who, in his definitive work *Jesus and the Disinherited*, wrote, "The masses of men [sic] live with their backs constantly against the wall. They are the poor, the disinherited, the disposed. What does our religion say to them?"[3] This crucial question will be the telos of this chapter: What indeed does evangelicalism say to these masses, and how can reconsidering liberation theology aid evangelicals' response to this vital question?

GOD'S UNIQUE UNITY WITH THE OPPRESSED

In the Old and New Testaments, God is intimately present with and actively working to liberate the oppressed. We also see God identify with the oppressed to the point where God says that when we neglect, disrespect, and forsake the least of these, we are actually doing these things to God. Referencing passages like Proverbs 14:31

---

[1] Martin Luther King Jr., "Pilgrimage to Non-Violence," in the *Christian Century*, April 13, 1960, 439-41.

[2] Martin Luther King Jr., "I've Been to the Mountaintop" (sermon, Mason Temple Church of God in Christ, Memphis, TN, April 3, 1968).

[3] Howard Thurman, *Jesus and the Disinherited* (Boston: Beacon Press), 4.

and Proverbs 17:5, biblical scholar Elsa Tamez says, "God identifies himself with the poor to such an extent that their rights become the rights of God himself."[4] Scripture repeatedly illuminates God's unique relationship with the oppressed. For instance, the only person within Scripture who is allowed to name God is a disenfranchised slave girl named Hagar. Hagar is severely oppressed—stripped of her freedom, dignity, and autonomy. Hagar's mistress, Sarai, barters her body, gives her as a concubine, and forces her to bear the child of a man she never has the volition to truly choose to be affectionate with. Hagar, robbed of her agency, is rendered a surrogate mother. In the midst of fleeing to the wilderness for a reprieve from her oppression, she is seen and met by God. After Hagar has been dealt with harshly by Sarai, God does not just meet Hagar spiritually but heeds her affliction, attending to her needs holistically. God communes with Hagar in an intimate way that we do not see anywhere else throughout Scripture. God allows her the power and privilege of naming the great I AM.

We also see Jesus intimately identify in this way with the hungry, thirsty, stranger, naked, prisoner, and sick in Matthew 25. These categories are not descriptions of spiritual impoverishment; they each speak to the physical and material reality of poverty, oppression, and social marginalization. The church must grapple with the fact that God makes no such proclamations about any other aspect of society. God's intimate identification—divine personification—with the oppressed is an irrevocable sign of a particular union with the least of these. The church cannot ignore this.

Theologian Daniel Groody writes in *Globalization, Spirituality, and Justice*, "God's concern for the poor and oppressed is one of the most central themes of the Bible. In the New Testament one out of every sixteen verses is about the poor. In the Gospels, the number is one out of every ten; in Luke's Gospel it is one out of every seven, and in James,

---

[4]Elsa Tamez, *Bible of the Oppressed* (Maryknoll, NY: Orbis Books, 2007), 73.

one out of every five."[5] Groody adds, "From a Christian perspective, whenever a community ceases to care for the most vulnerable members of society, its spiritual integrity falls apart."[6] Therefore, when we neglect the vulnerable, oppressed, and needy, we fail to be the church of Jesus Christ.

The church must seek first the kingdom of God. When we participate in God's ongoing work of restoration, we exist as the hands and feet of Christ in the world. Dietrich Bonhoeffer expounds on this by saying, "The Church is the Church only when it exists for others. . . . The church must share in the secular problems of ordinary human life, not dominating, but helping and serving. It must tell men [*sic*] of every calling what it means to live for Christ, to exist for others."[7] Few ministers have embodied the selfless disposition to which Bonhoeffer calls the church more faithfully than Dr. King. In a 1966 sermon on the good Samaritan, King declared,

> I choose to identify with the underprivileged. I choose to identify with the poor. I choose to give my life for the hungry, I choose to give my life for those who have been left out of the sunlight of opportunity. . . . This is the way I'm going. If it means suffering a little bit, I'm going that way. If it means sacrificing, I'm going that way. If it means dying for them, I'm going that way, because I heard a voice say "Do something for others."[8]

At its best, liberation theology crystallizes the cost of discipleship by illuminating the church's role in partnering with God's work of liberation and restoration in the world.

Liberation theology highlights God's emancipatory nature. It centers the experience of the least of these and illuminates how

---

[5]Daniel Groody, *Globalization, Spirituality, and Justice: Theology in Global Perspective* (Maryknoll, NY: Orbis Books, 2007), 32.

[6]Groody, *Globalization, Spirituality, and Justice*, 32.

[7]Dietrich Bonhoeffer, *Letters and Papers from Prison* (New York: Simon & Schuster Inc., 1997 [1953]), 282.

[8]Martin Luther King Jr., "The Parable of the Good Samaritan" (sermon, Ebenezer Baptist Church, Atlanta, August 28, 1966).

God—with the church—is working to forge freedom, justice, and liberation in the world. Liberation theology strives to illuminate the ways God invites the church to partner in addressing and deconstructing systems and structures that breed injustice, oppression, and death, where Christ instead intends abundant life to freely flow. Liberation theology seeks to hold the church accountable to its faith proclamations by reminding the body of the ethical implications of our faith proclamations. James Cone, a leading voice in liberation theology, echoes Bonhoeffer's conclusion regarding the church's call to sacrificial love when he says, "We [the church] must join the resistance by making solidarity with those who struggle for life in the face of death."[9] Bonhoeffer, while not a liberation theologian, theologically aligns with Cone by again saying, "The church has an unconditional obligation to the victims of any ordering of society, even if they do not belong to the Christian community."[10] Therefore, liberation theology implores the church to ask difficult questions; are we truly engaged in the "struggle for life in the face of death"? And, if we are, are we willing to engage in this struggle for those who do not belong to the Christian community? Liberation theology also nudges us to assess our lives honestly to see whether the gospel is informing and transforming our posture and orientation toward the least of these.

SACRAMENTAL PARTNERSHIP

One of the primary ways that God invites the church to participate in pursuing liberation is through the sacraments. Sacraments are freely given divine means of grace intended to order, transform, and re-member us into the likeness of Christ. The sacraments of baptism and communion ground and unify the church, giving sustenance for the wearisome sojourn to dual citizens exiled in this world. Blessed by the Spirit, these sacraments empower us to faithfully respond to the

---

[9]James Cone, *God of the Oppressed* (Maryknoll, NY: Orbis Books, 1975, new rev. ed., 1997), xviii.
[10]Dietrich Bonhoeffer, *Witness to Christ Jesus*, ed. John de Gruchy, The Making of Modern Theology (Minneapolis: Fortress Press, 1991), 127.

gospel and pursue righteous relationships with God, our neighbors, and creation. They mark us as God's own and commission us to bear witness to the good news in word and deed.

Baptism.

Baptism is a public proclamation that our lives are no longer our own. It is an invitation to die, a renunciation of self-centeredness, and an acceptance of the cost of discipleship. Baptism incorporates us into Christ—his death and resurrection—giving us a new identity, story, and family, commemorating a new life ordered and empowered by the Spirit. It liberates us from the sinful dictates of our fleshly nature, the dehumanizing ethos of worldly empires, and the powers and principalities that vie for our worship and allegiance. Baptism delegates us to make God's name known and God's love shown globally. It anoints us as disciples in the mold of John the Baptist, a peculiar people called to "prepare the way of the Lord," participating in ushering in the kingdom of God by doing justice, loving mercy, and walking humbly with God.

Communion.

Communion is a sacrament Jesus instructs the church to partake in. A divine banquet that unifies the global church, it is a nourishing, restorative meal that not only reminds us of what Christ did for us, but also informs what we are called to do for others. Communion is a transformative feast that empowers the church to live as peculiar people, a collective called to live, act, and respond in the world as Christ's ambassadors. It reminds us that the divine cupboard is sufficient for all; none are excluded and there is enough for everyone's need.

SACRAMENTAL ETHIC

The Spirit of God is alive and active in the world through the sacraments. They are not merely historic traditions the church preserves, but rather divinely orchestrated spaces where we are met by God and catalyzed by the Spirit to reflect the sacrificial love and justice of Jesus. The sacraments call the church to love its enemies, confront evil, and do justice. They compel us to live for something beyond ourselves. They arouse a selflessness within us, a new way of living that seeks the good of others before that of ourselves. The sacraments provoke us to form covenantal bonds of solidarity with people that we are socialized to distance ourselves from: the poor, the least of these, the other, and our enemies.

However, somewhere along the way the church began forsaking the justice *ends* of the sacraments in pursuit of ritualistic *means*. As a consequence, the evangelical church has an anemic comprehension of the sacraments today. This sacramental malformation corrodes our identity, retards our liturgy, and domesticates our witness in the world. We fail to realize that these divine gifts are more than an outward and visible sign of an inward transformation. Sacraments not only bestow divine grace on us, but they also commission us to live a cruciform life of faith, hope, and love. Sacraments are meant to shape, inform, and consecrate Christian ethics. Christian identity is sacramentally patterned, and our evangelism, activism, and missiology must be rooted within the sacramental confines we profess. The sacraments are not just sacred rites that we partake in; they are a hallmark of Christianity, events that anoint the church to embody its faith in the world.

The church's sacramental ethic transforms how we engage the world. The sacraments remind us of Scripture's call to place the interest of others before our own. Theologian Michael J. Gorman puts it this way: "The cross and resurrection both motivate and shape daily life. The appropriate life 'for' or 'toward' Christ is the cruciform life. Life 'for' Christ, is simultaneously life 'for' others . . . because the cross and resurrection were for others."[11] The sacraments root us in the selfless nature of God's love expressed in Christ. Jesus, the

---

[11]Michael J. Gorman, *Cruciformity: Paul's Narrative Spirituality of the Cross* (Grand Rapids: Eerdmans, 2001), 47.

archetype of our faith, embodied what it means to offer oneself to God as a living sacrifice and, as his followers today, our aim must be to pattern our lives after his faithfulness and sacrificial love.

Sacramental belonging.

When we partake in the sacraments, we are transformed, re-membered, and made new. The sacraments are divinely ordained to interrogate, disrupt, and transform the church's conformity to the patterns of this world. They give us renewed vision, elucidating our true citizenship. They fuel us to live unashamed for Christ into the countercultural ethics of the kingdom.

Scripturally speaking, God sacramentally troubles the waters of belonging. The sacraments are ordained by God to uproot the imperial ethos of belonging; they are meant to castrate the oppressive hierarchies empire constitutes. Daniel Groody defines empire as "power structures that benefit the elite, enslave the poor, and dominate the weak."[12] He goes on to say, "The notion of empire often describes political entities, but it is not limited to them. Symbolically, the empire represents any power that arrogates to itself the power that belongs to God alone, or any group or institution that subjugates the poor and needy for its own advantage."[13] Our failure to take empire seriously as a theological category has hindered our structural analysis, precluding us from confessing and repenting of corporate sin.

Baptism prophetically reconstructs the church's familial lineage. In these sacred waters, those whom Christians are socialized to fear, avoid, exclude, and persecute are loved, drawn near, embraced, and welcomed in as family. The sacraments scandalously reorder our lives, disrupting tribalism and our participation in reinforcing boundaries of segregation, racial purity, and moral superiority. The sacraments beckon us into kinship that we would never choose on our own, and God uses these implausible relationships to birth newness and abundant life.

---

[12]Groody, *Globalization, Spirituality, and Justice*, 34.
[13]Groody, *Globalization, Spirituality, and Justice*, 34.

The sacraments implore us to see our identities as covenantally bound to others, particularly accentuating our connection to those we are primed to see with suspicion, as the other and as our enemy. These divine gifts summon us into a cruciform life of contagion with the other, where inclusion is our orientation and we are transformed by communing with the least of these: the prisoner, poor, widow, orphan, and foreigner among us. Biblically, in the very places and unions we are socialized to circumvent, we encounter, experience, and receive God most profoundly. Salvation is often found in these stigmatized places, forbidden relationships, and prohibited eucharistic encounters.

SALVIFIC ENCOUNTERS IN UNEXPECTED PLACES

The gospel is inextricably wed to eschewed places and "unclean" people. God appoints the church to traverse fortified boundaries of belonging, to wade into socially detestable kinship. We see this in the life of Moses, when Pharaoh's daughter saves him from the Egyptian massacre that was decreed by her father. She defied an imperial decree, transgressed class and ethnic boundaries of belonging, and intimately identified with the other in treasonous ways. This prophetic act of faithfulness could have cost her everything: her inheritance, status, family, and life. Nevertheless, she remained faithful to what she knew was right, even in the face of this tremendous risk. Furthermore, in this story, we see Pharaoh's daughter led by the Spirit of God to break the law, disobey her father, and cause a social disruption. This does not fit nicely into our clean, neat, black and white categories as evangelicals; thus, we must reckon with what God provokes her to do here and wrestle with the theological implications of this passage.

Pharaoh's daughter was raised within a household, and culture, that taught her that Hebrews' lives did not matter. Everything around her trained her to see Hebrews as inferior and therefore expendable people. Nevertheless, the Spirit of God corrected her vision, convicted her heart, and revealed the truth to her: there are no expendable people within the kingdom of God! Not only did Pharaoh's daughter defy the imperial status quo by communing with Moses—a marginalized, ethnically subordinate, orphan—on saving his life, but she also saw Moses' identity as intrinsically bound to her own. She did not merely offer Moses charity, nor did she see him as a project or someone for whom she cares from a distance, but she authentically identified with Moses. She ultimately adopted him and chose to raise as her own son someone whom she had been discipled her entire life to see as the enemy. Within this perilous interaction, lines of belonging, purity, and family were all fundamentally reconstructed.

This subversive theme of being inherently bound to the socially contaminated is not only sustained, but expanded throughout Scripture. When Moses grew up, he too embodied a sacramental ethic of belonging to those whom he was socialized to disdain as subalternate. He, too, put his life on the line—opposing the imperial powers that be—to fight for justice, pursue freedom, and stand in solidarity with those he had the privilege of ignoring. The Spirit of God that stirs the sacraments penetrated Moses' apathy regarding the other and disrupted his comfortable life within the confines of luxury and excess. God compelled Moses to reexamine his life and all that he had been entrusted. Moses realized that he was blessed to be a blessing, that he had a responsibility to use his access to the master's tools to dismantle Pharaoh's oppressive house. God moved Moses from apathy to activism—to the point where he forsook the pleasures and prestige of the palace, to sojourn in solidarity with the oppressed into the desert for righteousness' sake.

When Christian ethics are sacramentally grounded and informed, God works through the church to inseminate freedom, induce justice, and birth liberation. As we see in these two narratives, divine revelation is paradoxically manifested in illicit communion. The Bible elucidates this uncanny truth and the incarnation corroborates it. Nevertheless, over the course of history, most of evangelicalism has failed to interpret, teach, and preach a gospel that attests to this countercultural reality. Given this reality, what role can evangelicalism play in resuscitating the dry bones of liberation within the Western church today?

RECONSIDERING INCARNATION

Our understanding of liberation is profoundly shaped by our biblical interpretation. The incarnation serves as the ultimate social transgression; the Creator became the creature, in order to dwell within, liberate, and restore creation. Jesus, in selfless abandon, took on flesh and a new orientation toward humanity. Christ became Emmanuel and was rejected; his body was tortured, broken, and crucified. Three days later, Jesus' desecrated body was resurrected and redeemed by God. Today, Christ's body serves as consecrated nourishment, the generative source empowering Christians to imitate his cruciform ethic of self-giving love and justice. The incarnation revolutionized communion, forever changing what it means to identify with (understand ourselves as innately connected to) the least of these, the other, and our enemy.

Moreover, we see the transvaluation of relating and belonging reach a crescendo in the life of Jesus. Throughout his lifetime, Christ breached and disrupted traditional notions of kinship and family by embodying a sacramental ethic of love, justice, and restoration. Not only did he contentiously commune with those rendered socially invisible—the infirm, the demon possessed, and prostitutes— but Jesus, the Word made flesh, was also an ignominy in and of himself. God could have enfleshed in any form, yet chose to enter into our world as not just one of us, but as one of the least of these. Jesus was born in an unsanitary manger, birthed to unwed,[14] impoverished parents, in the midst of state-induced domestic terrorism, causing his family to emigrate in order to seek refuge from the Roman Empire.

---

[14]Jesus' parents were unwed when Mary found out that she was pregnant with a child from the Holy Spirit. Soon after, Joseph does as the angel commands and marries Mary (Mt 1:18-25).

Jesus consistently lived his life usurping relational norms, contravening social stratifications, and refining the ethos of belonging; the church is called to embody this. One of the clearest scriptural illuminations of this is the grafting in of Tamar and Rahab, two members of the despised, "inferior," and notoriously adversarial Canaanite clan, into the direct genealogical lineage of Christ. Biblical scholar Craig Keener says that the Canaanites are depicted as "the bitter biblical enemies of Israel."[15] Stephen Humphries-Brooks, a religious studies professor, says that Canaanites were "to be offered to the Lord as a whole burnt offering of purification of the land to God."[16] Nevertheless, God repudiates cultural norms by welcoming the enemy. God not only identifies with the enemy, but covenantally binds them to Jesus through their incorporation into his family. This integration of the enemy into the lineage of Christ is merely a microcosm of how belonging to the enemy is epitomized and expanded in Jesus' crucifixion and resurrection.

What is more, even Jesus' death was indiscriminate; in death, Christ opened himself up and invited the world into his body, baptismally. The Bible says that Jesus died for the sins of the world "while we were still enemies." Therefore, not only did Jesus spend his life identifying with the enemy, he ultimately gave his life for the enemy. In the most radical expression of loving the enemy, the cross became the locus of belonging. Christ inaugurates a form of belonging in which no exclusion, segregation, or hierarchies exist.

In discussing the enigmatic nature of Christianity, Luke Bretherton asserts that it is a "consistent dynamic in the history of Christianity, those who take themselves to be at the center, have to turn to those on the periphery to understand the new work that God is doing."[17] God's

---

[15] Craig Keener, *The Gospel of Matthew: A Socio-Rhetorical Commentary* (Grand Rapids: Eerdmans, 2009), 415.

[16] Stephen Humphries-Brooks, "The Canaanite Woman in Matthew," in *A Feminist Companion to Matthew*, ed. Amy-Jill Levine and Marian Blickenstaff (London: Sheffield Academic Press, 2001), 141. Also see Judg 2:3-5, 21-23.

[17] Luke Bretherton, "Healing Babylon: Hospitality, Common Life, and Nature of Faithful Citizenship" (2015 Schaff Lectures, Pittsburgh Theological Seminary, March 26, 2015).

distinct revelation along the periphery crystalizes the gospel's sub-versive nature. God makes those who see themselves as the religious center dependent on those they deem unclean, summoning them into repugnant communion. As Christians ethically engage in stigmatized places and verboten relationships—that the world disciples them to evade—they bear witness to the love, mission, and movement of God.

Becoming Christlike, Scripture reveals, is the willingness to not only be with, but to become and ultimately to be transformed through self-giving relationships with the other and our enemies. Bonhoeffer, in his classic text *Life Together*, writes that Jesus came "to bring peace to the enemies of God. So the Christian, too, belongs not in the seclusion of a cloistered life but in the thick of foes. There is his commission, his work."[18] Bonhoeffer then quotes Martin Luther, the Protestant reformer, who said, "The kingdom is to be in the midst of your enemies. And he who will not suffer this does not want to be of the Kingdom of Christ; he wants to be among friends, to sit among roses and lilies, not with the bad people but the devout people. O you blasphemers and betrayers of Christ! If Christ had done what you are doing who would ever have been spared."[19]

Part of Luther's zeal arises from the fact that unique revelation occurs as we commune with the least of these, the other, and our enemies. This seemingly vile nature of communion mysteriously begets divine conversion, which is essential for the unregulated trans-formation of the Holy Spirit. The sacraments call Christians into spaces of uncertainty—liminal spaces where we live a life of contagion with the other. This communicable relating begets a radically alternative way of pursuing life together, where the *imago Dei* is rela-tionally manifested in unexpected ways. J. Kameron Carter concludes that "the image of God is a verb, not a noun."[20] Thus, within this

---

[18]Dietrich Bonhoeffer, *Life Together* (San Francisco: Harper & Row Publishers, Inc. 1955), 17.
[19]Bonhoeffer, *Life Together*, 17.
[20]J. Kameron Carter, "The Image of God" (CHIC 2015, Evangelical Covenant Church Triennial Youth Conference, Knoxville, TN, July 13, 2015).

analysis, the divine image is relationally revealed when the church's orientation is inclusion and its communion acts to destabilize the status quo. This thesis is corroborated by scriptural accounts that explicate it counterintuitively: God is most profoundly revealed and manifested amid fugitive communion with the other and our enemies.

LITURGICAL LIBERATION

This reconstituted understanding of the sacraments and incarnation must inform how we envision and participate in the church's liturgical calendar, particularly the seasons of Advent and Lent. Advent reminds us that we serve a God who intentionally chose to enter in. While God did not have to, God elected to intervene on our behalf. Compelled by love, Jesus—in selfless abandon—humbled himself forsaking comfort, safety, and heaven's *shalom* to liberate the world and stand in solidarity with humanity.

How does Jesus' life inform our understanding of solidarity? Do we see entering into the pain of our world—into the pain of others that we are not directly implicated in—as an essential element of our faith? Are we compelled into selfless abandon for the sake of the gospel? In light of Christ's sacrificial example, if we are unwilling to forsake comfort, safety, and worldly security, can we even claim to be following Jesus?

Lent reminds us that Jesus entered the world under the occupation of the fiercest empire in world history. In the midst of this flourishing empire, Jesus prophetically inaugurated the kingdom of God. His unflinching witness in the face of imperial power, which included the religious elite, threatened the very foundation of the Roman Empire. Jesus' countercultural ethic was so disruptive to the placebo peace promised by the *Pax Romana,* and the imperial status quo, that he was sentenced to the death penalty.

Therefore, we must understand that Advent and Lent are more than seasonal invitations to reflect on the salvific work of Jesus. These two periods are a reminder of the cost of discipleship. They are times where we are called to pause and evaluate how we are bearing witness to the kingdom in the midst of the US empire. The liturgical calendar is a gift of accountability, one that reorients the church by reminding us of our mission in the world.

We need these reminders because empires are manipulative and hegemonic. Empires are predicated on fear mongering. Whenever empires fear they are losing power or influence, they use coercion and produce propaganda. Empires satiate their citizens, intoxicating the masses into submission and compliance through the distribution of privileged trinkets. The possession of imperial assets fosters division, creating a sliding scale of access between the "haves" and the "have-nots." Those who have soon realize that they have a vested interest in the sustenance and maintenance of imperial stability. Members of the privileged population thereby become imperial ambassadors.

When one has access, privilege, and comfort within the confines of the empire, it becomes extremely difficult to divest oneself from it. When the empire is understood as the source of safety, security, and abundant life, it becomes an idol, whether consciously or subconsciously. Idolatry is anything that we give ourselves to other than God. Idols are not evil things in and of themselves, but they become bad as we begin to prioritize them over and against seeking the kingdom first. The gospel—most clearly elucidated through the incarnation and the sacraments—must disturb our propensity to acquiesce to imperial injustice and succumb to pledging our allegiance to the empire over and against the kingdom.

The Holy Spirit is at work within the church recalibrating our vision, granting us divine clarity. The Spirit frees us to see divine truth; although we live within a stratified world, we are all inherently bound together in covenantal solidarity. As a baptismal family, we are empowered by the Spirit to model what the pursuit of life together can and should look like. Our pursuit of life together must not be hindered or disturbed by imperial stratifications, markers, or boundaries of belonging. As the church, we are called to pursue life together in radical, countercultural ways that disrupt the norms of our fallen world. Our pursuit of life together is informed and ultimately made manifest as we eucharistically abide in Christ.

Choosing to seek the kingdom first is to live in a way that is foolishness to the world. Living in this countercultural way is costly. It will cause the world to hate us, just as it hated Christ before us. Jesus' costly decision to live in this manner was taken for granted by the ones he came to save and, as a result, he was persecuted, defamed, tortured, and crucified. Nevertheless, Jesus remained faithful to his mission, to God, and his neighbor; this faithfulness in the face of persecution is what birthed our liberation.

As Christ's followers in the world today, when we live in this manner, we too will be taken for granted by some of our peers. Will we allow their response to discourage and distract us from our mission in the world, or will we follow Christ's example? How is Jesus' posture before the imperial powers that be prescriptive for us today? As Christians, are our lives not intended to be patterned after Jesus? While we are not saviors (nor should we attempt to be), we are co-laborers with Christ, and as such are we not also summoned to fiercely bear witness to the kingdom in the midst of an oppressive empire?

Christ's faithfulness in the midst of persecution, which he *endured because* of his stance of solidarity with the other, is what induced the freedom that we now enjoy. While our efforts and solidarity can never be salvific, our choice to sacrificially stand with the other, remaining faithful in the face of persecution, can also birth liberation and freedom in the world today (from the effects of sin, not sin itself. We are not divine; we do not have that power).

While Advent reminds us that we live in the midst of the now and the not yet, Lent asks us if we are willing to bear the cost of discipleship, if we are willing to boldly bear witness to the kingdom of God in the face of the imperial powers that be. The kingdom of God has been inaugurated but it has not yet been culminated. We the church, as Christ's hands and feet in the world today, are invited by God to partner with and participate in God's work of restoration. Yet we are called to do so without fearing the imperial powers. As Matthew 10:28 tells us, "Do not be afraid of those who kill the body but cannot kill the soul."

When the incarnation is used as our ethical blueprint, we are forced to conclude that Christians are called to be people who choose to enter in—a peculiar people who elect to stand in solidarity with our neighbors and even our enemies—when everything tells us we do not have to. When we choose solidarity—especially at the expense of privilege, comfort, and social status—for the good of our neighbor, the peace and prosperity of our cities, and the furtherance of the kingdom, we become more Christlike. Choosing solidarity is a spiritual practice that prompts us to look not to our own interests, but to the interests of others. When we practice the spiritual discipline of solidarity, we strive to embody "the same mindset as Christ Jesus" (Phil 2:5).

As believers today, liturgical seasons like Advent and Lent remind us that we live in-between Christ's two comings. We live in response to Jesus' first Advent, when he inaugurated the rule and reign of the kingdom of God here on earth. As we await his second coming, we are not just here idly waiting, twiddling our thumbs and passing time; we are called to wait with expectation and anticipation. We are called to *active* waiting. Our waiting prepares us and the world for Christ's return. Jesus is the archetype; he demonstrated what it means to give our bodies as a living sacrifice. Lent reminds us that living prophetically for God might actually mean that our bodies are physically sacrificed. As we learn to fear only God and not the empire, Advent reminds us that we are ambassadors of liberation in a story that has already been written.

As we wait for the consummation of the story and comprehensive liberation, we wait in the mold of John the Baptist: preparing the way for the Lord. How we wait ultimately dictates how we live and we are called to wait with purpose. James Cone articulates it this way,

To resist evil is to participate in God's redemption of the world. Though evil seems more prevalent and powerful today than yesterday, people are still resisting. Resistance creates hope. Just as Jesus' resurrection was born out of his apparent defeat on the cross, so too the poor are born anew out of their resistance to suffering. . . . We must join the resistance by making solidarity with those who struggle for life in the face of death.[21]

The church is called to participate in God's ongoing work of liberation, not just watch it from the sidelines. The church must serve as a conduit to the world regarding God's care, concern, and love for the least of these.

EMBODYING SACRAMENTAL LIBERATION

In his seminal text *The Cost of Discipleship*, Dietrich Bonhoeffer writes, "When Christ calls a man [*sic*] he bids them to come and die."[22] The gospel is explicit: following Jesus requires dying to ourselves, the world's commodifying logic, and the imperial status quo. Nevertheless, Scripture also illustrates that this nature of dying begets rebirth, which for his followers today is consummated sacramentally. The sacraments are the church's nourishment for its sojourn down the narrow road. Yet, this is only true inasmuch as we heed these words of James Cone: "Theological concepts have meaning only as they are translated into theological praxis, that is, the Church living in the world on the basis of what it proclaims. This means that theology and ethics, though not identical, are closely interrelated: the mission of the Church is defined by its proclamation, and the proclamation is authenticated by the mission."[23] The sacraments must become indispensable ethical markers of Christian identity; if they do not, we risk reducing them to theological platitudes.

As evangelicals we know that the gospel must be proclaimed. The news is too good to keep to ourselves! However, our proclamation

---

[21]Cone, *God of the Oppressed*, xviii.
[22]Dietrich Bonhoeffer, *The Cost of Discipleship* (New York: Simon & Schuster Inc. 1997 [1959]), 11.
[23]Cone, *God of the Oppressed*, 34.

was never intended to occur exclusively through words. The gospel must be testified to in word and deed. What we invest in, prioritize, and pursue bears witness to what we truly believe and worship. The world is anxiously awaiting the day the church's actions align with our professions.

Somewhere along the way, evangelicals have become known for what we are *against* rather than what we stand *for*. *Evangelical* has become a doctrinally loaded word that is often perceived more as a political declaration than a religious affiliation. I, along with many others, am deeply troubled by how the term has been co-opted. We must take a sober look at our history and confess that all too often we have borne witness to an idol, a Western God who is apathetic toward oppressed people, rather than the one true God who is with, for, and acting to forge liberation for the oppressed and the world at large.

When Scripture is read in a way that takes liberation seriously as God's priority and a fundamental aspect of the church's mission, our interpretation of the text changes. The story of the good Samaritan exemplifies this well. Traditionally, evangelicals have interpreted this passage as one stressing kindness, charity, and empathy. However, King's interpretation goes beyond these themes. He says, "The first question which the priest and the Levite asked was: 'If I stop to help this man, what will happen to me?' But . . . the Good Samaritan reversed the question: 'If I do not stop to help this man, what will happen to him?'"[24] Going even further, Gustavo Gutierrez, the founder of liberation theology interprets this passage saying, "The neighbor [is] not he whom I find in my path, but rather he in whose path I place myself, he whom I approach and actively seek."[25] Evangelicals must learn to approach Scripture from a vantage point where we interrogate who we are seeking and how our seeking is sacramentally rooted within the faith that we profess.

---

[24]King, "Parable of the Good Samaritan."

[25]Gustavo Gutiérrez, *A Theology of Liberation: History, Politics, and Salvation* (Maryknoll, NY: Orbis Books, 1988), 113.

CONTRIBUTOR BIOGRAPHIES

Rev. Dr. Mae Elise Cannon is executive director of Churches for Middle East Peace and an ordained pastor in the Evangelical Covenant Church. Cannon formerly served as the senior director of Advocacy and Outreach for World Vision US on Capitol Hill in Washington, DC; as consultant to the Middle East for child advocacy issues for Compassion International; as the executive pastor of Hillside Covenant Church, located in Walnut Creek, California; and as director of development and transformation for extension ministries at Willow Creek Community Church. She is the author of *Social Justice Handbook: Small Steps for a Better World* (InterVarsity Press, 2009), which won the 2010 Outreach Magazine Resource of the Year Award in the category of justice. She is the editor of *A Land Full of God: Christian Perspectives on the Holy Land* (Cascade, 2017). She is also the author of *Just Spirituality: How Faith Practices Fuel Social Action* (InterVarsity Press, 2013) and coauthor of *Forgive Us: Confessions of a Compromised Faith* (Zondervan, 2014). Cannon holds an MDiv from North Park Theological Seminary, an MBA from North Park University's School of Business and Nonprofit Management, and an MA in bioethics from Trinity International University. She received her doctorate in American history with a minor in Middle Eastern studies at the University of California (Davis), focusing on the history of the American Protestant church in Israel and Palestine. She has also completed a doctorate of ministry in spiritual formation from Northern Theological Seminary.

Rev. Dominique Gilliard is an ordained minister of the Evangelical Covenant Church (ECC). Dominique serves on the board of directors for the Christian Community Development Association and the board of Evangelicals for Justice. Dominique is also the director of racial righteousness pilgrimages for the Pacific Southwest Conference of the ECC. The ECC named Dominique to its list of "40 Under 40" leaders to watch, and the Huffington Post named him as one of the "Black Christian Leaders Changing the World." Dominique is a graduate of North Park Theological Seminary, where he also served as an adjunct professor.

Dr. Drew G. I. Hart is an author, activist, and professor of theology in the Bible and Religion department at Messiah College, with ten years of pastoral experience. Hart majored in biblical studies at Messiah College as an undergrad, he attained his MDiv with an urban concentration from Biblical Theological Seminary, and he received his PhD in theology and ethics from Lutheran Theological Seminary at Philadelphia. Dr. Hart's dissertation considered how Christian discipleship, as framed by black theologies and contemporary Anabaptism, gesture the Western church toward untangling the forces of white supremacy and the inertia of Western Christendom, which have plagued its witness in society for too long. Hart finds the practice of reading Jesus not only for the church, but also against it, to be a vital dimension in salvaging Western Christianity from itself. Hart's work beyond teaching and writing has included pastoring in Harrisburg and Philadelphia, working for an inner-city afterschool program for black and brown middle school boys, delivering lectures and leading antiracism workshops, collaborating with faith-based organizers in his neighborhood, and doing a broad range of public theology. Hart sees his current role as a theology professor as an extension of his ministry vocation that began with pastoral leadership. His book *Trouble I've Seen: Changing the Way the Church Views Racism* was chosen as a 2016 book of the month by the *Englewood Review of Books*. As a text, *Trouble I've Seen* utilizes personal and everyday stories, Jesus-shaped theological ethics, and antiracism frameworks to transform the church's understanding and witness.

Rev. Dr. Peter Goodwin Heltzel is an ordained minister in the Christian Church (Disciples of Christ) and is the director of the Micah Institute and associate professor of Systematic Theology at New York Theological Seminary. He also serves as assistant pastor of evangelism at Park Avenue Christian Church in New York City. Rev. Heltzel holds a BA from Wheaton College, an MDiv from Gordon-Conwell Theological Seminary, and earned his PhD from Boston University. He also completed coursework at the University of Mississippi in Southern fiction and creative writing. These courses, combined with his childhood years in Mississippi, inform his work with a deep commitment to the power of words and music, to social justice and to a global movement of radical change and collective activism. A gifted writer, Rev. Heltzel has contributed to seven books as author or editor. He has published numerous articles in journals such as *Books & Culture, Science & Theology News, Sojourners, Political Theology, Princeton Theological Review,* and the *Scottish Journal of Theology.* Rev. Heltzel won a theological research fellowship from the Association of Theological Schools (2006–2007) and a Sabbatical Fellowship from the Louisville Institute (2008–2009). He is a participant in the Luce/AAR Program in Comparative Theology and Theologies of Religion. He serves on the Metro Commission on the Ministry and the Anti-Racism/Pro-Reconciliation Team of the Northeastern Region, Christian Church (Disciples of Christ).

Dr. Pablo A. Jiménez was born in New York and grew up in Puerto Rico. Prior to joining Gordon-Conwell, Dr. Jiménez served as senior pastor of the Iglesia Cristiana (Discípulos de Cristo) in Espinosa, Dorado, Puerto Rico. Dr. Jiménez previously served as pastor of the CCDC in Sonadora, Guaynabo, Puerto Rico; director of the Rev. Juan Figueroa Umpierre Bible Institute of the CCDC in Puerto Rico; and executive director of the Association for Hispanic Theological Education and manager of the Hispanic Summer Program. He has also taught in numerous positions, as professor of New Testament and preaching at the Latin American Biblical Seminary in San José, Costa Rica, and as instructor of homiletics at the Episcopal Theological Seminary of the Southwest, in Austin, Texas. He earned a BA from the University of Puerto Rico; an MDiv from the Evangelical Seminary of Puerto Rico; an STM from Christian Theological Seminary in Indianapolis; and a DMin from Columbia Theological Seminary in Decatur, Georgia. Pablo is the coauthor of *Pulpito: An Introduction to Hispanic Preaching* (Abingdon Press, 2006), among other materials. He is married to Glorimar and has three children: Antonio José, Paola Margarita, and Natalia Isabel.

Dr. Rajkumar Boaz Johnson is a professor of Hebrew Bible and theological studies at North Park University in Chicago. He grew up in the slums of New Delhi, where he encountered the realities of poverty and injustice. The son of parents from different castes, he was told to never reveal the identity of his mother's outcaste family. After studying Hinduism at Ramakrishna Ashram and being dissatisfied with the answers it provided, Dr. Johnson began to search for answers in other world religions. Jesus the Messiah, as seen in the Gospels, captured his mind and imagination. He realized that in Jesus lay the answers to questions that plagued his mind. Dr. Johnson earned his PhD in Hebrew Bible and theological studies from Trinity International University, his ThM in Hebrew Bible and Semitic languages from Trinity Evangelical Divinity School, his MDiv from Union Biblical Seminary (Pune, India), and his BA in economics from University of Delhi.

Sarah Withrow King is deputy director of the Sider Center at Eastern University, and an associate fellow of the Oxford Centre for Animal

Ethics. She and her family live in Philadelphia, and are covenant members of Circle of Hope. She is the author of *Animals Are Not Ours (No Really, They're Not): An Evangelical Animal Liberation Theology*, and *Vegangelical: How Caring for Animals Can Shape Your Faith.*

Jeanine LeBlanc is Mi'kmaq /Acadian and her people are from the Gaspe Peninsula of Eastern Canada. She is the wife of Dan Lowe, daughter of Terry and Bev LeBlanc, and sister to Matt and Jenn. She lives with her husband, Dan, in Edmonton, Alberta, Canada. She studied history, sociology, and anthropology at the University of Winnipeg, obtaining her bachelor of arts in history in 2001. In 2008 she graduated from Asbury Theological Seminary with her masters of divinity academic degree in anthropology. She has contributed two articles to previous issues of the NAIITS journal, one documenting the history of NAIITS and the other examining and celebrating some traditions of hospitality within the Maori context in New Zealand and the First Nations context.

Terry LeBlanc is Mi'kmaq/Acadian. He and his wife Bev are in their forty-fourth year of marriage. They have three adult children—twin daughters and one son. In addition to being the executive director of Indigenous Pathways, Terry is also the founding chair and current director of NAIITS: An Indigenous Learning Community. Terry holds an interdisciplinary PhD from Asbury Theological Seminary, specializing in theology and anthropology. Terry serves as adjunct professor at George Fox Evangelical Seminary in Oregon, Acadia University and Divinity College in Wolfville, William Carey International University, and Tyndale University College and Seminary in Toronto, where he also serves as program elder for the University BEd program. Terry has accrued over thirty-eight years of community work in Native North American and global indigenous contexts, including as an educator in theology, cultural anthropology, and community development practice. Author of numerous articles, papers, and assorted book chapters, Terry has won several awards for his varied writings. In June 2010, for his work on the creation of NAIITS, Terry became the twenty-eighth recipient of the Dr. E. H. Johnson Memorial Award for Innovation in Mission—an award he holds in common with such distinguished recipients as Archbishop Desmond Tutu. In May of 2015 Terry was awarded an honorary doctor of divinity degree from Acadia University.

Dr. Paul Louis Metzger is professor of Christian theology and theology of culture at Multnomah University, director of its Institute for the Theology of Culture: New Wine, New Wineskins, and editor of its journal, *Cultural Encounters: A Journal for the Theology of Culture*. He is the author of the following works: *Evangelical Zen: A Christian's Spiritual Travels with a Buddhist Friend* (Patheos, 2015), *Connecting Christ: How to Discuss Jesus in a World of Diverse Paths* (Thomas Nelson, 2012), *New Wine Tastings: Theological Essays of Cultural Engagement* (Cascade Books, 2011), *The Gospel of John: When Love Comes to Town* (InterVarsity Press, 2010), *Exploring Ecclesiology: An Evangelical and Ecumenical Introduction* (co-authored with Brad Harper; Brazos/Baker, 2009), *Consuming Jesus: Beyond Race and Class Divisions in a Consumer Church* (Eerdmans, 2007), and *The Word of Christ and the World of Culture: Sacred and Secular through the Theology of Karl Barth* (Eerdmans, 2003). He also edited *A World for All? Global Civil Society in Political Theory and Trinitarian Theology* (along with William F. Storrar and Peter J. Casarella; Eerdmans, 2011) and *Trinitarian Soundings in Systematic Theology* (T&T Clark International, 2005). Dr. Metzger blogs regularly at his column "Uncommon God, Common Good" at Patheos.

J. Nicole Morgan, MTS, is the author of *Fat and Faithful: Learning to Love Our Bodies, Our Neighbors, and Ourselves* (Fortress Press, 2018). Her work on ending antifat bias in the Christian church has been featured in various places including *Christianity Today, Sojourners,* and Moody Radio. She earned her master of theological studies from Palmer Seminary of Eastern University.

Dr. Emmett G. Price III is a leading expert on the music of the African diaspora, Christian worship, and the black Christian experience. Price is dean of chapel, professor of worship, church, and culture, and executive director of the Institute for the Study of the Black Christian Experience at Gordon-Conwell Theological Seminary. Born and raised in Los Angeles, Dr. Price received a BA in music from the University of California, Berkeley and earned both his MA and PhD in music (ethnomusicology) from the University of Pittsburgh. He also obtained an MA in urban ministry leadership from Gordon-Conwell Theological Seminary. He has spent much of the past few decades writing, lecturing, and conducting cutting-edge research on bridging the generational divide. A well-regarded scholar, educator, and public speaker, Dr. Price has the unique ability to capture the hearts and minds of the most diverse and versatile audiences with his compassionate sense of humor, his amicable intellect, and his quick wit. He is a noted print and broadcast media expert, as well as a widely sought-after keynote speaker and preacher.

Soong-Chan Rah is Milton B. Engebretson Professor of Church Growth and Evangelism at North Park Theological Seminary in Chicago. He is the author of several books, including *The Next Evangelicalism: Freeing the Church from Western Cultural Captivity* (InterVarsity Press, 2009). Rah is formerly the founding senior pastor of the Cambridge Community Fellowship Church, a multiethnic, urban ministry–focused church committed to living out the values of racial reconciliation and social justice in the urban context. He currently serves on the board of several organizations, including Sojourners, World Vision, and Christian Community Development Association. Rah received his BA in political science and history/sociology from Columbia University; his MDiv from Gordon-Conwell Theological Seminary; his ThM from Harvard University; and his DMin from Gordon-Conwell Theological Seminary.

Robert Chao Romero is an associate professor of Chicana/o studies and Asian American studies at UCLA, and a pastor. He received his JD from UC Berkeley and his PhD in Latin American history from UCLA. He is also a lawyer. His book, *The Chinese in Mexico, 1882–1940* (University of Arizona Press, 2010), received the Latina/o Studies Section Book Award from the Latin American Studies Association. It was also recognized in *Critical Mass: The Blog of the National Book Critics Circle Board of Directors* as one of the top ten small-press books published in the United States in 2010. Romero is also a pastor to activists. As pastor, he codirects the nonprofit organization Jesus for Revolutionaries (J4R), together with his wife Erica Shepler Romero. The mission of J4R is to train and mobilize activist students in issues of justice and race from a Christian perspective. Robert and Erica are also cochairs of the Matthew 25 Movement in Southern California.

Rev. Alexia Salvatierra is a Lutheran (Luther-costal) pastor, coauthor of *Faith-Rooted Organizing: Mobilizing the Church in Service to the World* (InterVarsity Press, 2013), and serves as adjunct faculty for six seminaries and graduate programs, including Fuller Theological Seminary, Azusa Pacific Theological Seminary, Eastern University, New York Theological Seminary, and El Instituto Biblico Virtual in Argentina. She is a doctoral candidate at Fuller in missiology. She also works as a consultant and trainer for World Vision, InterVarsity Christian Fellowship, and the Christian Community Development Association, as well as a variety of other national and international ministries. She has been a national leader in engaging evangelical churches in the struggle for immigration reform. She is also assisting pastor at Hope Lutheran Church in Hollywood.

Andrea Smith is a cofounder of Evangelicals4Justice and a board member of the North American Institute for Indigenous Theological Studies. She is currently chair of the Ethnic Studies Department at UC Riverside. The author and editor of several books, including *Conquest:*

Sexual Violence and American Indian Genocide and *Native Americans and the Christian Right*, her next book, *Unreconciled: The Christian Right and Racial Reconciliation*, is forthcoming from Duke University Press. She is also the cofounder of a number of organizations, including Incite! Women of Color Against Violence, and the Boarding School Healing Project. She previously served as the US coordinator for the Ecumenical Association of Third World Theologians. She is Southern Baptist.

Dr. Chanequa Walker-Barnes is a prophetic voice for healing, justice, and reconciliation. She has authored over a dozen journal articles and book chapters, as well as the book *Too Heavy a Yoke: Black Women and the Burden of Strength* (Cascade, 2014). Dr. Walker-Barnes has earned degrees from Emory University (BA, psychology and African American/African studies), the University of Miami (MS and PhD, clinical child/family psychology), and Duke University (MDiv, certificate in gender, theology, and ministry). She is an associate professor at Mercer University's McAfee School of Theology. A candidate for ordination in the United Methodist Church, she serves as the discipleship pastor at the Nett Church in Lilburn, Georgia.

Dr. Amos Yong is professor of theology and mission, and director of the Center for Missiological Research at Fuller Theological Seminary in Pasadena, California. His graduate education includes degrees in theology, history, and religious studies from Western Evangelical Seminary (now George Fox Seminary), Portland State University, and Boston University, and his undergraduate degree is from Bethany University of the Assemblies of God. He has authored or edited over three dozen volumes. He and his wife, Alma, have three children—Annalisa, a junior at Point Loma University; Alyssa, a graduate of Vanguard University; and Aizaiah (pronounced like the biblical Isaiah, also married to Neddy), who oversees the local missions initiatives at Azusa Pacific University—and one granddaughter (Serenity Joy, from Aizaiah and Neddy). Amos and Alma reside in Pasadena, California.

SCRIPTURE INDEX

OLD TESTAMENT

Genesis
1, *135, 137, 190*
1:1, *247, 261*
1:2, *190*
1:3, *251*
1:26, *137*
1:28, *138, 190*
1:29, *138*
1:30, *136*
2, *137, 140, 256*
2:18, *248*
3, *62, 171, 183, 185*
6, *251*
7–8, *138*
7–9, *140*
9, *141*
9:1, *135*
18, *252, 261*
18:20, *252*
19, *159, 261*
20, *252*
20:5, *252*
20:6, *252*
21, *253*
43:32, *258*

Exodus
2, *261*
2:23, *252*
3:4, *253*
3:7, *253, 254*
3:8, *253*
3:9, *215*
13:3, *273*
23:10, *138*
23:12, *138*
33:1, *262*

Leviticus
17:3, *138*
25, *102, 271*
25:10, *263*
25:42, *271*

Deuteronomy
8:3, *257*
10:18, *26*

Judges
2:3, *337*
3, *158*

Job
12, *144*
38:32, *136*
38:39, *136*
38:41, *136*
39:1, *136*

Psalms
10:14, *248*
13:1, *215*
19:1, *247*
33:20, *248*
36:5, *138*
50:10, *135*
65, *140*
66, *140*
98, *140*
104:24, *135*
110:1, *298*
119, *263*
119:45, *263*
145, *140*
147:7, *137*
147:9, *137*
148, *140, 144*
148:7, *136*
150:6, *135*

Proverbs
17:5, *328*

Ecclesiastes
3:19, *144*

Isaiah
1:16, *254*
11:6, *140*
41:1, *254*
43:20, *135*
58, *104, 326*

61, *104*
61:1, *321*
65:25, *140*

Jeremiah
1:9, *254*
7:16, *138*
7:20, *144*
29:5, *218*
29:7, *217, 218*
31:28, *255*

Lamentations
5:20, *215*

Ezekiel
16:49, *159*
36:9, *255*

Daniel
7:13, *298*

Micah
6:8, *195, 206*
6:9, *326*

Zechariah
7:10, *26*

New Testament

Matthew
1:18, *336*
4:23, *263*
5, *264*
5:3, *17*
5:4, *263*
6:10, *140*
9:9, *8, 9, 10*

9:12, *8*
10:28, *268, 342*
10:29, *144*
16:26, *101*
21:13, *300*
25, *206, 328*
26, *298*
26:47, *296*
26:51, *298*
26:52, *298*
26:55, *298*
26:63, *298*
27:15, *299*
28:19, *56*

Mark
1:14, *89*
1:15, *10*
2:15, *10, 263*
9:38, *6*
12:30, *26, 56*
14, *293*
14:43, *296*
15:7, *293*
15:11, *293*

Luke
1, *99*
1:46, *17*
2:52, *156*
4, *321*
4:14, *321*
4:16, *103*
4:18, *196, 263, 271, 300, 322*
4:18-19, *285*
4:19, *272*
4:21, *103*
6, *264*
6:20, *17, 263*

7:18, *7*
7:22, *322*
7:28, *8*
9:49, *6*
10:25, *5*
10:37, *6, 26*
13:12, *263*
17:21, *322*
19:41, *302*
22:47, *296*
22:49, *296*
22:52, *297*
23:2, *297*
23:5, *297*
23:14, *298*
23:18, *294*
23:25, *294*

John
1:1, *250*
1:12, *10*
1:45, *89*
1:46, *90*
2:1, *256*
3:3, *120*
3:16, *138*
4, *236*
4:46, *256*
5:1, *257*
6:5, *257*
6:11, *263*
6:35, *257*
6:48, *257*
6:51, *257*
8:31-32, *262*
9:1, *258*
9:5, *259*
9:6, *259*
9:7, *259*
10, *258*

10:7, *258*
10:9, *258*
10:10, *172*
10:14, *258*
11:1, *259*
11:25, *260*
11:43, *259*
14:6, *260*
14:12, *234*
18:10, *296*
18:31, *295*
18:36, *298*
18:39, *295*
19:30, *261*
21, *146*

Acts
1:8, *320*
2, *32, 318, 319*
2:1, *320*
2:6, *319*
2:8, *319*
2:11, *319*
2:17, *318*
2:22, *320*
2:33, *322*
2:41, *319, 320*
2:44, *104, 319*
3:21, *139*
4:32, *104*
5:16, *322*
6, *105*
6:1, *326*
10:38, *320*
13:39, *263*
15, *6*
16:25, *230*

Romans
1, *10*
1:14, *10*
3:22, *139, 263*
5:12, *139*
8:2, *139*
8:14, *195*
8:18, *190*
8:19, *139*
8:19-21, *170*
8:22, *131*
12:4, *173*

1 Corinthians
1:18, *303*
1:26, *99*
3, *181*
7:25, *98*
12, *181*
12:4, *323*

12:12, *104*
12:24, *105*
13, *29*

2 Corinthians
5:17, *121*
5:19, *132*

Galatians
2:11, *9*
3:22, *191*
3:28, *9, 10*

Ephesians
1, *140*
2, *181*
2:8, *76*
5, *181*

Philippians
2:5, *17, 342*
3, *9*

Colossians
1, *140*
1:15, *137*
1:19, *139*
1:23, *140*
2:8, *10*
2:18, *10*

1 Timothy
4:16, *16*
6:10, *101*

James
1, *10*
1-2, *9*
1:27, *9, 16, 26*

2, *10*
5:1, *326*

1 Peter
3:15, *206*

1 John
2:18, *7*
4:1, *7*
4:2, *7*
4:7, *7*
4:8, *234*

Revelation
1:5, *269*
4, *140*
5, *140*
5:13, *135*
19, *181*
21, *140*
21:4, *261*